BRATISLAVA

m. (in Vienna) AMELIA [AMELIE] SPANNAGL (1849-1922)

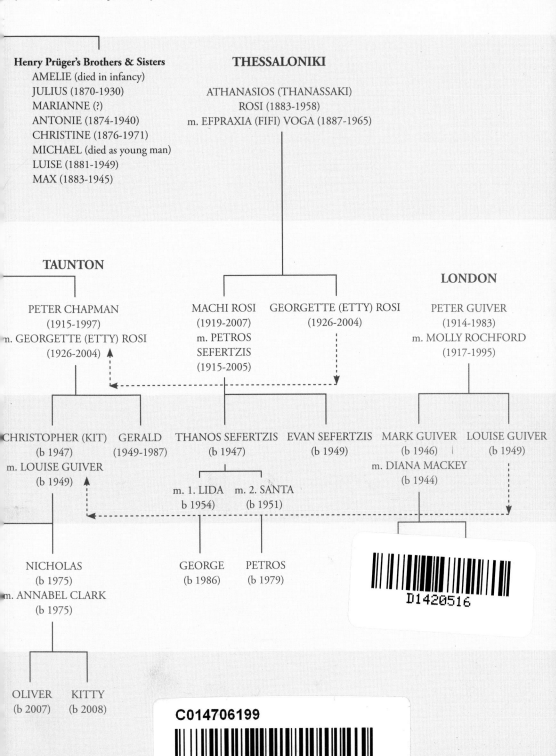

Henry Prüger's Brothers & Sisters
- AMELIE (died in infancy)
- JULIUS (1870-1930)
- MARIANNE (?)
- ANTONIE (1874-1940)
- CHRISTINE (1876-1971)
- MICHAEL (died as young man)
- LUISE (1881-1949)
- MAX (1883-1945)

THESSALONIKI

ATHANASIOS (THANASSAKI)
ROSI (1883-1958)
m. EFPRAXIA (FIFI) VOGA (1887-1965)

TAUNTON

PETER CHAPMAN
(1915-1997)
m. GEORGETTE (ETTY) ROSI
(1926-2004)

MACHI ROSI
(1919-2007)
m. PETROS
SEFERTZIS
(1915-2005)

GEORGETTE (ETTY) ROSI
(1926-2004)

LONDON

PETER GUIVER
(1914-1983)
m. MOLLY ROCHFORD
(1917-1995)

CHRISTOPHER (KIT)
(b 1947)
m. LOUISE GUIVER
(b 1949)

GERALD
(1949-1987)

THANOS SEFERTZIS
(b 1947)

EVAN SEFERTZIS
(b 1949)

MARK GUIVER
(b 1946)
m. DIANA MACKEY
(b 1944)

LOUISE GUIVER
(b 1949)

m. 1. LIDA
b 1954)

m. 2. SANTA
(b 1951)

NICHOLAS
(b 1975)
m. ANNABEL CLARK
(b 1975)

GEORGE
(b 1986)

PETROS
(b 1979)

OLIVER
(b 2007)

KITTY
(b 2008)

Kit Chapman

My Archipelago

The story of a family

MERCER books

MERCER books

First published in 2010 by Mercer Books
www.mercerbooks.co.uk

ISBN 978-0-9557127-1-5

Design by Reuben Wakeman
Family tree designed by Gill Whatmore
Printed in the UK by Butler Tanner & Dennis, Frome

For my grandchildren,
Daniel, Oliver and Kitty.

Contents

Preface

Families are strange and wonderful organisms. Bound by blood, they embody relationships which can be at once loving and nurturing, fragile and combustible. Every family is different, each one unique – but all confront difficulties and dramas common to the human condition. Tension and conflict are, perhaps, the most common themes – their source often driven by a shifting culture and the mores which divide one generation from the next. This book tells the story of my family – its great paradox being that while our problems are unique and personal in one way, in another, the issues I describe are universal.

The book would have been impossible to write without the rich source material at my disposal, much of it discovered after the death of my parents, Peter and Etty Chapman. In addition to my own papers, journals and diaries, and a family history written by my father, I fell upon a remarkable cache of letters, documents, photo albums and memorabilia which lent detail and colour to my narrative – the most significant being revelations about the death of my grandfather Henry Prüger, and an insight into Peter and Etty's extraordinary love affair.

Here and there in the text I have changed the names of some minor or supporting personalities. All are or were real people but, in these few instances, I felt it wise to protect their true identities. Also, one or two short passages have been adapted from my last book, *An Innkeeper's Diary*.

A host of kind friends and acquaintances have given freely of their time to assist or advise me in my writing. But my first thank-you must go to my late parents, Etty and Peter, whose "forgotten" archive has proved an invaluable source for this story. Other family members have also contributed: my brother-in-law, Mark Guiver; my English cousins, Nicky and Alex Chapman; and in Greece, cousins Thanos Sefertzis and Vassili Rementzis. My thanks also to Dimitri Dingas-Chardalias in Salonica and, on the island of Skiathos, Patra Mavropoulos, Taxiarchis Stivaktis and Stephanos Milis. In New York to my brother Gerald's dear friend, Ivan Chatman; to Sheri M. Goldhirsch, Artistic Director of Young Playwrights Inc; to Stephen Sondheim and Peggy Hansen; and to Don Lundquist at the Cathedral Church of St. John the Divine. And in Bratislava to Eric Assimakopoulos, Eva Kadlecik and Sonja Divé-Dahl.

The Gerald chapters were not easy to write. The process was helped immeasurably by my brother's Cambridge friend Peter Judd, now Dean of Chelmsford, who granted me access to his private correspondence and diaries, and who submitted himself to hours of questioning from this inquisitive author. My thanks also to The Rev. Dr. Anthony Phillips, Chaplain of Trinity Hall, Cambridge in the late-Sixties; Daphne Rae, widow of Dr. John Rae; Max Stafford-Clark, Artistic Director of The Royal Court Theatre when Gerald launched his Young People's Theatre Scheme; to Peter Spink, James Fahey and Wendy Gregory; and to David Bridges, archivist at Taunton School.

Many other good people have helped and supported my writing, not least, colleagues, friends and past associates of the family and our hotel, The Castle at Taunton. They are:
Anne and Mike Allen, Paul Aplin, Becki Beanland, Michael Blackwell, Stuart Carter, Cedric Chirossel, David Coubrough, Thérèse Duriez, Mary Gibbs, Richard Guest, Valerie Harper, Mike Hawkins, Alice Hodges, Kevin McCarthy, Adrian Miller, Sam Parkinson, Jon Peilow, Sarah Podro, David Prior and Elizabeth Williams.

A small band of literary friends cast their critical eyes over the manuscript. Collectively and in their different ways, they have been a profound influence on the shaping of the final text. First, I must thank my agent, Caradoc King for his sound advice and constant encouragement without which I might never have completed this work. Warmest thanks also to my English master, Michael

Parslew (retired!) who imposed a rigorous copy edit and denied my excesses with the English language. To Rosalind Daukes, Jacqueline Mann and Emma Kitchener-Fellowes for their detailed comments and observations. And to my publisher Tim Mercer and his team for producing this handsome volume.

A special word of thanks also to my secretary and amanuensis of twenty-five years. Gill Whatmore undertook the task of typing and retyping my hand-written manuscript through its many drafts. Indeed, she has performed the same task for all my books and I am eternally grateful to her.

But the last word is for my wife Louise whose love has sustained me through this four-year labour. Without her, there would be no family and no family story to tell.

Kit Chapman
Ashfield House
March 2010

Part One

Rise and Fall - The End of a Family Name

The Savoy-Carlton Hotel, Bratislava. Early 1930s

Diodati – Summer 2006

She died in her bed at dawn on St. Valentine's Day. In her clenched fist she held the gold cross inscribed with her name. We were taking a short break in St. Paul de Vence when the care home called – sipping an early morning tea at the time. But that was almost two and a half years ago and, since that day, I have failed to shed a tear in her memory. There is an emotional legacy, of course. After all, this was my mother. But although she gave me life, all that is left now is a raging heart – and a mind, obsessed and unforgiving, filled with recollections of a million hurts and injustices. Yet here we are, Louise and I, happily installed in the Aegean hideaway she created with her Peter (she always referred to my father as "my Peter" in company). I used to hate this place we were never allowed to use and I was all for selling it – but the boys stopped us and they were right. We have now made it our own, claiming some of our happiest moments here – Diodati, our escape. She would call it their "paradieschen" – their little corner of paradise. And so it has become for us.

This is the strangest conundrum : that I should choose to tell this story – a search perhaps for reconciliation – on an island that chokes on its emotional polarity. Some of our most miserable moments are etched in the stone terraces and pine trees of this house. Grim ghosts still linger in the resin we inhale with every breath. Yet, somehow, Louise and I – after decades of contempt and alienation – find a peace and a happiness, both tender and passionate, that is almost unimaginable. Each return is a renewal of love – for the place and for one another. A triumph of the human spirit, but one I sometimes find strange to grasp, like a magician's sleight of hand. Then I simply raise my head and gaze over a silver bay at some of the smaller islands of the Sporades, each protected by the monstrous cudgel of Skopelos, and I think, maybe this is a parable of beauty and the healing effects of rebirth. Diodati reborn. With the death of Peter (who found and built this place), so the house died. Over the past years, we have nursed it back to life and shaped it anew.

*

Today is perfect. Louise is still asleep and I write these words on the upper terrace we call Aristotle's. Not an hour ago Homer's "rosy fingered dawn" shot its stiletto-thin shaft of deep-pink light across a sea of the smoothest pearl-grey silk. The comforting stillness of the early morning is broken only by an occasional burst of song from an unseen bird. And in mid-view a Flying Dolphin rumbles furiously to port, its first call of the day. My desk, a small round table painted Mediterranean-blue in the style used in Greek village cafés, is shaded by four young pines thick with needles which diffuse the stealthy climb of the sunbeams. A mug of tea slowly releases my head of the final shreds of a deep, satisfying sleep.

I shall never forget our first arrival at the house thirty-five years ago. Louise and I were just engaged (questions arose about the sleeping arrangements) and the year-long construction, fit-out and decorations had recently been completed. The manner of our progress was a strictly choreographed affair directed by Etty. And so it was my father alone who met us at the island's airstrip and drove us out to Kalamaki, a lush pine-green peninsula attached to the island's southern flank. A low white-washed stone gateway heralded "Diodati" on a simple wood board and a hairpin driveway dropped steeply towards the house. From the top of the drive we glimpsed a rash of red roof tiles and that heart-stoppingly beautiful view across to Skopelos. Peter halted the car and we found ourselves beside a long flight of steps leading down to the rear terrace : a wonderland of bougainvillea, oleander, geranium, jasmine, orange and lemon trees. And there she was – between the double-panelled front door and the foot of the stairs – arms outstretched, floating in an ocean of chiffon, commanding our wild applause. Then, taking us by the hand, she led us in – instructing us to lead with our right foot "for good luck and the evil eye". Inside, two enormous plate-glass windows slid back into their wall cavities to reveal a wide stone-flagged terrace : the dress circle in our Aegean theatre and a living fantasy. Below us, the pinewood banked sharply to the shoreline and a blue-crêpe sea, surrounded by its islets of green brush, rock and sand, completed the stage set which dazzles us even now. It is a constantly shifting scene, always perfectly lit according to the time of day, season and weather. Even a thunderstorm over the bay holds us transfixed like helpless children.

*

I guess it is Diodati's timelessness, its other-worldness, that appeals to the imagination, is so soul-soothing. We may have claimed our tiny corner of Eden on this island, but changing times and the package holiday have – over three decades – flung this ancient sea-wrinkled community into the arms of voracious developers. From being victims of piracy to harvesting the tourist euro, the islanders today have never had it so good. For 700 years – from Byzantium at the time of the Crusades – they struggled under the yoke of Venetians, then Ottomans, whose protection they often sought from privateers who plagued the Aegean seas. After liberation in 1821, they gradually deserted their fortified settlement in the north of the island – once a ragged pile of 300 houses and 30 churches – to rebuild their town around the natural harbour in the south. They are a fearless, generous people with an unbending faith in their Orthodox Church and in their language – neither of which succumbed to those long centuries of alien occupation and terrible adversity.

Forty years ago this was a quieter place. Rather in the manner that the British invented the Côte d'Azur as a winter resort, so it was a small group of English buccaneers, tired of the grim winters at home, who first discovered the island and, seduced by it, decided to create a new life here. They based themselves at Kanapitsa on the Kalamaki peninsula – a rum bunch of writers, professional drop-outs and retired soldiers trailing MCs and DSOs after their names. The most basic of modern communications were non-existent, but true to their kind they went native and transported the materials for their house-building on the backs of caiques and mules. The island's main road grafted into the rock contours of its southern coastline only took shape in the sixties. By the early seventies this pack of convivial rogues was in full cry.

The one overarching memory I have of those early years – before Dom and Nick were born – is the social scene. Kanapitsa acquired the unmistakeable whiff of a tiny, forgotten British colony and the local taverna was its clubhouse. This is where the expats assembled at lunchtime and in the evening – and this is where vast quantities of ouzo and retsina would be consumed with the minimum fiscal pain. Upper middle class values, attended by their delicious little snobberies and conventions, prevailed and, at the start of the season, a relentless cycle of cocktail parties slipped naturally into gear. There was no escape. Practically every evening we shuffled either up or down long, steep flights of stone stairs to the terraces of the English villa owners. Not a Greek in sight. This was the land of the hooray hearty. My mother (token Greek, married to an ex-Indian army officer, so that was alright) loved these affairs and they loved her. Well, she was different, wasn't she? Unlike the faded, flabby matrons of Hampshire, Etty was striking, elegant, exuberant. She brought colour and a girlish gaiety to the scene. My father, on the other hand, hated these parties – although not once did I hear him confess his antipathy. Given a choice in the matter, Peter would have preferred to be left in peace : to read his books, check the water level of the butt that served the house, seek the evening cool of his pine trees, or just quietly reflect on his good fortune to be in such a place. Soon after the house was opened, he built a low stone bench on the cliff-top at the edge of the woodland. A quiet spot to sit, to stare and to dream.

Their pet names for one another were the Greek words for "mine" and "yours" (μου και σου) which often prefixed the German diminutive expression "chen" to give "mouchen" and "souchen". When they first met in Thessaloniki just after the war, my parents had German as their common language, Etty having been reared by Austrian governesses and Peter – for all his English public school education – being the son of an Austro-Hungarian hotelier from Bratislava. As a child, I very nearly grew up tri-lingual but in the end, it was the Greek and the English which stuck while their favourite terms of endearment were either German or Greek or the elision of both. For me, the charm of "mou" and "sou", "mouchen" and "souchen", is the suggestion of sharing, give and take, mine is yours : a simple mantra for a marriage. But for all the love and happiness she brought my father, he was the giver, nourishing her every whim and fancy. Etty loved her parties – both hosting them and livening up the hospitality of others – and Peter indulged her craving, happy himself to see his wife sparkle and attract a swarm of admirers wherever they might be.

Solitude and spiritual contemplation, while never openly expressed, were important to my father. An undercurrent of melancholy seemed to trickle intermittently through him – a characteristic Etty never recognized nor understood which, in some ways, may have been a good thing. She brought a joy and a vitality to his existence and he adored her for being her – his little Etty, his Ettylein. But her wilful spirit, evident from the earliest age, was a problem he was never able to contain. It brought me into violent conflict with her, troubled him to the core of his being and undermined my relationship with the father I loved and admired.

I pause a moment for no apparent reason and raise my disbelieving eyes to see a dolphin at play in the bay – a young one, I think, and quite alone. Has the child lost his family? Leaping gracefully out of the water, he is now heading out to sea. It is a sight to make the heart shimmer with joy – and, for me, a first sighting from these terraces. Peter swam with dolphins. Was it him? Those perpendicular leaps, four or five, like waves in greeting. For me? And then he was gone.

What was the struggle deep within him? The longing for peace to ease the turbulence, the hidden pains of long ago. (Then renewed and magnified by the death of Gerald.) What was it that so disturbed his soul to inspire his search for an Aegean hillside where finally he might find some peace of mind?

He never spoke of his fears and anxieties – the vampires of his early life which, now I come to reflect on these things, were obviously lodged in the fabric of his being. But then that generation – seasoned by war, austerity and the Victorian ideal – didn't. All I have is a consciousness of a sensitive, gentle man, spiritual in an unassuming way. A loving and devoted father certainly but one whose love was founded on principles, self-discipline and an ethic of "duty first" – values my brother and I were required to practise from the earliest age. His little catchphrases, like advertising slogans, still ring in my ears. Any display of timidity or "wetness" was challenged with the call : "Are you man or mouse?" – an injunction, not a question. A temper tantrum was squashed by the simple command : "Control yourself!" On the wall by my bedside hung a small glass-framed postcard - lines of a verse copied out in a long flowing hand which read : "Boys of spirit, boys of will,/Boys of muscle, brain and power,/Fit to cope with anything,/These are wanted every hour." A few more lines followed on this stoic theme but I do not recall them. The handwriting belonged to Henry Prüger, Peter's father – a man he idolized but hardly knew, a grandfather who died eighteen years before I was born, and a powerful presence who, in our family, had acquired mythical status.

His portrait hung in my father's office at the Castle – a painting I never much liked for the stony lifelessness bearing down from the wall. I first saw it as a child visiting my cousins in Torquay where my uncle Michael, Peter's elder brother, displayed the original above the fireplace in the drawing room of 'The Villa' – their house on the hill overlooking the Imperial, his hotel which in its day became a legendary playground for the rich. So my father had the portrait copied. And now a lingering guilt pricks me when, from time to time, I clamber into our attic at home and see this mythic image, gloomy as a wet February afternoon, stacked and redundant with the rest of the family's accumulated bric-a-brac.

Long ago, my father wrote a family history. I took little notice, glancing through it, finding it over-sentimental and anodyne. Henry Prüger lay at the centre of the narrative and reading it now, his story is pure hagiography. Certainly, he was a brilliant hotelier, lionized by his contemporaries, but he was also touched by some power mania, a control freak who could not brook failure and ultimately brought misery on his wife and three sons – Peter being the youngest and most vulnerable. Here was a man who would boast to his children about his initials which, he said, also stood for Horse Power and Houses of Parliament. In time, at the great hotel he created in his native Bratislava, he borrowed Napoleon's symbol of a busy bee and made it the family's logo.

As a thirtieth birthday gift, my father gave me one of HP's many cigarette cases. This one was particularly beautiful – slim, gold and gently curved to fit his breast pocket, its lid elaborately engraved in swirls and curlicues woven to form these two famous initials. Although it was designed to hold Turkish cigarettes, angled and at a squeeze, it took five Marlboro king size – my own poison at the time. Soft and smooth to handle in the palm of my hand, its subtle clip and spring mechanism opening the lid like a magic box, this was my pride and joy, my favourite heirloom. And then, some years later, it vanished; lost or stolen from a loose jacket laid above my head on an inter-city train somewhere between Paddington and Taunton. I was devastated. And stopped smoking soon after.

Prüger was a fervently patriotic son of the Austro-Hungarian Empire. He was born in Pressburg (now Bratislava) on 15th September 1867, the first son of Henry Anthony Prüger, a successful chef-restaurateur who had trained in the imperial capital, Vienna, where he met and married Amelia, a fearsome and fearsomely stout burgher's daughter fifteen years his junior. Amelia had barely celebrated her sixteenth birthday when Henry Anthony brought his bride home to Pressburg and after young Henry was born the following year, she gave birth to a further eight children. The family prospered, first by taking the lease on a resort restaurant by a lake a few miles out of town; then in the running of the Goldener Hirsch, an inn in the city's market place. By the time Henry Anthony died, in 1898, his eldest son had long abandoned the drudge of the family shop to chase stardom as an international operator in an age gripped by the extravagance of La Belle Epoque when Europe's grandest hotels were vying to outshine each other. Meanwhile, at home, Amelia assumed control as supreme matriarch, imposing her dynastic will on the sons and daughters of the new generation with Henry's two younger brothers, Julius and Max, as her principal lieutenants.

My father describes Henry Prüger as a "very dapper man" : he often wore a fresh bloom in his button-hole, sustained through the day by a glass phial of water hidden behind the lapel. Vain, perhaps, but driven and tough too : "He was of medium height, physically strong and well built – he once swam several miles down the Danube." After national service in the Hungarian army's artillery, Prüger – bold, ravenous, clever – set forth : to Vienna, of course, then France, Italy, Germany, the United States and Switzerland. By his early thirties, he was Deputy Director of the Grand Hotel National in Lucerne, the first specific appointment we have on record and this only because on 6th July 1901, the Chinese Emperor's ambassador at the Imperial Court of St. Petersburg awarded my grandfather a Silver Medal of the Double Dragon "for services rendered". The Gold, one imagines, going to the General Director. [In my father's account of this presentation, he mistranslates the French "Brevet", inflating HP's award to a gold medal where the citation clearly states "medaille en argent (silver) du double Dragon". I assume, in spite of the pomp, this was a small diplomatic courtesy on the part of the ambassador but it already suggests that Prüger was beginning to move in elevated circles.]

But his big break came in November 1903 when, at the age of 36, he was appointed General Manager of the Savoy in London, one of the world's great hotels and the most fashionable watering hole in high-Edwardian society.

*

Louise calls – the shade has gone from Aristotle's. The sea – now brilliant blue and still as a pool of virgin oil – is too tempting to deny. Grabbing our towels, we make our way through the woodland to the head of the cliff, passing the low stone bench which looks a little forlorn beside the green-painted shed we built last year to contain the paraphernalia of the beach. Fifty-eight steep steps lead down to an eccentric outcrop of rock and stone we call Puddleduck because in my father's imagination this sea-sculpted promontory bears a distinct resemblance to Jemima – a favourite character in the Beatrix Potter stories he used to read to Gerald and me and then to

Dom and Nick, his grandchildren. Here and there, clumps of samphire cling to the rocks matched in their determination by a gang of sullen sea urchins lying just below the crystalline surface of the sea. I wear rubber sandals for my sensible protection. Louise, braver than me, prefers to dive straight in and mind where she treads. The water, like a cool therapeutic balm, glides over our bodies as we swim around the bay, either to the left or the right, to one of the two sandy beaches which flank our headland. Breathless by the time we reach our destination, we crawl out and lie motionless, spread-eagled on the sand, beneath a sun which infuses us gradually with a rising sense of well-being. Occasionally our solitude is broken by a tourist's small craft being dragged onto the beach or by one of our neighbours tripping down for a midday dip. It's of little consequence. Back on Puddleduck, stretched out on our chaises longues, the drawbridge is raised.

*

I find myself drawn less by Peter's storyline and more by the volume of appendices attached to his family history. He must have spent hours raking through the archives at the Savoy – as did I many years later. The bundle of press cuttings for one month alone – September 1909 – has me gasping. HP's six year reign (there is no other way to describe it) established the hotel's pre-eminence and, in its wake, his own reputation and fortune.

From the day of his appointment, he set about upgrading the Savoy's rooms and facilities. Within two years he had more than doubled his bed occupancy figures which now touched or exceeded ten thousand a month. As if to make the point, he took out a full-page advertisement in the New York Herald in September 1905, proclaiming his success by publishing three years of statistics and endorsing the Savoy's status by providing a society-conscious city with a roll-call of his celebrity clients – hundreds of Dukes, Earls, Counts, Barons, Lords, Knights and Generals – all topped by no less than nineteen Royals and a Sultan. The foot of the advertisement carried his signature in bold type : "HENRY PRÜGER, General Manager".

The name would not have been unknown to New Yorkers. On both sides of the Atlantic, HP was being sought by aristos or parvenus, or just the plain super-rich, as an impresario of unusual talent. The most famous party he organized was probably the "Gondola Dinner" for the Wall Street financier, George Kessler. My grandfather flooded a courtyard in the hotel, dyeing the water blue and recreating the scene of a Venetian lagoon. The Hello! Magazine of the time - the society publication *Cartons Mondains* - reported the occasion in rather obsequious and inflated prose:

> "… the miracle was accomplished by a magician named Prüger who
> kills time by managing the Savoy. And he put live swans in the pond,
> live ducks, salmon trout, whitebait, and in the middle a floating dining
> room in the shape of a huge Venetian gondola.
>
> "The waiters each had his gondola, swiftly carrying the dainty dishes to
> the favoured twenty-four.
>
> "… Then, as in an enchanted dream, on the still, balmy atmosphere rose
> the rich mellow tones of the divine Caruso's voice …
>
> "The moon was shining brightly, by order of Mr. Geo. A. Kessler, for
> the American Nabob would have the illusion of Venice complete, and,
> after improvising the lagoon below, created an electrically ornamented
> firmament above …
>
> "Then I caught sight of … *Jumbo Junior* [a baby elephant] carrying to
> the guests … a cake, a *sweety* five feet high studded all over with electric
> diamonds and revolving all the time producing the most dazzling effect.
>
> "The floral decorations included : 12,000 choice carnations; 2,000
> Malmaison carnations; 17,000 roses …
>
> "One hundred white doves fluttered over the scene, and the lighting up
> comprised no less than four hundred Venetian lamps."

The bill for this intimate soirée came to £3,000 which in today's money would equate to about £170,000. But what the author of this ponderous article omitted to report was that the blue dye in the water poisoned the fish and killed all the swans.

Like the advertisement, Kessler's party also bore HP's signature. *Cartons*

Mondains ran the story one month before the paid notice appeared in the New York Herald and the photograph which accompanied the article pictured a flower-strewn gondola, host and guests posing stiffly for the camera, with a small "service gondola" in mid-field carrying a watchful Prüger.

What I find intriguing here is not the chutzpah of a brilliant self-publicist but the timing and his ability to milk an opportunity for a sound competitive cause. His arch-rival, and the man he succeeded as manager at the Savoy, was César Ritz. And at the time of these events, Ritz was building his eponymous hotel, primed to open on Piccadilly in 1906. Like his famous predecessor, HP knew the game was as much about patronage and personality as it was about the splendour of the fixtures and fittings. He must have been haunted by Edward VII's over-rehearsed claim; "Where Ritz goes, I go," when the greedy King was Prince of Wales. Prüger also needed friends out of the top drawer and he knew how to find them – flatter them.

By September 1909 HP was impatient to make his next move. Now forty-two and still unmarried – though he had been showing more than a passing interest in the Savoy's head housekeeper, Miss Nell Chapman – his consuming ambition was to create his own hotel, preferably in London. Ritz had already done it and his close friend Otto Goring was six months away from opening in Victoria. But his first move was to set up his family in Pressburg and the fortune he had been amassing at the Savoy was already being invested in property on the city's main square opposite the Opera House. Within three years, he had bought an apartment block and two existing hotels either side which he remodelled and integrated to make one large three-storey building to be rechristened "Savoy-Carlton". Meanwhile, his plans for London would have to wait. Leaving his indomitable mother, the Widow Amelia, to mind the family interests in Pressburg, Henry boarded the SS Mauretania in Liverpool and set sail for New York.

When the story broke, newspaper headlines went wild when editors of the nationals and London's Evening Standard discovered that a millionaire consortium of businessmen was paying Prüger fees of £10,000 – £560,000 today – to open New York's newest and most ambitious hotel and restaurant venture: "… a stipend somewhat higher than Great Britain pays its Prime Minister," boomed the Standard. "His departure removes one of the most striking personalities from the hotel world of Europe." On the day he left the Savoy for the last time, he was given a hero's farewell: "… the crowd of employees, Americans and hotel proprietors who saw him off stopped the traffic in the Strand and nearly filled the platform at Euston," reported the Daily Express on 27th September.

In all the excitement, there was one story the newspapers missed. Before Henry's departure for New York, Nell received a proposal of marriage from him. And this was an arrangement he could not afford to postpone. He had a rival for her hand. His senior lieutenant at the Savoy, the Assistant General Manager Herr Schwenter had also made a proposal. Poor Schwenter! As Prüger's deputy he doubted his chances of success, and HP had no intention of leaving the field open in his absence in the United States. As he sailed into the Irish Sea, Liverpool at his back, he was comforted by the knowledge that he was an engaged man. That Christmas, a happy but lonely bride-to-be did her familial duty. She sent her prospective mother-in-law a framed self-portrait: grand coiffure, enigmatic smile, a ball gown with an English rose attached at the bosom, a closed fan held lightly in her right hand – a composition magnificent in its Edwardian formality. Beneath, the inscription read, "With my love to Madame Prüger, Nellie Chapman. Xmas 1909".

*

All these events occurred in the decade before my father was born. Reading the history, it is obvious Peter was awestruck by his father. But the more I trawl through these documents in pursuit of HP, the more wary I become of the myth and the hyperbole. I want to like him but I find myself strangely disengaged, unable to discern the humanity of the man. Then, I know what's to come and perhaps this is obscuring my judgement. It even makes me angry that Peter's account of a terrible episode is thin; an excuse, a denial. I'm trying to be honest; I'm trying to be fair – but as I wade through the evidence, I feel

I am sometimes groping for the truth. A truth I seek only to inform a better understanding of my own father.

*

His brief fulfilled, Henry returned to London the following year to lead the design and construction of the RAC's new headquarters in Pall Mall. This was another grand project for him, bringing with it its own peculiar challenges. Digging the foundations, he discovered the site was floating on a spring. To solve the problem he turned to Otto Goring whose technical innovations at the new Goring Hotel had impressed him. His friend suggested he harness the spring water to create a swimming pool in the club's basement. And there it remains today.

This was also the year HP decided to delay no further his plans to wed Miss Chapman – still 'Lady Housekeeper' at the Savoy – and they were married at Corpus Christi Church in the Strand on 19th January, 1911. Nell, good-looking rather than pretty and almost thirty-four years old ('30' on the Marriage Certificate!), was the daughter of John Chapman of Uppingham, a plumber who, by the date of the wedding, had risen comfortably in life to define himself as 'Architect and Builder'.

I was nearly seven when – forty and some years later – Nell died but, still I hold the fondest memories of her; perhaps because I think I was her favourite grandchild. It was she who insisted on calling me Kit rather than Christopher, and it stuck. She lived in a small cottage in Little Common near Bexhill, Sussex with Maky, her Hungarian companion, who liked to refer to her as "my missus". In the Easter and Summer holidays, Gerald and I would visit with our cousins from Torquay : Avon Lodge, a name she chose to remind her of the big house the family had on the Thames at Pangbourne during the First War.

Seven. An age of sublime innocence. What did I know? Of her struggle? The battles she had to fight? The hardship? All I saw was a kindly old lady, grand and grey in her modest cottage, a long illness gradually wearing her down, reclining on her sofa in the drawing room with its French windows opening onto a garden she loved but rarely stepped into, preferring instead to watch the racing on television. How should I know that changing a city name signals a turbulent moment in the history of nations as much as it does in the history of a family? How Pressburg became Bratislava? How Prüger became Chapman? Half a century on and that happily oblivious seven year old has arrived at late middle-age. But is he any the wiser? Wiser about those events in the twenties and thirties that changed everything – ending with her eventual, inevitable capitulation and her return to Blighty with the faithful Maky. And her youngest, dearest Peter despatched to India before another war postponed their shy reunion by ten years. But these are just a few raw facts. What truths may lie behind the history, self-censored as it is by sentiment, are matters yet to be untangled.

For now, better, easier the seven year old tiptoe back to bed at Avon Lodge to be awoken in the morning by Maky with a cup of tea. Oh! The treat of it! And still I taste the sweet and milky maltiness of the brew. Then, minutes later, that savoury smell of frying bacon creeping up the staircase had this pack of hungry cubs tumbling into the dining room for breakfast. If the day was fine, there would be games in the garden or a trip to Hastings or walks in the surrounding fields and woods where, in spring, we were under orders to gather primroses for Granny. On wet afternoons, we were allowed to join her in front of the television on the strict understanding that we remained quiet and still. There was one occasion when I didn't. I remember it so well. She called me over to her sofa: "Kit", she said sharply, "you are to be smacked for your disobedience. Put out your hand." Sick with fear and remorse, I approached her and extended my hand. Perhaps she saw the contrition in her grandson's flushed and frightened face, she fixed me with her kind eyes and tapped me lightly on the wrist. From that moment, I knew how much I loved her.

For England in the early fifties, these were still post-war years of austerity. Like any other child of my generation, I was innocent of any regime of food rationing – besides, we ate so well at Avon Lodge. Maky, of course, did the cooking but as an Hungarian family servant who never mastered her adopted tongue, inventing instead her own Anglo-Bohemian patois, she was remarkably skilled in the ways of the English country kitchen – doubtlessly the result of Nell's careful tutelage. Back in the twenties, Nell had run an ambitious market garden on the family estate outside Bratislava. Her kitchen garden in Little Common, tiny by comparison and now tended by Maky, remained nevertheless a source of great pride for all the fruits, vegetables and herbs it supplied for her grandchildren's enjoyment. Memories swell up in a rush; tastes so fresh and aromatic they have never been equalled since: fluffy potatoes dug that morning redolent with mint; a white sauce bursting with the garden's parsley for a boiled gammon or a piece of cod; runner beans, broad beans and the sweetest peas and carrots; jams and jellies for tea from plums, greengages, blackcurrants and raspberries – the feast sometimes topped by the best Victoria sponge. And after tea there would be more games – our favourites being sardines, an amusing variation of hide 'n' seek, and murder-in-the-dark, a scarier version of the same – until, eventually, we were despatched to bed exhausted.

*

Piecing together the events of 1911, the year seems to elevate Henry Prüger to new heights within London's political and social milieux. Now married and settled in apartments set aside for him and Nell in the splendour of the new Royal Automobile Club, it was not long before the couple were being fêted by the good and the great of the capital. The Austrian ambassador, Count Mensdorff, threw a banquet at the Embassy in their honour with a menu that ran to eight courses ending with *Pêches Henry Prüger* – a dessert echoing Escoffier's famous invention at the Savoy for the diva, Dame Nellie Melba. Soon after, the ambassador was in touch again, this time to present HP with the equivalent of a knighthood from the Emperor himself: The Knight's Cross of the Order of Franz Joseph which he received "in recognition of his services in the field of public welfare and commerce". Finally, in December, Nell gave birth to their first-born son, Henry Michael.

Fourteen months later their second son – named Anthony after HP's father – was born and, as for his brother, the birth was recorded at the RAC in Pall Mall. These years before 1914 might have seen some of Prüger's energies directed towards his young family – after all, he was now in his middle forties – but I find no evidence of any interest in his domestic life. The job was left to Nell. He was too busy completing his portfolio of investments in Pressburg to create the new Savoy-Carlton under Amelia's matriarchy. And, that job done, he turned his attention to the search for a suitable property in London for an hotel which would outshine the Ritz. He found it. Better still, he found it in St. James's Street, a spitting distance from the palace César built on Piccadilly.

No sooner had the purchase been made – he ready primed to begin work on the development with his architect and design team – than Europe descended into its bloody war. Prüger now found himself an enemy alien in a foreign land. The choices he faced were momentous and the decisions he took would reshape the lives of his family and reach into the next generation. In the history, my father writes: "His friends, particularly those at the RAC occupying high positions in society and government, were most anxious to retain the services of this brilliant man. He had spent all his last, many, years in Britain and America and had married an Englishwoman. His sons were British by birth. Naturalization as a British subject would have surmounted all difficulties. The necessary papers were prepared and put before him for signature. Henry Prüger took one of the most important and significant decisions of his life – he refused to sign."

That was it! He makes an agonizing, life-changing choice – signing away his property rights, signing away his fortune – and I am left to imagine the turmoil that must have been pumping through his veins and, more poignantly, Nell's. I am his grandson. So what would I have done; knowing my wife was pregnant with a third child; knowing that I would lose my job and forfeit the valuable property I had just acquired in St. James's Street – shattering my greatest dreams? Knowing also that I had won the confidence of my sovereign and had been decorated by him. To turn my back on my country would have been a grotesque act of treason. My Viennese mother and her family in Pressburg would be horrified if I decided to switch nationality just because, in so doing, it happened to be convenient to my circumstances. No. I would have made the same decision. In truth, HP had no choice. To have done otherwise, to have signed away his own nationhood would have made it impossible for him ever to return home.

And Nell? How did she cope? What did she feel and think? Did Henry, in making his decision, suggest the family pack up and return to Pressburg? The embassy and consulate had closed and their staffs were repatriated. Should they do the same? Was it not the obvious thing to do? This is where, I think, Nell would have drawn the line. She could accept the politics and patriotism of his decision but, beyond that, he would have to accept that the security and well-being of the family were her concern. Somewhere in my head, I hear her saying: "If you want to go, go! I'm staying in England with the boys!" And then, I wonder: are the emotions of a mother transmitted to the child she is carrying in her womb? Is some deep primal force conveying this turmoil to the embryonic life growing inside her? The relationship is so fragile, tender and intimate, it is impossible to believe the unborn child – Peter, my father – was not affected.

*

Supported by his powerful patrons, HP avoided deportation and was allowed to remain in England with his family. Furthermore, his job and career prospects abruptly terminated, both enemy governments, British and Austro-Hungarian alike, found a role for him which ideally suited both sides. At the outbreak of war, thousands of expats, many of them working in poorly paid jobs as musicians, waiters and kitchen porters, now found themselves interned and in need of support. This was a responsibility the British authorities preferred to sidestep and one which Vienna could not avoid. A war help fund was set up to provide humanitarian relief for this displaced constituency and Prüger was appointed its principal; his task to provide hundreds of meals a day at feeding stations in internment camps and to organize clothing schemes for his impoverished countrymen and their dependants. Henry Prüger had a busy war.

Meanwhile, the family moved out of London. Exactly why, I have never discovered. Was it the job? Was he required to leave the capital? Was it the expense? I do not know. The other mystery is the frequency of their moves. Between 1914 and 1918, they relocated three times. Their first home was in Thames Ditton, near Esher in Surrey where Peter was born in March 1915. The following year they moved to Bexhill-on-Sea which must have endeared itself enough to Nell for her to return to East Sussex two decades later. The only photograph I have of the house reveals a modern, functional suburban box typical of the era which may have been a stopgap before the family finally landed in the handsome Thames-side manor at Pangbourne : the original Avon Lodge.

*

At home, on the landing outside our bedroom, Louise and I have hung two framed watercolours of Avon Lodge – paintings almost certainly commissioned by Nell. Perhaps she was searching for some sane and civilized antidote to the horrors and madness of war recounted each day in her newspapers. The theme of these pictures is blithely pastoral – two leafy, balmy, tranquil scenes of a family at play in high summer. The house is ivy-clad, surrounded by woodland, windows thrown open. A neat lawn bordered by box hedges, arbours and fruit trees slopes gently to the riverbank where figures dressed in white linen are watching a punt. A monochrome photograph of the same scene identifies Nell and her sister Fan reclining in the long, narrow craft and, in the painting, a reflection of the house shimmers in the water beneath them. The scene in the second watercolour is of a backwater by the side of the house. Another punt is moored alongside as three diminutive figures run toward it (Michael, Anthony and Peter?) while a grown-up standing in the boat holds fast to the bank – Henry perhaps.

These are more than an artist's impressions of a house and garden – a riverscape. It is a pictorial record of an intensely personal hue – to capture, as a diptych, the life of a family in its habitat of fairytale loveliness. It breathes harmony in an age of terrible conflict; beauty of life at a time of bestial slaughter. Is it irony or accident that the figures in each scene are divided in a particular way? The one with two English women, Nell and her sister, and the onlookers in white – a nanny or nurse with two young girls; the other, elsewhere in the same garden, depicting Henry, the loyal Habsburger, and his three sons. Elsewhere in Europe at that time, Passchendaele was raging at a cost of three hundred thousand dead and wounded – all for the sake of five miles of mud.

Seventy-five years later, when eventually my father and mother stepped away from the Castle to set up home on Somerset's Blackdown Hills, he named their house Avon Lodge.

*

At the end of the war, the old Austro-Hungarian empire collapsed and the map of Europe was redrawn. All Prüger had to show for his work directing the war help fund was a letter from the "Foreign Ministry In Liquidation" thanking him for his "practical assistance in the interests of our former co-nationals living abroad."

There was nothing left for him in England and in October 1918 the family set sail for the Hook of Holland to return home to Pressburg. It is at this point in the story – my father now three and a half years old – that I begin to glimpse events and their impact through the impressions of a childhood retold at first-hand. Peter's first recollection of his parents is distinctly Freudian, "sitting on a potty at the top of a flight of stairs at Avon Lodge, Pangbourne". Here and there in the narrative, he touches disarmingly on the traumas he suffered in his early years; that "life was difficult" and, as the youngest sibling, that he felt excluded, "not part of a group". Certainly, from my own childhood, I soon became aware of my father's uncertain relationship with Michael, his eldest brother by three years. Single-minded and strong willed, Michael was the family's brightest star and Peter, gentler by nature, admired him but feared

21

him too – a fear which fed the insecurities that shadowed his life from the beginning. In its detached and awkward prose, the history – written, we must remember, for family consumption – recalls two life-and-death incidents which would have terrified Peter the child but, at the same time, cast his older brother in the role of hero. The first drama took place in Pangbourne while the children were playing in the garden by the river. Tony, least bright of the three brothers but blessed with a keen sense of fun, fancied a swim in the bathing cage attached to the riverbank. It was early spring and the water was too cold for the intrepid four year old. So mother said no. Tony's reaction to this minor humiliation was to fill his toy watering can with hot water which he then ceremoniously poured into the Thames – and at this point, he fell in, panicked and nearly drowned. Michael's level head and quick wit saved him. He grabbed his brother's hand and shouted for help.

The second incident Peter describes – again as a sensitive child witness – left a more profound mark on him. He begins by recalling the journey home to Pressburg at the end of the war, looking through a porthole of the ship taking the family to the Hook of Holland and watching the other ships in the convoy surrounded by the protecting screen of the Royal Navy. "There followed the journey across a Europe in chaos," he writes. "The Germans, on the verge of defeat, could not have relished the sound of three little boys singing Tipperary and other war songs in their midst. Then the arrival in Pressburg followed shortly by the fall of Austria-Hungary, the revolution and the advent of the Czech troops. Everyone had been instructed not to look out of the windows. In the Carlton Hotel, Nell and her children were in their room when curiosity to see this new breed, the Czechs, marching into the town became too great for her and she peered out of the window. A soldier saw her, raised his rifle and fired. Luckily Michael again came to the rescue. He was at her side, saw the soldier and pulled his mother back into the room just in time. The bullet shattered the window and lodged in the ceiling." This was young Peter's introduction to the new state of Czechoslovakia.

Not long after their arrival, HP moved the family out of the Savoy-Carlton and they settled into a spacious villa in the countryside close to the city centre.

My father – ever conscious of his audience – paints an idealized picture of his childhood years in Bratislava (as the city had now become): tobogganing in winter, swimming in the Danube in summer, building camps in the woods, soccer with the garden staff. But underlying it all, there is also the sense that life was not remotely easy. Henry, having been isolated as an alien in England during the war, now found himself isolated again – this time in his own home town. The old Habsburg patriot hated his new masters and they showed little inclination to accommodate him. Eventually, an uneasy truce was forced upon them both. After all, he was a famous hotelier who owned the most prominent hotel in the city. As host, he had an obligation to welcome his guests be they Czechs, Slovaks or any other nationality – and they were not shy in enjoying the superior hospitality of the Savoy-Carlton. But in the privacy of his home, he had nothing but loathing and contempt for the new regime, refusing to allow anyone to refer to the city by its new name. For him it was, and would always remain, Pressburg or, in Hungarian, Pozsony. Living with this tension and in this atmosphere left their mark on his youngest son.

The politics and prejudices of those times were not the only point of friction. Nell now found herself bound to a culture which was at odds with her English upbringing and independence of mind. Her first meeting with Amelia was a disaster and set the tone for an icy relationship between mother and daughter-in-law. Local custom and politesse demanded the younger woman kiss the matriarch's hand. Nell refused and nothing her husband said would persuade her to change her mind. After this early skirmish, Nell kept her distance, devoting her life to the family, the house and the garden.

Of course, she would have been an asset to the Savoy-Carlton but any thoughts of her being involved in the management of the hotel were now blown to the wind – besides, the place was already overrun by Henry's brothers, sisters and related family members: Julius running the Café Savoy at one end of the vast edifice and their youngest sister Luise directing the Carlton Café at the other. Middle sister Christine and her husband Gustave Wellisch ran the hotel's two restaurants and the central kitchens, assisted by a platoon of Wellisch relatives. Youngest brother Max was office-bound as an administrator while his wife Elsa managed the laundry. And there, overseeing the whole, enthroned in her mezzanine office looking down upon the hotel's grand entrance hall, sat the awesome dowager-figure of Amelia. Nothing escaped her hawkish gaze and the sound of her voice would echo around the hall as if from nowhere – chiding, instructing, correcting some hapless employee or even, when the occasion demanded, directing Mr. Joseph, the concièrge, to escort an errant guest off the premises.

On the wall behind her hung the battle cry and rallying standard of the family's endeavour. No ordinary company logo this. This was a call to arms, a statement of mission. Branding with attitude. The legend, headed by the Napoleonic bee and framed by a laurel wreath, read:

EIN GROSSER GEIST GEPAART MIT UNVERDROSS'NEM FLEISSE LIES DIESES HAUS DEM PHOENIX GLEICH ERSTEH'N UND ALS SYMBOL VON DIESEM GROSSEN FLEISSE IST EINE BIENE ALLERORT'S ZU SEH'N.

(A great spirit coupled with unflagging industry caused this house to rise like the phoenix and as a symbol of this great diligence a bee is everywhere to be seen.)

There never was a more ubiquitous bee – printed, engraved, stitched and embroidered – on stationery and menus; china, glass and silverware; napkins, sheets and pillowslips. The bee – as the lady and her heir decreed – everywhere to be seen.

On 30th December 1922, after a stroke, Amelia died at the age of seventy-three. "So many people turned out for her funeral," writes Peter, "it almost became a state affair." In her obituary, the city's evening newspaper ran a lavish encomium ". . . another piece of Old-Pressburg is lost with her departure," it observed. "She achieved the stature of a truly great lady and in all circles of society she was valued for her untiring ability, her great experience and her generous personality."

*

By the time of the great matriarch's passing, the turbulence of the post-war years had subsided and Bratislava, Slovakia's principal city in the new Czechoslovakia, was growing as a political and industrial centre. Business was good. And Henry, denied his ultimate dream in London, now set his heart on transforming the Savoy-Carlton into a grand luxury hotel on a scale that would rival Europe's finest. His plan was to take the nondescript three-storey structure bolted together out of the three buildings bought a decade earlier and double its size to six storeys. The old apartment block – the middle section – would be razed and rebuilt with the entire façade then resurfaced as one, the whole suitably ornamented with balconies and cornices, mouldings and parapets. As a final touch, this magnificent new edifice would be topped by a seventh floor master suite, its roof crowned with a giant bee in glittering bronze.

To realize his ambition, HP had to borrow heavily and the banks were only too eager to provide him with the funds. By the mid-twenties, reconstruction work was well underway. But it was then that the economy began to sour. Business fell away. The hotel was hit by a cash crisis and, struggling to service his borrowings, HP raised additional finance just to meet his repayment schedules. He was not alone. Across Europe industry was beginning to feel the squeeze as the early signs of the coming depression gradually took hold. And all the while Henry's Czechoslovak bankers quietly enjoyed turning the screw on their old Hungarian adversary as interest rates climbed to 24%. At home, in their villa on its hillside above the city, there were occasions when Peter would overhear his father whispering his despair: "I *do* hope," he'd say to Nell, "I'll be able to see this through to the finish".

There is a photograph of the family taken in the summer of 1928. It is a carefully composed image – almost formal – but the body language in its very composition betrays the sadness and strain of a marriage at a low ebb. Husband and wife are seated on a white garden bench, a rockery as background; their three sons – white shirts open at the neck, sleeves rolled up – standing behind, half-smiling are looking straight at the camera's lens. Nell, on the left of the picture, is unsmiling, lost in her own world, staring blankly away to the right into nowhere. She has gone prematurely grey. Perched on the bench either side of her lap, she holds two adorable but solemn-looking Scotties, their ears pricked. Her only comfort. Henry looks equally distracted. Leaning lightly on the armrest, away from Nell, his left hand clutching the clenched fist of his right. There is not a glimmer of affection on display. Only a sense of estrangement.

One year later, three months before the stock market crashed on Wall Street, Henry Prüger committed suicide. Peter, now fourteen years old, was looking forward to the end of the school term when his godfather, Otto Goring, arrived unexpectedly at Dover College to break the news to the three brothers. They left school immediately to rejoin their mother and the family in Bratislava. "It was a miserable summer," wrote Peter. "The world we had known was at an end."

In the history, only the appendices provide some hint of the circumstances of the tragedy. My father's narrative record of the death is worse than anodyne, it is almost a denial – but, perhaps, I judge him too harshly. He had to live with the trauma from an impressionable age and for his generation, coming also from a Catholic background, suicide bore society's and the church's stigma. Even so, I struggle to understand why he carried such a weight of inhibition and pain to dismiss this terrible episode in one short paragraph of less than thirty words. He describes the severe strain of the financial burdens on HP and then, come the moment, concludes: "It was all too much and the worry of it all killed Henry. He died on 11th July 1929, two months short of his 62nd birthday."

It was not until after my mother's death that I fell upon the truth. Louise and I were clearing Avon Lodge – Peter and Etty's villa nesting on its steep slope over the Vale of Taunton Deane. On a high shelf in his old study, I discovered a large black tin deed box with "P.F. CHAPMAN" stencilled in white on the lid. Peter Francis Chapman, I thought, repeating my father's two Christian names to myself. He claimed his second name derived from Fan, his godmother, Nell's sister. Maybe. Equally likely, I think, Francis was given as a tribute to HP's beloved Emperor – Franz Joseph.

The box was unlocked and I had to lift it with some care to avoid its heavy contents spilling out over my head. Resting it on the floor of the study, I opened the lid to find dozens, perhaps hundreds, of documents: certificates of birth and marriage; army books – his officer's record of service, an officer's dress card, various ID cards and travel passes including one for the Khyber Pass, a smallpox vaccination certificate; old passports; Maky's will; a testimonial from his headmaster at Dover College; a testimonial from his commanding officer, Brigadier H.W. McDonald; discharge papers from the Indian Army and a letter of thanks for his service from the India Office; legal documents including the deed, signed by the three brothers, renouncing the family surname of PRÜGER. Near the bottom of the tin, beneath bundles of correspondence from Gerald during his years in New York, I found a short letter written in black ink on expensive vellum. The handwriting was unmistakable. I recognized it instantly from my childhood: the framed postcard hanging on the wall by my bedside, the lines of verse copied out in a long flowing hand: "Boys of spirit, boys of will,/Boys of muscle, brain and power,/Fit to cope with anything,/These are wanted every hour."

I had found a suicide note. Maybe there were others, I cannot tell. It reads - in shocking, ironic contrast to the poem:

My dear Hilda,

A terrible folly of mine smashed all what we possessed.

I come to you with the great request, please please help my poor wife and children.

Oh my boys, my boys.

I can't say more my heart aches for my poor Girl my boys and my brothers and sisters, it is too terrible for words.

Once more let me appeal to you.

Goodbye

Your unfortunate

Henry

I have not been able to uncover the identity of Hilda. A close family friend, perhaps? There is one touching postscript to this letter which otherwise leaves me in a tangle of emotions (from deep sorrow to extreme anger that HP's hubris should ultimately lead him to the premeditated dumping of his wife and children). Enclosed with the note to Hilda was a yellowed, crumpled cutting from the Times's court columns dated 20th January, 1911 announcing the wedding of Henry and Nell the previous day. The notice states that: "The church was beautifully decorated with chrysanthemums. The bride ... wore a travelling dress of sapphire blue velvet and a large black hat trimmed with feathers." Henry obviously treasured this cutting and for the eighteen and a half years of their marriage kept it somewhere close – possibly in his wallet – as a token of his love for Nell.

And the famous appendices? All in their dense Gothic newsprint – reams of obits, personal profiles and inflated valedictory notices, most oozing their soapy servility in a hochdeutsch whose strangled idiom defies translation. What do we learn?

Die Grenzbote, Pressburg's leading daily struck, in my reading, a more considered chord, running a long piece by a Herr Eugen Holly. It goes to some length to characterize Prüger, describing "a brilliant life" which ended "not brilliantly, but honourably in a space in the roof of his own hotel." Later in the article, Holly explains the petty bureaucracy HP encountered before obtaining the permissions he needed for the works to proceed. He continues:

"Right at the top of the building the work is still continuing; much is yet to be completed, with unfinished stairways, a confusion of wooden beams and scaffolding, a jumble of labour and effort."

"The project swallows up millions, costing more than originally calculated ... the bricks which were laid prove heavier than the hand which ordered them. Prüger, a man who always wishes to oversee, calculate and control everything himself, a man who tries to keep an eye on every detail – every length of wire and every new bell-push – finally loses his grip. Anxieties mount ... but this reserved man, thrown back upon himself, has such pride that he scorns any help, even in the form of advice. He remains a dynast, one who trusts himself and nobody else, but now he loses his clarity of vision, sees imaginary dangers around him, feels himself in the dark, wanders around upon the scaffolding of his dreams in the upper storeys of his giant building – a man searching for himself, but in vain." Finally, Herr Holly describes how Henry found his end by creeping into *"a hollow attic space in the highest story of Pressburg's grand hotel"*.

Whatever the Catholic Church's teaching on suicide, Henry was granted a grand and honourable funeral. Led by the Cathedral Dean and senior clerics of the city, one report claimed that the crowds at St. Andreas' cemetery could be counted in thousands. Diplomats, parliamentarians and councillors; the Chamber of Commerce, the Licensed Victuallers, café proprietors and employees; editors, publishers and even the loathsome bankers who caused him so much misery. They were all there to witness the cortège: Nell, Michael, Tony, Peter, the family following Henry's coffin flanked by eight head waiters of the Savoy-Carlton bearing lanterns. As I write this, I simply wonder about the thoughts – the terror even – of the innocent young fourteen year old, standing at the graveside, watching his father's heavy oak coffin wrapped in a black shroud being lowered into the earth.

*

In the aftermath of his death, the city seems to have been gripped, momentarily, by a fit of collective guilt. The Mayor wrote a toe-curlingly obsequious letter to Nell expressing the Council's condolences, acknowledging "the creative joy and wide vision" Henry brought to his "great enterprise". They also commissioned a bronze bust of the great hotelier as a fitting memorial to his life. But when they proposed to name a street after him, Nell decided their hypocrisy was just too indigestible. She declined.

This is what I love about my grandmother. Her spirit. Her gritty principles. Her determination in the face of adversity. No one doubted the strength of purpose behind that polished veneer of English reserve. So Nell now took control, rousing the family to do battle to rescue her dead husband's precious dream. Unfinished, the Savoy-Carlton was an unattractive asset anyway and armed with her defiant will she set about refinancing the project. She succeeded; works resumed; and by the turn of the new decade Henry Prüger's great palace was complete.

At the same time, Nell was determined that her three boys should return to school and complete their education at Dover College. Nor did she want any upheavals at home. In their holidays, they returned to the family's villa and estate outside Bratislava – a home life they had grown up with and enjoyed. But the debt burden – no less acute than before – now rested with her.

She coped. And when her youngest first set eyes on the finished hotel, he was awestruck – his description of the place ringing with the enthusiasm of an excited teenager: "It was quite magnificent," he gushes, "six storeys high, with a seventh in the middle, and a whole block long and deep. It had 254 bedrooms, (341 beds), two large cafés between them seating well over 300 people, billiard rooms, three restaurants, a cabaret and night club, and several large function rooms and a Winter Garden … and at the rear was the four-storey power station and workshops."

Peter's youthful pride in his father's achievement would never be sustained. As depression gripped the world, the financial pressures mounted like some rumbling storm, enveloping the family; incessant, insistent, emphatic. The horrible inevitability of it all never openly expressed or admitted. On one occasion, at home during the school holidays, Peter was alone in the house when the telephone rang. He lifted the receiver in the hall to hear the agitated voice of his uncle Max warning him that "The Flying Dutchmen" were on their way. These were the notorious fleets of bailiffs who descended on debt-ridden families like raiding pirates, stripping them of their possessions. Peter, terrified and with no one to turn to for help, began rolling up large Persian rugs and, driven by the adrenalin pumping through his veins, he dragged and shoved the heavy carpets through a trap door into the roof space. He returned downstairs for more, searching out the family's silver, antique objects, heirlooms, anything valuable the bailiffs might seek to snatch. Two hours later, sweat-drenched and exhausted, there was still no sign of them – nor did they come that day.

Nell waged her war for seven years but the thirties remained depressed and eventually the banks foreclosed. For the second time, the Prügers lost their fortune and their inheritance.

For Nell it was all over. Her only comfort was the knowledge that her three sons had completed their schooling in England and were now safely launched on the world. If she harboured any regret for her children, it was that she could not afford the university places both Michael and Peter might have won. With nothing to keep her in Bratislava, she salvaged what she could, packed up and returned home accompanied by her faithful Hungarian servant Maky. From that day in 1937 the Villa and its estate were abandoned – left to the guardianship of a local solicitor who divided the land into plots for development. Then came another war, the Iron Curtain and a communist regime which cast the family's rights of title into confusion. Since the lifting of the Curtain and the fall of the Berlin Wall, we, Henry's grandchildren – all of us – have been trying to engage the processes of Slovakia's arcane legal system to untangle the threads wound around our claim on the property. And so, seventy years on, this story still runs. But that is a tale for another day.

By the summer of 1937, Nell and Maky had settled into Avon Lodge, their cottage in Little Common near Bexhill-on-Sea in East Sussex. The year is significant for another reason. Peter was now in India and had been for almost two years working for J & P Coats, the cotton traders, when he received a letter from his brother Michael announcing that the family or – more accurately – *he* had decided to renounce the surname PRÜGER and, in its place, adopt their mother's maiden name CHAPMAN. The news came as a shock to Peter. He was hurt and angry that a decision of this magnitude had been presented to him as a fait accompli. The arguments and the motives for Michael's determination to change the family name are obscure. Peter's narrative on the issue, sensitive as it may be, is guarded and circumspect. That it ignited fresh tensions within the family is self-evident from the sparse facts in my possession. In all the years I knew my uncle Michael – himself an hotelier of genius and the architect who made the Imperial in Torquay the most famous hotel in England – not once did I succeed in persuading him to talk about his youth in Pressburg. This was in stark contrast to my father who loved to tell and retell to Gerald and me the happier stories of his Swallows-and-Amazons childhood. I remember asking him why, for Michael, "Brats" – as the boys called their home town – was a closed book. His reply was cautious, suggesting that at school Michael had been bullied for being a Boche. But I wonder if, as the eldest of the three brothers, his desire to bury this period of his life was not in some way linked to a deep unspoken resentment towards his father for the calamity he brought upon the family. Even his given names were not exempt from purification. He was christened Henry Michael – his first name carrying the burden of the patronymic (for so it seemed to become) of both father and grandfather. For the first twenty-five years of his life, family and friends knew him as Henry or Heini. Old Maky was confirmation enough. She frequently lapsed into the Pressburg vernacular referring to him as Henry – a habit which confused me as a child because I, with the rest of the world, knew him as Michael Chapman. But to Nell, her eldest was, invariably, "Henry Michael".

Then there is the deed poll itself. This suggests that a compromise was reached. That, in the end, the three brothers agreed to renounce PRÜGER in favour of de PRÜGER CHAPMAN (the French affectation "de" being an expedient alternative to the less acceptable Austrian title "von" – which HP declined to adopt when the Emperor decorated him with his Order of the Knight's Cross). In the event, Michael and his family, my cousins, never used the elongated surname and, a generation on, it has fallen from use with us.

And Nell? Where did she stand on this issue? Predictably, she would not be moved. Nell remained a Prüger until the day she died in January 1954.

*

The black tin deed box was not the only archive I discovered on the high shelf in my father's study. There were photograph albums too. With the history's self-conscious and arid prose, with the contents of the deed box, and now a pictorial anthology of Peter's early life, a new awareness began to dawn on me, a gradual realization of a special love-bond between mother and younger son.

In 1935, the year Peter sailed for India, Nell began to compile one of these leather-bound volumes – its brown starched leaves annotated in white ink with the title page dated and inscribed with the words: "Peter's Book". Below this simple heading she pasted a monochrome portrait of her twenty-year-old son. The most handsome photograph of my young father I have set eyes on.

Immaculately dressed in a dog-tooth sports jacket and carefully knotted old school tie, his dark brilliantined hair perfectly parted over a high forehead, full lips and strong, clear sculpted features, he looked the quintessential, dashing English gentleman. A peach, a plum, the apple of his mother's eye.

Two years before, he had left Dover College for the last time to spend a final summer holiday at home in Pressburg. His valete listing in the school journal read heroically of his achievements on the playing fields; of his colours and caps and trophies (now littered about my study). And, best of all, the University of London Matriculation Board had entered his name in the first division of the published examination pass list. A proud mother sent her son a telegram with the family's "heartiest congratulations". Peter deserved his holiday and he decided to spend part of it on the Danube. By now Michael had begun his training with a merry-go-round of placements in Europe's great hotels, so Peter and Tony mustered a group of friends to row a long boat down river from Passau in Germany to Bratislava – a journey of over two hundred miles which took the crew of six a week to complete. It was a journey chronicled again by Nell in an album of photographs taken by Peter & Co. and annotated in white ink.

The friends spent their first day exploring Passau and walking the countryside – the start to an adventure which began with an incident ringing with the sinister prescience of events to come. As they topped the brow of a hill bordering the river, they fell upon a mass rally of Hilter's brown-shirted storm troops, the SA, exercising in the valley below. "It was an unsettling sight," Peter recalled and the group retreated back to their boat. From then on, Nell's photo-journal records a week of vigorous rowing broken by visits to historic sites – notably Dürnstein Castle where Richard Coeur de Lion was imprisoned on his return from the Third Crusade – and bouts of serious drinking. One snap has her sheepish-looking son, skullcap askew, taking breakfast in a café at Dürnstein – the weary inscription observing: "The day after the night before." But by the end of the trip, Peter had acquired a skin bronzed deep by the Danube's sun and a final picture taken of him on the boat sees Nell's athletic Adonis in full rowing-strip crouched across the craft, oar tucked under shoulder, with the caption reading "Peter reckons he's a bit of a king in this photo".

That autumn, the holiday forgotten and with Peter back in London, the reality of living in 1930s' Britain hit hard. The young king of the Danube could not find a job. After two months of calling on dozens of companies, day after day, he was taken in as an office boy at a wage of thirty shillings or £1.50 a week. He survived – just – until J & P Coats called him to Glasgow for an interview with the cotton firm's trading division and on New Year's Day 1934 he began work as a management trainee at an annual salary of £140. Peter was euphoric: "The relief and joy at having at last found a job with a real future is quite indescribable". Mother also was relieved. She sent him £20 with which to open his first bank account.

Eighteen months later a post fell vacant in India and by October 1935 he had booked his passage to Bombay on the SS City of Simla sailing out of Liverpool. A fortnight before embarkation he was given leave to return home to say his farewells to the family – his final visit to Pressburg. A mother's instinct is a strange mystery. Nell knew she would be parted from her boy for a long while but some deeper sense convinced her the separation might be longer than even she imagined. To Peter's surprise, she insisted on returning to England with him. Saying goodbye was not enough. Nell wanted to be mother and do what mothers do because she knew this would be the last time. She wanted to go shopping with him – to make sure he was properly equipped for the tropics. And she wanted to see him off. "I could not understand her tears," he recalls, "after all I was off on a fabulous adventure! We waved until losing sight of each other. Little did either of us realize it would be almost ten years before we met again. I was twenty and a half years old".

On the long train journey back to London, Nell wept herself into a dull, uncomfortable sleep. On her return to Bratislava she bought another brown leather album and inscribed it "Peter's Book" in large white letters.

A postcard of the SS City of Simla shows a workaday vessel past its prime – not that this dimmed its passengers' will to party for much of the month-long voyage. Nell's chronicle of photographs sent home by her son reveals a carefree existence of shuffleboard, obstacle races and fancy dress parties in an all-male group made up mostly of young officers straight out of Sandhurst, seemingly oblivious of the fact that their ship was sailing into a war zone – Mussolini's invasion of Abyssinia (now Ethiopia). But the sight of Italian troop carriers, warships and submarines in Port Said and the Red Sea only added to the gaiety and romance of the trip.

As the Simla steamed across the Arabian Sea, Peter's senses began to be aroused. "Approaching Bombay, even a full day away," he notes, "one was aware of an aura, also a smell which was a mixture of spices and heat."

At the dockside, he was met by the local branch manager who entertained him to dinner at the Royal Bombay Yacht Club before driving him to Victoria Terminus to catch the Frontier Mail for the twenty-four hour rail journey to Delhi. This was a welcome oozing Empire and Nell's album throbs with Peter's images of colonial splendour and the symbols of power – Queen Victoria's statue in Bombay, the Prince of Wales Museum, the High Court, the General Post Office – huge edifices of Gothic extravagance.

For six months, "Peter's first home" in Delhi was a grand, colonnaded and porticoed, hotel called the Cecil, next door to the Delhi Club, hub of the local expat social scene. It marks the beginning of a period in my father's life which was pleasurable and stimulating. Released from the constraints and tensions of family, the turbulent currents stirred by his father's suicide and the withdrawal from Pressburg, India gave Peter a new sense of freedom. Nell missed her son but she understood and was happy for him. And in the history, his narrative sheds its self-consciousness and takes flight. Nell's care, the manner in compiling her pictorial anthology, not only expresses her love for Peter, it somehow chimes with the spirit of his own descriptive record of his life in India written fifty years later. For me, the album exposes this deep mutual affection. It is unspoken, undemonstrative – in its way emphasizing the power of their special bond. And, here and there, this is evident in a shared humour. Peter's bearer – his servant – Nazir Khan was a source of amusement which tickled Nell. Turbaned, richly moustachioed and white-suited, Nazir was an impressive looking man who, for my father's needs anyway, was over-qualified for the role. At home, Nell would open her son's letters from Delhi to find the latest crop of snaps and, occasionally as a bonus, a primitive cartoon in pencil or ink of "the great God Sahib being awakened by servant Nazir"; or Nazir preparing his Sahib's hookah; or Nazir assisting his Sahib into his tonga to take him to the office. Half a century on, my father wrote: "He brought my early morning tea and toast, put out my clothes and would also have shaved me in bed, bathed and dried me, and put my shoes on my feet and laced them, had I allowed him to do so! I must have disappointed him and he reached the conclusion that I was *not* a Pukkah Sahib."

By spring of the following year, Peter had joined the Light Horse, part of Delhi's Auxiliary Force, for no reason other than to ride – with the added benefit of expert instruction from a British cavalry staff sergeant. Riding became a passion – the pages of Nell's album filled with photographs of parades, picnics, gymkhanas and Peter exercising his horse Sullivan. Pictures of him in pith helmet, jodhpurs and polished boots are variously captioned "Our Empire Builder in India"; "Peter as Cavalry man"; and "His Excellency The 'Viceroy' Pips." (Pips being Nell's pet name for him.)

With the photographs, cartoons and the occasional press cutting reporting his gymkhana triumphs, Nell also removed the postage stamps from Peter's envelopes and pasted them into her book. By 1937, the head of Edward VIII had been replaced by the twin portraits of King George VI and Queen Elizabeth. It was also the year Peter transferred to Bombay – a posting and an urban life he found less agreeable to the country-style of living he had enjoyed in Delhi. He missed his riding and his beloved horse Sullivan. And life at work was complicated by a station chief who was a drunk. But he soon settled in, taking up rowing and rugby again as a member of the city's famous sports' establishment, the Bombay Gymkhana Club. When he smiled for the camera, his cheeks creased – a characteristic Nell adored – moving her to mark the words "Pips & his DIMPLE" beneath one sporty snap of him in his white flannels.

After the Munich crisis of 1938 and with war now inevitable, Peter rejoined the Auxiliary Force and was offered a commission in the Royal Engineers. With the rank of Second Lieutenant, he and his unit were charged with responsibility for Bombay's coastal defences. Letters home to mother were upbeat – he loved the army, he loved the uniform. He even loved the drills and the inspections as Nell noted with wry surprise in the latest rash of photographs she received. "Life in an army mess," he wrote, "amongst young, ebullient and high spirited subalterns was very jolly."

With the outbreak of war, he wanted to join the "proper army", and applied for officer cadet training. By October 1940 he had completed his course and, inspired by Kipling's poem *The Ballad of East and West*, he was accepted by the regiment of his dreams, Queen Victoria's Own Corps of Guides, "undoubtedly the finest regiment in the Indian Army."

And when they drew to the Quarter-Guard, full twenty swords flew clear --
There was not a man but carried his feud with the blood of the mountaineer.
"Ha' done! ha' done!" said the Colonel's son.
"Put up the steel at your sides!
Last night ye had struck at a Border thief --
to-night 'tis a man of the Guides!"

Lines I remember well. Not by reading them but for hearing them recited to Gerald and me as children.

It is at this point in Nell's biographical picture book that the story comes to an abrupt stop. Or, rather, she adopts a new, more reflective, retrospective approach to her quiet labour of love. Peter, no doubt, continued to write – but his letters contained no photographs. His war – about which he writes at great length in the history – took him to East Africa, the Middle East, Italy and finally, as a Major, to Greece.

Turn the page from a Bombay quayside mustering a platoon of recruits and I find myself staring at a picture of Nell, forlorn by the porch of her cottage in Little Common. The white ink, a cri de coeur "Still waiting for Peter. Avon Lodge 1939". Another, in her garden, hands clasped behind her back, is marked simply "Mother". The remaining photographs mounted across the twin spread of the album's brown sheets are of her lost boy: two in the garden at Pangbourne taken in 1916, a child clutching a lawn mower. One caption reads "Peter at 14 months, my Gardener". The other continues "already tired of gardening". A third is dated Bratislava 1922, showing a pious seven year old in a lace-fringed surplice over his heavy cassock, with the inscription "Peter as Ministrant". The last shows him floundering in deep snow – "Semmering, Austria 1924. First skiing lesson. First fall."

Nell had to wait another six years. As the war approached its end, Peter fell ill. The pressures and experiences of his long war collided with those of a lost youth and now they claimed their victim. He had a nervous breakdown and was evacuated out of Patras in southern Greece to a base hospital in Italy. It was six weeks before he returned to his duties and, shortly after, he was granted three months leave in England. The troopship carrying him home docked in Liverpool in May 1945. Now thirty, the emotion of his return after an absence of nearly ten years was overwhelming. He had written to Nell to alert her to his homecoming but he was unsure whether she had received his letter. He wanted to telephone from Liverpool but didn't, fearful that he might miss the next train bound for London. The same happened at Victoria Station where he found a train about to leave for East Croydon. When he arrived, he had twenty minutes to spare before his connection to Bexhill. At Avon Lodge, Nell answered the call. The few moments Peter spent speaking to his mother from the telephone box on the platform at East Croydon station that spring evening remained alive in his memory for the rest of his life.

"Hello Mummy," he began, "it's me. I'm home again."

"Who's speaking?" she replied.

"Peter."

"Peter? Peter who?"

"Peter," he insisted hoarsely, "your son. Peter!"

At the other end of the line, there was a timeless pause before her reply.

"Peter you say? Where are you speaking from?"

"I'm in East Croydon."

"What are you doing in East Croydon?" she said, instantly regretting the curtness in her voice.

"Changing trains. I'm on my way home and due to arrive in Bexhill at 10.30."

The impact of the news she was hearing began to well up inside her chest like rolling waves. She needed to stop herself.

"How silly of you Peter to take a train to Bexhill! You should have gone to Cooden Beach. It's much nearer!"

Mother and son were reunited that night. There was much to tell and much to hear. And Maky kept them fuelled with endless pots of tea.

Three months later, Peter returned to regimental life – in Salonica in northern Greece. He was about to meet the love of his life. And by the middle of the following year he and Etty were married. Nell now completed the final page of her album. Headed "Victory Year" in her familiar white ink, the page decorated with George VI postage stamps, she wrote the words "The beginning *and* end of Freedom". Below the inscription, she wrote a second heading "Peter's Marriage – June 2nd 1946" – "The end and beginning of his Freedom". Last of all, like melodies in counterpoint, where her title page carried his portrait, the young boy bachelor in sports jacket and old school tie, so the end page carried a portrait of the married Indian Army officer, his nineteen year old olive-eyed bride at his side.

*

Part Two

Early Skirmishes

Aristotle's Terrace

Alone again. Just the two of us – Louise and I. Family and friends have come and gone, spellbound and content, seduced by Diodati's balmy ether, convinced after all that life is beautiful. Last night we dined beneath a violet-tinged sky prickled by starlight, the air resin-scented by the pines, the floodlit woodland wrapping us in its reassuring glow (and an output of three thousand watts keeping the mosquito at bay!). Beyond, the sea was still, the calm occasionally disturbed by the puk-a-puk-a-puk of a fishing boat on its way to join a lantern-blazing daisy chain of vessels strung across the archipelago. On our terrace we sat side-by-side staring in wonderment out through the trees, sharing our thoughts. At last, after all these years of exile I was beginning to understand why this place was important to Peter – and we imagined them both, Etty and Peter, doing as we were now doing – staring.

At table, we were feasting on Patra's *yemistes* – fat tomatoes and peppers stuffed with rice and minced veal and seasoned with onion, mint, parsley, sultanas and pine nuts – the most aromatic and satisfying of Greek dishes. With them we drank a well-made sauvignon blanc from the uplands of Florina in northern Greece, a wine equal to the best you may find in the Loire valley. Perfection! Eating in this country – often mocked by tourists arriving home with stories of cold, oil-laden, indigestible food – is one of the nation's great offerings if you know where to find it. For the inquisitive it has a gustatory culture to rival Provence or Tuscany. And the fruit! Fresh, ripe and in season – cherries, figs, peaches, melons. You will never taste the true and sublime sweetness of these fruits until you have tasted them in Greece. This morning we breakfasted on peaches – their ripeness at perfect pitch so that each quarter of velvety skin eases lightly off the flesh like cream off a spoon. Then fold with yoghurt and honey and eat in the gentle, breezy warmth of the rising sun. It is an experience you will not repeat north of the Balkans. But where peaches nourish with their bosom-wholesomeness, green-nippled figs should be consumed raw, unaccompanied and, like sexual intercourse, in private – such is the sensual joy of this fruit when its red-pink sticky sweetness explodes out of its creamy-white flesh.

Enough fantasy for today! Who is Patra you may wonder? She was baptized Cleopatra but to dwell a moment more on the ambrosian metaphor, her aura, her spirit, is peach-fruit, not fig! For us she is as old as the house, a part of the house, a friend and a part of our life on the island. She had just turned twenty-nine when my mother discovered her working in a neighbour's villa. Now in her sixties, she remains as we have always remembered her; peach-plump and house-proud, motherly and the best cook in the Aegean; the irresistibility of her confections despatching us home to England with a few extra pounds about our bellies. But her comforting domesticity belies the nature of a deeper being – one who bears a quiet serenity and a strength founded on her Orthodox faith to which she gives three hours' devotion each Sunday and never fails to observe the multitude of feast days and fasts in the Church's busy calendar. If her religion is worn lightly, she leaves a firm sense of someone who is on excellent terms with her Maker. And like her faith, on matters temporal, her convictions and beliefs may be unspoken, held within the bounds of a strictly maintained discretion, but you know you are in the presence of a woman of unshakeable values in the conduct of her quotidian routines. Married to the indomitable Panayioti, father to their three grown-up children (and both proud grandparents too), she conforms to the island mores of family life where he, as head of the household, rules but where she, in reality, is the one who governs. Hers is a practical, earthly intelligence uncluttered by the sour breezes of social fashion or popular wisdom. For us, her charm lies behind those deep, soulful eyes which, set alight, sparkle with wit and fun. Patra loves to giggle – and it is laughter that unlocked her relationship with Louise. With no common language to ease the flow of communication, they communicate with ease – laughter replacing language as the conduit of understanding, Louise's determined struggles to grasp the rudiments of the Greek tongue fuelling more merriment. Two women, of two different cultures, of two different worlds, somehow able to pluck common chords to create a communion of hearts and minds in a manner which is essentially female in disposition.

*

Leap a generation back into the past and how different life at Diodati! Another world. A different cultural web.

A younger Patra would catch the morning bus out of the village to the stop by Kanapitsa and walk the steep peninsula track to the house – some forty minutes in the dust and heat of an Aegean summer. She'd cook and scrub and clean; change the sheets and towels, wash, tidy and make good as we set off for the beaches and boats. On our return, we'd find the table on the terrace beautifully laid – a small brass bell at my mother's place – in readiness for lunch. We'd shower and change and gather for a long drink; Etty appearing radiant in a printed ankle-length linen wrap-around with a matching top and bandeau about her raven hair. "The view! Oh, the view!" She'd ring the bell. Patra would appear with the mezethes – a taramasalata, zaziki, melitzanosalata, Kalamata olives, a choriatiki salata – while Peter poured the wine. In those days it might be a Demestica, a dull yellow, resinous liquid – drinkable enough then but not to be compared with the quality of Greek wines today. Again the bell. Patra would return, clear and present the main event : a rich and silky moussaka, or herby, spicy kephtethes cooked with potatoes and a tomato sauce, or her famous yemistes. The bell again. Water melon, cheese, baklava, kadaiffi . . . And so sated to our beds for a sleep while Patra cleared up and made her way back along the scorched track, a host of cicadas rattling in her ears. At the bus stop, she endured a long wait – one hour, sometimes two. Back then, the island only ran one bus and, on its return from the beaches, it would often be full, leaving her stranded on the steaming tarmac for another hour. This was the routine – six days in each August week – leaving Sunday for church, a rest and her family.

The routine today is altogether more democratic! A partnership of equals. Where Etty commanded, Louise assists – first by collecting Patra by car. She visits us once weekly and our day begins at nine o'clock with Greek coffee (*metrio* or medium sweet) and *koulouraki* (cookies) on the verandah of the family's comfortable home near the town's soccer ground. Here, Panayioti holds court in his chair, briefing us on the island's latest dramas, warning us of impending storms, alerting us to the local police's tariff for various motoring offences, and blaming the Albanians for most of the ills of the world. As Diodati's custodian-in-chief, he supervises our minor maintenance projects – calling up plumbers, electricians and carpenters, as and when, hectoring them noisily down a telephone line to the annoyance of his granddaughter, Panayiota, who calls down from her bedroom telling him to shut up because she is trying to study. Eventually, we set forth, piling sardine-like into our Hertz-hired Suzuki Jimmy, a mini-jeep which discriminates painfully against long-legged humans. At the supermarket, Louise and Patra nudge a trolley down the aisles in search of stock essentials and debate menus for the coming week before we head for Apostolis, the grocer at the top of Papadiamantis – the town's pedestrianized high street, thus named in memory of Alexandros Papadiamantis (1851-1911), the island's most illustrious son and one of Greece's great literary lions. Here we buy our fresh fruit, vegetables and herbs; the best feta, caseri and graviera cheeses to be found anywhere, and our wines – from a remarkable selection, itself a persuasive advertisement for the revival of Greek viticulture. Shopkeepers like Apostolis are all but an extinct breed in our homogenized, Tesco-rinsed world. A kindly, mild-mannered and scrupulously courteous man, his knowledge is encyclopaedic – keen always to explain the provenance of the products displayed at his deli-counter; encouraging you to taste different varieties of a generic cheese, or olive, or cured meat; recounting the methods of individual producers; dissuading you from choosing one particular item over another if, that week, he is not entirely satisfied with a delivery. His is the best kind of sales patter – a pitch which converts your over-indulgence into an act of moral worth, adding aesthetic value to the mundane process of doing the shopping.

At home again, there is no delay as the kitchen mutates into a kaleidoscope of colour, noise and smell – sounds of chopping and sizzling, the savoury aromas, and the chortling of what passes to be a Greek language class, all assail my senses high up on Aristotle's, the pine-shaded terrace above the villa. Patra is a natural, inheriting her gift from both mother and father who taught her that the preparation of good food was a matter of taste over technique. By her early teens she was cooking for the whole family, as she still does today, adopting us simply as members of her own extended household. And, for us, the great boon of her slow-cooked dishes is that they keep (in fridge or freezer) and are often better in the eating on the second or third days. So these marathon cooking days sustain us happily in gastronomic contentment for the best part of a week.

By one o'clock, or thereabouts, the job is done and Louise pursues her Greek instruction in the jeep ride back to the village where Panayioti is waiting for his lunch.

*

Patra is the beneficent link in this island story of two universes. Extreme universes they are too. The one of peace, happiness and reconciliation; the other of conflict, despair and division. For it was here on the island that the opening skirmishes took place all those years ago : the four of us drawn together on this tranquil Aegean slope, the magic of the new house, Louise and I not eight months married, Peter and Etty eager to share their dream with us. In recalling those moments of tribulation now, it is obvious that marriage was the catalyst that provoked the collision of wills which was destined to grow in force – even to the very end of Etty's life. But the seeds of her compulsion to control, to possess, were sown from the moment of our births – Gerald's and mine. A presumption that the child – infant or mature, married adult – must defer at all times to the parent regardless of the rectitude of the parent's behaviour. That respect was a commodity to be supplied on demand, irrespective of the parent's attitude toward the child. Yes, we were expected to adore her, an adoration which had to be unconditional. In return, she would lavish us with her love, but oh!, how that love was staked out by her rulebook. To challenge her was an affront to her motherhood; to criticize would be to betray; to tease would be to humiliate; to humour her was to embarrass her – or, at best, to perplex her.

As children, Gerald and I had to comply. To resist created a drama which regularly attracted a smart slap on the face and, with an explosion of wailing and tears, she would then smother us with her hugs and kisses. Emotional blackmail became a valuable currency for us. But, equally, we admired her as any child might with a mother so striking, star-like, even exotic – and even one possessed with the extraordinary power of inspiring feelings which swung (sometimes violently) between extremes of the deepest affection, and yes adoration, to the most terrible hatred. There was one brief and hapless moment when, aged six and in a state of misery, I laid plans to run away one night – plans which, it seems, were forgotten after a good high tea.

But from the moment Louise and I were engaged to be married, a new dimension in the family equation presented itself – one whose significance was, at first, masked by the euphoria of the announcement and the prospect of a wedding. No one could have been welcomed into the family with more joy and exuberance than Louise was by Etty – and before that warm June evening in 1971, the two women had never set eyes on one another. I had calculated it that way – as an ambush – because, by then, I had learned that bringing girlfriends home always began happily enough before fault lines developed with time and a greater familiarity. So in the planning of Louise's introduction, the only woman to whom I have ever proposed, the tactic was shock and awe. And it worked! For my father and mother, this was just another weekend visit to Taunton – except that on this occasion I was accompanied by a new girlfriend.

'Home' for my parents was a handsome duplex penthouse above the shop, and the shop was the Castle, a venerable forty-bedroomed hotel in the town centre, where Gerald and I spent our childhood years. Home for Louise and her brother Mark was a discreet ivy-clad mews house in a quiet Knightsbridge backwater. So on the day before our drive to Somerset, a Thursday, I had to fulfil my duty by presenting myself at number 4 Ennismore Gardens Mews to ask Louise's father for his twenty-two year old daughter's hand in marriage. Peter Guiver was a tall, fearsome-looking man with a penchant for immaculately tailored Savile Row suits and a reputation for detesting his daughter's boyfriends. Our romance had been more cyclonic than whirlwind – a courtship of six short weeks and I was merely a twenty-four year old cub executive in a large London advertising agency flogging Ariel soap powder for my clients Procter & Gamble. Making presentations to a line-up of grim-faced brand managers was a nerve-wracking business, but facing up to my prospective father-in-law, a man I hardly knew, was properly scary. Without the pips on my epaulettes or a healthy bank balance, I stepped into that mews house with a pretty flimsy pitch – so I decided to open with a grand gesture and presented Louise's mother, Molly, with an arrangement of expensive blooms from Moyses Stevens in Berkeley Square. The two then disappeared upstairs, leaving Mr. Guiver and me seated across a coffee table in the drawing room. His mood was convivial – a side I had not seen before – and to my relief he brushed aside my over-rehearsed presentation, confirmed his and Molly's delight at the match and, over a glass of iced Noilly Prat, quizzed me – not on my prospects but on his pet subject, the London restaurant scene, a favourite topic we held in common and which, curiously, seemed to set the seal on his blessing. Later that evening he took us all out to dine at Tiberio, a fashionable Italian eaterie off Curzon Street, where we celebrated not in champagne (a drink he had no taste for) but in a couple of bottles of a great white burgundy – an exquisite Corton Charlemagne.

It was midnight by the time I fell into my bed in Camden Town where I shared a house owned by a close chum who, coincidentally, had been at school with Louise. Mary Heaton-Armstrong was a feisty beauty with a habit of attracting undesirable lovers. She was also fiercely loyal to her tight circle of friends and it was she who forged the match between Louise and me. Lying in bed, incapable of sleep, my mind replayed the events of the previous six weeks like some surreal fantasy by Jean Cocteau. I had been working in the agency one Saturday in early May preparing for yet another deathly business presentation to my clients on Monday morning. By seven I had had enough. Feeling weary, bored and ravenously hungry, I called Mary (a wonderful cook) who at that time had taken a basement in South Eaton Place before her imminent move to North London. I was then flat sharing in Harrington Gardens with a live-in landlady – daughter to a wealthy banking family – who, nightly, entertained a platoon of dope smoking African American servicemen in her bedroom. Amusing company for a while, but when the cats acquired a taste for her ganja cakes and started crapping in the bath tub, I decided it was time to move on and I accepted Mary's invitation to join her in Camden.

I caught a tube to Sloane Square, bought a bottle of wine and found Mary in her kitchen preparing supper for four. I poured myself a large whisky and sank into an armchair mildly embarrassed that she had invited friends and I had not bothered to change out of an old pair of cords and a blue tracksuit top. Minutes later I heard the doorbell and a blonde with highlights hobbled in on crutches trailing a bloke called Richard. Mary introduced us … she and Louise had been skiing in Kitzbühel … a bad fall … titanium wires in the right leg … only just out of plaster … a pioneering Austrian surgeon … healing well.

There was no coup de foudre that evening, no seismic wave beneath my feet. Rather an immediate sense of ease in her company, the surprise and pleasure of discovering interests shared – in travel and in foreign film; in French and Italian singers like Gilbert Bécaud, Sylvie Vartan, Françoise Hardy, Richard Anthony, Ornela Vanoni, Jimmy Fontana and their songs : *Et Maintenant, Kilimandjaro, Il Mondo, J'entends siffler le train* and dozens more. Her father, mistrusting English universities, had despatched his daughter to southern France to learn French and to Florence to study Renaissance art. Meeting her for the first time, I found myself charmed by a natural free spirit and a translucent freshness about her features which, in my imagination, I compared with a thousand celluloid images of Catherine Deneuve. This was the effect she had on me. For days afterwards, the ease and pleasure of our togetherness were tempered by the enigma of an aura, an untouchable mystique so dazzling my admiration was set at a distance, engaged but detached like staring at a screen in a darkened cinema.

Over the washing-up Mary briefed me – leaving Louise in the sitting room deftly parrying Richard's clumsy paws. She had a number of suitors – none too serious – and they were beginning to irritate her. The skiing accident had given her time to think. "It's up to you, Kit," she whispered as we said goodbye. Outside, we flagged down a taxi and as we climbed aboard I turned to Richard suggesting the cabbie drop him off first before driving on to Ennismore Gardens. Sheepishly, he agreed.

The next few weeks were played out like some courtly game of chess – my advances gently stalled, her defensive moves teasing and testing my resolve. Each time I called to suggest dinner or a show or a picnic or anything, her response was ambivalent – a maybe, possibly or perhaps: "I'm not sure what I'm doing that evening … day … weekend …" It drove me mad! In the end I could stand it no more. I telephoned to say that I would meet her at 6.30 that evening in the bar of the Carlton Tower Hotel and replaced the receiver barely allowing her a moment to think of a reply. Arriving early, I sat at a corner table picking at a bowl of cashews unsure whether she would turn up. And then she appeared – wearing that smile of hers, a smile that reels on the edge between innocence and mischief. A waiter approached us and she ordered a Dubonnet and bitter lemon to my lager. When the drinks arrived, I wasted no time in launching my offensive – in effect, a declaration of love, but one which demanded an expression of her own true feelings because I was no longer willing to tolerate her ridiculous games of hide-and-seek. Her response took my breath away – I suppose because I was expecting her to prevaricate again or, at best, let me down lightly. But no! For the first time she was as bold and clear about her commitment to me as I had just been to her. Our love was sealed. I called the waiter to remove our drinks and ordered a bottle of champagne.

From this moment, our love affair moved impatiently forward without a plan or a timetable, without any sense of wise counsel or regard for the future or caution for our youthfulness. On her birthday I sent her twenty long-stemmed red roses with a phial of Guerlain's Chant d'Arômes hidden in the foliage. We re-enacted scenes from *Elvira Madigan* and *Un Homme et Une Femme*. I bought a wicker basket from Harrods, filled it with food from the deli-counters and took her boating up the Thames from Bourne End – mooring beneath a willow for our lunch. We dined at our favourite bistros in South Kensington and Notting Hill, and talked until we were the only people left in the restaurant. As May turned to June, we had begun introducing each other to our friends – two of mine inviting us to their Rutland farmhouse one weekend. Young, like us, they were already married and, I guess, I must have looked upon them as role models to provide me with encouragement and advice on the business of making a proposal. And so it was, on Sunday afternoon, that Louise and I stepped into the sunshine for a stroll in a gentle landscape which deserved at least an hour's exploration but which carried our feet no further than a few hundred yards. We lay on the grass verge of a field, the corn swaying silently in a light summer breeze as an old biplane, coughing, clearing its hoarse throat, ducked and weaved in the sky above us. And then (and this is no romantic fantasy – simply historical fact) as I sat up to utter the immortal words "will you marry me," the plane soared over our heads and looped the loop. Louise, overcome by the drama of the moment, lapsed into a state of irresolution and said she wanted time to think. It took her a week – perhaps the longest week of my life.

Eventually, I don't know when, I drifted into a heavy sleep. In the morning I awoke late with a jolt – disoriented for a second before that sudden rush to the head, the realization that we were an engaged couple, and that today I was driving to Taunton to introduce her to Etty and Peter.

More accustomed to riding in the passenger seat of an MGB or a Triumph Spitfire, Louise found my choice of motorcar an eccentric joke – especially for a thrusting young advertising man. But I loved my fourth-hand Austin 1100 Vanden Plas – its leather upholstery and walnut trim, the grandness of its bonnet and grill beguiling me with the illusion that I was driving a Bentley. That afternoon, as we cruised piously down the A303 across Salisbury Plain and into Somerset, the transition from the metropolitan-chic of Knightsbridge and Curzon Street to the parochialism of the English provinces was like a journey on the Starship Enterprise. Louise arrived in Taunton unprepared for the hue of a three-star hotel in a somnolent market town in the early seventies (for until 1976, and its transformation into something else, The Castle was still outside our family control). But she was warmly received and her nervousness soon dissipated over drinks on the penthouse's flower-decked terrace which seemed to her like an airborne bubble of continental enchantment compared to the views beneath the lofty castellations – a bingo hall, the bus station, a municipal car park. Only the distant sight of the Quantocks to the north, the Brendons on the western fringe and the Blackdown hills to the South – their contours accented in the sunlight and shadows of an iridescent evening – provided any hint of Somerset's pastoral beauty beyond the town's perimeter.

At dinner, more alien surprises. We ate downstairs in the hotel's baronial dining room. Here Louise found herself swallowed by a space light years from the glamour of Tiberio the night before. A grotesquely patterned carpet, its tendrils like antlers, clashed horribly with a turquoise ceiling emblazoned with golden stars, the two surfaces muted only by the cool whiteness of the starched table linen and a line of high windows draped with sombre gold curtains in heavy velvet held apart by tasselled satin ropes. John, the black-tailed bow-tied Irish headwaiter, approached us – his heroic belly straining to escape its gravy-smudged waistcoat, his breath reeking of booze. This was an evening that left its imprint in every tiny detail. Thirty-five years on and Louise still loves to remind me of the melon she ordered – the fruit cut like a boat with an orange slice speared by a toothpick to make a sail, its mast crowned with a maraschino cherry like some livid pimple; her lamb cutlets daintily presented with paper frills wrapped around the rib ends; and the "sweet trolley" – a squeaky chariot laden with sagging, sweating mousses, gateaux, pies, trifles and caramel creams. But the indifference of the menu was relieved by the pleasure of my father's magnificent cellar – his pride and joy (as it is mine today). We drank a hock out of tall, amber-stemmed glasses and a decent claret before returning to the penthouse for coffee and a nightcap.

We were approaching the moment of big bang – the point of ambush.

It was now past ten o'clock on this perfect summer's evening as we gathered once more on the terrace – all of us feeling relaxed and at ease. Louise's first impressions of Peter and Etty were reassuring: she found them kind, warm and good company – my mother fun, if a little overwhelming. But it was time for her to leave the stage and, on cue, she excused herself to go to bed. In my parents' estimation, Louise scored maximum points (then on first meeting new girlfriends usually did) and their spontaneous enthusiasm for her made my task simple. "We are very much in love," I said bluntly, "and I'm going to marry her." I had barely finished speaking when Etty leapt out of her chair and threw her arms around me screaming her delight in a gabble of Greek. With tears in his eyes, my father hugged me too – and as she rushed off to find the bride-to-be, she turned to him yelling "Mouchen! Mouchen! Champagna! Champagna! A winter wedding! A winter wedding!"

In her room, Louise had undressed and was stepping into a new baby doll (the fashionable nightwear of the moment). When the bedroom door burst open, the hurricane that swept in forced the nightdress into a tangle over her head as Etty, oblivious to the circumstances, embraced her and, taking her by the hand, ran back to the terrace where my father and I were laying out a bottle of Bollinger and four glasses … more hugs … kisses … tears … Then Etty – effervescing with excitement – disappeared again. Moments later she returned waving something, a small object, above her head. It was a ring for Louise – a gold band set in a twist with a single diamond and a pearl – which she thrust on her engagement finger. The fit was perfect. "It belonged to Nell," she said. "Peter's mother."

Louise was overcome. She loved the ring and said so – but there were two other, more urgent matters pressing upon her. Clad only in her baby doll she felt naked with embarrassment and before any champagne toast, she wanted to call home. Five minutes later, begowned and comfortable, she was on the telephone to Molly, her mother, before introducing the two Peters – Chapman and Guiver – who, after congratulating one another on the charm, grace and nobility of each other's offspring, discussed dates for a weekend visit to Somerset. The atmosphere atop The Castle fizzed with electricity and, duty done, dates set, we raised our glasses, drank deeply and retired to bed.

The great meeting of the two families was convened for a weekend in late June. As Peter and Molly Guiver drew up to the front of the hotel, a posse of porters swooped on their car followed by my parents, Louise and me. The first passengers to leap out were two Yorkshire terriers who, after three hours' confinement, advertised their relief noisily on the tarmac and threw the reception committee into a state of animated confusion. (My mother preferred cats.) Once the awkward courtesies had been exchanged, our attention turned to the boot which was spilling out Harrods' green carrier bags stuffed with the essential impedimenta dogs require on a weekend away from home – including a variety of old saucepans filled with chicken livers and other delicate morsels. It was a comic display which unnerved Etty whose public face and acute sense of status would have been better served if her staff were seen to be handling a neat line of Louis Vuitton holdalls.

Inside, the housekeepers had prepared the best suite in the hotel: finest Irish linen on the beds, the fluffiest towels and robes in the bathroom, fresh flowers on the dressing table, a private bar, ice, chocolates ... and a view overlooking the garden with its twelfth century remains of the castle keep and moat walls. Peter and Etty escorted their guests to the door – Etty proclaiming that "the Queen Mother once powdered her nose in this room!"

The weekend passed off well enough – difficult, really, for it not to have done, although a meeting at teatime on Saturday to discuss the wedding lit a fuse which, unknown to us, would smoulder for five years before a convulsion of terrifying force erupted, tearing our two families apart. Etty's child-like precocity – regularly excused as her natural enthusiasm and excitement for life – too often regressed into thoughtlessness and insensitivity. Over tea that afternoon, her girlish silliness irritated Peter Guiver – a fastidious and particular man who took exception to anyone who overstepped his boundaries.

He was a devoted father and husband, worshipping his wife whom he addressed simply as "Moll". With few close friends, and intensely private in the conduct of his affairs, he was careful to make a clear separation between the family and matters of business to which he applied his own forensic judgement (never putting his trust in bankers and accountants). Even in the management of his family's finances, investments and trusts – as I would learn in time – his way would be to arrive at decisions based on the business case, knowing in the long haul that this could only be to the advantage of family members. Short-term sentiment had no place in his calculations because he knew this never paid off in the end. And the astuteness of his business mind came in equal measure with the keenness of his human instincts which showed remarkable prescience in his analysis of our family – my mother in particular. As the day of the wedding approached, at home in London one evening, he and Molly were discussing their daughter and what her future held. "She'll have a difficult ride with a mother-in-law like that," he confided, "but if anyone can handle it, my Sparrow will."

Louise shares many of her late father's instincts and the spirit he spoke of to Molly, often characterized by a native facility for a sharp retort, whetted the edges of our teatime gathering in Taunton six months earlier. Sitting together in the polished antique comfort of the penthouse's drawing room, the meeting opened with Etty declaring breezily that she hated the English expression "daughter-in-law". "It is so cold, so formal," she continued. "I am warm-hearted. I am continental. Now, Louise is my daughter." To which Louise replied: "Etty, I think I only have one mother". The jibe was lost on her – it just didn't register and besides she was too excited about plans and preparations for the wedding – a grand party already booked for early December in the ballroom at Claridge's in Mayfair, a party at which she would star.

As the discussion progressed, the mood on Peter Guiver's face darkened as Etty chattered on about the family's connections with the Savoy Hotel Company and how her Peter knew the General Manager at Claridge's. For all my father's gentle efforts to restrain her, she was behaving like a foal cavorting in its paddock out of control. But it was her pronouncements on the make-up of the guest lists that finally sharpened the atmosphere in the room. Where the Guivers, on their side, imagined a list not exceeding seventy-five, Etty – flicking through the index cards on her Christmas list – wanted to invite le tout Somerset – some three hundred and fifty addresses. And when she suggested the reception would be livened up by the strains of a Viennese string quartet playing a repertoire of waltzes, Peter Guiver snapped. Mustering a rictal smile and lobbing a candy-coated missile, he shot back. "Can we just be clear whose daughter's wedding this is?" he growled. "And who's paying for it anyway?" We all laughed stiffly and Etty, stung by her humiliation, left the room to call for more tea.

That evening we gathered once more in the drawing-room. My mother, eager to present her new "daughter" to their grander friends, had organized a dinner party (dress black tie) which, as I recall, included the MP for Taunton, Edward du Cann, and his wife Sallie among other members of Somerset's county set. Now, Mrs. Chapman's dinner parties in the Castle's penthouse were renowned for their splendour, their generosity and a large George III mahogany table set with the family's silver, glass and candelabra. For the hotel on a busy Saturday night, these occasions were a trial – depriving the restaurant of its senior staff and distracting the chefs who were honour bound to keep paying customers waiting while they prepared and despatched the food for the party upstairs via a dumb waiter connecting basement and roof. But for the chosen ones selected to attend the Chapmans and their guests at these glittering soirées, it was a privilege which came well rewarded.

When Peter Guiver walked in – Molly on his arm – my mother pounced. Impeccably groomed in a double-breasted dinner jacket, his habit was to wear a silk handkerchief in his breast pocket folded carefully to form a flat inch-wide strip along the top. Etty – giggling and flirtatious, telling him how handsome he looked – plucked the handkerchief free, shook it out and stuffed it back into his pocket like wilted rose petals. She had taken her revenge. This was one of those momentary vignettes in life that stick like a scar on the memory. I was there, standing next to her, ready to greet my prospective in-laws when it happened and I remember wincing inwardly, shocked, embarrassed, angered by her behaviour. These were our special guests – strangers whom she had never met until the weekend – and her display of pique, more typical of an over-indulged six year old, was quietly locked away in Peter Guiver's mind. Hurriedly, I led him away to introduce him to the other guests while my mother took Molly in hand.

The dinner, with its mix of stately formality (waiters in white gloves) and convivial good humour, advanced merrily to that point after pudding where the hostess rises to invite the ladies to retire leaving the chaps to "put the world to rights" over a decanter of port and a humidor bristling with Havanas. This was Louise's first experience of an archaic boudoir ritual my mother never failed to invoke at her parties and one which rarely strayed from its fixed formula, even in the subject of the conversation – the chatter ringing with adulation for Etty as she held court from her dressing table while the other women sat on the big double bed taking turns to visit the bathroom. It might begin with the dress she was wearing (she possessed a fabulous wardrobe), and on this particular evening it was a cream silk chiffon gown hand-stitched with beads and pearls. "Etty, what a gorgeous dress!" says one. "It's utterly divine!" says another, "Where did you find it?" For my mother, this was the signal, the green light, the starting gun for the story of her life. How she met her Peter in Thessaloniki ("He is not just my husband. He is my lover, my father, my mother, my brother, my sister. He is my pillar. He is my everything."). How she came to England as a nineteen-year-old bride just after the war. How her Mama and Papa prepared her trousseau – filling a line of trunks with fine linens and beautiful dresses. And how, even after bearing two boys, she still carries the figure of a teenager, never putting on weight which is how she comes to wear her lovely gown.

I remember at Avon Lodge (the one on the Blackdown Hills. Their Avon Lodge. Not Nell's). Pictures, pictures, pictures everywhere. Pictures in expensive silver frames. Posed, stylized portraits of Etty in those famous dresses. I have them still. There is one studio composition taken in the early fifties: a stunning strapless ball gown with a tight black velvet bodice flowing outwards like surf into a white silk skirt gathering falling black leaves stitched randomly into the fabric. Her hair is in the style of the period: a centre parting with the ends of her rich raven locks curled into bundles around the temples and the nape of the neck. Another has her seated on a sofa in the penthouse – her luxuriantly decorated Christmas tree in the corner. She wears a strapless number again – this one in cerise silk taffeta, frilled around the bust. A second Christmas portrait reveals her in a long-sleeved black dress dotted with a myriad diamond sparklets, a black velvet choker about her neck and a white feather boa by her side. And another classic pose: this one, taken in the Castle's dining room, sees Etty standing in profile, head held high, back-lit almost in silhouette and framed by the restaurant's huge bow-window.

All these, and others counted in dozens, displayed at Avon Lodge. More framed images of herself than the rest of her family. Hardly any of Louise. Some of me. More of Peter and Gerald. Where did it all come from – this look-at-me-me-me? The oft-proclaimed love of Peter deployed as a foil for her self-adoration. This subconscious urge to display a family mosaic with her at its centre and, by extension, to express how she saw her position within a society from whom she craved equal approval. There is another vignette etched on my memory. It came much later, after Louise and I moved from London and joined the family business. I had begun to promote a series of cultural events – wine, music, theatre and so on – to fill the Castle's beds over bleak winter weekends. On one Saturday evening, a throng of sixty black-tied gastronomes gathered in the hall for champagne before a gala dinner. Then, like a great chorus revolving in unison, our eyes turned upward to the head of the stairs as my mother – *ravissante en trousseau* – swooped down, paused, and spread her arms wide to embrace the applause before continuing her progress. It was an entrance worthy of a Garbo, a Dietrich, a Monroe.

After her death, clearing cupboards and drawers at Avon Lodge, I fell upon an old, yellow-stained envelope stuffed full of loose black and white photographs. There were three of her mama and papa, Fifi and Athanasios Rosi, who, in the manner of most educated Europeans of their class, liked to travel. One is of the couple in Paris; the second taken in the Piazza San Marco in Venice – a pigeon perched on top of my grandfather's homburg. And the third is a post-card size picture of him in the spa town of Karlsbad in the summer of 1927 where they were taking the waters at the famous thermal springs. The remaining photographs, a dozen and more, were of Etty in her early teens including four beautifully composed soft-focus studio portraits. But what I found most striking was the parcel of informal snaps of this adolescent child – on the beach, in the countryside, at her boat club – posing like a Vogue model, the pubescent solipsist. Where was her beloved sister, Machi? Her friends? Her aunts, uncles, cousins?

At Avon Lodge, when I used to visit her, I was sometimes tempted to make some remark about the multitude of her self-images scattered around the house and the relative paucity of silver frames devoted to the rest of us. But I knew perfectly well it was never worth the punt - just to unleash a furious volley of shock, indignation and denial that I would even think of making such an extraordinary accusation against my own mother! Dramatic scenes of this order would usually end with a final injunction, her coup de grâce: "Christopher, you are mad!"

*

The days and weeks chasing the date of the wedding (Friday, 3rd December, 1971) raced by. As Louise, her mother, her father and her brother Mark set about the preparations in London, so Etty laid her own plans to celebrate the marriage of her διαδοχος (her "son and heir"!). Before the summer was out, she and Peter had hosted our official engagement party – a splendid roof-top affair for thirty at the Castle – in addition to dinners and lunches for their own circle. In August, when we visited them at Diodati, she threw the cocktail party of the season with Patra on overtime in the kitchen dishing up a succession of delectable mezethes as my father and I dispensed the ouzo, Demestica and retsina. And for her finale (having been denied her Viennese string quartet at Claridge's), she issued invitations to the Guiver family, the bridesmaids, close friends and relations for a "Bouzouki Evening" in Taunton on the Saturday night after the big day.

As for me, I had the novel challenge of coming to terms with the Catholic Church. While Louise belonged – her membership endorsed by an education at one of England's thoroughbred convent schools – I came with the disadvantage of being a baptized Anglican: an impediment to our union which Rome defined as a "mixed marriage". To marry in her Church – as Molly, a devout Catholic mother, would wish for her daughter – I was obliged to submit to "instruction" which I was happy to do because I was curious.

Our first meeting with the Church was disastrous. The priest maleficent. We had gone to Warwick Street in Soho – to the Church of Our Lady of the Assumption and St. Gregory, an eighteenth century chapel which had once been attached to the Portuguese embassy. It could be no other because, a generation before, this is where Peter and Molly Guiver were married. So, hearts overflowing with faith, hope and charity, we began an interview which ended with my bride-to-be reduced to tears and made me lose my temper with the very authority on whom we relied for permission to be wed. The approach was more inquisition than interview, the zeal of this sad and sclerotic priest driving him to expose Louise's transgressions as a Catholic. Had she done her "Easter duty"? No. When was the last time she had been to Holy Communion? She couldn't remember. When had she made her last confession? At school because she had to. Did she attend church on Sundays? No – sometimes. I sat in silence listening to this interrogation, hearing Louise's voice shrink into a meek whisper. And when he had finished, the man's final judgement – so secure in its divine hubris – came with the force of satanic lightning: "Then you are a bad Catholic!" My patience was spent. "And you are a bad Christian!" I replied. His body turned slowly in its chair. Pausing for a second, he glared at me, dark purple shadows like storm clouds around his narrow eyes. "Mr. Chapman," he said, "did you know that one in three mixed marriages end in divorce?"

But our Father Maleficent was a venal beast – his thin, moist lips anticipating the jam on this sweet and tempting teacake. Besides, Molly was a Rochford – a well-known Catholic family name – and her Uncle Clement, now long retired, had served the Church as a much loved canon and had been the celebrant at her wedding. I signed a cheque and the deal was done.

Now we had to find a sympathetic priest to undertake my instruction and one who might perform the marriage rites. While a kindly old Irish monk patiently led me through the meaning of the seven sacraments and engaged me in a lively debate about the complex notion of transubstantiation in the Eucharist, the search for the man who would marry us proved hazardous. At times I felt like a blind man walking hopefully down a potholed pathway.

Over supper one evening in Camden, Mary offered to introduce us to a friend she trusted and admired – a Jesuit called Father Anton. When we met him I was struck immediately by his spiritual charisma. Soft spoken, warmly reassuring, he listened to the story of our experience in Warwick Street. In the weeks that followed I fell under his spell, felt I had won a friend, that he understood. He, I suspect, saw a convert within his grasp rather than a young man in love who just wanted an honest priest to marry him. Finally, I came to the naïve conclusion that we had found our man and I invited him to officiate. Almost instantly I realized I had made a terrible mistake – for at that moment he turned up the volume on his iron dogma, a shrill propaganda full of hate and contempt for all the Protestant Churches, demanding that I must now accept Catholicism as the only Christian truth. We had a furious argument and I have not seen him since. So, in the end, dear old Uncle Clem, aged eighty-two, was brought out of retirement and he did the job.

The invitation read "2.30 o'clock" and when the half-hour struck old granny Guiver, Peter's mother, shouted at me from her seat across the aisle: "Christopher, she's late!" (Ripples of laughter.) The two Daimler limousines – one carrying Molly and the bridesmaids, the other father and bride – had been separated by the Friday afternoon traffic. So the police sent Molly's car looping around Golden Square to avoid gridlock in Warwick Street. Inside, the expectant congregation had more than organ music to keep it entertained. A small coven of tramps – regulars who used the church as sanctuary from the perils of Soho's street life – grunted and belched at the back. The wardens offered to send them packing but we didn't see why they shouldn't enjoy the spectacle with the rest of us.

In the front pew, I waited patiently – Gerald, my best man, at my side, Peter and Etty behind us. They had arrived fifteen minutes earlier fresh from their suite at Claridge's where we had spent the previous evening. Etty did not disappoint. She entered the Church on Peter's arm *en grande tenue* in a pillar-box red tunic dress topped off with a large black fur hat which, in its military inspiration, placed her somewhere between a Russian Cossack and an Hungarian hussar. (The point is she looked magnificent.) Escorted by an usher, slowly they made their progress down the nave greeting their friends, smiling at the other side, and when they arrived at the chancel steps, Gerald and I received her with elaborate embraces.

The choreography of the bride's mother's entrance was not so much discreet as invisible. Suddenly Molly was there next to granny having tiptoed down the side of the Church nodding on the way at St. Anthony, her favourite saint, because he was the benevolent mystic who always found everything she mislaid from her chaotic handbag. Glancing at her – looking shy, a little nervous, even vulnerable in her neat Hardy Amies suit and pillbox hat – everything about the way she presented herself suggested a natural modesty and an innate, deliberate desire to dress down, not to diffract any light away from her daughter on this special day. She looked lovely and somehow, through this sense of her demureness, she radiated an innocence and purity I found beautiful. As I write these words and think back on her life, all my recollections are of a wonderful, selfless woman whose only wish was to nurture and care for her family – always listening, encouraging, teasing, consoling – but also a woman firm in her principles and quick to reprimand our transgressions or redirect our waywardness. Yes, I loved her. And as the years rolled by, Molly came to represent for me everything I admired or ever wanted in a mother but never found in Etty. Finally, she came to fill all the unrequited longings of a son who, somewhere along the way, lost his mother. A strange conundrum, this. Mine who despised the English appellation "daughter-in-law" and wanted to possess Louise as her own. And I, alienated from her and adopting my mother-in-law to the role because I loved her as a son might his own mother.

These, the musings on a day thirty-five years ago – the early telltale signs of a turbulent estate to come in the affairs of this family. But not that day – where hearts were flying high as the floral displays and the incense-drenched atmosphere infused us with an unusual sense of piety. And look!

The congregation is standing and the organ has struck its opening chords, annunciating the arrival of the bride. On our feet now, Gerald and I turned to stare down the length of the nave. Then I saw her: framed in the glaring light of the west door, a sylphid apparition in diaphanous white, cataracts of irradiated veil billowing in the breeze and, around her, six bridesmaids fussing to control the ebb and flow of the fabric. When they had done their best (it seemed an age) and fallen into line – resplendent in blue velvet "Doctor Zhivago" hoods and cloaks – Louise gripped her father's impatient arm and the procession set forth. I strained for a glimpse of that elfin smile I had grown to love and as they approached I noticed that her troublesome veil was crowned by a fabulous diamond brooch of ribbons tied in bows like a luminescent butterfly. A family heirloom. The sight of her, feeling her close to me, the two of us together at last, side by side, had the effect of putting me at ease. I began to relax and so did she.

And so we were wed – although there was one uncomfortable moment when Uncle Clem, our superannuated canon, lost the thread in his book and, reading upside down, I found myself gently directing him away from the funeral rites and back onto the marriage pages. Then, during the address – eloquently delivered by Anthony Phillips, an Anglican friend who had been chaplain at Gerald's Cambridge college – we were surprised by another minor distraction. Looking up into the apse, I noticed a small hatch had opened and, from behind the aperture, a pair of dark mocking eyes scanned the Church. Within seconds the hatch slid shut again but there was no mistaking the bearer of those prying, maleficent eyes.

As we emerged from the sacristy, the register signed, the Church vibrated with the organist's urgent playing of Widor's famous Toccata. The tramps took fright and vanished – and we glided down the aisle like a pair of swans. At Claridge's we cut the cake to whoops of applause and Gerald had them choking on their champagne with a ridiculous story about my tonsorial entanglements with hairdryers: this, remember, was the Age of Aquarius and long hair. These were also the days, mercifully, when wedding receptions were kept short and sweet. So, at six the toastmaster despatched us upstairs to change – Molly and the bridesmaids in pursuit, weeping torrents; Etty in party paradise – and within the hour we were heading west out of London bound for the Cotswolds in my beloved Vanden Plas. With another client presentation scheduled for the following week, the only honeymoon I could offer Louise was a weekend break – three nights at the Whately Hall in Banbury, a cosy hotel owned by a family friend. Next morning – late – our breakfast arrived with a tap on our bedroom door and a maid entered bearing a tray laden with toast and croissants, juices and coffee, eggs and bacon. Perhaps the sight of us lying in our four-poster, fresh after a night of lovemaking, was just too much for the young trainee. The tray slipped from her hands and fell to the floor with an almighty crash. And so began the long adventure of our married life.

*

With marriage came the mortgage – ours was on number 24A Oxford Road, Putney – a two-bed Victorian half-basement with a patch of lawn at the back, a glass door leading to it from the spare room. Our first home. Happiness for £8,000. It was a handy address too. The number 14 bus route started from the top of the road; the High Street was a short stroll away; a launderette fifty yards from our front door dealt with the washing and, on the corner, Mr. Malik and his family kept their small store open for the people of the neighbourhood from dawn till late, seven days a week. Just beyond Malik lay Wandsworth Park and the river.

As for my advertising career, advancement was driven by a shameless cupidity – itself in the nature of the trade – as I hopped like a tart out of one agency into the next. After soap powder came cigarettes and garishly packaged junk snacks; then deodorants and hairsprays; and finally more soap until I was sick of the game – its shallowness and vacuity. The malaise set in after Dom's birth and I remember pushing his pram around Wandsworth Park thinking what a mug I was busting a gut hawking cans of gunk or stuff that damaged your health for the sake of an inflated pay packet. Perhaps I took it too seriously but, for me, the corrupted passions, the faux-glamour, the fabricated hype that fed this world sucked the soul dry – drained me of value which, in the language of marketing, assumed an entirely different definition.

My Damascene moment came one day in a Manchester conference hall where I was required to present a campaign for a new hairspray to several hundred salesmen. Their boss, the client company's sales director, followed my pitch with the unveiling of the product – a role he played with all the fervour of an evangelical preacher at a Bible Belt rally. Laser beams strobed the stage. The sound system blasted us with Beethoven's *Ode to Joy*. And as the screens parted to reveal a mountainous display of tin cans, waiters poured in from side doors and distributed glasses of cheap fizz to the faithful. Raising his glass in a Nazi salute, their boss proclaimed the toast. A toast to an aerosol spray that would keep your hair looking cool and beautiful even unto the Apocalypse!

It would be a little more than a year before our move to Somerset and, meanwhile, still in pursuit of the advertising shilling, I moved on one last time.

*

Last night the island was hit by a powerful storm. Spectacular lightning strikes illuminated the archipelago casting demonic silhouettes of rock and sea in shades of black, purple and grey. The electricity in the sky plays a macabre game with the imagination and the terrifying crackle of the thunder moments before an ear-splitting boom convinces you that mortals somewhere have incurred the fury of the ancient gods on Olympus. Even Diodati – built to withstand earthquakes – rattled like some flimsy shanty. In bed we clung to one another – twins in the womb – as the rain flayed the paintwork on the shutters and the terraces turned into raging wadis.

By daybreak the skies had cleared and the sun rose undisturbed, once again casting its rose-tinted light on the sea. We ate our breakfast in the courtyard by the kitchen door – coffee, fruit and porridge for a little ballast after the terrors of the night. The scent of wet jasmine, its sweet fragrance distilled by the morning sun, seemed to prompt our collected memories and our conversation drifted back to the days when breakfast on this very spot was a well-rehearsed ritual conducted by Etty and Peter.

We would awake to the urgent sounds of domestic preparation: the table being laid with its muddy grey-green set of Denby earthenware (naff today, in vogue in the early seventies!); my mother also setting the breads, the Tiptree jams and the cereals, including my father's Grape-Nuts – essential to the proper functioning of his digestive system. Peter's routine was to make the coffee – Nescafé instant – but prepared in a manner which alluded to the real stuff. So he would take the tall Denby coffee pot, heap in a generous serving of granules, pour on boiling water, insert a long-handled wooden spoon and then, by clapping the palms of both hands either side of the handle and rubbing them vigorously back and forth, rotate the spoon at Magimix speed inside the pot. The job done, we would then hear his call – a call as familiar to me in childhood before the start of the school day as it was now as a married man on holiday: "Breakfast is on the table!" And, of course, the ingrained habits of his army discipline would ensure the timing of the call was exactly regulated. At Diodati, it came each morning at nine o'clock.

If I have one consuming memory of those times, it is of that breakfast table. This pretty courtyard, spilling over with its massed colours of geranium, bougainvillea and oleander, always seemed to be the chosen field of confrontation – the field of battle. I don't know why. Perhaps because Patra was not expected until later. The first of these skirmishes came in the summer of '72, the wedding eight months past, now a fading dream and, with that, the beginnings of a new consciousness looming – the realization of a new dynamic inside the family structure: Louise. A younger woman, an independently-minded daughter-in-law, a threat to the status quo.

The events which ignited this breakfast head-to-head were beyond trivial but, like all the fights in our family, this one illustrated my mother's unique moral universe and her habit of using Peter as her instrument of delivery. To challenge her was to court danger and conflict. But conflict was inevitable unless you were prepared to be suffocated and have the oxygen of a free life squeezed out of you.

The problem started with a drinks party at the Whittle-Martins, an engaging and lively family who owned a house on the hillside above us. Like the rest of the villa-owning set on the Kalamaki peninsula, they were doing their turn on the social carousel that was the August "season". And, as I recall, it was a jolly party largely on account of a strong contingent of twenty-somethings whose outlook on life had yet to be infected by the mustiness of their plum fruited mums and dads. Towards the end, as people began to filter away, a group of us decided to move on and hit the town for some supper and, later on maybe, a club. Deep down I could sense a collective urge to escape our old dears for a few hours of uninhibited fun. When I told my father of our intentions, he seemed relaxed, even pleased for us. Etty, unsure how to react in public, just looked surprised.

Next day, retribution descended like the gathering storm: first the black clouds waiting to spit their dankness, then the break; the crackle and, finally, the explosion. The customary noises of breakfast in preparation were muted, a cold silence cloaking the atmosphere inside the house. My father was not to be heard and only occasionally did we hear the indistinct murmur of Etty's voice. There was no call to table. When Louise and I emerged from the bedroom we knew we were in trouble. Peter, wearing the mask of a walrus, looked nervous, his eyelids drooping sadly over his eyes. Etty bristled, primed to shock like a high-voltage current. She turned to me. And with the patronizing authority of a primary school teacher, she said: "Come and sit down, your father wants to talk to you!"

We sat and my father cleared his throat. Whenever he had something difficult or unpleasant to say, he would betray his nervousness with a mild stammer. There followed a monologue in a tone of regret and disappointment – dismay at our behaviour the previous evening – that they had made arrangements, booked a table for the four of us to dine at a local taverna – how rude we had been to go off without a thought or care for them – that we were, after all, their "house guests", here only for a short spell. "Your mother's gone to great lengths to make everything nice for you," he continued, "and this is how you treat her! With ingratitude! The least you can do is apologize."

As my father's theme gathered pace – Louise and I sitting in silence, incredulous – Etty now chose her moment. Turning on Louise she said: "I'm sure you don't behave like this when you see your parents in the South of France."

"Of course we do," she replied. "We're always going out without them. The last thing they want is us hanging around their feet!"

This was a direct challenge and Etty didn't like it. She ran for cover.

"Don't contradict me!" she snapped. "Listen to what my Peter is telling you."

"House guests" indeed! I refused to apologize and we left the table, seething. Argument had been futile and when I suggested the table booking was a convenient fabrication, there was an outburst of denial and indignation. The taverna had been planned as "a surprise"!

Louise, more than I, was stung by the ferocity and injustice of this spat. But these things were set to become part of the complex maze of my mother's egomania which, over the years, we would learn to manage, not always with success. Etty never gave us space in territory she claimed her own. And Greece was definitely her territory. This was her country, her house. Your pleasure as her guests had to acquiesce to her will, be on her terms. Always welcomed, yes, but Louise and I were never permitted to use Diodati for a holiday unless they were present. It hurt. And her manner and speech, even her spoken accent, were contrived to fit the circumstance or adjusted to suit the environment. On the island she would lapse into the vernacular with Patra and the locals but assume a grander tone for those whose rank she regarded as more exalted. In England it was much the same, adapting her accented English to suit the audience. And with us, when she ascended her moral spire, her voice rose to a pitch of imperious sovereignty.

This was Etty my mother. A woman with a panoply of raw instincts and instant emotions; where there was no scope for subtlety or discretion except in the art of manipulation on a Machiavellian scale. Her mind contained not an ounce of reasoning power and where she expressed an opinion on the affairs of the world, it would be one which had been rehearsed for her in sound bites by Peter. People, however, were commonly judged on first acquaintance.

She took to them or she didn't. They suited her purpose or they didn't. Whoever they might be, each one would be slotted into a pigeonhole and each compartment would carry a crisp, simple label. In this way she created her own picture gallery of familiar clichés. So-and-so might be classified as "erudite" or "a bore". "Sympatico" or "antipathestatos". "Distingué" or "basse classe". "Handsome" or "ugly", etc. So, if you were an ugly basse classe antipathestatos bore, there was little hope for you! Snob? Heaven forefend!

Our holidays at Diodati as Peter and Etty's "house guests" ground to an end some years later – a denouement sparked by another cocktail party. By now Dom was with us – a spirited two year-old and first grandchild who gave his grandparents enormous joy. At breakfast that morning, the table was set in its customary manner and Dom – perched securely in his high chair – bashed haphazardly at his boiled egg with a spoon as Peter tried to peel the shell and dunk his toasted soldiers into the yolk. Talk turned to the evening's arrangements. Some ship-owning Greeks who were raising funds for a new medical centre on the island were throwing a grand charity do at their villa and Etty had accepted their invitation. This, after all, would be the apex of the season's social calendar. I groaned inwardly and, glancing at Louise, I could see that she was equally exasperated at the prospect of another drinks party. So we declined – a refusal which was greeted with predictable horror.

"But they are related to the Onassis family," protested Etty. "We have to go. It would be rude not to support them in such a good cause."

"Yes, fine," I replied, "so you must go. We don't know these people. We have never met them. And they certainly won't miss us among their hundreds of guests."

"No, you must come," she insisted. "I have accepted now and said we would all go. Anyway I have already booked Patra to baby sit."

Louise now intervened. "But I don't want Patra baby sitting. We will be very happy staying behind looking after Dom."

Peter sat in his chair speechless. The argument was already out of control as Etty accused Louise of selfishness, reminding her again that we were guests in her house – a phrase that was painting our minds crimson with fury.

"Etty, I'm sorry but we don't want to go," Louise repeated. "There is no obligation on us to go. Please, just leave us alone!"

"What's the matter with you?" Etty's attack was turning nasty. "Do you have your periodo," she sneered. "Why are you so capricious? You are so cold and English. Why can't you be more like me? Continental. I am so easy, warm-hearted, vivacious!"

In the decades that followed, this stream of invective, in these exact words, became an often-repeated battlecry whenever the two women clashed. Words that still echo in our ears, they cut Louise to the quick – but she could do little more than stand her ground. For the moment, at that breakfast table, Louise had reached the limits of her patience. She shot up and grabbed Dom from his high chair. Etty lunged forward in an attempt to sit him down again. Louise was incandescent.

"Don't you dare touch my son!" she screamed and ran into the house clutching Dom.

I found her at the foot of the woodland overlooking Puddleduck, our rocky headland, staring out to sea. Dom was cradled in her arms. Looking disconsolate, his little hand was wiping tears from her eyes. "God I hate this place," she whispered. "I just want to get out." We sat in silence trying to regain our calm – the three of us snuggled close, drawing comfort from our despair. After a while, we heard the engine of the Beetle start up – Etty driving to the village to shop. I hoisted Dom onto my shoulders and we made our way back up the steep track to the house. On the terrace, Peter sat reading – or attempting to read – his face more walrus-like and despondent than I had ever seen.

Private conversations with my father without Etty present were rare. Embedded inside her darker instincts, there seemed to be a deep desire to ration the development of any bond between father and son – mistrusting me, I think, more than him, suspicious, even jealous, of my motives. It was much the same between Louise and Peter. Quietly they adored one another. But if Etty caught Louise talking separately to her Peter, she immediately broke into their space and changed the subject – drawing her away. All part of my mother's obsession to control, fearful that in some indefinable way we posed a threat to her. Ironically, she often came close to confessing her tendency, although she would never have recognized the irony. It was expressed in another of her commonly repeated mantras. Whenever the family were gathered together she often boasted proudly: "I now have you all under my wing!" It was a sentiment which always touched Peter who saw it as an expression of maternal affection.

But that day on the terrace was one of those rare occurrences. Father and son talked. His eyes looked pale and watery. He hated rows and in his gentle manner he appealed to me to come to the charity do for the sake of family harmony. "Life is just not worth living otherwise, Kit." He was right and he was wrong, but he was my father and I loved him. So we relented and once again Etty claimed her victory.

Nor was she shy in her moment of triumph. By now the sun was rising high and hot. Scooping Dom back onto my shoulders, I made my way with Louise down to the bay to the left of Puddleduck. We swam and sunbathed on the deserted beach feeling the heat of the sand beneath our towels, Dom in his cotton sun hat gurgling contentedly in a rubber dinghy between us. But the loveliness and solitude of the setting did little to salve the wretchedness gnawing at our guts like maggots. Then, as the sun began to soothe our bodies with the analgesia of its rays, we heard the cooing. We froze on our towels. "Coo-oo! Cooee!" I opened an eye. Again, "Coo-cooo!" We looked up from our towels. Suddenly the peace of our beach was transformed into a Hollywood set. There was Etty resplendent in her bikini and matching sarong, a bandeau across her forehead held tight by large sunglasses; an expensive beach bag swinging from her arm. Striding over the sand, dipping her toes in the sea she called and waved, and I half-expected Cary Grant to make his entrance. But there was only Louise and Dom and me. Smiling broadly, she called and waved again, her eyes shining in triumphal celebration.
"How lovely!" She cried. "The family all together! I've brought my camera. I must take some photographs!"

That evening we presented ourselves at the Konialides' house – a beautiful villa sculpted into the landscape in its own secluded bay at the end of an avenue of olives illuminated by flares. At the door, a line of black and white uniformed domestics held trays of drinks and directed us out to the terraces where Louise and I were introduced to our hostess, Madame Konialides. As I shook her hand, she turned to my mother.

"Etty!" she exclaimed in immaculate English. "I can't believe you have a married son! You are far too young!"

Etty hooted with pride. "And a grandson as well!" continued Madame K echoing the words of her guest. "Congratulations. I wish them good health and may they bring you great joy. Now have you met ..."

*

In the early years of our marriage, incidents like these came and went. Some confrontations were narrowly avoided by the biting of lips; others threatened just beneath the veneer of family equanimity; while still others erupted with the inevitable outcome of one or both of us being cast as villains of the piece. And when the prodigal son quit London to join the family business in Taunton, the accumulating impact of these mini-dramas began to penetrate our souls, lodging inside us like a cancer of the spirit. Gradually, we scaled down our trips to Diodati, leaving Dom and Nick, our second, with their grandparents as we set off to explore other parts of the Aegean for a few days before returning to collect them. And yet, as the boys grew older and joined us on our Greek island excursions – when Diodati itself fell off the itinerary – we could not travel freely without my parents in close pursuit, Etty determined to orchestrate our holiday plans on her native soil.

We yearned for a little space of our own. We longed to escape the spectre of febrile tension that seemed to grip us when all we wanted was to be alone. These feelings had a strange and unpleasant effect on me. I came to project my unhappiness beyond my mother. I came to loathe Greece and all Greeks, quarrelling with taxi drivers and shopkeepers and, most particularly, with uniformed authority – customs officers, airport officials, even the police. In the end, we turned our backs on the country. I had had enough. And we began taking our summer holidays in Tuscany – a region we had fallen in love with years before Tony and Cherie Blair discovered its fields of sunflowers, its soft curvaceous countryside dressed in that limpid terracotta light. Florence became our favourite city and the name we gave our beloved black labrador. In Tuscany we were alone, we could be ourselves.

But this sense of alienation and contempt persisted, and our self-imposed exile from the land of my mother endured for years before we returned. And when we did, it would not be to find Diodati pristine, glorious and gleaming white as we had always known it. With my father gone by then and Etty adrift and lost in her own closed world, we would be coming in search of reconciliation – only to find a house strafed by the weather, unswept, unloved, and in an advancing state of disrepair. It was then that we set our hearts on a mission of renewal.

*

Part Three

Cabin Trunks and
the Secrets of the Box of Lindt

Etty at nineteen

On the evening of June 1st 1946, a Saturday evening, Peter Chapman was alone in his bedroom at the Excelsior Hotel on Omonia Square. His best shoes and a tin of boot polish lay on newspapers spread on the floor. The housekeeping department had lent him an ironing board and he was busy pressing his uniform. On the bed, the silver buttons and badges of a major were arranged in a neat line, all polished and shining, and next to them his leather belt lay buffed to perfection – its buckle proclaiming that this officer belonged to Queen Victoria's Own Corps of Guides, the finest regiment in the Indian Army. As he passed the iron over his khaki trousers, he was disturbed for a second as a momentary shiver ran down the length of his spine. He was happy – happier than he had ever been in his life – but for that brief second, his body was gripped by a strange sense of loneliness. Or perhaps it was fear – for his happiness was of a kind he had never felt before, a warm feeling of contentment. And deep within his heart, a great hope for the future seemed to underscore his sense of blissful ease. Yet, around the edges of this happiness, invisible demons gnawed at his mind whispering that he might not deserve such good fortune.

Only five days before, the ship carrying him, Etty and her family from Salonica to Piraeus had nearly been blown out of the water by a floating mine. Others had been less lucky. But now the Rosi family – Athanasios and Fifi, their two daughters, Etty and her elder sister Machi, and Machi's husband Petros – were safely installed with their relatives in Athens, excited as the day of the wedding approached, fussing over the final preparations and visiting St. George's in the district of Kipseli, the church where the marriage would take place – there to light candles, to pray and to harass the priest about the exact positions of the enormous floral displays.

Surrounded by all the members of her family and relishing the palatial surroundings of her cousins' Kipseli mansion, Etty was behaving like an impossible child, fizzing with electricity – her animation driving her bookish sister mad. Only her father seemed able to temper her excitement, his dome-like baldness and keen gentle eyes discharging a calm owlish wisdom which she could not ignore. He spoke to her in a quiet reassuring tone. She would listen and, for a while, leave everyone in peace until the anticipation of the wedding took hold once more. And if no-one paid attention, her fervour would reach a pitch where she was tempted to sprint the short mile from Kipseli to her Peter holed up and alone in Omonia Square. Only the thought of displeasing her father and the conventions of family and Church curbed her rashness. In the end it was enough to dream her romantic dreams, to replay the moment this dashing Englishman proposed to her in his army jeep – and she just nineteen years old. Now she could lie and revel in the warm glow of their love for each other. Hers was a happiness free of inhibition, her thoughts running wild and carefree, oblivious of the disquieting reminiscences plucking at Peter's happiness as he stood over the ironing board in his room at the Excelsior Hotel.

His mind began casting restlessly over the momentous events of the past eighteen months. His nervous breakdown and his evacuation out of Greece to Taranto – a base hospital in the heel of Italy. His brief return to duty – this time in Salonica – before being sent on leave. He recalled his troopship bound for Liverpool crossing a smooth Bay of Biscay when, on 8th May, news of VE day came through. And then his train journey south and the reunion with Nell, his mother, after a separation of ten years. It was a vivid and tender moment. But, in too many ways, those three months' home leave unsettled him.

Seeing his brothers again – Michael, the eldest, and Tony – reawakened memories of the difficult years in Bratislava after their father's suicide. The spectre of 'The Flying Dutchmen' – the bailiffs – threatening to strip the family home of its furniture haunted his dreams; nightmares where those bailiffs morphed into Hitler's Brownshirts on exercise in the fields outside Passau as, leaden footed, he and Tony tried to escape back to their boat on the Danube.

Then London, the Depression, the long struggle to find a job and his euphoria when the cotton traders, J & P Coats, offered him a position as a management trainee. And, finally, India, the war and the years of separation.

Now, in the aftermath, everything had changed. Michael – signed off as unfit to serve in the armed forces because of a rugby injury at school – had built himself a reputation as the glamorous host of the Imperial in Torquay, an hotel which was bringing gaiety and a taste of luxury to a country tired of being blitzed by the Luftwaffe. But the two younger siblings had returned from the fight weary, nursing their own personal battle scars.

When Peter came home to Nell, it was Tony who met him on the platform at Bexhill station. As he stepped off the train, he did not recognize his second brother. Then the shock rising in his belly began to twist like a knife. Tony had been wounded at Arnhem. A wireless set abandoned by the Germans – booby-trapped. It blew off half his face and the fingers of his right hand. After many long months of hospital treatment, skin grafts and psychiatric care, Tony had been discharged to convalesce with his mother and with Maky, her faithful Hungarian retainer.

Peter, in his war, did not suffer the horrific wounds of his brother but his experiences had exacted their toll. He had seen fighting in Eritrea and Abyssinia, been part of the brutal campaign in Italy and had witnessed "the indescribable waste of war … the dead and the hellishly wounded." In the family history, he writes of "an unforgettable moment standing at a corner of a salvage dump in the Western Desert and seeing, in both directions, south and east, for miles row upon row of smashed tanks, guns and vehicles." And then, towards the end, there was his tour of duty in Greece – a country which had suffered cruelly under German occupation. Starvation was widespread, thousands died and infant mortality reached 95%. Young men fled into the mountains and joined the resistance, preferring to go down fighting than to starve to death. But after the German withdrawal in October 1944, the guerrilla bands polarized into left and right wing factions, and a tentative and nervous Greek government, backed by the British, was now confronted with a new threat from the leftist national resistance movement EAM/ELAS. It was not long before the British, supported by sections of the Indian Army and charged with the task of bringing peace and stability to a nation torn apart by war, found themselves embroiled in a bitter civil conflict. For Peter, the strains of this new mission finally overwhelmed him.

Back home and trying to reconnect with his half-forgotten family, searching for what might pass as normality, endeavouring to lay new foundations for his life and a future, he was lost – confused by a surreal world of partying in the ballroom of the Imperial one evening and coming to terms with a family fractured by war and separation the next morning. Michael (or Henry Michael as Nell called him) had married, and his wife Tim had produced a daughter Nicky – his first niece now three years old. They welcomed him to Torquay and plunged him into a round of dances and dinners where young girls were paraded for his inspection. "Was there a conspiracy?" he wondered. "Are they determined to marry me off?" Returning to Bexhill, he took Nell and Tony and Maky on drives into the countryside and to the sea – to Hastings, Eastbourne and Pevensey Bay. Then there were visits to London – staying at Claridge's with Michael and Tim. It was a glorious holiday. Everyone had been kind and generous. He had had fun.

Yet somehow, somewhere, something was wrong, did not quite fit. Once again those old childhood fears and uncertainties resurfaced – the feelings of exclusion, of not belonging returned to simmer uncomfortably on his consciousness. He did not feel at ease with his family and the source of his awkwardness was his relationship with Michael whom he had never quite forgiven for renouncing the family name – for consigning the senior line of the illustrious House of Prüger to oblivion. But he admired his big brother's style, his dash and success. And the splendour and prestige of the Imperial impressed him in much the same way as, fifteen years before, he had been awestruck by his father's tragic creation in Bratislava – the Hotel Savoy-Carlton.

This was the ragtag barrel of emotions churning inside his mind as he leaned over the ironing board to press his uniform on the eve of his wedding.

He forced himself to stop. He knew he was prone to moments of melancholy. But this burst of ruminative heartache was silly and self-indulgent. The war was over. He was in love and happy. About to be married to his Etty, a girl eleven years younger, still a teenager, and full of energy and innocent beauty. Her youth and freshness offered him a new life, new hope for the future. She was his liberation – from the hell of war and from the confinement of his own troubled youth. In her he had found his release from the knots and fetters of his own family, from the past. Etty was something different. She brought him a happiness he had never believed possible – a purity and a zest for living that was the perfect antidote to the trials of his early life. Her naïvety, her vivacity, her goodness refreshed his tortured soul. And for all the trauma suffered by Greece in the past five years, she seemed untouched by the vicissitudes of war. Instead, she radiated optimism and romance – everything he needed, at last fulfilling his elusive unconscious yearnings. But did he deserve her? Did he deserve such good luck? Still the demons nagged.

In England, in her Sussex cottage near Bexhill, Nell understood her son. In the photograph album she kept of his life, she prepared to write the final page in her familiar white ink. Beneath the title "Peter's Marriage – June 2nd 1946," she inscribed the words "The end and beginning of his Freedom."

*

He spotted her immediately – captivated by the laughter springing from her dark olive eyes. She was standing in the centre of a group of Greek guests at a mess night he had organized shortly after his return from home leave. It was already autumn in Salonica and he was pleased to be back in regimental service. Although a year had passed since the German withdrawal, there was still work to be done restoring peace and order in northern Greece. In many remote regions outside the city, people continued to live in fear – believing that the Germans remained as the occupying force or that their area was under the control of EAM/ELAS or some other resistance movement politically hostile to them. Part of the army's role was to reassure these communities, not least by distributing food and supplies to villagers who were half-starved and clad in rags. But as second-in-command of his battalion, one of Peter's more agreeable duties was to direct the mess committee, the body charged with organizing dinners and parties for prominent locals.

On this particular October evening, Athanasios and Fifi Rosi and their two daughters were among the battalion's guests. Peter stood bewitched; so struck by the sight of Etty – her vitality, the striking features, those eyes – that barely two words passed between them all night. Instead he stared, frozen like a rabbit caught in the beam of a powerful headlamp as his fellow officers circled, hovered and whispered their exaggerated attentions on her. To his delight, a few days later, he and his friends received a return invitation from Mr. and Mrs. Rosi to take tea with the family at their house in Queen Olga Street – a handsome fin de siècle villa bordering the Bay of Salonica. More visits followed, he grew attached to the family and they became friends.

*

Athanasios Rosi, my maternal grandfather whom Fifi my grandmother always called Thanassaki, was a shy hero of the Greek nation; a courageous man who put his life, and that of his family, at risk during the occupation and the political troubles that followed. As head of the northern division of the National Bank of Greece, he was a taciturn and high-minded chief executive whose clients included a large constituency of Jews many of whom he saved from deportation to the Nazi death camps. Then after the Germans left, Salonica for a while fell under the sway of EAM/ELAS until relations with the national government collapsed and the crisis escalated into civil violence on the streets in what became known as the "December Events" of 1944. In his office, Thanassaki feared for the Bank's gold reserves and – with British assistance – he conspired to clear the vaults in secret and ship the gold to safety in Athens.

My recollections of my Greek grandparents are the recollections of a child of the fifties. They remain clear but none more vivid than those of Fifi who provided for us, Gerald and me, spoiling us in the manner of Byzantine princes. Well, her noble bloodline has been traced back to the military rulers

Amelia Prüger, my great grandmother.

Henry Anthony Prüger, my great grandfather.

Nell Chapman, my grandmother.

Henry Prüger, my grandfather.

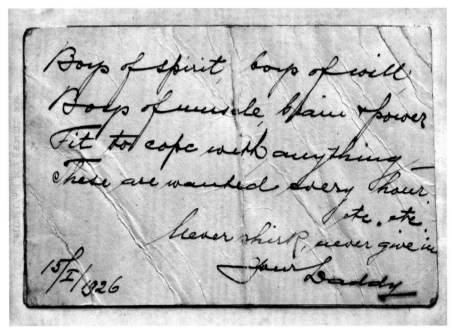

"Boys of spirit, boys of will…." My grandfather's framed dictum passed down the family line to hang above my bed as a child.

Henry Prüger's suicide note.

The famous "busy bee" logo.

The Savoy-Carlton in Bratislava, circa 1930.

With my cousin, Nicky, in 2007 outside the hotel, now rebranded the Radisson SAS Carlton.

With my love to Madame Prüger
Nellie Chapman.
Xmas 1909.

Watercolour of the original Avon Lodge. The Prüger family's Thames-side manor at Pangbourne during the First World War.

The second Avon Lodge. Nell's cottage in Little Common, near Bexhill-on-Sea in East Sussex.

Opposite: My grandmother, Nell, newly engaged. She presented this portrait to her future mother-in-law, Amelia Prüger, for Christmas 1909.

Peter in the summer of 1933 at the end of his long rowing expedition on the Danube – from Passau to Bratislava, a journey of over 200 miles.

The three Prüger boys: Peter, Tony and Henry Michael.

Nell outside her Sussex home in 1939. "Still waiting for Peter".

Maky. Nell's faithful Hungarian companion.

At home in Bratislava, summer 1928. Tony, Henry Michael and Peter. Seated, Nell and Henry Prüger betray the strain of a marriage at a low ebb.

Peter, my father, the sportsman.
Dover College 1932.

J. G. Whorwell,

7. BENCH ST.
DOVER.

of Constantinople in the fourteenth century and several of her antecedents were strung up in public by the Ottomans to deter dissent. For all her aristocratic credentials, Fifi was short, plump and adored. Her hair jet-black. Her eyes bright glistening olives. Her skin pale, smooth, translucent like fine porcelain. When she wrapped us in her arms it was like falling on soft silk pillows. Her hands, with their expertly manicured and varnished fingers, betrayed her status in the cushioned, privileged society to which she belonged. Supported by her team of uniformed servants, she was admired in Salonica as a generous and accomplished hostess. And her talents as an embroiderer once hung behind glass frames on the walls of Avon Lodge – Peter and Etty's home in Somerset.

Visiting the family as a child just a few years after the end of the war, the enduring impression still branded on my consciousness is the extreme contrast of conditions which existed side by side: privilege and poverty; the well-fed and the starved; the comfortable and the desperate; the upright and the maimed; the beauty and the ugliness. Scars on my mind. Salonica was a wreck. Its people broken. Riding down its parched, burnt streets, all I saw were beggars in rags and crippled children. It was a painful, unpleasant sight which left me frightened, ill at ease. You could almost touch the fear – and you could smell the decay on those streets. I could not understand why. Five, six, seven, eight, every year we came – Gerald and I – and it was still the same.

Queen Olga Street was a wide boulevard running parallel with the seafront, ornamented by a line of once gracious, now faded late-nineteenth century villas: two-storey mansions of elegant proportions, large windows and cool verandahs. Each was set in its own garden which gave onto the sea. Thanassaki and Fifi lived at number thirty-two, a house distinguished by its large oval plaque suspended from a first-floor balcony which indicated that this was the residence of the Norwegian Consul – an honour bestowed on my grandfather by a grateful government. Like the others in the street, the house was in grave need of repair. The grand iron railings surrounding the property were flaked, rusted like charred matchsticks, and the garden was a wilderness of scrub, weed and dead earth. For all its lost grandeur, at least the place limped in sympathy with its tattered city. But once we had run the gauntlet of dust and decay, breathed the stench of the streets, raced by the beggars and bent bodies; once we had closed the front door behind us and entered the cool of the house, a new world opened before us. One of polished wood, delicate lace and old silver; furnishings dressed in immaculate summer-white linens; refreshing breezes off the sea; and sweet, mysterious smells from the kitchen. Food was at the centre of this charmed universe; our grandmother, "Yaya", always pressing something delicious into our tiny mouths gaping like fledglings in a nest.

Unlike England where rationing had become a way of life, self-denial a good habit and drabness a state of mind, here in this wrecked city, in my grandparents' home, there was not the remotest sense of scarcity or deprivation. Here was only plenty, prepared and served by a small retinue of cackling peasant women who had the infuriating habit of pinching our cheeks (the traditional Greek custom of showing affection towards children). It was worth the pain. We ate wonderfully, feasting on all those dishes we continue to enjoy today when we sit with our young family on the terrace at Diodati.

And much like our life on the island today, our childhood routine in Salonica would follow a similar pattern. After lunch we would be despatched to our beds for a mandatory siesta – a deeply civilized habit we have now adopted. Then at six, Yaya would come to wake us – even now I can feel the smooth, soft luxury of the fine linen sheets that swathed our tiny naked bodies. No ordinary wake-up call this. Nothing as banal as a cup of tea or a lemonade. Yaya Fifi would present us with a *glyko* (a sweet) – an exotic delicacy offered on a long silver spoon so rich that decorum and common sense dictated that a spoonful a day was quite enough. A tall glass of iced water necessarily accompanied the *glyko* to cleanse the palate after ingesting this blissful confection. My favourite was *kerassi* (cherry), the scarlet fruit glistening in a syrup which spilled slowly over the edge of the spoon to create a slick of pinkness on its small cut-glass dish. I can taste the fruit now – the deepest, sweetest essence of cherry – cloying, sticking to my tongue and the roof of my mouth. I wanted more. She would never say no – just chuckled with pleasure, pinching my cheeks (more gently than her servants), saying, "Avrio, avrio pethi mou" – tomorrow, tomorrow my boy.

Our annual visits to Salonica were not confined to Queen Olga Street. There were other members of the family to whom we had to pay homage. The most important of these were my great-uncle Petros, Fifi's brother, and his wife, my aunt Cleo. Cleo was enormous, rouged and so heavily powdered that when she shook her jowls, the atmosphere misted like a halo about her lunar features. Her ample frame was rendered in an ocean of silk. Her neck, wrists and fingers runkled under the weight of gold and precious stones. Uncle Petros was deaf as a diamond but lived like a pasha. He was a voluptuary, a sensualist who devoted his life to women and food. But if he made me feel uneasy, Cleo terrified me. Still, for all my misgivings, I soon learned that a visit to their opulent seventh-floor apartment high above the promenade was an occasion not to be missed. Cleo's hospitality was legendary.

In the backstreets, not a hundred yards from the apartment building, the grimmer reality of hungry children scavenging in gutters and tired old men begging for small change passed us over. Sitting on Cleo's flower-strewn balcony, gazing over the bay – the sea dotted with American warships – maids offered wine, ouzo and spicy *mézéthes* to the grown-ups while Gerald and I practised the art of shelling pistachios which we gobbled greedily. Then lunch – a formal ritual at the damask-covered dining table laden with dishes of giant crawfish. For me *astakós* was the ultimate gastronomic luxury: fatter, sweeter than any English lobster I have ever seen since. We ate them cold, with fresh mayonnaise or olive oil and lemon juice. They were fantastic, and just thinking about them makes me salivate. Cleo would pick lustily at the dense flesh and then rinse her podgy, jewelled fingers in warm water poured into glass bowls, rose petals floating on their surface, which the servants had placed on napkins by each table setting.

To follow, there were vast plates of fruit – slices of water melon, peaches, grapes, figs – and then a stunning selection of pastries delivered that morning from Flóka, Greece's most famous patissier, with its bustling cafés in both Athens and Salonica. I would wait for this moment. Twelve months I would wait. And each time its consummation would be the most perfect, the most sublime moment of my life. The pastry of my dreams looked like a Big Mac: two round buns made of fine, airy-light sponge and filled with a delectable chantilly. The top bun was coated, éclair-like, with chocolate, and its exquisite squidginess demanded that we ate it with Cleo's set of beautiful ivory-handled pastry knives and forks. Five decades on and the taste of that cream bun still lingers, humming quietly about the contours of my palate.

*

This was the childhood world my mother grew up in – a world where good things were magicked from nowhere, issuing forth each day on silver trays and bone china as naturally as the light of the rising sun on the Aegean Sea. A world so cushioned and comfortable, so detached from the reality of the streets outside, it became a fantasy. Even the education of the two Rosi girls – Machi and Etty – would be the province of private tutors, governesses imported from France, Austria and England. Thanassaki adored his younger daughter, nicknaming her "Koutzi Mou" – an abbreviation of "Mikroutziko Mou", my Little One. He loved Machi too, but her intellect, her passion for books, politics and argument were not the qualities expected of a young lady of her background. Etty's extrovert charm and femininity, her carefree pursuit of fun and games were a welcome relief from a wicked, violent world. She charmed her father, his heart melting with the pleasure of her sunny optimism, and he would see to it that nothing intruded to unsettle her happiness or that of his own.

*

Peter was beginning to enjoy his regular visits to Queen Olga Street when, in December 1945 – three months after his return from leave – he was transferred to Brigade HQ in the port of Kavalla, a tobacco trading centre in Thrace ninety miles east of Salonica. He missed the company of the Rosi sisters and soon after his arrival he decided to organize a dance at the mess inviting Etty, and Machi who had recently married the son of a textile mill-owning family. Another Peter, Machi's Petros, had been recalled into service by the Greek army to counter the threat of insurgency from EAM/ELAS. On the day of the party, a warrant officer was despatched in a staff car to collect the three special guests. They were installed in the Victoria Hotel in Kavalla. "Not very good," wrote Peter in a message to Etty, "but the best here and quite clean." In the campaign to win hearts and minds, this was Peter's first public function at the Headquarters Mess and he was anxious to see the evening go down well with the local brass hats and grandees. And, as the new boy in town, he also needed to impress his CO, the Brigadier, who stood with him at the entrance to greet people as they arrived. The moment he spotted Etty striding into the mess flanked by Machi and Petros, he felt a rush of blood to his head. She looked fabulous, dressed simply in a long ball gown falling lightly off the tips of her shoulders, held in at the waist by a wide belt, her dark luxuriant head of hair, parted at the centre, cascading in a flood of curls and waves onto her back. When the band struck the opening bars of the Blue Danube, he asked her to dance. But his mind was split in too many directions and he could not stop his eyes sweeping the floor to check all was well, the joy of seeing Etty again muted by his duty as host.

Over a whisky and soda at the end of the evening, the CO declared the party a success and Peter retired to his quarters to find his bed for a sound night's sleep. Next day, when he awoke, he found the town gripped by an icy breeze, but the sky was bright and cloudless and he had promised Etty a walk in the countryside. By mid-morning his jeep was racing past fields and tobacco plantations into the hills behind Kavalla. This was the first time the two of them had been alone together – no Machi as chaperone – and for the first time in Peter's life, there was a quickening awareness that in Etty he had found a woman with whom he could talk freely, without restraint, without inhibition. Just being with her felt like the most natural thing in the world. And his nagging discomfort – the feelings of being a misfit in his own family – began to peel away like a dried scab on an old wound.

So it was in these hills that their great love took root – a love pursued with such intensity that, in the spicy gossip of the officers' mess, a romantic mythology was spawned and grew into a rich repertoire of apocryphal stories; the most famous being credited to the CO himself asserting that Peter had fallen into Etty's arms as he parachuted out of the sky to liberate the Greek people from the Germans.

But the urgent rhythms of their love – fuelled by a dozen telephone calls a day and frequent visits to Salonica on "important army business" – suddenly came to an end when Peter fell ill with hepatitis on the same day that the Division received orders to return to India. From his sick bed, he now had to plan the movement of the Brigade to Salonica – transport, supplies, feeding, medical provision, the whole circus; and from there too organize its embarkation onto troopships bound for Karachi. With a departure date fixed for the middle of February, there was no time to delay and by the first week of the month he was fit enough to meet shipping officers in Salonica to lay the final details of his plan. On the evening of the fifth, he called at the home of the Rosi family in Queen Olga Street and took Etty for a long drive in his jeep, heading south out of the city towards Agia Triada and the lighthouse marking the point at the mouth of the bay. He proposed. She accepted. And they embraced. In the history, Peter noted the moment: "My life was changed," he wrote. "Euphoria, dancing on air, what happiness!"

Next morning, Thanassaki broke his routine and was not to be found in the walnut and marble splendour of his office at the Bank. He remained at home with Fifi and his daughters. At the stroke of ten, Peter presented himself at the house to ask permission for Etty's hand in marriage. The interview, which took place in the privacy of Thanassaki's study, lasted over an hour – far longer than was necessary as the amiable banker was quick to welcome Peter's overtures. But the young officer felt duty-bound to confess to his prospective father-in-law that he was a man of limited means and doubtful prospects with no civilian employment to return to in England. The older man sat quietly and listened unperturbed. He had admired Peter from their first meeting. He trusted him. And he knew his Koutzi would be loved and cared for in the manner he would wish for his favourite girl.

The excitement of the engagement was as effusive and chaotic as any Greek celebration might be. With the Brigade's imminent departure for India, Peter was a busy man – and now he was obliged to run the gauntlet of hospitality with the many branches of Etty's family. Sumptuous dinners followed fabulous lunch parties, and at a pace set by Uncle Petros and Aunt Cleo who were determined not to be out-hosted by any other uncle, aunt or cousin. In a city starving and distressed, even Peter stopped to wonder from where all the good food was conjured. But for one evening they escaped the chattering horde and stole a moment for themselves to exchange rings and gifts. When she was a child Thanassaki had given his daughter a gold cross inscribed with her name. Etty now presented it to her Peter. She hung it around his neck and he wore it from that day to his last.

*

The wedding was set for May – a date which paid little heed to the obstacles that would confront Peter in a new world coming to terms with an uneasy peace. On the morning of February 28th, when the troopship docked in Karachi, his men, a brave and disciplined force of comrades composed of Hindus, Sikhs, Pathans and Punjabis, received a heroes' welcome home – then only to find their country gripped by a conflict that would lead to its violent partition into the two states of India and Pakistan. But for Major Chapman, the years in India and his tour of duty in the uniform of an officer of the Guides were drawing to a close. The moment had come for him to choose between being demobbed in India or England and, as there was nothing to keep him in India, he decided to accept a free passage home.

But in making his decision he soon found himself being harried by the unbending arm of the civil service. His journey was scheduled for April 20th and he was instructed to prepare for embarkation out of Bombay on a troopship bound for England. His request for a passage via Greece – "to get married" – was dismissed as preposterous and irregular. Pulling rank with the Army's headquarters in Delhi – through his CO, the kindly Brigadier – failed to impress the officials. But in the end they were given no choice in the matter and issued authorization documents when the General commanding the Division ordered Peter to be posted back to Greece on "official army duty" – the "duty" being to conduct negotiations with the base paymaster in Athens on unit funds which had been affected by the devaluation of the Greek drachma.

So when the troopship sailed from Bombay late on that bright April afternoon, Peter was on board, his papers authorizing him to disembark in Suez, his thoughts only for Etty to whom he had written each day since he kissed her goodbye on the quayside in Salonica. On deck he gazed out across the Arabian Sea. Behind him India was disappearing for the last time.

*

Now I must pause in recounting the tale of Peter's homeward odyssey – for by some immaculate intervention in the progress of my writing, the Fates seem to have been whispering in Louise's ear. She has made an extraordinary discovery. She has found the letters – dozens of them; thirty-five alone from Peter to Etty, most dated between February and June 1946, between the date of their engagement and the day of their wedding.

I have read and re-read the family history – a pedestrian text too short on detail. I have filled the gaps from pictures, notes, albums and my own recollections and insights; from hearsay and snippets of information from relatives and other archives; from my father's black deed box – a treasure trove revealing Henry Prüger's suicide note. But in clearing Avon Lodge in Somerset, there was no sign of any cache of love letters – unique, precious documents, the best primary evidence, rarely discarded, usually tucked away somewhere safe, and then forgotten or lost. I thought we had lost them and I put them out of my mind. It is two and a half years now since Etty's death; since we cleared the house and put it up for sale. But no sign of those letters – until, that is, last week when Louise decided to sort out the αποθηκη (apotheki), a large white-rendered shed by Diodati's main terrace used to store garden tools and outdoor furniture. At the back, hidden beneath decades of accumulated bric-a-brac lay two old cabin trunks scuffed and caked with dust. On the lids, in faded white paint, she could just make out the moniker "MAJ. P.F. CHAPMAN". She called me to help her drag the trunks into the late morning sun warming the terrace. We lifted the lids. Inside we discovered a mass of boxes and tins, pictures, books, silver cups, campaign medals, army gear, badges, school colours and caps – even drinks' coasters branded with the famous Red Eagle of the 4th Indian Division and a kukri, a Gurkha's curved machete. It was in an old 500 gramme box of Lindt chocolate assortments, its top decorated with gentian and edelweiss, that we found the letters. They were all loose except for one packet of thirty-five individually numbered air mail letters bound in yellow silk string and enclosed in an envelope printed with the title ΕΘΝΙΚΗ ΤΡΑΠΕΖΑ ΤΗΣ ΕΛΛΑΔΟΣ (NATIONAL BANK OF GREECE). The envelope was clearly marked in blue-black ink in my mother's hand: "Letters from my Mou in India 1946". The rest were letters from and between the two families – twelve written by Nell and thirteen from Etty to Peter although some appear to have gone astray as Peter's correspondence suggests he received at least sixteen.

I have now read the contents of the box of Lindt – my tightly scribbled notes running to a dozen sheets of legal pad. The discovery has had a strange and emotional effect on me, and I have needed a couple of days to absorb the significance of my reading. At one level the letters confirmed my instincts and beliefs. But gradually their impact, their texture, their revelations seeped into my consciousness to magnify my understanding of my parents and their relationship. Now I have a kind of proof; I have the evidence. And in some ways I have found myself afraid to confess that the evidence was disturbing, shocking even. Peter's and Etty's was not just a great love affair, it was an obsessive, consuming passion. And it was also a lopsided, unequal relationship – my father enslaved by his "Grecian Goddess", my mother, spoiled and indulged as a child, now placed on a high pedestal, an avatar to be worshipped by her uxorious consort.

Here below, I shall try to present a flavour of these letters with their blend of passion, tenderness and poetic metaphor; also Peter's need for his mother's approval and, in her letters, Nell's advice to her son and her words to Etty.

First Peter to Etty.
No. 2 At Sea, 19 Feb 46

My one and only Grecian Goddess,

… Koutzi mou! To me you are like the gentle wind in the trees, like a shaft of sunlight that comes through stormy clouds and lights up my soul like the fresh, bright green grass of England with delicate rose petals on it … Before I fell in love with you, I was like a sailing ship in the middle of the ocean with not a breath of wind, drifting aimlessly along, not knowing where I wanted to go and feeling that there was no object in life. Now it is as if a fresh strong breeze has come, I can feel the ship moving along swiftly through the water …… I am with you always, my darling. A million kisses and more, Peter.

Before Peter left Salonica, Etty asked him to make a number of purchases of items that were unobtainable in Greece. These included a particular brand of natural lipstick, Ponds Cold Cream and a white bathing cap. By letter no. 4, the troopship was passing through the Suez Canal and Peter reported that these things were not to be found in either Port Said or Suez. He was also showing increasing concern in case Etty – whose English was not as fluent as her sister's – did not understand his letters. So he explains that from now on he will give an alternative English word or its German equivalent in brackets ("a = alternative English") and ("g" = German"). In letter no. 5, the ship now sailing down the Red Sea, he talks of his happiness and imagines Etty's preparations for the wedding. Is she in Athens? Is she preparing her trousseau? Then he reflects on the past two years of his life: "1944 was a very bad year for me. Everything went wrong and the year ended with me in hospital!" No detail. No explanation. He does not tell Etty about his nervous breakdown. He continues: "But I have great faith in 1946. It will be a wonderful, marvellous, most beautiful year! And why? Only because of you, my Grecian Goddess, my one and only Schnabelchen!" (My father adored Etty's distinctive nose! Schnabel is "beak" or "bill" in German.) The letter ends: "Darling, sweetest 'mou', your picture, your cross and your ring always remind me of you, your beauty, gentleness, goodness, sweetness and also your devilry! And I hold you in my arms and kiss you all day and all night. There was never anybody on Earth like my 'Cleopatra'. Your, 'Anthony'".

By letter no. 7, the ship had entered the Indian Ocean.

No. 8 At Sea, 25 Feb 46

My own sweet Darling,

One of the things which I cannot stop wondering about is the reason why I, my miserable self, should have been blessed with the fortune and grace of receiving the love of a person like you. I mean this in all sincerity. What you see in me I really cannot imagine. For, honestly, to me Etty you are the personification of all that is good, sweet and lovable. I know that I have told you all this before, but it still "worries" me to a certain extent! You are so good, so kind, so sweet, so beautiful, so sensible, capable and intelligent, above all, so lovable that I really cannot believe that you are to be my wife. I am not worthy of you. Possibly this knowledge will help me strive and make even greater efforts to satisfy you and to make you happy. It is often said that the most dangerous and difficult time of any marriage is the first year. This will be even more than usually true in our case. You will be in a strange land, amidst strange people, far from home and it will be just during this first year of our life together that I will be at my busiest, trying to establish a position for myself, and, therefore with the minimum of spare time to devote to you. A great deal depends on my family. I know that. But also I have complete faith in them and I know that they, too, will do everything possible to make you happy. But my brothers are busy men, wrapped up in their own affairs and my mother is an old, sick woman who is now tied to her house for most of the time. Being an invalid, too, she suffers a lot and has, of course, all the disabilities of invalids in general.

You have no idea how I am longing to arrive in India if only so as to get her letters (and yours too, of course!!) to see what she has to say about our engagement. It is more than likely, too, that by the time you get this letter you will have had a reply to the letter you sent with your photograph. Remember? I posted this on about 10th February.

…Write to me often, my Goddess.
Your humble and devoted Peter

The box of Lindt did include Etty's letter to Nell of 10th February. She would have received help drafting it from both Peter and her sister Machi. There is a formality and a restraint here that masks Etty's true voice beyond the uncertain fluency of her written English which would have been polished up for her.

32, Queen Olga St. Salonica, 10th February 1946

My dear Mrs. Chapman,

I expect that by now you will have received Peter's letter telling you of our engagement. It came very suddenly, but Peter and I are so happy. We have known each other a long time and we both thought very carefully before we decided to be together for our whole life.

I love my Peter very deeply and I am prepared to do anything for him, just to see him smile and be happy. I hope you will understand me and that you feel what Peter means to me.

I am a Greek girl, but I was brought up by foreign nurses and later on I had an English lady who spent all the summer holidays with us at our country farm in the hills, until the beginning of our war in 1940.

I received a careful education and I speak French and German. I am doing my best to improve my English! I am used to foreign customs because of my father's position as the consul for Norway in Salonika. We are acquainted with all the foreign consuls and especially with the British Consul General, whose daughter is my sister's best friend. I have often been to Vienna for long visits, but I was only a child then. I have only an elder sister who is married to an ex-officer of the Greek Army who is a cloth mill owner.

Peter loves you so much, he has told me all about you and how very nice and dear you are and I am sure that it will be very easy for me to love you and to call you "Mother" if you allow me to do so.

Please, mother dearest, will you give me your blessing and say that you agree to our engagement?

Yours affectionately,
Etty

Nell's reply.

Avon Lodge, Little Common, Bexhill O/S, Sussex Feb 19

Very dear Etty

Your very charming and sweet letter came as a great and joyful surprise to me yesterday afternoon, just as I was starting off to a Bridge party – am afraid I was very "distrait" all the time. Your face and words coming between me and the Cards. You see, I had not received Peter's letter, but it came this morning.

I think that first of all I would like to thank you for loving my Peter, thank you most sincerely for making him so happy, for after all, that is what all true Mothers wish for, is the Happiness and well being of their children, and Peter is very dear to me. It may be because when he was young up to 9 or 10 yrs, he was not so robust as my other 2 sons and I remember that I was very nervous about him when he had to go to Boarding School, however I made friends with the Matron and she understood.

He was at College till he was 19 and I only saw him at holiday times and then came the big break when after joining Coats Firm I saw him off at Liverpool Docks for India. When the ship sailed away I felt my heart was nearly broken but I could still hear his pleasing worlds "Only 4 years Mummy, it will soon pass". Little did I then dream that 10 years would pass before I saw him again and so from a shy student of 20 yrs old – but very brave and earnest – he came back to me a man of 30. 10 yrs of lost happiness for me, and so much of lost sweetness which is Peter's great charm of character – but I had great consolation that he seemed still unspoilt. The same naïveté of spirit still so young. I was so afraid, Etty, of what India, with its glamour would do to him, but no, and people here who met him for the first time all remarked "He is so young for his years". This devastating and terrible war has ruined so much that was beautiful in our lives, it is up to ourselves, to keep on searching for beauty and make our own Happiness – and in as simple a way as possible – I wanted Peter to marry, to make a life of his own. Roots, Branches – someone to care for him and be his helpmate as I cannot be here for ever and still wish to see as much of him and his Happiness as I can. I often said, "There are so many English girls but the one I wanted was, the one who would understand and love him and you are the one, dear Etty, it seems for he has told me how very much he loves you.

I hope your engagement will not be too long. I shall welcome you with open arms and am sure the rest of my family here will do the same.

Must now end up and will write more of our family later on – meanwhile kindly convey to your Mother, Father and Sister my most affectionate regards and greetings – as for you, sweet Etty, a warm hug and kiss and every blessing possible and may we meet very, very soon.

From Mother to be.
Helen [Nell] Chapman

Next day, Nell wrote to Peter – a "FORCES LETTER" in its singular shade of khaki addressed to "Major P.F. Chapman, c/o Lloyds Bank Ltd., Hornby

Road, Bombay, India. Its postage was 1½d (a penny ha'penny) compared to 5d (five pence) for her letter to Etty the day before.

Avon Lodge, Wednesday Feb 20th

My darling Peter,

On Monday afternoons post the Regt letter arrived bringing the big and surprising and joyful news. I was just starting off to a Bridge Tea, but was so excited went without several necessary articles. When I returned I again read Etty's very sweet letter then I rang up Torquay only to find H.M. [Henry Michael] was In London. We have had an excitement here by the birth of a son to Henry and Tim. Now you have given us a cause for rejoicing for from her letter and picture I can see for myself what a lovable and perfectly sweet little girl she is.

Today I have sent letters also Ettys and picture off to H & T and they will see as I do that you are a very lucky boy and needless to tell you, my very dearest and best of sons, how happy, how thrillingly happy, I am that the girl you love, loves you too and I feel it will be a perfect marriage. I do not mind in the least that she is not English, all the better for you my dear, she is better educated and well brought up, I only wanted to be sure you found the right one. Someone who will understand and love you like I do, who will take care of you when I am no more here for I have had precious little of you in my life. So, please Peter – do not have a long engagement. I don't believe in them. Marry as soon as you are demobbed. God bless you my dearest and sweetest Peter. Maky is <u>delighted</u> – she at once placed Ettys picture by yours and says she <u>knows</u> she is the sweetest darling. All for now darling am longing to get your next.

Much love
Mother

Then a second "FORCES LETTER" from Nell to Peter eight days later – a deep and thoughtful message to her favourite son. Her great happiness for him seems to be tempered by her own anxieties. And her troubled heart, I suspect, has been stirred more by memories of her own marriage than by the austerity of the times. For me, reading this letter was like watching a volcano erupt in slow motion. In three short sentences, Nell sheds light on a dark family secret which has lain buried for seventy-seven years. In giving Peter her advice, the letter begins to untangle the mystery and explodes the myth surrounding Henry Prüger.

Avon Lodge, Wednesday Feb 28th – 46

Dearest and best

Your dear letter "At Sea" Feb 18th reached me safely and I do feel so sorry for you my darling – being so long without news.

My pleasure and contentment at your Engagement and Plans, you will know – for Ettys letter brought tears to my eyes and I do not cry easily – she must be a most sweet and charming girl – and as the Greeks are known by everyone, our Govt included as the one race in Europe who is sincerely and wholeheartedly pro British – I do not feel at all that I shall have a "foreign" daughter in law. I shall love her all the more and try to make up to her, the loss of her beautiful country, for our Land is anything but these days. With this austerity everything is shabbiness and poor rations.

My advice as to what and how much to tell ones wife is always tell her the truth – about everything – when she asks you – a wife wants to be at one with her husband, not to be put off with excuses – that denies trust and causes dissension. Does she know about your Father? He was a fine man and you have no reason to be ashamed. You get all your Brains from him, he was a most unselfish, noble and fine character, but should never have married.

Your Plans for Marriage. I quite agree – snatch your happiness when it comes your way – there is so much misery in the world at present.

Much love my dear one and God be with you. I am very anxious these days, these troublesome days.

Your very loving
Mother

"Always tell her the truth," Nell advises. And then asks: "Does she know about your Father?" What does she mean? Why might there be any suggestion that Peter would not have spoken "the truth" about his father? But, in thirty-five letters to Etty, with frequent references to Nell, there is not one mention of his father. "He was a fine man and you have no reason to be ashamed." And again why should there be any suggestion that Peter might be ashamed? Why did Nell feel she had to reassure her son that HP was "a most unselfish, noble and fine character"? And then the final phrase. Those last five words … "but should never have married". I could not believe what I was reading. Through the fug of eight decades of spin and cover-up, slowly everything seemed to come clear. The pieces of the jigsaw fell into place. In 1929 the whole of Europe was feeling the stranglehold of economic collapse. The financial pressures on HP, this titan hotelier, as his reconstruction of the Savoy-Carlton approached completion, were enormous – but not unusual for industrialists and entrepreneurs of the time. To me it seems unlikely that this great burden in itself drove him to his death – a death, I discover, that was suicide, a word never uttered in the family, the truth hushed-up. Now I learn that a darker secret may lie beneath this truth. Is Nell hinting that her husband was not the marrying kind? He … "should never have married" … "never have married". These words began to haunt me. I went back to the black deed box and reread Prüger's desperate letter: "A terrible folly of mine smashed all what we possessed … I can't say more my heart aches for my poor Girl my boys and my brothers and sisters, it is too terrible for words …" The "folly"? What was the "folly"? A moment of madness, perhaps – driven by the strain of his business worries. Henry Prüger, I suspect, may have been a repressed homosexual and Nell knew it. The incident, whatever it was, would have set light to a scandal and ruined his reputation at the centre of Bratislava society. He had disgraced the family name and he could no longer face his wife, his children, his brothers and sisters with any sense of dignity. The shame and dishonour were too great for a proud man to endure. He crept into a roof space at the top of his hotel and hanged himself from a beam.

1929. Nell's annus horribilis. She was now left with the task of managing the crisis. She needed to bury the scandal and protect her three boys who were coming to the end of the summer term at Dover College and looking forward to their holidays on the banks of the Danube. Peter was only fourteen. Nell, I am sure would have been especially sensitive in the way she handled this devastating news with her youngest. We know he was her favourite, and we know he was less "robust" than her two older sons. She was anxious about how he would cope at his English boarding school so far away from home and she went out of her way to befriend his matron. Of the three, Henry Michael, five months off his eighteenth birthday, was mature for his years and Nell may well have looked to him for support through this terrible period. My guess is that either she or another member of the family – one of HP's brothers, Uncle Julius or Uncle Max – would have taken Michael into their confidence. However the news was broken, it hit the young man very hard. Whereas Peter and Tony were more forgiving, their brother's attitude was to bury Bratislava and all it represented in a supreme act of denial. His feelings of betrayal struck deep and he ended up reinventing himself as Michael Chapman – renouncing the family name, discarding the patronymic, avoiding all talk about his early life. Where I would often hear Peter and Tony lapse into German, not once did I hear Michael speak his father's first language.

But this sense of shame and betrayal also affected Peter. In the correspondence with his beloved Etty, he ignored his mother's advice and avoided all reference to his father. It was too messy, too horrible – and Etty was too sweet, beautiful, good and kind to be contaminated by his shame. This, tragically, is where his insecurity and lack of self-worth are rooted. This is why time and again he keeps returning to the same theme in his letters: "I am not worthy of you," he writes. And: "I cannot stop wondering … why

I, my miserable self, should have been blessed with the fortune and grace of receiving the love of a person like you".

On 27th February Peter wrote his last letter to Etty (no. 10) before docking in Karachi. He is excited, bubbling with the prospect of receiving his post, anticipating news from his family, impatient for their reaction to his engagement. He tells Etty that he has written a "birthday letter" to his mother who would be entering her seventieth year on 6th March. "The pen went with a 'schwung' [swing]," he writes, "and I think it was a good letter! What I said about you I will not repeat as it would make you blush!" He continues: "I am longing to arrive in India so as to get my mail (a = letters) both from you and my mother – to see what she has to say."

On the same day, three thousand miles away in Salonica, Etty also wrote to Peter. Her mind is preoccupied with preparations for the wedding and she seems to feel more at ease expressing some of her more intimate thoughts in German. For all their passion, sentiment and sincerity, Etty's letters are light and frothy – perfectly in tune with the language of a teenager in love. There is nothing in them to echo the soul-searching agonies of Peter's correspondence which seem to pass over her head.

32 Queen Olga St. 27th February 1946

Own Mou,

Today I am tired and I am not in the right mood. I am longing for you, for your kisses and your tender words, I miss everything so much, my Mou.

Petraki mou I nearly finished my preparations in Salonika and I am leaving for Athens probably next week with Gods help. There I will make ready the rest of my trousseau, this means sheets, dresses, hats etc. I will order all my dresses in Athens because they make them smarter … I hope to be back in Salonika about Eastertime. Darling Mou I have such joy in preparing those things that I can not describe it to you. I think sometimes that I am dreaming, so wunderschön ist es *und doch wahr* [it is so beautiful and yet true]. ... *Es kommt bald die Zeit, wo wir <u>ewig</u>, glücklich beisamen bleiben, my own Mou. In Gedanken bin ich immer bei Dir Peterle.* [The time will soon come when we shall live happily together for ever, my own Mou. You are always close to my thoughts Peterle.] *Come to me soon. I love you poli, poli* [Greek – very much].

A sweet love kiss from your Sou.

*

For the next seven weeks – March and much of April – Peter was based in Lahore. He instructs his bank, Lloyds in Bombay, to forward his post and cables but, to his growing frustration, nothing arrives until mid-March – nor is he successful in his search to find Etty's white bathing cap and lipstick. The only good news to come through is his official permission to marry which he receives on March 8th – his thirty-first birthday. At last, in his letter of the 16th (no. 17), he tells Etty that the parcel from Lloyds Bank has arrived. "My mother is <u>so</u> pleased about our engagement," he writes quoting Nell's letter of February 20th at length.

This small package of correspondence from Bombay, like a pair of bellows, fanned the flames of Peter's passion. There are moments when his letters to Etty burn like a raging furnace. The framed portrait she gave him is perched on his desk and he worships it, his intense feelings crackling through every line on the page: "I sit here looking at you and thinking of you until I literally tremble (g = zittern) – so then I must go out for a walk!" No. 19 continues: "... my beautiful golden Greek Goddess, my Cleopatra, my Juliet, my Delilah ... I want to take you in my arms and hold you and kiss you and never, never let you go again." No. 21: "Every time I look at your big picture, my heart almost stops, such is the thrill and the wonderment and the joy at seeing such a lovely, beautiful being, with such divine inner light. Yes, that inner light of yours lights up your face and shines through those perfect deep eyes of yours, seeming to bring joy and a blessing to me."

Not until March 24th (letter no. 24) does Peter begin to explain the bureaucratic wrangle he is locked in with the authorities to arrange a passage to England with a stop in Greece to attend his own wedding. And, anxious not to alarm Etty, he is careful to reassure her that, with the intervention of his CO, the good Brigadier, he had arranged a meeting at General HQ in Delhi to hatch a spurious plan which would see him posted back to Athens "on duty". All would be well. She was not to worry.

The following day, a letter arrived from Henry Michael. For weeks now, Peter had been waiting to hear from his brother whom he describes to Etty as "the head of the family." I had always been conscious of my father's sense of awe – even a slight fear – for his bright and glamorous elder sibling – and this deference is apparent in his words to Etty: "I wanted very much to know what he would say about our engagement," he writes (letter no. 25), and then goes on to replay Michael's slightly patronizing remarks. "We are delighted," his brother begins. "You certainly sounded like a love sick maiden in your letters, however we think Etty looks a sweet thing and feel sure you will both be very happy."

At the end of the month, with only three weeks remaining before his departure, Peter set off for Bombay to pack up his civilian clothes and the other belongings he had put into safe storage when he joined the army. And on the return journey to Lahore, his plan was to travel via Delhi to see GHQ about his posting in Greece. The next letter to Etty (no. 26) is written from his room at the Taj Mahal Hotel in Bombay. It is hot and humid, he tells her – confessing that as he writes he is sitting naked under the ceiling fan and "still I am absolutely wet with sweating." But the good news, he reports, is that he has at last completed her shopping list and bought "<u>two</u> nice white bathing caps and <u>four natural</u> colour lipsticks."

With less than two weeks left before embarkation, Peter began counting the hours and his letters to Etty became more urgent. "I am getting so excited now," he writes on 9th April (no. 30). "Ich kaum es nicht aushalten!! [I can hardly bear it!!] It is terrible, awful. Every nerve in my body, every drop of my blood is shouting 'Etty, Etty, Etty, Etty' all day and all night long." And three days later (no. 31): "I am like a kettle of hot water on a stove. Every day the heat of my love for you gets greater and greater. Now I am boiling and all the water is boiling over, out of me! It hurts, es schmertzt! [it hurts]. Looking at your photograph now, you seem to come alive and I want so terribly to take you in my arms, Koutzi mou."

His final letter to Etty from India (no. 35) was written four days before he boarded the troopship in Bombay. Below I have transcribed it in full. Peter's vision.

H.Q. 7 Ind. Inf. Bde, c/o H.Q. Lahore Area, Lahore, Punjab, India 16 April 46

Mou,

It is now after ten o'clock at night. I am sitting all by myself in the room I share with Willy Brooks. The lights are out, except for the table lamp on my desk. The doors and windows are open because it is hot and the ceiling fan is swishing above my head. From outside come a lot of noises, frogs croaking, cats and jackals calling – because there is a full moon and it is almost as light as day.

Tonight, too, is the re-opening for the summer season of the officers club here. It is a nice place, full of light and colour and friendship and joy. I was going to this party. Some others and I have just finished having dinner before going there. But towards the end of dinner you were so terribly close to me, I felt I had to talk to you and to tell you about the beautiful Vision I have had. So when they went away I excused myself saying I did not feel well. I must talk to you and tell you what I have seen. This is it:-

It is in Heaven, just before 5th October 1926. God turns to St. Peter and says "I want to make something extraordinarily beautiful now." And God calls all his Saints, Archangels and angels around him. Amongst these are some well-known people. And God says "You, Benvenuto Cellini, you will construct the _form_. And you Michael Angelo will be in charge of the _head_. You will obtain and spin the feathers of a Raven, silk with the softness of Moss for the hair. Eyebrows you will *make from black Swansdown, eyes you will obtain from topazes from Celestial China. The cheeks and skin you will construct from the petals of Lilys. The teeth from the most perfect Pearls in Heaven and the mouth from the sweetest red Roses. The ears you must make from mother-of-pearl and the neck you will model from the columns of the Parthenon in Athens" – Turning again to Benvenuto Cellini, He says "When constructing the <u>form</u> you will use the finest Marmara marble – <u>and She must be tall</u>."*

The Holy Spirit then said "And <u>her</u> Heart? What is that to be?" And God said "Her Heart will be in the form that you made the Annunciation to <u>Mary</u> – in the form of a <u>Dove</u>." And to the Holy Mother, He said "Because <u>She</u> will be a girl, to You I entrust <u>her</u> character – make it like yours." Then Jesus turned to the Holy Father and said "And what of <u>her</u> Soul?" And God replied "<u>Her</u> Soul. I give it to you to make." And so <u>She</u> was made. And God decided that because <u>She</u> would be modelled from the ancient and beautiful Goddesses of Greece, She would be a Greek. So St. George said "I am the Patron Saint of Greece, also of England – may <u>She</u> be called after me?" God said, "So be it – <u>She</u> will be called "Georgette". Then St. George said "And who will be her Mate? As I am also Patron Saint of England, will he be an Englishman?" The Heavenly Father said "Yes, he will be an Englishman."

At last St. Peter said "What will be the name of this Englishman?" So God said "He will be called after you, Peter."

And so, on the 5th October 1926 was born a most beautiful, wonderful and sweet maiden, and her name was Georgette Rosi.

<u>Saint (???) Peter</u>

Many years later, under different circumstances, and in a place on the other side of the world, Peter would have a second vision. Again it would come at a time of emotional tumult.

But this will have to wait. For now I must return to the story of his journey home.

*

As Bombay shimmered off the horizon and the troopship steamed towards the Gulf of Aden, Peter's thoughts drifted from the joy of the coming reunion with Etty to a more practical question. His battle with the bureaucrats over his passage was as nothing to the challenge of dealing with his luggage. The regulations were clear. An officer was permitted only such baggage as he himself could carry. His army gear alone might have been manageable. But he now had to transport his pre-war civilian wardrobe along with his books, pictures, sporting trophies and all the impedimenta essential to the life of a young bachelor. Waiting to board ship in Bombay, he had stood before a line of cabin trunks, wooden boxes and leather suitcases all branded boldly "MAJ. P.F. CHAPMAN" in white paint – inhospitable lumber which, he realized, would become his inanimate companions until he landed in England. The horror of shifting this private cargo around the eastern Mediterranean seaboard and onward blurred into a long dark nightmare of dockside ruffians, pickpockets and street urchins as well as soldiers who were marshalled like mules to assist him. And to add to his ordeal, in every port he was confronted with bands of troublesome officials – the Army's Movement Control – who seemed determined to thwart his travel plans. After his arrival in Suez, he was sent to Cairo and billeted in an officers' mess for a week. From here he moved on to a transit camp in Alexandria only to find that no ships were sailing to Greece. From Alexandria the next set of orders despatched him to Port Said where he discovered a small and dirty coaster waiting for him. But a customs investigation delayed the tramp's departure for another five days.

Time was passing. It was already mid-May; the day of the wedding was upon them and the family had settled in with their relations in Athens. They waited. And waited. And still there was no sign of Peter. After his final cable from Port Said, Thanassaki decided to postpone the marriage and by the time Peter disembarked in Piraeus, they had all returned to Salonica. He followed in haste – but not before undertaking his "official duty" with the base paymaster in Athens who had already been briefed by GHQ Delhi. It was a straightforward matter and the two officers completed their business in the time it takes to down a couple of whiskies on the mess verandah.

*

After one false start, the revised arrangements for the wedding were rushed through in less than seven days. On May 28th a notice was posted in the "FORTHCOMING MARRIAGES" listings of the Daily Telegraph. With the mournful omission of an acknowledgement to the late Henry Prüger, it read: "The marriage of Major Peter F. Prüger Chapman, youngest son of Mrs. Helen Chapman, of Avon Lodge, Little Common, Bexhill-on-Sea, and Georgette (Etty) Rosi, younger daughter of Mr. and Mrs. Athanas Rosi, of the Norwegian Consulate, Salonika, Greece, will take place in Athens on June 2." Next morning – Wednesday – seventy invitations were despatched hurriedly to family and friends who were asked to attend St. George's church in Kipseli at 10.30 am on Sunday.

St. George's – more basilica than church and dressed in a luxuriant mass of flowers – made a perfect stage set for the Orthodox ceremony with its colour, its ritual and tradition of floral coronets held above the heads of bride and groom: she in a simple period gown of pale cream silk; he immaculate in uniform – leather belt, buckle and buttons polished to a high shine. For Peter, one memory more vivid than any other would remain close to him for the rest of his life. "It was those eyes," he would say, "those eyes looking up into mine".

By midday, the Rementzis family, Etty's favourite Athenian cousins, were greeting guests at their Kipseli mansion. After the feasting came the toasts and Peter, unable to contain his happiness, found himself speaking far too long, a dilemma made worse by Machi who was required to interpret every phrase and nuance into Greek. It didn't matter. The family and their friends fell for the rich diplomacy of his words as he promised to name their first-born son George in tribute to the patron saint of both Greece and England, and the reigning kings of their two glorious nations. He kept his promise. I was christened Christopher Henry George.

While the celebrations in Athens spilled into the afternoon, at home in Little Common, Nell was pressed for time – writing to the newlyweds and determined not to miss the 5.30 post from Bexhill. Over the previous three months, she had written frequently to both of them – her letters to Etty packed with news of the family and advice on how to cope with the rigours of post-war England. March had been a bitterly cold month … "don't forget darling," she wrote on the 15th, "you are <u>not</u> coming to a lovely warm country – not even in summer is it very warm – am so afraid you will loathe the climate and I must confess that I hate the cold weather myself – that's why I'm writing this on my knees before a blazing fire – as this small Cottage has <u>no</u> central heating … So dear heart, as you are about your trousseau, don't overlook warm things and sturdy good shoes." By May the weather had warmed up and Nell was more cheerful … "Am enclosing a few snaps of your future home," she tells Etty. "We [she and Maky] live for our flowers and our garden now is a mass of colour and beauty."

But on this particular day, she was being rueful and reflective.

Avon Lodge
June 2nd 1946
Your Wedding Day

My darlings both,

On this day of all Days it is a little sad for me that I cannot be with you but my thoughts are with you <u>all</u> the time, and all my Blessings and Good Wishes for your future particularly Good Health, and with all that, one can battle with many of the Cares of Life. There are always "ups and downs" in most people's lives, but there must be some Rain, otherwise we should not enjoy the Sunshine. Well, let us *hope there will not be too much Rain, as we are having in England just now – the wettest May for 50 years! But Maky gathered the first Sweet Peas this morning and she has been to Church to pray for you both and also yesterday Saturday – we took your first Communion Candles (3) September 15/1924 all decorated with flowers and ribbons for Mother Mary's Altar also beautiful flowers – and Prayers were offered for you both – I feel I am a very lucky woman to have such good children … It is now Noon 12 o'clock and with you in Athens 2 o'clock. Are you already married – you did not tell me the hour!!*

I hope you have both been photographed in Wedding Dress. Etty must be lovely in White!! And keep all snaps and all wires – I must make a Book – so bring picture of church. Arrange with Michael where to stay if you come thro London. He will Book for you – but all is very expensive, so take care! Aunt Fan just arrived so must end quickly – she sends her love also Maky.

Kisses and hugs to you both and come home soon.
Mother

But Nell's pleas for an early return home went unfulfilled. Travel across Europe remained a complicated business and besides, there was the honeymoon: a week at the luxurious resort of Kifissia in the cool of the hills north of Athens and a week at a simple beachside taverna on the island of Poros. Here Peter and Etty were billeted with a poor and half-starved community who survived on a diet of olives, olive oil, tomatoes, cheese and rough bread. But the locals befriended the young couple and made them welcome with what little they had – hospitality which Peter was able to return with some of his army rations. It was here, on this Aegean island that I was conceived.

On their return to Athens, the romantic bubble burst as the realities of the times resumed play. Reporting to Force HQ, Peter learned that he and Etty would not be travelling home together. His orders were to board a troopship sailing out of Piraeus in the next forty-eight hours and she was to join a transit camp for the Greek wives of British servicemen – there to await a second ship which would be commissioned when the numbers in the camp justified its departure. The notion of abandoning Koutsi Mou to a spell in a camp full of Greek women of uncertain pedigree was unthinkable. Thanassaki and Fifi would have fainted in horror. Peter had to act and lost no time going in to bat with the "old boy" routine. A number of his colleagues at Force HQ remembered him and after some friendly banter and a few pink gins, they were persuaded to find Etty a seat on an RAF flight to Northolt leaving Athens within the fortnight.

The next headache to grip Peter's fevered mind was the recurring nightmare of his baggage. At a stroke it had doubled in volume. On top of his own gear, he had the additional freight of the trousseau to shift: large wooden crates packed to the brim with bedding, linens – even carpets and silver – as well as Etty's considerable wardrobe. To aggravate his predicament, Peter's itinerary was not a straightforward passage from Greek port to English port. The ship sailed for Marseilles where he was obliged to commandeer a lorry to transport the trunks and boxes to a transit camp. Here he waited two days until the order came through to transfer to the railway station. Another lorry. More loading and unloading. The train rumbled nervously into a long French night across an unseen war-worn landscape. Arriving in Calais, he repeated the drill: another lorry, another transit camp – until a ship was found to ferry him and his cargo across the Channel.

The tense denouement of Peter's nightmare was finally played out in a customs' shed on the dockside at Dover. He knew the place well. For a moment he was struck by past memories of his school days – returning to college with his brothers after their holidays in Bratislava. He thought of his father and shuddered. Now he stood at a counter, army kitbag and haversack at his side. Behind him rose a cliff face of wood and leather daubed "MAJ. P.F. CHAPMAN" like the white-painted signatures of an incontinent graffitist. Before him stood a customs' officer whose eyebrows bristled in astonishment.

"Moving house are we, sir?" enquired the customs' officer shaking his head in disbelief. "Bring 'n buy sale maybe?"

"I've just got married, officer," replied Peter. "These are all my wife's belongings, her trousseau …"

"Trousseau?" interrupted the officer. "Some kind of wedding cake is it?"

"Wedding presents, clothes, bed linen, table linen, that sort of thing," he tried to explain. "Look officer, here is my marriage certificate, discharge papers and my travel warrants."

The uniformed official was not impressed. He'd seen it all before and he was determined to pursue the interrogation.

"Look sir, let me try and believe you," he said. "Supposing we put a value of £1,000 on this little lot. What would you say to that?"

"That's very fair, very fair, officer," assented Peter quickly, knowing the value had to be much higher.

"Excellent sir," smiled the customs' officer. "We're beginning to make some progress here. Now sir, with twenty percent purchase tax and then there's your customs' duty, I reckon that comes to £400 owing." [About £11,000 at 2006 prices.]

Peter's jaw dropped. His heart began pounding. That kind of money was beyond him and he began to plead with the man: he'd just got married, he'd travelled from India via Greece; all these boxes and trunks were to set up home; they were not goods and stock to set up a new business – definitely not, he insisted.

"Yes sir, of course sir," said the man, a cynical twitch curling around the edges of his thin lips. "But you've just agreed that these goods are fairly valued at £1,000, sir! That's £400 to pay!"

Peter was desperate and braced himself for an unpleasant confrontation as the official started to lose patience.

"Look sir," he snapped. "I'll call my superior and he can sort this out."

A few moments later, a tall bearded officer appeared, his cap and sleeves encrusted in gold braid. Wearily Peter rehearsed his story again while the blank-faced beard and braid listened. They eyed one another; the senior official in silent scepticism, Peter in silent prayer. At the end of a pause of a lifetime, the man began to speak.

"I see that you are declaring a bottle of ouzo," he said without betraying the slightest hint of irony. "The duty on that will be nineteen shillings and fourpence [96½p]. Kindly pay it sir, and get this stuff out of here." He made a grandiose gesture at the pile of wood and leather. Peter muttered a brief thank-you, paid the money and a platoon of porters wheeled his cargo to the railway office for forwarding to Bexhill. His great odyssey was over.

For Nell the waiting was also nearly over. Her dearest and best was coming home at last and the anxious anticipation of his arrival seemed to her more poignant than his homecoming the year before. He was returning a married man. His beautiful bride was expected in a few days and the excitement of meeting her was unbearable. There was so much to learn, so much to prepare. She sent Maky off to bring in the harvest of fruit and vegetables in the kitchen garden, and she bullied the shopkeepers in Little Common to stretch the rations.

When Peter's taxi drew up by the gate at Avon Lodge, Nell was there to greet him. She took her son into her arms and held him in a long embrace, careless of the tears streaming down her cheeks. Linking arms she ushered him into the house while Maky busied herself with his kitbag and haversack before returning to the kitchen to prepare their tea. Two days later Peter travelled to Northolt to meet Etty's flight. By early evening he was back and his young wife – fearful of her strange surroundings in a foreign land – was welcomed with the same warmth and affection as that of a mother reunited with her lost child. After the years of strain and fracture, the hardships and accidents in a world torn apart by war, Nell had found her peace. She was content. Her family complete. Together once more.

*

Part Four

The Castle

The Castle Hotel, Taunton. 1950s

I am sitting on the low stone bench at the head of the cliff above Puddleduck.
As I draft these words in the soft shadows of the day, the majesty of the view
fills the soul with wonder, the archipelago swathed in a halo of mellow amber
light. I love this moment before nightfall. And the symbolism of the place –
Diodati's tiny woodland refuge – begins to stir inside my mind.

The writing of this story has revealed so much about my father. The
memories were always there, I suppose, buried under layers of semi-
consciousness, beneath the glib acceptance that children have for their
parents and their past. Now this family tale – the telling of it – has brought
me closer to him as I begin to understand the man. Where my mother's
personality offered the world an unambiguous display, a glaring exposé of
raw temperament, my father's shyness and reticence – his unshakeable sense
of duty to wife and family – obscured the darker forces troubling his heart.
If I had built Diodati, it would never have occurred to me to plant this seat
in concrete and stone when a deck chair, beach towel or cushion might have
done just as well as a means to enjoy the view. No. Peter wanted a permanent
throne here. He sought witness in his own lifetime – a symbolic shrine to
his unrequited search for peace and harmony. A sanctuary from the pain of a
family in conflict.

So this was his place. This is where he came to find the exquisite calm of a
temporary truce in the struggle of his existence. And he would come at this time
of day – just to sit alone and stare; reflect and absorb the infinite soothing beauty
of his private seat. Now I am sitting in his place (not entirely undisturbed as
the honk and rasping brakes of the last municipal bus bounce a thousand yards
across the bay to remind me of a clamorous world beyond). But I feel his close
presence – as though the two of us are seated side by side in conversation. He

tells me how he came to Greece and found his freedom. He could not believe his luck. In Etty he discovered the promise of happiness and a future – they were married and he brought her to England. The early years were grim, grimmer than he ever imagined. But sustained by the power of their great love they survived. And twenty-five years later they returned to find their plot by the Aegean Sea – here to build their *paradieschen*, their little corner of paradise. Diodati was an act of thanksgiving for the fulfilment of their romantic dream. It was Gerald who suggested they named the house after Byron's villa on the shores of Lake Geneva. And so it was. Diodati, the God-given, the place where they could close the door and lie in each other's arms for ever. Diodati gave them eternity on earth.

*

As he watched the passengers disembark at Liverpool docks – a long crocodile slowly making its way towards customs – Peter was struck by an acute sense of déjà vu. He could hardly miss the diminutive but plumply elegant figure of Fifi accompanied by two porters wheeling a dozen outsized packages. She approached a phalanx of uniformed officials standing like Doric columns behind a line of trestle tables. One passenger, twelve boxes! But Fifi was prepared. While her French and German were fluent, she had only a limited grasp of English and as she boarded ship in Piraeus, Thanassaki passed her a sheet of starched notepaper on which he had printed four English words for her to rehearse on the voyage, warning his wife as he did so to expect a showdown with customs in Liverpool. Come the moment, the exchange with her stern-faced adversary was brief, almost perfunctory. Standing before her, he pointed at each box and fixed her with an inquisitor's eye. On the first enquiry, she paused before replying in her halting guttural voice, "Food for ze baby!" The man nudged his index finger methodically along the line of packages. To the second, again she said, "Food for ze baby!" And to the third, the fourth, right on to the last, the monotone response was the same, "Food for ze baby!" The officer was in no mood to challenge the lady – besides, it would have been impossible to make himself understood and, with a flick of his forearm, he waved her through.

It was already late in the afternoon on a chilly day in early March and Peter, who had not seen his mother-in-law since the wedding the year before, was anxious to spoil her and to make a fuss of her welcome to England. But Fifi, travel weary and salt-caked, was in high spirits – happy to have arrived at last, making light of her rough passage across the Bay of Biscay. Anticipating her exhaustion, Peter had booked rooms at the Adelphi – an hotel, he thought, which would provide his adored mother-in-law with a favourable first impression of her daughter's adopted country. As they stepped out of their taxi and into the lofty interior, she stood for a moment to take in the vast expanses of marble and mirrors, the moulded ceilings and the statuary. But after a pot of tea and a slice of Madeira cake beneath the magnificent chandeliers in the lounge, Fifi was ready to press on. She needed to be with Etty. Her daughter's first-born was already overdue.

All Fifi's and Thanassaki's instincts told them there were problems. Etty's letters home and those written by Peter to his father-in-law were dutifully upbeat but they could not disguise the rigours and discomforts of the times. After an hiatus of seven years, Peter's reacquaintance with civilian life came as an icy shock to the system. In the army, living was taken for granted. He didn't have to worry about a job that paid enough to cover the rent or household bills or a wife with a baby on the way. And what of Etty and the English? They were different; they did not exude the enthusiasms and spontaneity of Greek people. Etty mistook English stoicism and reserve for coldness, unfriendliness. They lived in a small flat in Torquay and Michael and his wife Tim were her family now. Did they like her? She wasn't sure; they paid little attention and were quite unlike her uncles, aunts and cousins in Salonica and Athens. Nell loved her – that she did know – but Nell lived in Sussex. And rationing! For clothing as well as for food? She could not understand ration cards – why she should be restricted to one egg, one chop and an ounce or two of butter a week. The shopkeepers in town soon got to know this feisty young lady who feigned incomprehension and used her Greekness and pregnant state as weapons to stretch her entitlement.

There was also the sensitive question of household servants. Etty had grown up with them as a necessary means to the normal functioning of everyday life at home. Now, in post-war England, there were none – things had changed. In an extraordinary apologia, Peter wrote to Thanassaki in the summer of '46 with an explanation of the difficulties. He had made promises which he now discovered he would be unable to keep and he felt a deep moral duty to make his confession. "Life is very very difficult in England these days," he began. "All the workers are controlled and made to work in factories … and it is quite impossible to get servants for private houses. Even in the very best families they have no servants and the mother and daughters must do the cooking, the washing and everything else." Finally, he concluded, "So you can imagine how strange Koutsi Mou finds it. A hard form of life from that to which she is used … [but] she is quickly adapting herself to her new surroundings … and I am sure that she will be really happy here."

A few months later, with the advance of Etty's pregnancy, Peter did employ a home help. Her name was Bessie and she introduced her young mistress to the rudiments of household management – but it was an appointment the master could ill afford. Now, with the pregnancy reaching full term, Fifi knew Etty would want her mother on hand to see her through the birth. There was no time to lose and she dismissed Peter's thought that she might prefer a night's rest in Liverpool before continuing her journey. Within the hour, they had checked out of the Adelphi Hotel to catch an evening train for Torquay – a long and uncomfortable night-trek in a railway carriage that was grimy and broken; its windows boarded up, its upholstery shot to pieces. The dilapidated rolling stock of a nation distracted by the imperatives of the war effort. Fifi understood and dispelled Peter's embarrassment with her babbling good humour.

On the Monday morning of the tenth of the month, two days after her mother's arrival in Torquay, Etty entered a private nursing home in Falkland Road. At six o'clock that evening I was born – soon to be christened Christopher Henry George. Nell, who immediately called me "Kit", had also travelled to Torquay from Sussex to hail the birth of her favourite's first-born. From her bedroom at the Imperial, she wrote a note to her daughter-in-law.

Imperial Hotel
Torquay
Tuesday March 11/47

Dearest and Sweetest Etty,

What a very clever girl you have been!! I do think it was the glass of sherry that I advised you to drink on Sunday night … I am so happy for your Happiness and also for Peter. I am so grateful to God that you passed your great Ordeal so bravely and got over it all well, that dear good Dr. Lees deserves <u>all</u> our gratitude too – God bless him!!

Thank you darling for your sweet letter, but you must now Rest and not be writing too many letters, remember that your Body has received a shock and so do Rest as much as possible.

Sleep – is a great Restorer!

Peter has been to see me and told me <u>everything</u> – but I am longing to come to you myself and to see my beautiful Grandson, but Dr. Lees said "not yet". Sweetest love and kisses and hugs and to the darling <u>all</u> my Blessings.

Mummy

*

Frank Isaacson sat on the long sofa in Michael's office, a panelled room like a secret command post strategically sited behind the reception desk at the Imperial Hotel. He inhaled deeply on an untipped Player's Medium Navy Cut – a cigarette he held tightly between his thumb and middle finger. His trilby was perched mole-like beside him and as he leaned back the smudged waistcoat of his mid-brown suit strained to contain his well-fed torso. A sallow skinned man with features the colour of tobacco, Isaacson examined his business partner's younger brother through rimless spectacles and expressionless eyes. Wet behind the ears, he thought. Still the man was fresh out of the army. Pregnant wife. Needed a job. Can't deny big brother wanting to give him a leg-up. He and Michael had just bought a controlling share in three café-cum-bakeries – two in Newton Abbot, one in Teignmouth – to add to their growing portfolio of shops and small businesses in south Devon, and they needed a safe pair of hands to manage their new acquisition. It was Michael who suggested the meeting to introduce Peter to Isaacson.

They seemed an unlikely pair. One the suave, charismatic hotelier. The other the East End barrow boy who'd hawked meat the length of the Thames Estuary before turning respectable as a butcher-businessman of substance. They had met in the early months of the war when Michael was finding his feet – determined to attract a well-heeled following with the promise of good food and a class act in his dining room overlooking Tor Bay. He needed a canny supplier to source the goods. Frank delivered where others couldn't or didn't know how, and Michael asked no questions. In time, a mutual unspoken respect blossomed as the two men registered one another's cash-generating usefulness. Isaacson, the terrier, chased the opportunities – a fishmonger in Brixham, a grocer in Paignton, a café in Dawlish, even an employment agency for foreign domestics in Torquay – while Michael, the purse-minder, checked out the numbers and planned the financing of each new deal. Thomas Jones & Son (Newton Abbot) Ltd., the mini-chain of three bakery-cafés, was their most substantial investment in the partnership's brief existence. Old Man Jones, tired of the drab conventions of the day, had offloaded seventy-five percent of his business to fund one last dissolute fling in the bordellos and opium dens of the Orient until he was finally declared insane. This sudden exit denied young Mr. Frederick, his disaffected son, the full inheritance he was expecting – a betrayal which came at the very moment when trade in the family firm was gathering a head of steam.

As the meeting with Isaacson proceeded, Michael – straight-backed and leaning forward across his neatly ordered ping-pong sized office table – chose not to dwell in any detail on the background and circumstances of their acquisition of T. Jones & Son. And, for his part, Peter buried the misgivings he may have harboured on first acquaintance with his brother's business associate; nor did he want to think too deeply about the prospect of working alongside a disenfranchised café proprietor. Instead he disguised his desperation for a paying job with a show of enthusiasm, ready and keen to accept anything they offered. Besides, on the face of it, the proposition under discussion looked exceptionally generous with the ownership of the business split equally in four tidy parcels: Fred Jones clinging possessively to his minority holding, Isaacson and Michael taking twenty-five percent each, leaving Peter the balance of the shares as a sweetener to his brief which was to manage the outlets and keep a watchful eye on young Mr. Fred who was already showing signs of dissent inside the new regime.

Later in the day – a bleak afternoon in early January 1947 – Peter left the Imperial on foot and, cocooned in a thousand thoughts, walked home to the tiny flat he and Etty had taken in the weeks before Christmas. Living at the hotel since their arrival in England had become too much of an imposition on Michael's generosity – it was time to find a place of their own and begin to prepare a home for their first-born child. Rising skyward on its steep slope commanding the bay, Number Four Bay Fort Mansions in Warren Road deserved its title. The views were magnificent – unveiling a Devonian littoral which Michael liked to call the "English Riviera". At once excited and terrified, Peter – ever the soldier marching purposely up the hill – had telephoned ahead to announce the news: he had accepted the job and was starting work in the morning.

As he unlocked the door to the flat, Etty rushed into his arms – "Bravo, my Mouchen!" she called clasping his head between her hands, adding in German "They are lucky to have such a wonderful man." In the background, he could hear a kettle whistling and Bessie shuffling about the kitchen, a faint whiff of burnt toast drifting through the open door. The domestic had come with the flat – joining the young household at the same time Peter had deposited a quarter's rent and picked up the keys from his landlord. He was paying her for twenty-five hours' help a week – more than he could sensibly afford. But he worried about Etty and the loneliness she would endure while he went out to work; he worried about the child she was carrying; he worried about her happiness in a strange country, a cold climate. And sometimes it troubled his sleep. Bessie salved his conscience – she would be company for his darling wife and a support in this new servantless society.

It was, perhaps, too soon to make judgements – but even Peter was ready to concede the possibility that the two women were like distant constellations heading for collision. Etty's universe was founded on her mother's model: a benign regime of strict codes where staff came to understand that every process had its procedure and every item belonged in its place. Bessie – the older woman by an indeterminate decade or two – was a herdsman's daughter from Stoke Gabriel and unversed in the finer arts of the scullery or parlour. A good woman of earthly virtue, her talents were more practical for the day, her responses to the needs of the home more soap 'n water. Little things were beginning to rankle. Etty liked her cupboards and drawers lined with smooth white paper designed for the purpose, just like Fifi did in Salonica. But Bessie seemed incapable of folding the sheets precisely to size. Her dusting was thorough but she did not share her mistress's aesthetic eye, rarely returning framed pictures and silver heirlooms to their designated spot or at the correct angle. And in the kitchen she saw to it that the family's rations were simmered to a colourless slick or roasted to a black infinity. How they missed the gustatory treats of Queen Olga Street. In bed at night – gentle now with their lovemaking for fear of disturbing a heavy womb – they lay entwined in each other's arms, Peter caressing Etty's long dark hair as she retold him Bessie's latest follies for the umpteenth time. He reassured her, whispering in a low comforting voice: to give Bessie time, that soon Mama would be with them, that she would bring good food and help their well-meaning housemaid adjust her bucolic ways.

*

To Michael's relief and Frank Isaacson's surprise, the new managing director of Thomas Jones & Son appeared to make a promising start – and no one was more relieved or surprised than Peter whose early fears were based on his professional innocence. He had no knowledge of restaurants or baking, and he knew nothing of his legal and licensing obligations as a director of a catering company. India had taught him the difference between whisky, gin and Alsopp's lager. But he had no idea what distinguished mild from bitter or Bass from Guinness. He knew sherry came in a variety of shades of brown and that port was red. But he was unsure of the colour of wines made in the Moselle Valley or the Rhineland. So Fred Jones, the very man he was charged to spy upon, became his mentor and in spite of his sloth and Peter's industry, the two colleagues slipped into an agreeable modus vivendi. Meanwhile, board meetings were dominated by Michael's and Frank's thirsty ambitions for a rapid expansion of the group and before long Peter was opening new branches in Torquay, Brixham and two in Exmouth.

But by the middle of the following year, the business began to falter and the bloom on the fruit began to sour. Branch managers seemed to be thriving but their prosperity failed to match the returns flowing into head office. Profits fell short of their budgets or toppled into losses. And young Mr. Frederick's lethargy melted into a stagnant pool of self-satisfied idleness. The once breezy atmosphere at board meetings – customarily held around Michael's large office table – now grew darker as normal courtesies were abandoned and replaced by the politics of the bear garden – Isaacson aiming his volleys of sniper fire at Peter in language brewed on the streets and alleys of the East End. Michael was more circumspect but his impatience with his brother's performance was palpable.

Peter felt stung; exposed, vulnerable. With the passing months and for all his efforts to turn the business, his sense of isolation grew more acute as he fell into a spiral of helplessness, frustrated by his lack of experience and training in the trade. Those who were best placed to provide him with the direction he craved were not there. Fred Jones had thrown in the towel and was nowhere to be found. Michael was too busy steering his great hotel to international glory. But for Peter, the pressures of his failing chain of cafés were not confined to the business. On the home front, his domestic finances were in a mess. As his meagre reserves trickled out of his bank balance, rent payments were becoming an issue and Bessie's employment looked more and more like a luxury too far. And in spite of the difficulties, he did not dare approach his fellow directors for an increase, or even an advance on his salary. He was living in a state of despair and the demons of his youth returned again, revisiting him in the dead hours before dawn. He shared little of this with Etty, seeing no reason to weigh her down with worries he believed were of his own making. At the end of the day, when he locked the flat's front door behind him, he found his solace in the comfort of being reunited with his wife and child. Their company alone made him happy and Etty's natural vivacity revived his battered confidence. Life took on a surreal quality – or so it seemed to him – as his existence became an interminable cycle of struggle and conflict, then peace and quiet: a bizarre twenty-four hour clock measured by days shrouded in dark oppression and evenings illuminated by sunbeams of joy – Michael and Isaacson cast as mythical ogres, Etty as the Greek goddess liberating him at night, restoring him at home.

Then, in the spring of '49, at a moment when the tide in his business relationships had descended to its lowest ebb, Etty announced that she was pregnant again – a second child, expected in November. If there was any rejoicing, it could only be heard by Bessie at Bay Fort Mansions. On the telephone from Avon Lodge in Little Common, Nell – true to her nature – greeted the news in words of love and support. "But Peter," she added, without disguising her concern, "how are you going to cope?" For the past year, her two sons and their joint enterprise had become a source of great worry to her – she had seen it all before in a previous life. At the Imperial, Michael and Tim were less sanguine about Etty's announcement. While Tim kept her counsel, Michael accused his brother of irresponsibility. "Are you completely off your head?" he raged. "You marry a foreign girl barely out of her teens and bring her to a strange country blighted by war. I set you up at the hotel, then I set you up in a business where things aren't working out. You produce a child and live in a flat that's just about suitable for a bachelor because that's all you can afford. Now this news. Crazy!"

Michael's temper was legendary. At the Imperial, the staff nicknamed his outbursts by his three initials – to suffer an HMC was to receive a verbal caning you were unlikely to forget. Peter turned on his heel and left the office humiliated and defeated. Walking swiftly through reception, he crossed the marbled hallway to the gentleman's locked himself in a cubicle and buried his inflamed cheeks and eyes in the palms of his hands. Weeping like a child, the storm in his head shot through his body as it heaved and convulsed out of control. He had no defence. His brother was right. Perhaps he shouldn't have married.

In the flat in Warren Road, Etty had no need to be told of Michael's attitude to her news – she could feel the froideur whistling across Tor Bay. For her, the reaction – or absence of one – from her brother-in-law and his wife served to confirm her earliest instincts. They represented everything she saw in the English character: aloofness, distance, icy cool. "They are cold and unfriendly," she confided to her Mama. "Not like me – warm hearted and vivacious!"

When Peter resurfaced – some days later to Etty's alarm – he realized they would have to move home. For a while he toyed with a plan to buy on a mortgage to rescue his rent payments from evaporating into the sea. But the arithmetic could not be reconciled. Finally, to his relief, his landlord offered the family a larger flat at the same rent. Forfeiting their fabulous view, the new flat at St. Ronan's, a house in Lower Warberry Road, was situated in a residential quarter elsewhere in Torquay, but it came with the bonus of an attractive garden.

On Wednesday, November 7th, Gerald was born in a frantic rush – the nursing home propelled into a fevered spin by my younger brother's impatience to land on the world. And when he did so, his entrance was made with all the scale and drama of a grand Shakespearean production: russet-faced, hairy and dark, vital, shouting and waving his arms to command the attention of his audience. But Gerald was not what Etty was expecting. Gerald was meant to be a girl. By her bedside, Peter held her hand and reassured her of his own joy at the birth of a second son. "I am so happy my Koutzi," he said softly kissing her forehead. "It's a beautiful Greek boy. You must be very proud as

I am." From Little Common, Nell set about writing her congratulations and, in her innocence, hinted unwittingly at the simmering tensions between her two sons and daughters-in-law.

Postmark – Bexhill-on-Sea 2.30pm 8 Nov 1949

Avon Lodge
Thursday

Dearest and most loving Ettylein,

Your dear letter just arrived and am writing at once, as I feel so happy that you feel well enough to write, but take care my darling, and do not be writing or seeing too many people, "You are not out of the wood yet" and with the Milk coming in, you must be as quiet as possible. What a pity that Tim is not there. I had a letter from Michael, he did not seem to be sure about getting away …

So the "Younger Peter" is black eyed and Hair – a real Mother's boy!!! I wish I could have seen Kit's face he will get more and more interested later on. How nice that you have a sunny bright room – do be wise and stay there as long as you can and as necessary – the weather here has been vile lately – so wet and stormy impossible to go out.

I have phoned round to all my friends to tell them of my 5th Grandchild* and all send heartiest Congratulations and love. I have just finished a Pullover for myself. "Old wool" remade and a vest and then comes Gloves and the new Blue Pram Sett for "His Highness" I have the wool you bought when here. We have a new Bird Table and it is lovely to watch them – Maky must make you one in your new Garden. How you will love to get in a new House and in the Spring, lovely to have a garden for the Boys.

Much much love and warm Kisses to you and "Kleine Peter" – only take care and keep quiet, and do not eat too many Grapes like last time and give the Baby "tummy ache".

Maky sends sincere love and congrats.
Mummy

(* By this time, Tim had given birth to three children: Nicky (Nancy), Michael and Tim's only daughter, born October 1942; Richard born February 1946; and Guy born March 1947 – twelve days after my birth.)

*

With the onset of winter, Peter's anxieties mounted – a succession of unexpected reverses piling one upon another compounding his state of distress. Like Sisyphus, he felt condemned, trapped by some eternal punishment. It was only after the family's move to St. Ronan's that he realized the rent, unlike Bay Fort, now excluded his utility bills. As the weeks passed, the weather turned more bitter, wet and cold. Gerald and I, Etty – we all suffered from it – my father confining us to one heated room. In the end, Bessie had to go – her departure feeling more like the sad abandonment of a faithful old retainer than a hard necessity. But the savings on her wages kept us in heat and hot water. Gerald's birth also precipitated an urgent need to acquire more things for the home – clothing, bedding, furniture – extra cupboards and drawers, for which Peter had to arrange a bank loan. Then to his dismay, and Etty's horror, Gerald went down with bronchitis and was rushed back to the nursing home. It took a fortnight's care before my baby brother was declared fit to return to the bleak comforts of St. Ronan's. A merciful relief – but for my father another bill landed on the doormat, one more to add to the pile.

And so it was that the early months of 1950 were among the darkest in Peter's life – not even Etty's youthful confidence and radiant love could sustain him. By the late spring, his ancient insecurities – stirred by those traumatic events in Bratislava twenty years before – erupted into a state beyond the sleepless nights he had been suffering. He now felt physically as much as mentally unwell and, on Etty's insistence, consulted his GP who put him on Dexadrine – an amphetamine routinely prescribed to bomber crews during the war to keep them awake at night on air raids over Germany. "Wakey-wakey" pills, as the airmen called them, were the last thing Peter needed and they triggered a second nervous breakdown.

Etty was stunned. She had never seen her Peter in this state. At first her emotions dissolved into turmoil – she did not understand. In the hospital, she laid siege to the doctors, matrons and nurses – anyone who would hear her pleading. "Why?" she kept asking. "Why has this happened to my Peter? He is a strong man. He is my pillar. Why?" The medical staff were solicitous and did their best to comfort her with cups of sweet tea and advice, but she neither drank the tea nor listened to their words. Gradually, her shock and confusion turned to a seething rage. Scooping Gerald up into one arm and grabbing me by the hand, she strode out and headed for the Imperial. At the desk, the startled receptionists scattered like dust in a storm as she swept into Michael's office unannounced. Michael, taken aback by her sudden entrance, rose to his feet. She glared straight at him – fearless, unblinking, her eyes on fire. "If my Peter dies," she gasped, "I'll shoot you!"

Of course, in the interests of politesse and diplomacy, this episode goes unreported in my father's history. But over the next two decades, as Gerald and I grew up, the story – always retold by Etty, never by Peter – became totemic of the uneasy distance that separated us from our cousins in Torquay. To visit them in the school holidays was presented as a duty rather than as a pleasure. In the naïvety of childhood, a parent's propaganda is accepted as gospel and only later was I able to shed these prejudices and make my own judgements – about Michael, about Tim, about the family in all its rich complexities.

I cannot describe with any certainty Michael's reaction to his sister-in-law's threat of violence, but as his nephew, I do have grounds for exercising a little imagination. Etty's ambush would have startled him but, I suspect, not for very long. Michael was a natural showman – a lady's man who enjoyed flirting – and he would have charmed her into submission by showering her with flattery – a tactic she found irresistible. Fifteen years her senior, he had an eye for her dark Mediterranean good-looks and secretly admired her spirit. Unlike Peter, she was never in awe of him and she possessed an uncanny, almost animal way of teasing him – stinging his most vulnerable spots by lapsing occasionally into the German vernacular, knowing he would understand, knowing he would only respond in English. I was always conscious of an unusual frisson in their relationship, an unexpressed sexual tension that was locked well beneath their exterior emotions – although, sometimes, when she was feeling playful, she would call him "ein Schmutzmann" [a dirty old man]. But somehow, I think it was their shared foreignness that appealed to her – to them both. Tim she branded pejoratively as "English" and, ergo, "cold" – a favourite theme that would echo through our lives and end up reverberating around Louise. In Etty's imagination, Michael was definitely not "English". He was as Austro-Hungarian as her Peter – ergo continental and warm-hearted. Equally Nell their mother qualified by marriage! In my mother's world, there was never room for grey ambiguity – she only dealt in primary colours.

It was inevitable, then, that after the move to Taunton which came at the end of that difficult year, our childhood excursions to Torquay would be rationed to the minimum necessary for the correct observance of the family tie. The journey by car – a black Austin 16 with a curious sun visor attached to the top of its windscreen – took about an hour and a half and Sunday lunch at the Villa, my aunt and uncle's house raised high on a hillock behind the hotel, would be our stageset for the day. These were not relaxed occasions – an awkward edginess crackling silently around the dining room. Michael, "Head of the Family", presided at the head of the table, carving the roast beef quickly, expertly from a sideboard behind him. Peter sat straight-backed in his chair as if he were attending a regimental dinner. Clearly, my father was on his best behaviour and, in the mind's eye of this child, conducting himself strangely. Etty played the rebel – talking too much in a high off-key manner I found faintly embarrassing. Tony, at the other end of the table, sat speechless, looking glum as a toad. And Tim held the whole disjunctive gathering together by being demure, sweet, kind and hospitable – virtues my mother ignored – while us young cousins tucked into our food mindful not to leave so much as a green bean or a sprout idle and uneaten on the edge of our plates. By four o'clock Etty was pressing Peter to leave for home: "παμε [let's go!]," she'd whisper, always a little too loud – her favourite Greek injunction.

Visits to our cousins – Nicky, Richard, Guy and Alexander, Michael and Tim's youngest – were more unbuttoned and fun when Gerald and I went alone and stayed over in the Villa for a few days. We would wake up to a grand peal of chimes from the wall-clock in the hall and breakfast would produce the juiciest, meatiest pork sausages. I mention these brief interludes only because they allowed me to observe Michael Chapman, the great hotelier, in action. I was smitten by his aura, his style, his brio – a hero worship my mother held against me when I joined the family firm in the late '70s, convinced I shared too many of my uncle's evil ways. But I admired him all the same. Watching Michael run the Imperial was extraordinary – leading, driving his team – harrying, cajoling, inspiring them to do better. Never once in a trade awash with graduates of the HMC school of hotelkeeping have I met one who did not acknowledge his panache nor thank him for their training. At his famous gastronomic weekends, I would sit in a corner of the ballroom or at a table in the restaurant and watch him glide like a matinee idol from one party to another – tickling, humouring, kissing the hands of dowagers and rich widows, puffing the egos of politicians and industrialists. It was a dazzling piece of drawing room theatre.

Every moment of his working day was conducted at speed with a short break for lunch in the Villa – late, after we had eaten with Tim. The drill was well rehearsed and precisely timed. At midday a platoon of waiters in long white aprons filed out of the hotel kitchens and marched briskly up the steep driveway to the house bearing silver trays of cloche-covered dishes above their shoulders. This was lunch! At two o'clock Michael would arrive to take his place at a now deserted dining room table and Tim would serve him his food. This was a domestic ritual I recall for one reason alone. By his setting at the head of the table Tim would place a telephone by his right arm, alongside his tumbler of water. Never out of touch. And within fifteen minutes he was away again.

*

By mid-summer Peter had begun to find his feet again. His adventure as a café entrepreneur in partnership with his brother was accepted by the family as a disastrous experiment and dissolved. Nell, whose health was failing, had been desperately worried for her youngest, pleading with Michael to help him search for a more secure future. Michael needed no persuading. He felt guilty and, at least, indirectly responsible for his brother's condition. He also needed to appease Etty who quickly discovered an aptitude for fuelling his sense of shame. In early July he suggested they take a drive to look at an hotel in Taunton, a market town on the A38 trunk road a few miles across the Devon border in Somerset. "They're looking for a resident manager," he said. "It could suit you."

The idea appealed to Peter – especially as the job notice came with a promise of board and lodging – and on Sunday afternoon, leaving Gerald and me in Tim's care, he and Etty set out on the fifty-five mile run from Torquay. They had never visited Taunton before and as they drove slowly down North Street, the town's main thoroughfare, they spotted a dirty scalloped glass canopy overhanging an equally grimy edifice next to Burton's, the outfitters. A limp sign advertised a dark-dank entrance to the "Castle Hotel". Their hearts sank at the sight of the place and the hopes they had been nursing in their imaginations evaporated in seconds. They were on the point of abandoning their mission when Peter noticed a medieval archway set back from the street, leading away from the Burton's store. Curious to see what lay beyond, he turned the car and drove through the stone arch. On the other side he emerged, like a child of Narnia, into a bright sunlit green and fell upon a real castle – all turreted and castellated and bearded in luxuriant clusters of wisteria. In a trance, they stopped and stood and stared. What passed between them I cannot say, but I doubt they would have begun to divine the significance of their chance discovery. Here before them was their future, their future home and life's work. Like Diodati, the Castle would become their legacy to us – Louise and me – to become part of our lives as it was part of theirs. To inspire us, worry us, thrill us, frustrate us, consume us. Their lives and passions live on in us today rippling through the reeds of two generations. One continuous stream defined by two places.

*

The false introduction in North Street turned out to be a back door – public access from the town centre to the hotel's lounge bar. But stepping inside the Castle by its porticoed main entrance on the Green hardly provoked an instant cry of 'Eureka!' There was nothing here to compare with the allure and gilded charms of the Imperial. As they walked into the hall, passing first through a revolving door which creaked eerily on its axis, they found themselves in a tall deserted cavern of courtly decrepitude. And as their eyes adjusted to the gloom, they encountered neither guests nor staff, save for one shy receptionist who ignored them. My father – a man who loved making lists – began to compile a mental inventory: an uncarpeted foyer; a dirty wood floor; dust encrustations on the grand staircase; cobwebs clinging to the antlers of the stags' heads – spiders at home in the corners of ceilings; high walls decorated with the old fire marks of insurance companies; a dismal, poorly lit, uncomfortable lounge; furniture in disrepair; a dining room still displaying the detritus of the lunch service; gravy-stained cloths left on tables; lights innocent of lampshades – naked bulbs dangling from ceiling flexes. After the unexpected surprise of the Castle's great Gothic frontage, everything they saw behind its magnificent façade now struck them with grim disappointment. The more so for Etty who found the English fondness for taxidermy sinister and barbaric – a prejudice associated with the superstitions of the Greek evil eye rather than the traditions of West Country stag hunting. Some years later, after the death of the owner, Mr. R.G. Spiller, my mother's first unilateral act at the Castle was to remove all the stuffed heads – a decision she took without reference to his widow, Mary, who was incensed by the insult to her late husband's memory. But for my father, the sheer dreadfulness of the hotel inspired him to apply immediately to Mr. Spiller for the post of resident manager. Recognizing also that the Castle was an historic monument and a major local landmark, he saw the potential. "Whatever I did was bound to be an improvement!" he wrote. "This was a wonderful opportunity for a green manager."

Peter's application succeeded amid tears of protest from Etty – but this was one battle where his will prevailed. Then having consoled her with the comforting thought that the job came with their board and lodging, Mr. Spiller's offer, he learned, only included accommodation for the manager – not his family. My mother, Gerald and I would have to be found rooms in the town – with the rent paid out of his annual salary, the princely sum of £600 [£14,400 at today's values].

This was a major blow to the family's hopes but in spite of the setback Peter accepted Spiller's offer and agreed to a start date in mid-October. My father then took a brave risk. He refused to contemplate any move to Taunton where he was separated from his beloved wife and children. Instead, he decided to take us all to Salonica for an extended holiday with Fifi and Thanassaki. His strategy was almost naïve in its simplicity. He would move into the Castle as planned in the autumn, work hard at the job, make his mark and win over his demanding proprietor. "By Christmas," he told Etty, "I shall have Spiller eating out of my hands!"

Later that July, we boarded the Dover-Ostend ferry and for the next two days and three nights we rumbled across Europe by rail. I was an innocent three year-old ignorant of recent history – the Soviet blockade of Berlin had been broken the year before and now the Continent was gripped by the Cold War. All I remember is a sense of fear rising inside me as tensions heightened at border crossings. They would take an age – our train lying stationary for hours as dullards in uniforms checked passports and papers. But the platform vendors did a brisk trade selling hot German sausages – or "Heisse wurstl!" as the Austrians called them. Dunked in "senf" [mustard] eating these delicious frankfurters became a family ritual on our long rail journeys to Greece in the years that followed.

The break in a warm Aegean climate gave my father the tonic he needed to regain his health, his nerves and his confidence. By the middle of August he was ready to travel home to England – a tearful farewell for Etty who was having to come to terms with a separation which would endure for at least four months and possibly longer. But there was a purpose to his early return. Before starting in Taunton, Peter needed a crash course in hotel management with his brother supervising his tutelage. Back at the Imperial, Michael set out a two-month programme of training with short stints in the reception and bill offices, the control department to learn bar and kitchen stocktaking and cellar management, and a spell in the accounts office. He was a conscientious student, making detailed lists of duties as he progressed. By the fifteenth of October, a Sunday, he was ready to take on the Castle Hotel.

Arriving by train from Torquay in the early evening, Peter was met at Taunton station by Mary Spiller. After introducing him to the duty receptionist, the head porter and the head chef, she handed him a large bunch of keys and left – a formal induction to the new job that was completed in less than five minutes. In his history, my father records that he spent the first fortnight "examining every room in the hotel" beginning with the bedrooms – sixty-two letting rooms and seven more occupied by staff. He continues: "All the rooms were thoroughly checked over from the door handles, numerals, hinges, locks, bolts, beds, mattresses, furniture and furnishings, and cleanliness down to the very last detail. There were over 400 deficiencies."

Public rooms – in equally bad shape – received the same scrutiny, every fault itemized with military thoroughness on his clipboard. A careful survey of the fabric of the building uncovered more nasties – leaking roofs, faulty plumbing and a desperate need to rewire. Basic housekeeping and cleaning regimes came in for a major shake-up. Linen was not always despatched to the laundry – sheets frequently given a quick iron and replaced on the beds. Changing into a set of blue overalls, Peter himself led the attack on cleansing the hotel from its battlements to its cellars and he hired a team of pest controllers to rid the place of cockroaches, mice and a plague of ants.

My father was never a man to harbour grudges but there is one story of the time which seems to cling to his memory like a magnet. A few weeks into the new job, Michael came to see his brother in Taunton – his first visit. He was joined by Frank Isaacson and the three erstwhile colleagues lunched together in the musty loftiness of an almost deserted dining room. After they had eaten, they moved to the lounge for coffee where Isaacson sank into an old armchair – a piece of furniture whose four legs now made their last stand and collapsed beneath his weight. In an uncharacteristic moment of schadenfreude for Peter, the playground bully who had inflicted three years' terror on his life had received his comeuppance.

But the battle of those years had passed. Peter's new challenge lay in his campaign to win the confidence of his proprietor, R.G. Spiller. Old "RG" was a local builder who owned the company which bore his name. The Castle lent him an extra air of gravitas and civic status; but notions of hospitality – welcome, comfort, a clean bed, good food – were, in RG's mind, no substitute for promoting the virtues of strict economy in an age of shortages and post-war austerity. Indeed, in the running of his hotel, Mr. Spiller believed it was his patriotic duty not to spend any money. So, bath water was limited to nine inches; envelopes were re-used and re-addressed with economy labels; refuse was tossed into old cardboard boxes rather than tin dustbins which were deemed an unnecessary expense; and at eight o'clock in the evening the kitchen shut down to the stentorian roar of the chef's call "Gases out!" The only invoices RG was pleased to sign off were those for food and drink supplies – and the steeper the bills, the happier his temper as they indicated at least that business was buoyant.

In these circumstances, a showdown between proprietor and new manager was inevitable and it came rather sooner than either of them might have expected. After Peter's first experience of the hotel four months earlier, he decided to order a few potted plants to lighten the gloom of the entrance hall and bring a little cheer to the welcome of new arrivals. While the staff, excited by the novelty of the idea, were impressed by the exotic greenery adorning the foyer, Mr. Spiller was not and, after a sharp tap at the door, he walked into Peter's office without waiting for a reply.

"I see the front hall's full of plants, Chapman!" he snapped. "Was this your idea?"

"Yes, Mr. Spiller, it was," replied Peter. "The place needed smartening up."

"The place is perfectly smart enough, young man. How much have you spent on this little exercise?"

"Very little, Sir. Less than £2."

"They're a waste of good money!" retorted Old RG, his blood pressure ramping up. "Send them back and demand a refund."

"That would be a mistake, Mr. Spiller," said Peter politely. "The hall badly needed cheering up. This was an inexpensive way of doing it."

"You don't know what you're talking about, m'boy! Send them back immediately!"

"I'm sorry, Sir. I'm not going to send them back!" responded Peter, determined to stand his ground.

By now RG's cheeks had turned scarlet – his eyes popping with fury. "Chapman, I am instructing you to return those plants. You are not paid to argue with me. You are paid to do as you are told."

The confrontation had now developed into a test of wills and my father knew he was pushing his luck. His situation was precarious. He was broke and he was in no position to risk his job. For a split second his thoughts turned to Etty and his obligations to his family. But in spite of the trials of the previous three years, he now revealed an inner strength and a conviction which steeled him for the fight. He had begun to win the respect and affection of a hard-pressed staff whose morale and pride had been rubbed raw. To give in to Spiller, he felt, would be to let them down and damage his own authority at a moment when he had found confidence in the new direction he was taking the hotel. If he stood aside now, he could see no future for himself. For the first time, my father was discovering a real sense of belief in his abilities – and, possibly to his surprise, a growing sense of his emotional affinity with the Castle.

"Mr. Spiller," he said in a tone which underscored the proprietor's name, "I'm sorry to disagree with you. I am not paid to do as I'm told."

"Then what the devil do you think you are being paid for?" Spiller interrupted.

"I'm being paid to run this hotel. And part of that job means making the place attractive to your customers. At present it is not. These plants are a tiny step towards improving your business! So, with your permission, please allow me to get on with the business of running the hotel."

For several moments Spiller stood rigid – glaring, dumbfounded by the words of his young manager. Eventually, sighing in resignation and lowering his voice, he said: "Then get on and run the bloody place!" Turning on his heel, he walked out of the room. No more was said about the plants.

Some weeks later, on Christmas Eve, Old RG came to see Peter again. On this occasion his mission was very different. He informed his manager that he had just sent a cable to Etty in Salonica extending a welcome to her and her two boys to join Peter as soon as she wished. Rooms would be made available for the whole family in the hotel. But he was a cunning old fox and the toll he exacted for his largesse was to trim Peter's annual salary from £600 to £400 [£9,600 today] – a penalty which did nothing to mute my father's happiness at the prospect of a long-awaited reunion with his family.

And so 1950 – a momentous year that had begun with great drama and calamity – ended in glad tidings and joy. After Christmas Nell, who had suffered in sympathy with her dearest son, wrote a long letter to Etty in Greece. And even Maky, in her unique Anglo-German-cum-Hungarian pidgin, appended an affectionate postscript. This letter – the last in the box of Lindt, written three years before her death – carries for me a particular poignancy, perhaps because she knew she did not have long to live. Its tone, her thoughts and preoccupations add up to a sweeping overview of her life at that time – from rueful observations on the family she loved to worries about war with the Soviet Union. But with its lingering sense of finality, Nell also expresses her love for Etty – the girl who brought happiness to her boy – revealing a desire to confide in her daughter-in-law about her visit to hospital to have an X-ray: "I have not told Peter or Henry & T – My spine is not too good …" This from a woman whose generation was taught never to complain. But in Etty she seemed to strike an endearing intimacy which she did not find with Tim. Casting back to my own childhood, my memories of Nell are of a gentle, special, loving grandmother. Her affection and warm approval of Etty provided her with the comfort and confidence in old age to open up – not only to express the fears she had about her health but also to write freely about her worries for Peter: his loneliness and his melancholy. Then with an emphatic line drawn below the last word, she makes a simple statement "Peter is 100% <u>good</u> …" – a sentiment which resonated throughout his life; not always to his advantage, and not always in the interests of his endless search for peace of mind. Sometimes his goodness was caught in crossfire, wounded by the emotional battles fought between Etty and Gerald, Etty and me. But all of this will come in its own time. Gerald and I have some growing up to do first. Meanwhile, here is Nell's last letter. It is an effort for her to write. By the end she is tired.

Avon Lodge
Little Common
Dec 30 1950

My darling sweet joyous Etty
Your dear letters arrived safely yesterday – and they made us both very happy. Your letters breathe your joyous and gay spirit just as Machi's show her sweet and sympathetic nature. It does me so much good to hear from those who belong to me, for I am always thinking of my dear and loved ones and it is a real Red-Letter day when I get news. It was so lovely to hear all about Kit and Gerald, the things they do and say and all about yourself and your gay parties – and to imagine that Kit has grown 2 inches!! That is what the wonderful sunshine and fresh air does! The weather here is appalling – very cold, wet, snow and <u>no</u> sunshine but my Heart is singing today for I have hopes of seeing you very soon and those beautiful Boys. Sometime ago I asked Peter if you could not all come to me for a while till things

were settled and when he replied he told me of his hopes that he would get you all with him again in the "Castle" – and then on Xmas Day – oh! that Joyous Day! when he told me that all was settled and that Mr. and Mrs. Spiller had offered the Suite of Rooms that they had sent you Cables – I am quite sure that Maky and I danced round with joy as much as you did at the great news and it is also possible when Peter comes to meet the "Plane" – he will bring you down here to see me if only for a few days. All this grand news after such a troublesome year was my greatest Christmas Gift – for you can be sure that what happens to you and Peter and the Boys is my first consideration. So now as long as there is no war, things look on the up and up and rosy. I hope there will not be War – I do not think Russia really wants war with Europe at any rate we will not spoil our Xmas/New Year with horrid fears. The Villa family all rang me up too on Christmas Day – first Tony – then Nicky – Richard and Guy – Henry and Tim – all very gay and jolly. They hoped to see Peter there at New Year.

I regret to say that Tim does not write me the newsy letters about the children which I should enjoy – so I hear very little of them – Henry never writes to me, nor does Tony. It is nice to get letters, but one has not always time nor inclination to write. I asked my sister Fan – Auntie May and Alice Woodcock all to write to Peter, as my Heart ached for his loneliness and they all did and he seemed so pleased. My Peter has a lonely nature and I am so pleased your dear Mother and Father recognise that and appreciate his good qualities. Peter is 100% <u>good</u> and am so thankful that the Spillers have recognised that and give him the credit for what he has done. Henry sent us good things to eat and drink – so we ate Pheasant on Christmas Day and Plum Pudding and a small bot Champagne – Maky and I and she got a little tipsy and was too funny for words. I slept till after 5 o'clock and did not hear the Kings Speech. Peter sent Maky £1 and me 2 pairs stockings – Tony sent notes – I made him a Pullover, it looked quite nice. I must begin to make for my Kit. I had to go to the Hospital this week for an Xray – no results so far. I have <u>not</u> told Peter or Henry and T. My spine is not too good but as long as I rest its not so bad. Must end, with all good wishes for the New Year and I hope it will not be long before we see you here. Please convey to your dear Mother *and Father and Machi and Petros my good wishes. I cannot write more for the moment. Loves and Kisses to Boys. Did the Boys get the Gloves?*

Mummy

Darling Etty!

I thinking on you somacs you no and di best of al. I hope thas you koming hir mit ti Boys. Gerald is a lovli Boy! Shend Kûsse for Mrs Rosis from mi. Kom home sun dir Etty. Kisses for Boy and for you.

Your Maky
XXXXX

*

By early January 1951, my mother, brother and I had been living as comfortable exiles in Salonica for almost six months. In that time, I had "grown two inches" and two months before, in November, Gerald had celebrated his first birthday with a family gathering at thirty-two Queen Olga Street. From photographs taken of the occasion, this was a party conducted in a manner decreed by Fifi – in other words with immaculate ceremony. Only the best would do for her new grandchild. So the dining room table was laid with embroidered linen and matching napkins, a silver samovar gleamed on the sideboard and Gerald sat propped up on an ornately embroidered cushion before a salver bearing an elaborate gateau illuminated by one candle. He makes an adorable picture – his rush of dark curls as yet untouched by a pair of scissors, his chubby face drifting across four snapshots from looks of bewilderment to expressions of enchantment and joy.

But at another level, these photographs speak for the values of the family and the power of the tie of blood. (My aunt Machi was always invoked as my only "blood aunt".) So these six months in the fourth year of my life made,

I believe, a profound impression on my psyche and sense of nationhood – a formative period which seemed to establish my Greekness, my sense of the motherland and my connection with her more persuasively than if we had returned to England in August as my father had done after his holiday. Now, at last, the moment had arrived for us to be reunited with him and for me it is a moment still etched on my memory. He travelled to Heathrow to meet our flight and as we emerged from customs, I found myself staring at a tall stranger who was my father. He wore a military-style khaki raincoat with a large collar and a belt pulled tight around his middle. He looked so alien – a classic officer-class Englishman – and I was overcome with shyness. In my hand I carried a wood-crafted model caique – blue and white with a red trim, a farewell gift from Yaya Fifi and Pappou Thanassaki – and as my father lifted me into his arms, all I could do was hold up the model for him to inspect and blurt out one word: "Βαρκα!" ["Boat!"] I had lost my English. Greek had become my natural language, my mother tongue. And Greece had become my country.

The little Greek boy inside me remains embedded in my soul. The idea that England – my home country – is in part a strange place, the mild sense of foreignness, still quivers somewhere within the contours of my conscious identity. As a child, particularly at school, I felt different from other boys – they were English, I wasn't quite English. I didn't fit and it made me uncomfortable, less confident. And even though my father's lineage was deeply Mittel-European, in my own psyche I have never felt the same powerful blood connectivity as I do with Greece. To me, my father always represented true, pure Englishness – just as he did at Heathrow Airport that day all those years ago. Perhaps this sense of rootedness in my mother's country explains why later, when relations between us soured, I turned away from Greece. As she became alien to me, so did I begin to deny my motherland. Now it is changing again – the power of the blood tie! My return here, to this Aegean hideaway – after her death and after the long years of self-imposed exile – is turning into a journey of rediscovery.

*

Part Five

Growing Pains

Kit at one

Old RG's unusual display of goodwill at Christmas – his promise to accommodate the whole family under his castellated roof – proved to be a gesture circumscribed by the limits of his generosity. That dreary January in 1951 we moved into a modest suite of rooms overlooking the garden on the second floor of the hotel: a double bedroom converted into a living room; two small singles – one for my parents (their double bed wedged into a corner), one for Gerald and me; and a bathroom. Later, when my brother outgrew his cot, Spiller allowed us to take the remaining two rooms on the landing – one as a bedroom for me, the other as a tiny dining room – and our wing became a self-contained flat. The absence of a kitchen in this arrangement did not bother my mother, the cosseting of willing servants in her childhood denying her the need or the desire to learn to cook. Life at the Castle Hotel became a fair surrogate for the style to which she had become accustomed in her ample home in Salonica. Beds were made, the laundry despatched; rooms cleaned, shoes polished – and meals were delivered from an unseen basement by a rope-hauled dumb waiter.

With the family settled, my father – energized by our return – set out to reburnish the fortunes of the Castle while my mother watched over us with the assistance of a round and jolly ginger-haired Scottish lady whom we called Nanny. This was an appointment made less out of necessity and more in deference to Etty's upbringing but it allowed her to be catapulted into local society – her natural vivacity and elegance attracting the attentions of the leisured ladies of Taunton while Somerset's starchy county set were won over by her youthfulness and Mediterranean charm. I remember lying in my bed at night listening to her parties – the gaiety and laughter spinning down the corridor to my room as she teased her guests about their English inhibition over cocktails – "gin and It" or "gin and French" were the thing! Eventually they would disappear down the hotel's great staircase to the dining room. Silence. Then Gerald and I would drift off to sleep.

In those early years there was one particular role my mother took upon herself – a task she carried out with obvious love and dedication – and it is only now that I have come to realize it. Indeed, I doubt I would be able to recount this part of the story with any conviction if she had not appointed herself archivist to her two young boys. Her modus operandi was eccentric, but in its way effective, and in clearing Avon Lodge in Somerset after her death, Louise and I discovered that her filing system was constructed around a galaxy of boxes within boxes, like Russian dolls. Hat and dress boxes were preferred. Into these were packed old chocolate boxes like the Lindt assortment we fell upon in Peter's cabin trunks. Open sesame! To Lindt we must now add After Eight, Suchard and even a wooden box of Epicure crystallised fruits from which spilled hundreds and thousands of little treasures ascribed to her children: notes, letters, box camera snaps, handmade booklets containing neat lists of friends and family, countries visited, sports played, books read, poems liked and films seen; there were crayon scribbles, drawings, paintings, raffia mats and a myriad of other handicrafts; and there were string-bound bundles of school reports. The After Eight box, a handsome red one-pound carton, also contained two special gems: a padded jewel compact enclosing ribbon-tied locks of blond hair and my first milk tooth; and – a late discovery – one more "last letter" from Nell, this one addressed to me:-

Avon Lodge
Little Common
Xmas 1952

My darling Kit,

I send you this 10/- note [50p] for Mummy to put in the Post Office Bank for you. For I am very proud of you, my dear one, You are my clever Boy! I saw the Sums you made & it made me feel very happy. Have a good Xmas & enjoy yourself!! I wish you were coming to me!!

Maky sends you her love & so do I with many warm kisses.

Your loving Granny.

Thirteen months later, on the twenty-fifth of January 1954, my darling Granny died.

*

Nell's pride in my arithmetical prowess showed all the sweetness and generosity expected of a devoted grandmother, but her son my father was less sanguine about my early education. In his estimation, the Beehive – a late Victorian mansion on Wellington Road – was a disastrous beginning to my academic career. The school was run by a deep-throated, muscular woman called Miss Gange who, later in my youth, returned to coach me in the basics and social niceties of lawn tennis. That Miss Gange should have been re-employed suggests my father eventually concluded that my lack of progress at the Beehive was more my problem than the school's.

So at the age of six I was transferred to Thone, the preparatory institution attached to Taunton School, where I came under the sway of Miss M. Lowman-Lang, mistress of the Kindergarten. Miss Lang was stick-thin and tall, her grey-strafed hair plaited in a bun. She held herself erect in a posture which could be Maggie Smith, earnest and stern except that her smiles betrayed the clucking care of a mother hen – and this was most of the time. Her brood – some twenty boys – sat on miniature chairs at three rectangular low tables designated A, B and C. A-graders, the bright elite, were her favourites; Cs were less favoured. And when I took my seat in September '53, I was placed at the lower end of table C. Now Miss Lang believed little boys prospered best under a regime of strict routines, drills and learning by rote. By nine o'clock on any weekday morning, a casual passer-by walking along Staplegrove Road on the western fringes of the town might well have been entertained to the plainsong of a score of little voices chanting their times tables. From here Miss Lang would hurl us into an intensive round of instruction in oral composition, word building, reading and writing. Then – after the milk break – came history, geography and scripture. This would take us to the lunch break, a rest and a softer afternoon of art, nature or music.

At the end of my first term at Thone, my father received a long buff envelope containing a tightly-worded report – a document which was icily conclusive in its appraisal of my scholastic ability. The word "backward" – adverbially qualified, here by a "very", there by a "rather" – appeared no less than four times. Oh dear! Of course in this age of twenty-first century enlightenment, political buzzwords like 'positive discrimination' govern our behaviour. Fielding a word like "backward" in a six year-old child's school report would be condemned as a damaging and heinous slur. A posse of bureaucrats would descend on the school. The teacher would be suspended pending an investigation. Disciplinary procedures would ensue. There would be an almighty rumpus. But this is an unlikely scene. Instead, today's child would be referred to educational specialists who would run a number of tests of the kind our son Dominic was put through before he was diagnosed dyslexic – a genetic affliction I now know is all my fault.

Now is now and different from then. Then the only remedy was to persevere or else sink. Some dark instinct inside me, nourished by my father's encouragement, persuaded me to persevere and engage in the struggle which, from that moment, took up residence under my skin, fuelling my life force and driving me forward. There were early dividends. With the new term I gradually won the approbation of Miss Lang who rewarded me with promotion and by the summer I was sitting with the best on Table A. But there were failures and disappointments too. After the beneficence of Miss Lang's Kindergarten, it took me two academic years to claw my way out of Thone's B-stream to join the A-graders. And then, to my father's dismay, I failed my Eleven Plus. As the school gathered cross-legged on the floor of the assembly room before the headmaster, Dr. Reginald Headworth-Whitty, a Dickensian figure of heroic presence and a fondness for wielding an old plimsoll, his sonorous voice intoned our fate as if it were the Day of Judgement. After declaring each candidate's name, he paused before uttering one of a pair of two-syllabled words: "Grammar" or "Modern". Working his way down the alphabetic list, he arrived at the Cs. "Chapman," he boomed. "Modern!"

This portentous ceremony went straight over my head. I had no idea of the significance embodying these two words until I learned that the shock of my failure had reverberated around school and home to a degree that Dr. Headworth-Whitty took it upon himself to appeal to the education authorities. Suddenly, I found myself being hauled to a local secondary modern school for an afternoon of additional tests. The exercises were various and included being seated beside a nice lady who presented me with a pictorial storyboard.

"In this picture," she began, "what time of the year do you think it is?"
"Summer," I replied.
"Why do you say that?" she asked.
"Because the flowers are out?"
"Anything else?"
"There are leaves on the trees," I added nervously, "and the people are wearing summer clothes."
"Do you think the sun is shining or is it cloudy?" she pressed.
"It's a sunny day," I retorted.
"How do you know?"
"Because of the shadows of the people and the trees" ... and so it continued. I never learned the outcome of these tests and it mattered less for this fortunate son whose worried father was determined to muster the means and pay the price of a public school education. And so my career at Thone ended much as it had begun, with a report which acknowledged my struggle but noted the shortcomings: a weakness in interpreting written questions linked to a lack of fluency in reading – problems which affected my ability to complete exam questions in the time allowed, depressing my final grades. Mr. G.K. Johnson, my senior form master, concluded: "... he advances by strenuous

and conscientious work more than innate talent."

These difficulties – my undiscovered dyslexia – became a burden I was destined to carry throughout my years at Taunton School and when I began life as a boarder at the age of thirteen, my dutiful letters home occasionally echoed my latest moments of angst. Entering the school's third year in September 1960, on the twenty-fifth of the month I wrote to my parents with my new Parker fountain pen – a gift for the start of term. "Dear Mummy and Daddy," I began, "I am in 4A and my form master is Mr. Dewdney (Dewdrop) … I have lots of new books and the form reader is 'Oliver Twist,' it has 509 pages in it, I do not know how I am going to finish it … I am afraid that Tuesdays are going to be very awkward days because the three preps for that night are due in the next day and I have rugger on Tuesdays. Wednesdays have exactly the same problems. I think I am going to find it very difficult to finish." A week later I write: "I have found a good place to read 'Oliver Twist', it is in the fiction library, it is nice and quiet there."

This confession – the great saga of my academic trials; the years of tribulation along the road to, first, 'O' Levels (eight taken, eight passed), then 'A' Levels (three taken, three passed) and university beyond (an ordinary B.Sc.) – is made only in remembrance of my dear father. Lord! How he suffered on my behalf! From the moment Miss Lang's report declared me "backward" to the day I packed my school trunk to join my boarding house, he bent his heart and mind to the nurture of my education. He became my coach and private tutor.

There was a routine of course – and timings had to be as precisely gauged as military manoeuvres. On our return from school, Etty would insist we changed out of our uniforms before sitting down to a high tea which was conveyed by the dumb waiter to the second floor chambermaids' servery, then transferred on trays to our tiny dining room next door. The spread would begin with a hot or cold dish: salads (shredded carrot and bleeding beetroot I recall) with cold cuts of beef or ham (chicken as a special treat), or fried eggs, bacon and baked beans. Then crumpets and buttered toast kept hot and limp beneath silver-domed warmers; crust-trimmed cucumber sandwiches cut into fingers; bread and butter with Tiptree jam; a chocolate gateau, a sponge roll or cupcakes. And the entire feast generously lubricated by two pints of gold-top milk. For the dumb waiter to deliver silver-top would have been considered a grave transgression as the lower-grade fluid might inhibit the healthy development of young teeth and bones. And tea remained strictly a beverage for grown-ups. When we had filled our tummies and drained the last drop of milk from our Peter Rabbit mugs, the trays were restacked for their return journey into the bowels of the hotel and Etty's trousseau tablecloth was exchanged for my father's old army blanket upon which I would lay my homework.

At this point my mother took Gerald off for his bath as my father sat down beside me to do battle with the three Rs. An hour's supervision and tutelage were about as much as he could afford to give – and certainly I would endure – before bathing and changing to return downstairs to greet his new arrivals, tour the dining room and ensure his Irish maitre d' was moderating his artless blarney and nightly ingestion of stout. But for that one hour my father was all mine and as the contents of the big red box of After Eight spilled out around me, the memories of those looping labyrinthine hours on the army blanket ballooned inside my head. English prep. And the topic of the moment had been King Arthur and his knights. The instruction to the class now was to write our own ballads of the tale. I was so proud of mine – a poem which ran to nine four-line stanzas – that I recopied it into my private notebook signing it "by C.H.G. Chapman," then, conscience pricked, I added in parentheses "with the assistance of my daddy." The value of that assistance – as the sample verses here might hint – was, I recall, a whisper short of a hundred percent.

At Christmas all the nobles met.
Nearby them in a glade
Was found, embedded in a stone,
A wondrous shining blade.

Upon the hilt in Latin words,
Was writ for all to see,

"The one who pulleth out this sword,
The King will surely be."

Then Dukes and Earls and all those there,
Each gave a mighty heave.
But though they tried their very best,
The sword refused to leave.

Maths prep. And the topic of the day had been fractions which, for this pupil, were as sinister and terrifying as the freezing mists in an Exmoor winter. For my father, a man of Herculean patience, one simple question drove him to fall on his knees in supplication – his arms folded on the blanket, his head propped on his hands as he begged me to grasp the logic and allow the penny to drop. The question was this: "What is a quarter of ten?" It was a question whose answer eluded me in spite of the painstaking step-by-step rehearsal my father led me through, not once, not twice, but a dozen times. A logical process which ended with the plaintive wail: "And so Kit, what is a quarter of ten?"

"One and three quarters!" I tried. By now my responses had become like a pair of dice I was hurling across a baize.

"Kit!" My father pleaded, resuming his pitch in desperation. "Let's try again. What is half of ten?"

"Five."

"And what is half of five?"

"Two and a half," I repeated confidently.

"And so WHAT is a quarter of ten?"

"Two and a quarter?" I parried with a wince and a shrug.

*

My father's devotion to my education reached far beyond the drill and drudgery of an evening's homework. His tactics were often wonderfully creative in their attempts to engage his sons' interests, to fire our young imaginations. Inevitably, they would also reflect his own particular loves – history and geography being favourite subjects at Dover College. One novel initiative was to encourage me to collect stamps and it was only after Louise discovered two packed albums at the bottom of a Harrods' hatbox that these carefully assembled folios revealed their perpetrator's strategy. Leafing gently through the pages, it soon became clear that my father's purpose was to teach me the geography and history of the British Empire and Commonwealth – with one curious diversion which explored the issues of the Third Reich. The philately of Greece was not included in this curriculum. So on Sunday afternoons and in school holidays, khaki blanket spread before us, he would sit beside me as we mounted the stamps onto their designated pages – country by country, in alphabetical order, from Aden to Trinidad & Tobago, with the Ugandan collection presented under the heading "Kenya, Uganda and Tanganyika." To illuminate our travels around the dining room table, a map of the world, largely tinted in a shade of dusty pink, denoted Great Britain's dominions and, as an incidental aside, my father would point out those territories once colonized by France, Germany and Italy.

The imperial collection was instructive in two ways. The reigning monarch's profile on each stamp gave a clue to the era of issue. And the designs – many featuring sequences of exotic images – opened my eyes to the economies, politics and cultural diversity of each country. Aden introduced me to dhow building, salt works and camel transport. Australia celebrated the Queen's coronation in 1953 and the Melbourne Olympics in 1956. Ceylon's stamps illustrated star orchids, king coconuts and wild elephants; the ancient ruins at Madirigiriya and the Temple of the Tooth. In the Gold Coast, a steam train hauled manganese from a mine; natives were pictured breaking cocoa pods while a young Elizabeth II looked on benignly – and in the Falkland Islands, George VI smiled serenely at a pair of cocky penguins. In India, the crowned head of King George V looked regally solemn on a stamp marking the inauguration of the Council House in New Delhi in 1931. In Malta, the theme was a series of historic monuments; Jamaica presented a banana plantation and a view of Kingston Harbour while Kenya, Uganda and Tanganyika displayed a variety of African wild life and civil engineering projects like the Owen Falls Dam. But perhaps the prettiest was also the simplest – a beautiful sky blue stamp from Rhodesia & Nyasaland showing a diademed Queen Elizabeth bathed in a soft rose halo.

Of all these collections, the most impressive for me came from Great Britain herself – pages of stamps bearing the heads of every monarch since Victoria; some unashamedly jingoistic such as the magnificent pair of George V Crown and Half-Crown stamps portraying a defiant Britannia, trident outstretched, astride a chariot drawn by three rampant stallions. Others celebrated our national landmarks: the Silver Jubilee of George V in 1935; the centenary of the first postage stamp (a penny black) in 1840 with twin profiles of both Victoria and George VI; the Olympic Games in 1948; the Festival of Britain in 1951, and the Golden Jubilee Jamboree of the Boy Scout movement in 1957.

Leafing through these folios today – two albums which have lain dormant in a hatbox for half a century – I find myself pinched by nostalgia, gazing at the stamps through the eyes of the child who spent all those free hours with his daddy wet-sponging dozens and hundreds of translucent adhesive tabs before mounting them hesitantly into their proper position on the page. Like holiday brochures, the images are a mix of the exotic, the romantic, the grand and the glamorous. They fill the imagination with a sense of wonder about far-off places. But for me these places assumed a more intimate connection because they had been given to me as places that belonged – or, in some way, were linked – to my father's country of birth, my country of birth.

Peter, throughout his life, always expressed a keen sense of national pride. He believed the British Empire was a good thing. Like many of his generation, he held notions of colonialism which, fifty years on, are considered naïve and dangerous in a new world order where the values of self-determination, independence and democracy too often become entangled and confused in a swamp of post-colonial tyranny, economic chaos, oppression and even genocide. My father held a deep affection for India, frequently telling Gerald and me about his life and experiences there before Independence in 1947. He was a proud servant of Empire, proud too of its legacy and the values colonial rule left behind. The stamp collections were his way of sharing some of these values with his sons, teaching us a little about the history of Britain along the way. It rubbed off.

Perhaps it was his love of country, his old-fashioned sense of English fair play and his tolerance which explain the sudden embolism that was the collection of stamps issued by the Third Reich – a predictable miscellany glorifying the face of Adolf Hitler, his Nazi symbol, the swastika, and propagandist images of young men in jackboots or raised arms in salute to "Ein Volk. Ein Reich. Ein Führer." His hatred of the regime – as much discussed with us as his love of India – predated the war to the fateful boating expedition he and Tony organized on the Danube. Peter was eighteen and had just left school. It was at Passau at the start of their journey downstream to Bratislava when they ran into a brigade of militant Brownshirts and the memory of the incident never left him. Some months later, in the winter of the same year, Patrick Leigh Fermor, another eighteen year-old, set out on his famous hike to Constantinople – a journey immortalized in his luminous works *A Time of Gifts* and *Between the Woods and the Water*. The two young men – one on foot, the other river-borne – shared many of the same sights and impressions on this stretch of Europe's greatest waterway. And both novice adventurers experienced the occasional discomfort of a brush with the rising temperature of the Nazi terror.

*

Growing up on the Danube, it was almost a given that the three Prüger brothers would acquire a passion for rowing. My father loved all his sports and at Dover College he claimed the school's colours for rugby, running and boxing. The irreducible tie of a healthy body with a healthy mind – 'mens sana in corpore sano' – was part of the culture of his upbringing. "Boys of spirit, boys of will,/Boys of muscle, brain and power,/Fit to cope with anything,/These are wanted every hour." The words are still burned on my memory: Henry Prüger's framed injunction passed on by his youngest son to hang beside my own childhood bedstead. But while the spirit and the will in me yearned to fulfil my grandfather's nostrum, I proved to be a hopeless sportsman.

To fail in track, field and gymnasium at an English public school – anyway in my time – stigmatized the pupil, reducing him to a common drone amidst the übermensch who strutted their stuff in tasselled and braided skullcaps, striped blazers and fancy ties. These fellows were further rewarded with praetorian authority which conferred upon them extraordinary powers over the lower orders who cooked and skivvied for their pleasure. And if we transgressed, we were beaten – mindful to thank our tormentors for their trouble. These were the unhappiest days of my life – my problem being an over-refined sense of injustice and a simple hatred of a system which considered sport its holiest canon. To be selected as one of your first team's fifteen players in the field on a Saturday afternoon made you a hero. To sing an unaccompanied solo as head chorister in chapel on Sunday morning marked you out as a queer. Alas, I was that chorister. And proud of it too – I loved the repertoire. But no, apart from the sexual fumblings initiating any adolescent schoolboy confined for months in a joyless male institution, buggery never won me over to its attractions.

As a timid, hesitant and sometimes sickly pubescent, not once did I detect a hint of disappointment in my father's frustration at my lack of sporting prowess. While Gerald emerged as the higher talent both in the classroom and on the sports field, Peter never failed to encourage his eldest and, in spite of my struggles, I always sensed his love and his pride in all my endeavours however minor. But, swimming and tennis aside, two pursuits at which I did not excel but quite enjoyed, I loathed games. I came last in any race; could not vault a horse or walk the beam or climb a rope. I was admitted to the swimming squad but the coach had to put me through a body-building regime of lifting a bench suspended from the parallel bars in the gym before I could begin to master press-ups as part of my circuit training. But the worst hell was rugby and my letters home occasionally complained of my greatest fear and hatred: being pitched into a game as a forward. In October 1960 I wrote, "In rugger I played left centre. As it had been raining the ground was muddy and the ball was slippery, I dropped two passes which were pretty lousy. Just because of this I was changed to second row at half time. I expect this means I will stay in the scrum for the rest of term. I am mad, exofrenon [Greek: ἐξωφρενον] and all the other words put together, I refuse to play any more, of course I'll turn up but I will NOT try."

At times my father must have found my weediness tiresome – but he never showed it nor gave up on me. He was appalled at my inability to climb a rope and had one fixed to a steel beam in the hotel's garage, working with me to explain the simple technique required to scale the wretched thing. A forlorn hope. And at weekends, with Etty, he would drive Gerald and me up into his beloved Blackdown Hills – to a favourite field a mile or so from Avon Lodge, the house they would buy thirty-five years later. Here, we ran like lunatics back and forth passing an oval ball to each other, kicking it and taking instruction on the most effective methods of tackling an opponent. My mother cheered from an imaginary touchline and my father was back at Dover College on match day.

A strange thing – thinking now of those Sunday afternoons on the Blackdowns; and so long ago: a lost age, a recurring dream as I sit here, today, on Aristotle gazing at an archipelago still in semi-silhouette two hours after the first sunbeams broke over Skopelos – and my thoughts drifting home to those rolling beech-cloaked English hills south of Taunton. The town, still manfully trying to shake off its sleepy provincialism, lies in a wide valley encircled by the most magical uplands. Of these Exmoor and the Quantocks raise landscapes of commanding majesty and drama: all crag and combe, heather and moor; wild ponies and proud deer; rushing rivulets and bent trees. The Blackdowns are their quieter, softer neighbour – their charms more subtle, seductive and feminine; their contours more graceful; the sod and woodland deeper, richer, greener; and their villages and hamlets less tourist-trodden; communities close-knit, mindful of their own. This was a rural habitat better tuned to my father's disposition – where he found a greater sense of peaceful escape. And, in the end, it is why he bought the family plot in the churchyard of St. Peter & St. Paul in the parish of Churchstanton.

For as long as I remember, from my childhood to their final ailing years at

Avon Lodge, this small, remote Norman church became a spiritual landmark in my parents' quotidian routines. This is where they would park their car to walk a circuit of lanes and returning, sit awhile in one of the ancient box pews to say a prayer before the journey back to Taunton. Close by – perhaps two miles from the church – lies the abandoned military airfield at Smeatharpe, a base the Americans used to prepare for the D-Day invasion in 1944. It was here, on the aprons and landing grounds that my father taught me to drive – a course of lessons which began with the words: "Now Kit, you must understand that a motor car is a lethal weapon." Some weeks later, to my astonishment, he allowed me to take off up the main runway and it was not until I had reached a speed of eighty mph that he quietly asked me to pull up.

It was hardly surprising then, that when in my father's judgement the moment had come to induct his son in the ways, whys and wherefores of sexual intercourse, he chose the family's customary Sunday afternoon walk on the Blackdowns as the place to conduct his delicate but essential tutorial. I was an innocent – ten going on eleven – but the use of the word "fuck" had emerged into general circulation in the school playground and, blithely, I carried it home. For Peter this was an alarm call: time to sort me out. But he needed a ploy to detach me from Gerald. Judging the Churchstanton circuit inappropriate, he chose a beautiful route which circumnavigated a mature beech wood. Parking the car in a lay-by and invoking a tone of mock-spontaneity and playfulness, he suggested that Gerald and Etty walk in an anti-clockwise direction while he and I take the clockwise route. At the point where our paths crossed, we would know we had reached halfway and duly note the time.

Like pairs of explorers undertaking a scientific experiment, we set out and after the excitement and greetings of the midway rendezvous, my father gathered his thoughts for his first foray into sex education. He had prepared himself. Even in my innocence, I was impressed by his gentle dissertation – a lesson which took care to be clear and explicit without sounding smutty or trivial, attempting to define the emotions of love and sexual attraction, emphasizing the importance of respect, the moral responsibilities and the dangers. His correctness and friendly formality seemed to strike the right chords. But out of it all, one single word stuck in my impressionable mind: it was the term he used for the male seed – spermatozoa! The word rang with operatic magnificence. To my ears, it sounded wonderfully romantic, marvellously poetic. In bed that night I repeated the word to myself, rolling it musically in my mind, intoning it, varying the chromatic phrasing over its five syllables like Don-Gi-o-va-nni. Somehow my father had succeeded in conjuring a vision of sex which was heavenly – an ethereal act, the ultimate consummation of human existence. But I could only dream. Another decade would follow before I put this lyrical union to the test – a fulfilment which came, blissfully, in a small flat high above the crescented terraces of Notting Hill with a girl from Cheshire.

Meantime, those awkward years leading up to my voice breaking (a minor tragedy for a treble chorister who never made the grade as a solo tenor) produced an unwanted coda to the Blackdown Hills' sex lecture. To my excruciating embarrassment, Etty found the onset of male puberty a strange and immensely entertaining phenomenon – her naïve curiosity running unfettered to the point of obsession. At frequent intervals – at school and at home – she would light up her feline grin and challenge me about the current state of gearing between my legs. Oblivious to the emotional and hormonal turbulence of my approaching manhood, she fielded the same German diminutive for the purpose: "Have your *bällchen* dropped yet?" It was hopeless – I was rendered defenceless. Repeated objections to her line of attack were met with a shrill volley of giggles telling me not to be so silly and English. "What are you embarrassed about?" she trilled. "It is perfectly natural!" Peter, often present when these exchanges took place, would look on benignly and smile – he loved my mother's uncomplicated directness – for him it was all part of the koutsimou charm that had captured his heart in Northern Greece.

Recollections of my mother through these sensitive years of growing-up seem to be tinged overwhelmingly by embarrassment when a sense of pride in her style, her brio, her élan might have been the keener emotion. She was very different from the other school mums who, I think without exception, struck me as older, duller, dowdier – but also more motherly which is perhaps what I missed. On formal occasions – a Sunday chapel or a school play or a prize giving – Etty would turn eyes, her effervescence demanding attention, her taste in hats fuelling the cruellest derision. Unlike the twinset and tweedy predictability of the others, she always struck an elegant and fashionable line in her choice of wardrobe. And my contemporaries, observing the contrast, would sneer: "There goes Chapman's mum!"

*

For Gerald and for me, these formative years in the fifties and sixties seemed to divide distinctly between the two phases of childhood and adolescence – each period set within its own particular institution under its own particular regime and, in each case, the institution influencing the regime, neither especially liberal. As children, we may have called the Castle home but it was also a functioning hotel under my father's direction. There were disciplines and mores which, as his sons, we were obliged to respect. When we reached the age of thirteen, we entered Taunton School as boarders and another regime took hold of our lives.

Visiting the homes of school friends – like the times we used to visit Nell in Little Common – was both strange and liberating. For a start my senses were captivated by the novelty of a domestic kitchen out of which poured wondrous smells of simmering stews, buttered mash or minted new potatoes. My first experience of a Bridgwater mum's toad-in-the-hole was unforgettable – I had never tasted anything quite like it as the dish never appeared on any menu at the Castle. There our days were strictly ordered – we were not allowed to loiter on the premises and during school holidays the place was put out of bounds. Breakfast, like all meals, was delivered by our elderly and groaning dumb waiter and Etty, mindful of our diets, would administer a daily dose of cod liver oil which, later, was replaced by a thick, viscous substance called Radio Malt. As tea and coffee were banned substances for growing boys, like the ritual at teatime, our Peter Rabbit mugs brimmed over with gold top and we were not despatched to school until the final drop had disappeared down our little throats. As we left the flat, satchels of completed homework hoisted on our backs, there would be one parting instruction repeated religiously every day: "Say good morning to the staff!" A small courtesy too often overlooked and a habit which remains entrenched in me to this day.

I never entirely understood my parents' obsession with the importance of a high consumption of milk and it became an issue – showering me with more embarrassment – when I started to board. On my first exeat, they were shocked to discover their son thinner, paler and a sadder specimen of the offspring they had so lovingly nurtured. They complained to my housemaster and, with no notice, I suddenly found myself being pricked and prodded by the school's medical officer in a series of tests which showed no evidence of a terminal disease. The answer, my mother concluded, lay in an extra pint of gold top delivered each day to the house dining room which, inevitably, inspired a new campaign of ribaldry from my ghastly peers. And beyond the special delivery of milk lay the gustatory culture of the tuck box. Together they seemed to assume the status of metaphor, magnifying my sense of isolation, my foreignness. At home my middle-European and Eastern Mediterranean heritage were much discussed – a proud history instilled into the fabric of the family. At school it was different. I was different. Standard provender for the Celts and Anglo-Saxons included processed cheese wedges, condensed milk, baked beans, peanut butter, Bovril or Marmite and Heinz Sandwich Spread, while my private larder's stock list read like a Fortnum & Mason hamper: a Colston Basset Stilton, a tin of Kalamata olives, an Hungarian salami, Scottish smoked salmon and a jar of Tiptree Strawberry Jam. One fretful letter home complains: "I have eaten all the olives already. Some of the other boys could not stand the smell and had to go miles away from me."

*

Differences, differences! Perhaps more illusory than real but real enough to a child feeling trapped in a web of disciplines framed by the hotel he grows up in; of continental notions of appearances and family honour (a Greek must never lose face!); of treats rationed and restrictions imposed. The Castle's acre of garden designed around its twelfth century ruins – stone chambers, a moat wall, the keep and a Norman well – gave my brother and me an adventure park to play in, but not too freely because it was shared with the hotel's paying guests. There was also the modern wonder of a television to watch but only for an hour after tea on Sunday afternoons because the hotel's single set stood sentry-like in a corner of the smoking room beside the men-only public bar. Then who would be watching *Muffin the Mule, The Flower Pot Men* or the *Lone Ranger* at that time of day?

And what of honour and reputation and face? Just as Gerald and I were instructed to say "good morning" to the staff as we left for school, so we were put on guard never to do anything or say anything that might cast the slightest blemish on the family's good name – secrets and confidences always signalled by my mother's forefinger drawn sharply down her pursed lips. Obedience and deference towards one's elders were the accepted values which we bore like a greatcoat across our tiny shoulders. There was nothing wrong with having a good time – invitations to fancy dress birthday parties at the Castle were swiftly taken up by our classmates' mums who competed madly to see their sons carry off a tube of Smarties in the best costume category. But even pleasure and fun had to be kept within bounds. To let one's hair down too far was to court dishonour and shame. If there were one watchword to recur in the manner of our upbringing, it would be my father's constant call to exercise "self-control" in the conduct of our lives. Wise counsel, indeed, but in the first two decades of my life – whether at school or at home – "self-control" in practice never needed much rehearsal as direct control came imposed by a higher authority. At times I found the regime oppressive. Whether it came from the institutionalized brutishness of an English public school or the beneficence of the family home, there seemed little space for free expression. Freedom ultimately meant escape and rebellion and these would come in their own good time. Meanwhile, hating its constraints, I tolerated childhood as an inevitable if pointless state of being. I yearned for adulthood because grown-ups had all the fun; grown-ups had power; grown-ups were free. Children, it seemed to me, lived in a state of siege. At the time, and though we were close, I never revealed my feelings to Gerald – I guess because we accepted our lot for what it appeared to us: normal. Much later I would discover that he had felt every bit as suffocated as I had been.

These feelings of entrapment inside a closed regime were never more evident than life during the school holidays – the very moment when freedom, or a sense of it, might take flight in the imaginations of little boys. Instead, the routines of the scholastic calendar gave way to a breathtaking agenda of structured activity administered by Etty who organized our every waking moment – apparently for our greater benefit. With home shadowing a busy hotel, this strategy was probably sensible even if Gerald and I passed much of the holiday simmering silently with resentment. But it was a strategy taken to excess. There were tennis lessons with Miss Gange of the Beehive. There was riding instruction by a military dictator who forced us to assume ridiculous postures on the backs of ponies as they trotted round his paddock. There was swimming coaching in the municipal pool with a white-vested, pop-eyed tyrant who blew his whistle at us like a manic referee. Worse still were the ballroom dancing lessons in a barren first-floor studio under the tutelage of a middle-aged matron with bad breath and pudgy hands. Finally there was French tuition in our tiny dining room from Monsieur Trevette, a ghostly-figure with a dove-grey pointed beard who dressed entirely in black: black suit, heavy black cape and a wide-brimmed black fedora. As he glided into the hotel trailing white horses of pipe smoke, Monsieur Trevette conjured a romantic vision of a nineteenth-century philosopher-poet. He also displayed a recondite charm of the kind you often find in cultured Frenchmen. My mother thought he was wonderful and, towards the end of our hourly sessions, she would tap at the dining room door and offer him a glass of sherry – Tio Pepe being his tipple. Kind and cultivated though he may have been, Monsieur Trevette failed to teach us much of his native tongue. Not because we did not pay attention. We did. His way inspired polite conscientiousness. I think he was just a little too highbrow to connect with a pair of young brothers bored and irritated by their parents' insistence that they submit to these pedantic tutorials.

*

The business of managing the Castle was a mystery to us in those early years. Home and hotel were partitioned territories and all we knew was that our daddy worked cripplingly long hours in his bid to drag the place out of its post-war doldrums. A four-year programme of renewal began with the re-roofing and rewiring of the entire property and ended with the installation of amenities essential to the comfort of the modern traveller. For the first time, the Castle was able to offer its visitors bedrooms with hot towel rails, electric razor plugs and bedside telephones – but guests who needed more than a basin with two taps and a bar of soap for their ablutions were still obliged to share a bathroom with their neighbours along the corridor. That amenity – the conversion of forty bedrooms to include their own private bathroom – was planned in phases as a later development.

If Gerald and I were distantly aware of these works in the 1950s, we were ignorant of their significance on the canvas of my father's rising career. When they were complete, the celebration to mark the hotel's renaissance was choreographed as an elaborate pageant in which he was determined to see his boys take leading roles. For him I think, this was an unconscious expression of a deeper instinct taking hold – a desire to see the Castle as a life-long mission. It resonated with memories of his own father, the transformation of the Savoy-Carlton in Bratislava and the Prüger family's involvement in the running of the hotel. At this signal moment, he wanted to feel that the father he admired but never quite came to know would be proud of him.

The party, a cocktail reception for a hundred local worthies, took place in the newly-decorated hotel lounge – a cavernous space on a mezzanine floor at the head of the first flight of the great staircase. Outside, two Tudor page boys in hose, doublet, cape and feather-trimmed cap waited impatiently as toasts were proposed – the speeches echoing to polite laughter. Two senior members of staff dressed as beefeaters stood guard, anxious to keep their charges quiet and hidden from view. Between them, they carried an enormous model of the Castle constructed of plywood, paper Union Jacks fluttering on pencil sticks above the north and south towers.

A tinkling of glasses, a rush of applause and the master of the Taunton Vale Harriers sounded his horn. The major, a veteran of the North African desert, had adopted this habit before going into battle and his bravery, I was told, had earned him the Military Cross. But at this particular moment, I was not feeling especially brave. Trembling inside my hose and doublet, I followed the Tudor tableau into the room. I mounted a table, unfurled a parchment manuscript and in a high treble voice intoned the cry "Oyez! Oyez! Oyez!" proclaiming the Castle officially open. Gerald, on cue, turned towards the model's barbican. Lowering the drawbridge and raising the portcullis, he withdrew a bouquet of roses which he presented to Mrs. Spiller, the proprietor's widow – old RG having died the year before. The assembled great and good erupted in cheers, and the pageant made its stately exit.

Later that night Peter took Etty into his arms. They made love. Exhausted, their final caresses and their whispers, replaying and replaying the day's events, soon dwindled into silence and rest. But for Peter other thoughts lingered before sleep overcame him – thoughts like a host of vampires which kept returning to taunt him but which he would never share with his wife. That evening she had brought him joy enough in supporting his landmark triumph – a moment which had planted the early foundations of the family's future. Now memories of the past flooded into his mind – of his mother, the grief of her death two years before still raw, and of her loving, praising letters. Yet for all the encouragement and advice she had given him, he could not shed the gnawing melancholy biting his soul, the hints of family dishonour which consumed him each time he recalled his illustrious father. Beneath his sense of elation, he felt torn and troubled.

*

During these formative years, my own troubles and anxieties weighed heaviest in the seemingly eternal stretches as a junior in my boarding house. Life at Taunton School condemned me to some Sisyphean hell. Then, as the onset of adolescence ushered in a new self-awareness, rebellion at the injustices of this barbarous institution crawled wasp-like inside my belly. I had just turned fourteen when I committed my first act of anarchy – the object of my silent rage being an assistant housemaster who took his pleasure in the company of a long, supple cane stalking the corridors after lights-out. The slightest evidence of movement or voices from a dormitory and he would burst through the door, smack on the lights and rip the covers off the nearest bed expecting to catch some poor soul in mid-masturbation. Ordering us out of our Spartan cots, we'd line up and each in turn bend over an iron bed frame. Before leaving the room, he would turn and smile, a driblet of spittle oozing from the corner of his lips.

Never in my life – then nor since – have I felt hatred and humiliation like this, an emotion so intense that I was bent on action mindless of the consequences that might ensue. One Sunday morning, working the lengths of the breakfast benches, a fellow mutineer and I roused the oppressed to march in protest and proclaim the house's solidarity by parading banners beneath our tormentor's study window. But when we gathered at the assembly point after chapel, no one showed – the demo had shrivelled to a gang of two. Undaunted, we proceeded to chant our slogans until, minutes later, we were summoned upstairs and submitted to a thrashing so violent the weals on our bums refused to heal for several weeks. Reports of the incident spread throughout the school. Something must have been said, for in the end our stand against this monster was not in vain – guilt and conscience reforming his ways. He stopped the nocturnal corridor patrols and his attitude towards me became sickeningly amiable.

But the scars lingered within this sensitive rebel's spirit and, it seems, were noted by the headmaster, one J.G. Leathem, an old-fashioned classicist who enjoyed a drink and whose end-of-term report observed: "I hope he is happy, for he doesn't always look it!" Two years on and his theme hadn't changed. "I find him courteous and he is obviously industrious," he scrawled. "Is he taking life too seriously?" My housemaster and a succession of form teachers peddled much the same message ... "He would be happier and more successful if he could rid himself of his tendency towards over-anxiety" ... "Lack of confidence does much to give the impression of a lack of energy" ... "Worrying could easily impair his results" ... "If he is to do his intellect justice, he must develop a more robust attitude." And so on.

The moment I entered the Sixth Form, the greater freedoms and privileges of seniority seemed to transform my outlook. The mood changed and the ever watchful J.G.L. suddenly spotted a happier young man: "He is shewing much more poise and assurance," he wrote in the Spring of 1964 – and by the end of the year he had concluded that I was "a very civilized person!" It was a view endorsed by my housemaster who now branded me as "intellectual and socially mature beyond his years." All very well – but, of course, not good enough for promotion to the prefects' corridor. The job description didn't fit – my extra-curricular interests lay in choral music, the debating society and a few minor roles on the stage. And occasionally, I even engaged in French conversation with like-minded chums – just for the fun of it.

*

As I struggled to cope with my A-level syllabus – a diet of Homer, Euripides and Herodotus; Virgil and Cicero; Molière, Racine and Flaubert – a new distraction insinuated itself into my life. It began at an inter-school debate with us playing away to the local girls' grammar and a motion which read: "This house believes that, in humankind, the male of the species is superior to the female." I undertook to propose the motion and as soon as I rose to present my wittily crafted arguments I realized that even Cicero's silver oratory held little chance against a hall jammed with two hundred girls and only a minor cohort of chaps from Taunton School. With the motion roundly defeated, the girls took pity on me and, all at once, I found myself rather taken by my principal opponent – and she with me. Her name was

Diana from the nearby town of Wellington and she possessed a very grand surname I forget which rhymed with Agincourt. I remember her as petite and blond and finely-featured rather than pretty. It was a passing fancy – one of sweetest innocence which came to nothing but was, in its way, a touchingly poignant beginning to my youthful and sometimes turbulent relations with the female of the species.

Now Miranda from Kent was an altogether more challenging prospect – a dark haired siren, enigmatic and exotic with large, limpid eyes which captured my romantic fantasies and played them like puppet strings. She was the sister of a fellow-pupil and her parents booked the Castle on their visits to Taunton. Miranda blew either very hot or very cold – warm was not a temperature gauged by her blood group. Smitten, I initiated a correspondence – spending hours on Sunday afternoons drafting and redrafting letters which, I felt, needed to strike that delicate balance between interest and restraint. From the first posting, the agony of waiting chewed me up. Each morning at breakfast, the duty prefect would distribute the mail, and each breakfast would end in disappointment; until weeks later – and by now I was in a state of despair – her neat handwriting on a blue envelope at last stared up at me as I munched my bread and marge. Reading her letters became a private ritual undertaken in a hidden corner away from the house in the school grounds. Imagining each page tinctured with her scent, I would read and re-read, analyse and re-analyse, earnestly trying to determine the beat of her heart. But she gave little away and the small encouragement these letters held came only at the end when she would close her meaningless chatter with an anodyne "fondly" – or more audaciously "with fond love".

The school holidays and a rendezvous in London kindled the flames. I met her train at Victoria Station and she pressed her hand into mine – the lightest of touches which shot up my arm like an electrical bolt. We took a cab to the Curzon Cinema, ignored the movie and spent two hours locked in an awkward embrace. Then dined at a bistro in Shepherd's Market before ending our evening at the Park Lane Hilton's 007 Bar where her hip and thigh movements on the dance floor hinted at the promise of extraordinary energy if ever it were translated to the bedroom. Of course, it was a promise never fulfilled. She had a late train to catch. And at our next meeting, with no warning, she chose to end it all anyway by the simple expedient of introducing me to her new beau. Crushed, I limped away and that was the last I saw of Miranda.

*

Casting my mind back to those years – that period of transition between the claustrophobic shelter of school and the freedoms of university life, from boyhood to approaching manhood – my existence seemed to be consumed by twin obsessions, destined for collision but racing instead on parallel tracks. First there was the urgency of A-levels – long hours spent in my study or in the library; the weight and labour of my texts instilling in me a fear of failure; late nights and early mornings driving me to complete a piece of Greek prose composition or a French essay or a translation of Virgil's Eclogues. And then there was the breathless urgency of the chase after a pretty girl; the hapless confusion between sexual desire and romantic love; and the latent realization that my parents' example was important to me. I imagined their love – demonstrative and openly displayed – as a fantastic coup de foudre, and I wanted the same for myself. But equally, I was desperate to be rid of my virginity – a state which denied me the worldliness I also sought. A friend at school swapped me a Durex for five Woodbine. It remained in my wallet, crumpled, sealed, unable to win a commission. My father encouraged me one holiday in Greece – slipping me a pack of three which fell into neglect, never seeing service. I met plenty of girls; I felt at ease in their company – but a rash of sweet kisses and a line of unhooked bra straps were about the sum of my progress.

Then in the winter of my final year at Taunton School, it happened! Not the loss of my virginity which seemed bent on surviving intactus far into my dotage, but the headlong fall into the real thing; or so I believed. And the setting for this love-match was written to a suitably romantic script. Ever since his own youth, my father had been a keen alpine sportsman – now he wanted his two young boys to breathe the air of the Bernese Oberland and experience the thrill of the ski slopes. As he and Etty could not afford the cost of a winter holiday, we children were despatched into the care of Swiss friends who took us to Grindelwald for two weeks each new year. By our middle and late teens we were judged old enough to travel unaccompanied – by which time the pretty village of Verbier, in the French-speaking Alpes du Valais, became the resort of choice. It was here, on New Year's Eve, in Verbier that it happened.

The night before the big party, Gerald and I were drinking hot chocolates after supper in the gemütlich surroundings of our chalet-pension when a chipper young man two or three years our senior walked over from his group and introduced himself in the strangulated vowels of an English army officer. His name was Clendon Daukes and he and his family, having spotted two lost souls, were wondering if we might like to join them for the festivities on the following evening. I accepted immediately. Crossing the room to their table he introduced us to his parents and to his younger brother and sister – David and Jenny – who, we learned, were twins. At the time the family lived in Paris as father – a lieutenant colonel – had been seconded to NATO. On first acquaintance I found Colonel Daukes reserved and high-minded; *un homme sérieux* whom one addressed quite naturally as "Sir", while his wife shone quietly with that classic English radiance and luminosity you see in fine eighteenth century portraits hanging in grand country houses. To my relief their daughter and two sons affected none of the polite formality of their parents and themselves appeared relieved that they had been joined by company of their own generation. Clendon was at Sandhurst, exuberant in his ambition of becoming a general. David and his sister were students in London and to me Jenny, whom I had noticed earlier in the day, was the most ravishing creature I had ever set eyes upon. Now they had invited us, two complete strangers, to join them. I could hardly believe my good fortune. Jenny! There she was – three feet away from where I was sitting: a blush and a freshness to her cheeks; eyes sparkling with humour and kindness; the smile on her rose-tinted lips giving me instant heartache. This was one of those moments in a young man's life that hangs suspended in the memory like a gossamer wing caught in a pocket of warm air – helpless, lost, unknowing where it might fall.

Twenty-four hours later, as the lanterns around the nightclub dimmed and the eight-piece band rose to a crescendo heralding the New Year, an act of spontaneous combustion in twelve drumbeats found us wrapped in each others arms. Still seventeen, I was in love for the first time.

What do I say about Jenny? Well, ours was less a love affair, more an affair of two young hearts, the youthful passion of two innocents. We met in Paris. We met in London. And we visited each other's homes. But finally my teenage ardour went unrequited and the relationship slipped imperceptibly into a close and enduring friendship. Certainly, those are years I look back upon with tenderness and affection. We still meet at family gatherings although the main link now is with David, her twin brother, and his wife Rosalind, Jenny's friend from their college days in London. It was to David and Rosalind's Rutland farmhouse that Louise and I escaped that famous weekend in June 1971 when I attempted a proposal on the grass verge of a cornfield as a vintage biplane rolled and looped in the skies above our heads.

*

My last day at Taunton School was glorious – a moment to savour, my lungs pumping with an intense feeling of freedom after years of submission to an institution whose values and culture I had despised. Now I could look forward to a life over which I had greater control. Driven by my own impatience, I was being propelled away from the narrow parochialism of a town and a home environment which, for a decade and a half, had prescribed my behaviour and outlook. I was bound for London – a city I had already tasted and bitten – seduced by the allure of its vibrancy and sophistication. This was the mid-sixties where the Beatles and the Stones ruled. London was swinging and I wanted to strut down Carnaby Street and the King's Road in a satin shirt and a kipper tie.

My mission in the autumn of '65 was to enrol as a freshman at a new university – so new, indeed, that it hadn't been built. As its hillside campus slowly mushroomed in the shadow of Guildford Cathedral, the University of Surrey's charter sprang out of the less edifying purlieus of Battersea Park Road where its red-brick technical college offered a B.Sc. degree in hotel administration, a four-year course of study and industrial placement modelled on its famous equivalent at Cornell in the United States. Years before, inspired by the drive and élan of my Uncle Michael at the Imperial in Torquay, this is the direction I had chosen – and, perhaps, just as well because Oxbridge or one of the other ancient academies I may have aspired to attend were almost certainly beyond my intellectual reach. And so that October I found myself pleasurably installed on the south bank of the Thames and had only to stroll across the river to find myself amid the bars and boutiques of Chelsea. My digs may have been a grim concrete high-rise on Albert Bridge Road but as halls of residence go it was the Ritz compared to Taunton School and good enough for me to call home in my first year as a student.

I loved it. Four years that would unfold as some of the most carefree in my life. There were surprises too. I discovered to my astonishment that the physical exercise I had shunned as a schoolboy had been an eccentric aberration. Overnight I became manically sporty as an enthusiastic member of the boat club and eventually made the grade to win a place in the University's 2nd VIII – no small achievement for a fellow under-endowed with the weight, muscles and athletic physique of a natural oarsman. But I trained hard – in the gym, running the perimeter paths of Battersea Park and, at weekends, on the water at Richmond. It was exhilarating; and exciting to be counted a member of an elite corps at college – all of us distinguished by the exclusive white, purple and black colours of our ludicrously elongated club scarves.

After Albert Bridge Road and over the next three years my digs drifted more upmarket. Joining forces with my cousin Richard, Uncle Michael's eldest son, who was studying for the same degree, we linked up with our companions to share a variety of flats around London: in Victoria, Ebury Street and, finally, Westbourne Terrace in Paddington. As I recall, our weekly rent in those days was a princely £6.

By now, circumstance and sentiment seemed to be gently nudging Jenny further and further away from my affections. Like butterflies, others fluttered in and out of view but none to compare. At home in Taunton, my parents took more than a passing interest in the ebb and flow of my amours – my mother's enquiries often persistent and almost proprietorial. They adored Jenny and with David and Rosalind, the Daukes became lifelong family friends. But nervous of Etty's scrutiny and her habit of interrogating new girlfriends, I was careful with my weekend invitations, knowing perfectly well who might qualify and who was less likely to pass the test.

And then there was the issue of my unyielding virginity – a private preoccupation which was becoming a personal embarrassment and a slur on my manhood as, more than ever, I felt the influence of my peers at college who, it seemed, were fornicating furiously while I loitered among the library shelves pretending to research Keynesian economic theory. With the arrival of the long summer vac, I saw my opportunity – or thought I did. All those of us who had survived the first year and planned to return for a second were sent off to find work – a real job in the real world. And here I had a clear advantage over the rest. Uncle Michael's celebrated gastronomic weekends at the Imperial had furnished him with a gilt-edged address book to the finest hotels and restaurants in France which he now put to good use on behalf of his son and nephew. In June, as England was bracing herself to host the World Cup, Richard and I crossed the Channel and travelled southward through France to work the season as *stagiaires*: my cousin at L'Oustau de Baumanière, the multi-rosetted gastro-shrine at Les Baux-de-Provence and I at the Martinez in Cannes, a sumptuous marble palace on the resort's palm-fringed Croisette.

In the course of those summer months the Côte d'Azur deftly exposed my naïvety and struck my innocence a final blow. Cannes was a deliciously wicked town which now anointed me in a rite of passage rather different from the one I may have anticipated. Grand hotels like the Martinez dealt in a rough trade below stairs and pretty white boys from London were fair game in that crucible of heat and sweat, anger and resentment – a dozen nationalities, creeds and colours from around the Mediterranean Basin re-enacting Byzantine feuds in a stinking basement while plutocrats, starlets and heiresses sipped champagne on the flower-decked terraces above their heads.

I was cast as a commis in the terrace restaurant; my job to carry plates of food from the kitchen on vast trays, then clear from my station's sideboard but never to approach a client's table. Chefs de rang served at table; maîtres d'hôtel took the orders and directed the show; sommeliers presented and poured the wine; and at the pinnacle of this mighty pecking order, the restaurant manager – a vile little Napoleon called César – cruised down the ranks of starched linen, glass and polished silverware, doing his oleaginous best to harvest his baksheesh. As a commis I was required to wear a white apron beneath a white patrol jacket. On my first day I dressed with care, folding the long apron to knee length for fear of tripping if it hung much lower. Within moments of setting foot on the marble floor, César pointed at me from the far side of the terrace, curling his extended forefinger in sharp staccato movements. As I approached him he lunged at me, grabbing a tuft of sideburn, twisting the hair viciously and pulling my head down until my nose hovered six inches off the floor. "Jamais!" he barked. "Never enter my restaurant again unless your apron covers your ankles!" And to emphasize his point, he gave my ankle a sharp kicking.

Later that evening I was given a second rude awakening. My strict training regime with the boat club had failed to prepare me for this, but by now I was wilting with exhaustion, sweating heavily under my commis' tunic and my feet were in agony. Carrying a heavy tray of empties out to the *plonge* (the wash-up), I paused to catch my breath. From the other side of the hatch, a pair of hands seized my wrists and one of the plongeurs, an Algerian, hissed at me in broken English: "You wan' come bed with us?" Grinning broadly, his mate looked on and nodded encouragement. I turned on my heel and hurried back to the restaurant pursued by a barrage of rich invective in a dialect I did not recognize. Another young English commis had been telling me grim tales of the perils he encountered living in the staff dormitory block across the goods' yard by the back door. I was more fortunate. Thanks to Uncle Michael's acquaintance with the owners' of the Martinez, I found myself billeted in a large airy room at the top of the hotel with two trainees from the accounts office. But I still had to run the gauntlet of the back-of-house and eat in a staff canteen where the food dished up was made marginally less execrable by a policy which granted each one of us a bottle of rough wine a day. Cannier heads made friends with the kitchen and bribed the cooks with beer and cigarettes for a decent meal.

I survived. Perversely, I found myself slipping into a bracing rhythm, a personal survival curve to cope with a fifteen-hour working day which, aided by the esprit of the team, I rather enjoyed. By midnight, our nerve ends strung taut by the pressure of the service and the abuse flung at us by the chefs across the hotplate, we were all too hyped to fall straight into bed. So a group of us would wander into town in search of a late-night drink. It took me a while to acclimatize to the bar scene in Cannes but at a time when homosexuality was still illegal in England, gay sex – and, indeed, prostitution, dope and every other illicit pleasure – appeared to be rife on the Riviera; a startling revelation for this nineteen year old neophyte. But it wasn't quite the pleasure I was in search of, and on one memorable evening I fell into conversation with a friendly barman with whom I decided to flex my French. Observing that there were an unusual number of "PDs" (the accepted vernacular for "*pédérastes*") in his club, he sweetly pointed out that he was one too and why should I mind? His bar was a favourite haunt for the gay community of the town. I decided it was wise to move on.

After my unpromising start, in time I began to win favour with César who decided to promote me to commis sommelier – a decision which was greeted with Gallic disgruntlement by his maîtres d' who complained that my Englishness and, therefore, my ignorance in the art of wine service would undermine the integrity of the restaurant. I was pretty chuffed. The new job released me from the drudgery of fetching and clearing trays and, at last, I was passed as a suitable candidate to engage diners at their tables. There was one unique bonus to my elevation. The raising of my profile whet the edges of ancient Anglo-French rivalries with a waiting team now thirsting to shaft the upstart from across the Channel. With England hosting *La Coupe du Monde* and the home side pitted against West Germany in the final, they thought they were on a winner and I accepted bets for cash, beer and cigarettes from all of them. In the event, I made a small killing.

It didn't always go my way – I made some embarrassing blunders which sent César and his Maître Sommelier into a frenzy, delighting the others. Wine in the glass was speckled with dust as I attempted to draw corks from the necks of bottles and found them crumbling on the screw. Crisp tablecloths were spotted red by rogue droplets spilling off the lips of bottles lifted prematurely from their glasses. And more embarrassing still was the day I lost my concentration pouring a glass of rosé for an Italian television star. She was lunching with her lover on the hotel's private beach where the team from the terrace ran a canteen for the rich and beautiful who sought shade and a little refreshment after a morning's intensive sun therapy. My client was a Roman madonna in a bikini innocent of much in the way of structural support and as I leant over her right shoulder to pour the wine, my eyes fell upon a view of unsurpassed magnificence, her peach-down bosom beaded with sand. It was at this point that I forgot myself. Moments later the rosé had overflowed leaking a puddle of pinkness across the table. César was off duty that day. Her lover did not complain. And I lived to serve another lunchtime.

*

Cannes – sizzling vat of temptation – opened my eyes but left my loins still and hungry. The summer of '66 passed without a result – the hours we worked limiting my opportunities which, when they arose, I was never shy to explore. A tall, striking, auburn-haired American girl came closest to the holiday fling I yearned. Her name was Virginia – Gini – and on the evening we met she was wearing a white Dior trouser suit over a wild flamingo-coloured blouse. Chaperoned by her aunt, the two women were travelling through Europe in the footsteps of the grand tour and, for two nights, they had checked into the Martinez. At dinner on the terrace, they seemed pleased to find an Englishman taking care of their drinks – but, with Gini, it soon became obvious that the easy chatter at the table hinted at an eagerness and an intent beyond polite conversation. At the dispense bar I took a book of matches and scribbled a note in the inside flap: "Shall we meet for a drink later?" Returning to the table I knelt down as if to pick something off the floor and placed the matches by her wine glass. And when her aunt disappeared to powder her nose, we agreed to meet at the Festival, a popular bar on the Croisette, at midnight. It was a beautiful flying romance but no sooner were we holding hands than she was heading for Florence and I was being transferred upstairs to spend my final weeks on the floors as a room service waiter.

*

Blooded but not quite the initiate, I returned home that autumn to begin the new academic year glossed in a veneer of worldliness tinted green around the edges. There was still some growing up to be done. At least by the start of my ten-month placement in the trade – in the spring of the following year – I knew what might be in store. In those days the Berkeley – crowning the head of Berkeley Street – was an elderly dowager of an hotel sneering at its rival across the road, the Ritz on Piccadilly, before its owners, the Savoy Hotel Company, decamped to Wilton Place in Knightsbridge and built afresh. For all its exquisite grace and outward show of good manners, the culture of the hotel differed little from life below stairs at the Martinez. It could be a rough place.

For my first three months' training I was posted to the kitchen – a subterranean furnace, its grimy floor tiles scattered with sawdust, its ceilings strung with long spindles of fly-paper hanging like amber stalactites. The mood in this airless dungeon trembled with a simmering hostility which put me into a permanent state of fear and made me alert to the flashpoints that seemed to erupt from nowhere. It was a febrile, menacing place where hierarchy seemed to be turned on its head and where territory determined the nature of power. In the morning, the head chef sat magisterially in his glass cage conferring with his sous chefs. At midday the general manager would descend the long stone stairs to pay homage to the chief toque over a glass of champagne. And as the waiters began appearing at the hotplate waving their scrawly chits, a sous chef would bark the orders: "Ça marche! Quatre couverts! Deux consommés! Deux terrines! Un rognon! Un turbot! Deux gigots!" According to the command, each chef de partie – the section heads responsible for the larder, the sauce, the fish, the roast, the veg – would shout back "Oui chef!"

This was the disparate gang that ruled my strange new underworld. They behaved like medieval warlords – cursing, swearing, spitting venom – each minded by a platoon of commis chefs who were required to declare absolute fealty, supplying their master's needs, usually in pints of beer to sustain him through the service or to provide cover when he slipped out for a cigarette. If any commis trespassed into another's section or was deemed to have insulted the chef, there was trouble. Disputes disintegrated into sporadic battles – sometimes fought with the crowbars used for lifting hot iron rings off the raging stoves. Knives, always to hand, were another ready weapon. On one occasion I saw a Spaniard spout fountains of blood from a twelve-inch wound running the length of his arm. And on another the sauce chef – a big German – hurled an Italian commis from the larder onto the burning range. Turf wars which subsided as quickly as they arose while the chef de cuisine sipped champagne and the sous chefs looked the other way.

As a junior commis – and, worse, a management trainee, I was a target for a ritual debagging and bog-flushing in the staff changing room. I escaped only because fear and an instinct for survival found their own camouflage in anonymity and the protection of the veg chef, a tubby Frenchman who was retiring at the end of the year after three decades' service with the company. The younger cooks respected him and they left me alone. After twelve long weeks in this pit, if I learned anything it was to make his *purée de pommes de terre* into a smooth, silky, buttery ambrosia.

From here I progressed to the cocktail bar where I mastered the subtle nuances of mixing the perfect dry martini (stirred, never shaken). Thence to the restaurant where I was relieved to discover a marked improvement in my wine skills. And, finally, after a succession of quick hops through stock management, control and accounts, I landed in reception: a space in the Berkeley's front hall furnished with beautifully crafted art deco desks behind which well-spoken and immaculately groomed young men sat in morning dress or dinner jackets depending on the time of the shift. The dinner jacket I had – now I needed to find the suit and on a trainee's stipend of £8 a week, this was likely to be an expensive investment. But I was in luck, my height and build matched the departing receptionist whom I replaced and he sold me his suit for £9. Four years later I was married in it.

I had now entered a different world – hardly believing that a few feet beneath the Wilton weave of the carpets lay a kitchen where tribal feuds and vendettas were as much a part of the daily routine as the pursuit of gastronomic excellence. Here I was in my pressed suit, a white handkerchief arranged just so in its top pocket, a sober tie carefully knotted, greeting guests, checking them in and escorting them to their suites. And all in a genteel atmosphere of peace and harmony; a graciousness and a serenity for which our clients (never "customers") paid a handsome sum. The gentility of the place also promoted a predisposition to high camp – its expression rising and falling on a scale determined by the client's title or position in society.

This was the domain of Mr. Symington-Clyde, the deputy manager whom, entre nous, we called Maurice (the accent falling with heavy emphasis on the second syllable). Mr. Symington-Clyde looked upon himself as the guardian of the Berkeley's unique standards. Nothing escaped this pedant's eye. He would appear rattling an enormous bunch of keys, his hair cropped and brilliantined, a jewelled pin holding his tie in a priapic curve as it emerged from his stiff collar. He examined us carefully one by one – an inspection which considered the shine on our shoes, the state of our manicure, the angle of the silk handkerchiefs in our top pockets (which he adjusted personally), and the cut of our hair: "Time for a trim, Mr. Chapman," he pronounced flicking the top of my ear.

Dear Maurice would whip himself into a terrible lather on the days Mr. Fornara, our silver-haired and suitably patrician general manager, received a visit from the head of the Savoy Company, the legendary Sir Hugh Wontner. Fifteen minutes before Sir Hugh's expected arrival, the deputy manager would stand sentry by the hotel's entrance and as the great man stepped across the threshold, Maurice bowed a low and reverential bow before proceeding to walk backwards in long, exaggerated balletic steps, bowing again with every third reverse stride. As they approached the reception desks, we all rose from our seats and, in unison, we bowed our heads adding the words "Good morning, Sir Hugh" as he glided into Mr. Fornara's office. The door closed, Maurice heaved a sigh and headed off to the managers' dining room for a coffee and a cigarette.

Underneath the formality and the theatre, we were a lively, spirited group. I enjoyed the work and struck up a friendship with another management trainee, a Scot named Fraser Brown. The two of us were the youngest in the team and it wasn't long before I noticed that an Italian colleague had a blinding crush on him and was now beginning to make passes at me. Umberto Barella was kind, charming, extremely funny and shameless in his open adoration of Fraser. But he was also a drunk and regularly reported for duty smelling of alcohol and expensive cologne: his moon-face bloated and bald, cheeks blotched crimson and his big, doleful eyes swimming like saucers of olive oil. We teased him and he loved the banter, seeing our attention as a sign of affection which, in its way, it was. For all his sins, Umberto was an immensely likeable man although we could see that beneath his good nature and bonhomie there lay a greater angst and turbulence. Then one day he failed to show for work. A blanket of silence descended on the circumstances of his disappearance; the cause of his fate remaining unclear – the hotel, of course, keen to avoid a scandal. But word leaked out. Reports suggested he had been drinking in a pub in St. James's. After closing time he had been followed and in the early hours of the morning he was found in a gutter in Duke of York Street, drunk and battered. An ambulance rushed him to hospital but he never regained consciousness and died at noon that day. The police treated the case as murder and a man in a checked shirt was sought for questioning. Here the story fades, ending without a conclusion.

I shall always remember Umberto. And in the years that followed I would have good reason to recall this episode and reflect on the tragedy of his life; the waste of his death.

*

It was at about this time that I met Allegra – one Saturday evening at a twenty-first birthday party. I don't remember where except that it took place in a large house in the Home Counties. No great beauty, she wore the preppy good looks of an English public school education and her personality bubbled with a breezy coquettishness – a sexual energy which attracted me to her. Inevitably, she had little difficulty infecting the other males at the party with the same enthusiasm. Everyone wanted to dance with Allegra. Talk to Allegra. Flirt with Allegra. Towards the end of the evening, as the music slowed to a languorous, groping smooch, I seemed to have won the contest for her attention. Coiled together like bindweed on the dance floor, we searched slowly for each other's lips. Within a week we had become inseparable and the heartbreak of Jenny which, for so long, had refused to let me go, at last began to ease.

Allegra cooked for a living. She had passed through the Cordon Bleu school in London and had found a job serving smart lunches in the boardroom of a firm in the City. My evenings off-duty were now spent with her – at the cinema or at a favourite bistro, and it wasn't long before she invited me to supper at her place – a cosy garret high on the slopes of Notting Hill in Elgin Crescent. Her flatmates were away; we would be alone. I brought wine. There was candlelight and there was music. The anticipation was fevered. We ate. We drank. We fell into bed. The earth moved and the trumpets sounded! Hallelujah! Rejoice! At last! Next day, when I left for work, I padded up Ladbroke Grove like a liberated tiger. I had come to the Sixties late – Radio Caroline, Sergeant Pepper, the Pill – but I had got there in the end.

From this moment I was overtaken by a terrible urgency – a need somehow, to make up for lost time. I could never be sated. Like a greedy child gorging chocolate bars, I wanted more – and Allegra was no less eager. She moved flats which was better for me as her new place put her within two short stops on the Piccadilly Line. After a day spent humouring Maurice Symington-Clyde, I would race out of the Berkeley to Green Park tube station, leap up the stairs at Knightsbridge and hurry along Brompton Road to Beaufort Gardens – another lofty garret she shared with her friends.

The months passed and I returned to University for my final year – an intensive regime of study in the science and theory of modern management practice. By now Allegra and I were an established suit and our friends had begun to look upon us as a couple set for the long haul. At weekends we would often drive to Taunton to visit my parents or to rural Cheshire from where her family came and still kept a pied-à-terre after their move to London. Strangely, I never felt at home on these long hikes up the M6. Cheshire life was achingly social, its people charming enough but not quite sincere – a distinct whiff of cliquey self-satisfaction permeating its drawing rooms, an undercurrent often spiced with the hint of a tryst here or an affair there.

What did we care? We were happy and carefree, making the most of metropolitan living. We even hatched a plan to provide the capital's society hostesses with our services as cook and butler. One classified advertisement in the Evening Standard and, to everyone's astonishment, our modest adventure took off. But with the approach of my finals, the enterprise was short lived. And, closer to home, my attachment to Allegra was now beginning to set off alarm bells. My mother had a close friend who was acquainted with the Cheshire set I had been mixing in and she began whispering in her ears. Whether the stories had legs I cannot say but they were enough to confirm my parents' own misgivings and, at a stroke, Allegra was declared persona non grata in Taunton. Fearful that our relationship was heading for the altar and determined to put an end to it, my father called me home for the weekend. Suddenly, the clock had rewound to my childhood. I was under their spell again – doing as I was told.

We sat in the penthouse – their airy sitting room at the top of the hotel – my father in his tall wing chair, me on the bergère sofa. It was, I remember, a difficult and painful interview – as much, I think, for him as it was for me. True to his nature, he spoke gently, never once criticizing Allegra, nor did he allude to the gossip Etty had been hearing. I had little to say, overcome by a temporary paralysis as I sat and listened; part of my mind sinking into a state of denial, another into confusion, and another still being persuaded by his sheer reasonableness and common sense when he expressed his concern about my degree, my future prospects and the need to make my way in the world before settling down. He went on to field the old clichés of pebbles on the beach and fishes in the sea, my inexperience and the risks of commitment at such a young age. In short, I must realize that there was no future with Allegra and it was unfair on her to suggest there might be.

I tried to explain that I had made no promises but, in truth, I knew I was in pretty deep. Allegra's parents had practically adopted me as a member of the family and her mother had begun dropping hints. I was riding a flood and refusing to admit I needed a lifebelt. My gut curdled into knots as a feeling of wretchedness swept through my body. I was lost – reality and truth like hostile aliens ambushing me out of a cloudless sky. I refused to believe my emotions were out of control – blinded by what my father saw as a mad, sexually-charged infatuation. Besides, my twenty-first birthday had been and gone and I was mature enough to regulate my own private life. I resented this brutal intervention. Slowly he talked me round and through all the emotional bruising and pain he succeeded in touching some deep instinct inside my heart to persuade me.

I agreed to the split but in my distress I didn't know how. Should I meet Allegra? Tell her to her face? My father was emphatic. No, he said, better to write her a letter. I offered no resistance and he went on to help me draft the words. By now I was living flotsam washed up in my own head and I returned to London in a daze, unable to think or do anything more than creep quietly back into the house in Westbourne Terrace, ignore my flatmates and close the door to my bedroom.

The fallout was swift and unpleasant – Allegra's humiliation cruel – the letter a cowardly act. She saw through it and heaped her contempt upon my shame and guilt. That night in bed I made a solemn vow never to allow my parents to interfere in my private life again.

Time passed and in spite of my misery I seemed to have acquired the knack of finding an occasional companion to share my bed. But these were joyless moments and I'd wake the next day wondering why I'd bothered. Then, early one evening I was sitting in the kitchen at Westbourne Terrace, eating toast and sipping a mug of Nescafé when I heard the doorbell ring. My cousin Richard answered the call and a sound of footsteps approached down the tiled corridor. I felt the light touch of a hand brushing the nape of my neck. I knew those fingers and I knew the voice. "Hello Kit!" she said.

It was fatal – our repressed passions exploding into flames once again; our lovemaking taking on a new piquancy, this time as an illicit union to be kept secret from the meddlesome gaze of parents. But it could not endure for long. Our lives had moved on, the original foundations of the affair fractured by events. I was graduating and had landed a peach of a job with a leading London advertising agency. Our trust in each other had been shaken and we were both beginning to drift into other relationships. It was over.

A year later, in the spring of 1971, I met Louise.

*

Part Six

Gerald's Great Struggle

Gerald as Richard III at Taunton School

Diodati – Summer 2007

Difficult to believe that a year has passed since I began this family tale, sitting here at my blue-topped table on Aristotle's. It's early morning, my favourite moment in the island's day, and my thoughts now turn to Gerald, my brother. It is time I told his story.

Awake before dawn, I make myself a mug of tea and climb the long flight of geranium-clad steps to my perch to watch the sun rise. Framed by the terracotta pantiles of the house below me, a clear sky above and the young pines either side of the terrace, I sit awestruck to witness one of nature's great majestic pageants. A five-minute show of heart-stopping beauty. The bay is a rippling chiaroscuro of stained glass as a single bird heralds the approach of daybreak and, way off in the far distance, the massed voices of seagulls clamour like kettledrums. Otherwise perfect peace. At a few minutes after six o'clock, the first fiery beam bursts into view – a crimson spike shooting off the mountain ridge above Skopelos. Then the sun – a vast burning globe – appears to move slowly to the right, rolling along the crest of the massif until the cliff gently lifts it into the sky at an angle of forty-five degrees. As the minutes pass, Homer's rosy finger, evident from the first, expands from stiletto to spatula – a shining milky-pink ribbon streaking across the sea to divide the archipelago in two. It is a sight beyond creation. Beyond scientific understanding. A vision that deserves worship.

As I stare, this brilliant shaft of light, like a maritime border – a liquid frontier post separating the landward side of the bay from the open sea – leads me to wonder about the mystery of family and the ties of blood. How two siblings, brothers, emerge from the seed of one father, the womb of one mother, share the same expanse of water and yet, like the islands before my eyes, are different in shape, each belonging to its own unique universe.

This notion of unity and division suggests itself again with my mother's conscientious assembly of her children's archives – her boxes within boxes. Mine came in a large dress box, Gerald's in a Harrods hatbox – and within each were the chocolate boxes revealing their myriad of little treasures. When I opened these two cardboard troves side by side, the most striking discovery was our baby hair lovingly preserved in jewel compacts: my first trimmed locks tied with a white ribbon, Gerald's – in greater profusion – wrapped in tissue paper. Mine blond, Gerald's dark as Kalamata olives. Each compact containing my mother's embossed visiting card – "Mrs. Etty Chapman" – where, on the back, she had written: "Christopher's lovely hair 1948" and "Geraldo's lovely curls! August 1951." I do not recall my first haircut but it took place sooner after my birth than Gerald's whose first date with a pair of scissors I do remember because it nearly broke my mother's heart, such was the emotional tremor that shook the family.

The four snapshots of Gerald taken at his first birthday party in Salonica in November 1950 already celebrated my brother's head of luxuriant curls. By the summer of the following year his hair was out of control and Etty had taken to planting a kirby grip in his forehead to restrain the massed crop from cascading into his eyes. Worse, to my father's embarrassment, Gerald's angelic looks inevitably misled friends and acquaintances into thinking he was a little girl. And so his gorgeous locks were snipped, then delicately wrapped in tissue paper and deposited with my mother's card in their compact: a precious memento – a token of what might have been – along with a trio of pearly-white milk teeth. The ambiguity resolved, at last I knew I had a brother, my parents a handsome second son and the family's life settled down once again.

*

From the moment of his birth, Gerald's vigour and joie signalled a personality and a drive which promised to touch all our lives. Recognizing herself in

194

him, my mother in particular saw a child destined to shine. She was in thrall to him. And by the early years of his passage through Taunton School, his intellect and his artistic sensibilities soon became evident. At the end of his spell in Miss Lowman-Lang's Kindergarten – the youngest pupil in her brood – Gerald emerged top of the class with a full bag of A grades – a position he rarely vacated in the next eleven years.

It was through this period of our childhood and adolescence – before university, independence and careers led us down different paths – that my brother and I were closest. And in growing up together we shared the same feelings of restraint – the controlling force exerted by Peter and, especially, Etty on our lives. Of course we loved them, but the nature of that love was founded on an unthinking sense of duty and we would often express our devotion and obedience in richly embroidered language because this is what Etty expected. One early letter from Gerald begins: "My dearest, lovable, most affectionate, most wonderful in all the world Mummy ..." It became a charade – a game, I think, my brother played more convincingly than me. But as children we never discussed the darker emotions lying hidden within our souls. This is how life was; this is what we knew. Much later – after he had left Cambridge – Gerald would unburden his heart in a long and distressing essay to his father.

Letters, letters – dozens of letters spilled out of the Harrods hatbox. All these in addition to the string-tied bundles I had discovered at the bottom of Peter's black deed box along with Henry Prüger's suicide note and other family papers. My brother was a remarkable correspondent – a habit which began even before Miss Lang had completed his instruction in the basics of English spelling. His first letter was addressed to the North Pole and read: "Dear Father Christmas, Will you please bring me a red and gray spays sut and a pocit nife. Love and kissis xxxx Gerald." But progress was rapid and as he rose through the preparatory school, his compositions were winning prizes – a literary success, I am sure, which owed something to his ability to communicate and interpret his subject with exquisite precision. He had just turned nine when he wrote to Peter and Etty from Grindelwald in Switzerland where we skied each year with family friends who acted as our guardians for a fortnight over the New Year holiday. My father was adamant that, as children, one of the essentials of a healthy constitution relied on regularity in the digestive system. As this was Gerald's first trip to Grindelwald, the importance of regularity had been drummed into him and so, in writing home, he was anxious to reassure his daddy that he had been functioning satisfactorily in this department. The final paragraph of his letter read: "I am doing KAKA nearly every day, <u>nearly</u> because we have to go to ski school straight after breakfast, so I try to do it in the afternoon. Love and many kisses, Gerald. PS Kit sends <u>his</u> love too."

Trawling through this extraordinary cache of early letters I was struck by the fast emergence of Gerald's intellectual and artistic curiosity – an articulate voice which hinted at a precocity, except that this was never an aspect of his character apparent to me. He was a carefree child – natural, fun, high-spirited and, to my father's occasional dismay, full of mischief. The two of us were affectionate brothers – protective towards one another – and I was never self-conscious about his special gifts. We enjoyed each other's company even if, at times, I behaved like a typically bossy big brother, sending him off in search of string, crates, boxes and the other materials we needed to construct our camps and obstacle courses amid the twelfth century remains of the Castle's gardens.

Naïve and oblivious to Gerald's rising star though I may have been, a number of signs marked him out as a young boy touched by unusual promise. Where I collected stamps, he created his own museum – a collection of artefacts from coins to shells and fossils and archaeological pieces, all logged, labelled and displayed in a large glass cabinet in his bedroom. Summer holidays in Greece mixed island beaches with ancient sites: the Acropolis in Athens, Delphi, Olympia, Epidaurus, Mycenae, Knossos – we visited them all and Gerald, guarded closely by Etty, would lift sculpted fragments strewn like debris which ended up in his cabinet at home. Today, spread on the table in front of me, memories of these family holidays flood back as I stare at a set of 10x8 photographs taken of Gerald, aged eleven or twelve, striding through the Temple of Apollo in the blazing August heat. Etty is by his side wearing a white headscarf and enormous sunglasses – Audrey Hepburn in

Breakfast at Tiffany's, except this is Delphi not New York City. They make perfect paparazzi snaps. Ideal for the pages of Hello! or Paris Match. The photographer, a local stringer, is clearly mesmerized by the pair. Meanwhile Peter and I are nowhere to be seen.

By now Gerald had graduated to the senior school and on his thirteenth birthday he wrote to Peter and Etty from Loveday, his boarding house, to thank them for the presents they had sent him: "Oh, Daddy and Mummy, what a lovely surprise you gave me. I had always wanted such books as the Illiad (sic) and especially the Aenied (or how you spell it). They will give me endless pleasure in reading them." And in another letter the same term, he tells them about his success in an auction of house newspapers: "I managed to get all the Sunday Times of the whole term for 7/3d [36p]. As this includes the paper, the magazine section and the colour section, it was a fair bargain."

But for all his winning ways – both in the classroom and, more modestly, on the games field – in his junior years at Taunton School, Gerald was bullied – a problem I never suffered to any great degree beyond the usual sneers and sniggers, and the rough and tumble of the dormitory and locker-room. Gerald, I suspect, became a target because some hooligans saw him as too bookish, too clever and too damn pretty – his dark Mediterranean looks setting him apart from the rest. As his brother, I became increasingly concerned and alerted Peter and Etty in my own correspondence home: "I think you must talk to Gerald because he is being bullied by boys at school," I wrote. "I am sure he is being hurt although he does not say so." Gerald's response came in a forlorn mixture of stoicism and despair: "… certain people have just picked on me and it gets me down," he complained in answer to his parents' concerns. "It is not so bad when you are new but now senior boys are simply beastly to me. Oh well, I suppose it will wear off some day, but sometimes I just get sick of it and wish I was with you. The reason that I don't go to Mr. Wright [Gerald's housemaster] is all to do with being a border [sic] and I must face up to it myself."

Gerald's misery was soon eclipsed by an arena that would grow into a passion and become his life's work – the theatre. The break came when he was cast as Dr. Lupin, a drunken parson, in the junior play – a production of *Sweeney Todd, Demon Barber of Fleet Street*. Both housemaster and J.G. Leathem, the head, praised his performance in their reports at the end of the spring term of 1963. "He delighted us all," enthused Mr. Wright. "I liked his acting," scrawled JGL, "especially his clear diction." By the autumn of the same year Gerald was close to turning fourteen when he won his first part in a major school production of Ben Jonson's *The Alchemist* – as Ananias, a Deacon of Amsterdam. The play posed a worry for the adolescent actor. "My voice tends to change tone and register sometimes," he explained to Peter and Etty, "but I think I have mastered it. I must speak lower than my normal voice and keep it in the same pitch and tone with differing volumes to avoid being monotonous." He continued: "I am rather proud of myself in that I have to speak the most famous line in the play – 'Thou look'st like Antichrist in that lewd hat.' I shall therefore certainly make a good show of it. Just as a matter of interest I shall be wearing a dog collar; a straight front and long sides wig, and a lovely huge Puritan hat!" Two years later, as he entered the Sixth Form, Gerald was topping the bill and being lionized by the school establishment. "His Richard III was a tour de force for a boy of his age," exclaimed his housemaster.

*

Gerald's transition into the Sixth Form was a seamless continuation of his academic superiority at the school – particularly in English. Although the alphas and the prizes chased him all the way, a deeper predicament was rising to the surface of his moral consciousness. With the retirement of J.G. Leathem in the summer of 1966, the new academic year saw the arrival of Dr. John Rae as headmaster. Ambitious, radical, controversial, Rae was only thirty-four when he was appointed and then remained in post for a brief four years before moving on to become famous in the seventies and eighties as headmaster of Westminster School. At Taunton he was quick to make his mark – roughing up the dinosaurs in the staff common room and expelling a ring of dope-smoking seniors. If he had an aim, it was to nurture academic excellence and in Gerald he saw a bright and engaging student whom he was keen to promote for early entry into Cambridge. He and his wife Daphne had already established a friendship with Peter and Etty through their visits to the Castle during the interview and appointment process – and, besides, Peter was a school governor. Sadly, John Rae died in December 2006 before I could speak to him but Daphne's memories of Gerald remain remarkably vivid: "He was an extremely handsome young man," she told me. "John liked him enormously and he was excessively polite to me. I shall never forget watching him walking in the school grounds with Etty – his arms linked through hers. He was the only pupil I ever saw to show affection to his mother in public – he had a tremendous adoration for Etty."

*

The precise facts surrounding the turbulent events of that autumn term in 1966 are unclear. Gerald had entered the upper sixth still two months short of his seventeenth birthday. In addition to his A-level syllabus, he was working hard on his early entry examination for Cambridge, receiving one-on-one tuition from his English, French and history tutors. The school's expectations were high and Gerald was feeling the pressure – the burden of fulfilling the hopes of his masters and headmaster resting heavily on his young shoulders. And then, one Sunday afternoon, he was caught having sex with a younger boy. Reporting to the headmaster's study, John Rae caned him.

For Gerald this traumatic episode was set to haunt him for the next eight years – a dark moment in his life which filled him with shame and guilt and a profound sense of self-loathing. It became an incident he submerged beneath his consciousness until he told his friend and confidant Peter Judd, a fellow undergraduate at Trinity Hall who, after leaving Cambridge, took holy orders and is now Dean of Chelmsford. I knew nothing of these events until earlier this year when I met the Dean in London to talk about my brother. Daphne Rae also recalls this incident and confirms Peter Judd's impression that Dr. Rae would have spent time with Gerald – giving him a Christian-cum-theological perspective on homosexuality. This was also a period in our social history when, technically anyway, male homosexuality was still a criminal offence. While attitudes were changing, they remained hostile and, in an English public school, shockingly hypocritical. But where many a headmaster might have expelled Gerald, Rae, who would have been troubled by Gerald's affair with a younger boy, was more understanding. He wanted to help his star pupil.

But, in Gerald's heart and mind, the moral struggle he faced was huge. He had already embraced Christianity and attended church as an Anglican. With John Rae's words ringing in his ears, his great trial now was to unscramble and make sense of the confusing mores of the times. The Wolfenden Committee had sat and reported a decade before; decriminalisation through the Sexual Offences Act stood within a few months of receiving Royal Assent; but still the old views about homosexuality persisted: that it was a social evil, a perversion, even a contagious medical condition requiring treatment. In Torquay, Uncle Michael suddenly found himself confronting the problem with his youngest, our cousin Alexander who, aged twenty-one, bluntly and bravely 'came out'. His father's reaction when he heard the news was to march his son down to the family doctor. In Taunton, Michael's brother reacted quite differently – each man, in his own particular way, finding the wounds of 1929 reopened, painful echoes of the secret life of their own father. When John Rae met Peter and Etty to talk about Gerald, my father lapsed into a deep reflective silence while my mother smothered her initial shock in a display of complete incomprehension. "Why? Why?" she cried, ultimately convincing herself that this was just a passing phase in her son's progress towards manhood, a trivial incident quickly forgotten.

The emotional tangle now coiling inside Gerald's whole being bore its inevitable consequence. His application for early entry into Cambridge failed – a disappointing result, his tutors surmised, owing to his inexperience. A year later, in the autumn of 1967, Gerald returned to Taunton for one final term to sit the English Open Examination for Cambridge. This time he sailed through narrowly missing an exhibition. In December, Dr. Rae sat down to write Gerald's last headmaster's report:

"He has been an outstanding senior member of the school community. He has achieved that very rare goal of being an influence for good without remaining (as some senior boys do) tied to the narrow world of school affairs; he has been loyal to the community without losing his individuality.

"I am sure he will do well because he combines ambition with a strong personality and sensitivity to the needs of others. He does not need good luck but I wish him it all the same! I hope we shall see something of him in the future."

J.M.R.

*

Much like the pattern Peter and Etty adopted with my own education, during Gerald's sixth form years, they packed him off to Lausanne in Switzerland for part of the spring and summer holidays to improve his grasp of the French language. His long letters home – often running to eight or ten pages of tightly written narrative – reveal a wonderful mix of gossip, news and cultural exposition. At times they also betray the early signs of a recurring melancholy and loneliness which would dog him throughout his life.

At that moment in the summer of '66 when I was being introduced to the fleshly attractions of the Côte d'Azur, Gerald was mounting a higher plane. In one letter he writes: "… I have become increasingly aware of truth and beauty, of what is required at the right time, of honesty of mind and soul, and the more I open my eyes in this way the more I develop a sense of values, of proportion, the more I clarify my ideas, and assume a sensibility for certain things which I never had before. This clarification of thought will, I hope, lead to clarification of expression, to a more balanced and worthwhile life, to a confidence in myself and other people that will overcome these bouts, often long ones, of mental and spiritual lethargy."

But Gerald's introspection comes and goes with his state of mind. In

Lausanne he lives with M. et Mme. Noir and family in their large house on the Avenue de Rumine. His descriptions of the family's routines and habits ["I have shaken hands God knows how many times."] are minute and often quite comic: "I was told," he writes, "that cette maison 'est un peu extraordinaire' and showed the various eccentricities like the *very special* way one must open the WC door!" And later he pokes fun at the rituals of the house at meal times: "The conventions governing eating are quite impractical, BUT VERY POLITE!! Each item of food – e.g. meat, carrots, salad, etc. is eaten separately and in two rounds. In other words one begins with carrots – having eaten this, one eats a second lot of carrots. After this two lots of meat, then two lots of salad. C'est très drôle!"

Gerald is also quite calculating in the messages he wants to send home to his parents – and in particular to his mother. In a letter he writes after watching the World Cup final on television, he describes his curriculum at the University and his fellow classmates – a group of students drawn from all over Europe: "I'm sitting next to the Greek girl [one Louise Papayannis] that I told you about in all my lessons. She's really very nice and we have great fun together speaking Greek so that no one else understands a blind word of which we're talking! There are also masses of Swedish girls…" Brightly crafted words which ring a trifle hollow coming, as they do, little more than a month before his fateful autumn term at Taunton School when calamity strikes him down.

In the Easter holiday the following year, as he is preparing to sit his A-levels, Gerald returns to Lausanne and the Noir household one last time. He writes two letters home – the tone in each contrasting starkly with those of the summer before. Gone is the breezy gossip about the classroom or the doings on the Avenue de Rumine. In their place Gerald is flexing his critical faculties – in essay form rather than as correspondence to his parents – on subjects ranging from philosophy and politics ("Ibsen was not so far wrong when he said 'The minority is always right'.") to contemporary plays, films and concerts he has attended. More poignantly, he uses two Ingmar Bergman films – *The Communicants* and *The Silence* – as scarcely veiled references to his own emotional and sexual turmoil. The films – part of a trilogy – deal with loneliness, spiritual emptiness (*The Silence* referring to God's silence) and emotional isolation – classic Bergman themes. Scornful of the romanticism of "the Zhivago and Lawrence type" of film which Peter and Etty adored, Gerald rues their popularity "at the expense of the stark reality and symbolic poetry of Bergman." Of course, Peter and Etty would have hated Bergman but Gerald now is determined to inflict his personal analysis upon them. "The theme of the film [*The Silence*]," he begins, "is, quite bluntly, sexual perversion; and 'the silence' itself is the lack of meaningful rapport between humans that leads to sexual perversion."

Later in the essay, for fear his besieged audience might still miss the point, he drives home this "misanthropic idea" by referring to Nicol Williamson's solo role in Gogol's *The Diary of a Madman* which he had seen in London a month before: "It was an incredible performance of a man whose control over his desire of self-indulgence in order to overcome his loneliness leads him to insanity."

Receiving this letter-essay in Taunton, the first page of eight dated neatly "14.iv.67", Peter and Etty's reactions were predictable, needing little imagination on my part. My mother, lost in the maze of Gerald's words, would have been oblivious of any real message which, besides, would have blurred into an instinctive sense of pride at the erudition of her clever boy. Throughout her life, almost regardless of the circumstances, however dramatic, she had a favourite Greek motto, a mantra she constantly repeated: "όλα ωραία, όλα καλά" ("all is beautiful, all is well"). Life's little complications best smothered in laughter and good cheer. My father, quiet and reclusive at these moments, would have been shocked, the pain of Gerald's commentary drilling deep into his heart, disturbed that his seventeen year old son was capable of writing in these terms to his parents.

Gerald knew exactly what he was doing. He wanted to hurt, shock, shake them because he yearned to be heard and understood. After the events of the previous autumn, he was angry and frightened, his feelings of vulnerability turned into a self-hatred which he transfered onto them as a reaction to the controlling regime of his upbringing. In defiance of their conservative middle-class habits, this was his first major assault on their bourgeois values. Certainly he loved his parents, but it was a love mixed with huge resentment. Now he wanted to make a raw appeal for what he described as "the lack of meaningful rapport between humans" – a plea for the understanding he could neither feel nor see in Peter and Etty: their "silence". Like an echoing cry in the dark, Gerald was searching for the truth about himself and, in that search, he was grasping at the truths of Bergman and Gogol.

*

1968. The weather in Vienna was bitter – "Siberian", Gerald called it. He'd just arrived at the Prinz Eugen, an unprepossessing modern four-star hotel opposite the Südbahnhof, a ten-minute tram ride from the imperial splendours of the centre. Herr Direktor Thaler, who – through the family's connections – had agreed to take him on in the reception office, greeted him warmly and an elderly porter showed him up to a small room on the second floor. Small, perhaps, but Gerald liked it because the room had everything he needed: a good radiator to keep him warm, a wash basin, a large bed, a table and chair, a telephone and a chest of drawers.

It was mid-January and business was slack, his duties light. By the end of the first week, he had registered for a course of fifty German lessons at the University, opened a bank account and joined the choir – composed, mostly, of students from the Musik Akademie – of Christ Church, the Anglican church next to the British Embassy. He also joined the library of the British Council. With a nine-month gap to fill before going up to Cambridge, he was determined to make the most of his paternal ancestors' great capital city. The atmosphere of Vienna, he tells Peter and Etty, "still lingers with the ghosts of Franz Joseph." In no time he takes the city to his heart, seduced by its unique charm, characterized in his imagination by the squealing brakes and clanging bells of the red trams.

At work Gerald soon grows bored. With little to do in the reception office, he fills the dull hours of his shifts rehearsing his German verbs and memorizing his lists of vocabulary. "I've come to be able to speak incorrectly but fluently quite quickly," he says, promising to write a letter home in German. Off duty he sets out to explore, visiting the Spanish Riding School, the Hofburg, the Belvedere Palace and all the main churches: "My impression of these," he observes, commenting on Vienna's ecclesiastical architecture, "was that they looked rather better outside than in." Predictably all his other spare moments are consumed by the performing arts – Schiller's *Maria Stuart* at the theatre, concerts of Beethoven's symphonies and the excitement of securing a ticket to watch Karl Richter conducting the Bach St. Matthew Passion. But he is outraged by the advertised prices of seats at the Staatsoper: "Not only immoral," he complains, "but contrary to good artistic policy!"

In the early weeks after his arrival, the enthusiasms Vienna inspires in his impressionable mind are tempered only by a worry about the food which he finds expensive and not always to his taste. But even this little problem dissolves when he discovers the Musik Akademie's communal dining hall where he is able to buy three courses – a soup, a main and a pudding – for just eight Austrian schillings. From now on he adopts a simple benchmark for judging menus posted outside eating places: the cost of a Coca Cola; a price, he finds, which varies between four and five and a half schillings. At the Musik Akademie, a Coke is only three schillings. And for those occasions when he feels a little peckish, he keeps a supply of oranges and macaroons in his bedroom.

But it is to the Church that Gerald turns for much of his social life – a community he describes as "very odd, but immensely stimulating" thanks largely to the charisma of its forty-two year old chaplain, Peter Spink, who – with all his evangelical Protestantism – goes affectionately by the name of Father Peter, and whom Gerald brands firmly as "an awfully good man." It was by a chance series of coincidences that I came to meet Father Peter some years ago. At the time, he was running the Omega Order, his pioneering inter-faith movement based at Winford Manor near Bristol. If I had known then what I know now, I would have paid more attention to his gentle efforts to tell me about my brother. But, lost in my own preoccupations, I missed the moment and I regret it. Father Peter is eighty-one now and a victim of

Parkinson's although the disciplines of his faith refuse to allow the disease to overcome his resolute spirit. For me, it just made talking about the rape a little more difficult.

It began innocently enough. Gerald had made friends with two Austrians – waiters at the Prinz Eugen – who took him out one evening to Grinzing, a pretty village-like suburb of Vienna famed for its Heurigen, its wine taverns. In a letter home, he takes up the story: "The wine proved even more potent than I imagined and after only half-a-litre I was pretty far gone – but in a nice way! My tongue really loosened then, and I was speaking in German v. freely." Inevitably, an account of the events that followed is omitted from the letter to Peter and Etty. Back in Vienna, the two men cornered him – helplessly drunk – and raped him. Traumatized he turned to his confessor.

Father Peter faced a distressed and lonely eighteen year old boy – a young man sinking under the weight of a guilt which was undeserved; split in his mind about his family, unhappy with the way he had to partition his life which he saw as a living deceit. Etty and Peter knew there had been a crisis. Peter, privately, made his own broad estimate of the circumstances. And an appeal to Etty's Orthodox faith through Father Peter – as much an appeal to the heart – persuaded her to accept Gerald's position that this was a matter to be dealt with by the Church and the grace of God. For now Father Peter set about the task of soothing and mending a fractured soul. He helped Gerald understand the meaning of God's grace, that it was a condition he must allow to develop and grow within himself: "Start where you are with what you 've got," he told him, "and begin to build bridges within yourself."

This was the province of Peter Spink's special gifts. He led lost souls through their crises by helping them make meaningful connections, positive contacts. His life's endeavour in the inter-faith movement aimed to achieve a greater understanding between the Churches through the expression of the human spirit. For him, the foundations of human understanding began with a common spirituality. That's what counted. And this is where he succeeded with Gerald. When he was invited to say the Anglican Mass in the Greek Orthodox Church in Baden, he took Gerald with him and introduced him to the Bishop. A little later, a lighter-hearted, happier son wrote to his parents: "I'm now teaching a Greek girl English conversation five times a week (200 schillings income every week). Her uncle is the Bishop of the Greek Orthodox Church in all Austria, Italy and Hungary – very posh!"

Father Peter also recognized Gerald's love of theatre. One of his last stage successes at school had been in T.S. Eliot's *Murder in the Cathedral* – a play which made a profound impression on him. So he needed little persuasion when his chaplain asked him to direct his own production in the Church. For Gerald this was an exciting break and, in Taunton, Peter and Etty – anxious to support their son – laid plans to travel to Vienna in May. Would it be a black tie occasion? they wanted to know. "No!" replied Gerald. "The occasion will most certainly *not* be one for dinner-jacket, not in a church anyway!" He sees the play "mostly as an act of worship rather than dramatic entertainment," and then adds: "I think, I hope, T.S. Eliot would agree." (Given the poet's Anglo-Catholic leanings, he probably would.) But Gerald knows his parents, knows their love of dressing-up, and sensing he may have sounded too scolding in his injunction goes on… "This does not mean that Daddy need not bring his dinner-jacket. On the contrary, if you want to go to the opera, or to a concert… you will almost certainly have to wear a dinner-jacket."

A month later, two weeks before the first performance, his tone is more subdued. He confirms the arrangements he has made: tickets for the opera, a hair appointment for Etty at the Bristol. And then he adds: "I expect you heard from Kit that *Murder..* has fallen through. It was a great disappointment to us all but it could not be helped." There had been difficulties in casting and rehearsals – the Chorus proving especially problematical.

The renewed bout of melancholy seems to have started a little before, with Easter – the pressures of his work on the play and its significance colliding in his mind with the meaning of Holy Week. He felt the burden of his beliefs challenging him and it had made him ill. His words home on the sixteenth of April are brief and vague: "I was feeling a little low after last week, not only because I had been unwell, but also being Holy Week, there were lots of things happening and much to think about"… Contemplating Christ's agony and confronting his own? Wondering about the Resurrection and asking what hope of rescue there was for himself? The living betrayal of his own beliefs? His worthiness of accepting the Eucharist? The reconciliation of his faith, God's grace and his sexuality? There had been temptations which he had successfully resisted. "I've made friends with the young chef (he's only about 25)," he tells Peter and Etty in an earlier letter, "so he sometimes gives me extra things to nibble!" Later, much later – after Trinity Hall – he confides in his undergraduate friend Peter Judd that the chef fancied him, wanted to bed him. Gerald declined and regretted it. "What a fool I was," he tells his friend. And the forgiveness of sins? Is there infinite forgiveness for sins infinitely, wilfully repeated?

*

Gerald's letters from Vienna in that winter and spring of '68 show my brother as a master of light and shadow and disguise – feeding his parents stories he knows will ring with approval, dancing around the edges of his darker secrets and anxieties. He is better playing the game away than at home where so many of my recollections are of rows and shouting matches and doors slammed – and always for the most trivial reasons: the length and cleanliness of his hair; what he wanted to wear (a Che Guevara T-shirt); what Etty wanted him to wear (a suit); the girls he should dance with at parties (he'd choose the fattest and spottiest just to annoy her). But the Vienna correspondence reveals a son who is devoted and loving, clever at engaging his parents' enthusiasms in his own cultural pursuits (raving about a Tosca or Nureyev dancing *Swan Lake* at the Staatsoper), and diverting their attention away from his inner struggle. In response Peter and Etty rise to his artistic and aesthetic passions by sending him cuttings from the English press and going to plays which he urges them to see.

Yet the many contradictions of his existence would become a defining aspect of his personality: the bohemian who was equally at home with luxury and extravagance; the red-blooded socialist mixing amiably with plutocrats and industrialists. "All the world's a stage" and he could play any part on it – a theatrical chameleon at ease in any costume. Vilifying the bourgeoisie and drinking from their cup. Screaming at his mother and adoring her. In Gerald's political mindset, the offer of a free ticket to the Opera Ball at the Staatsoper – the most glamorous and expensive in Vienna's winter season of society balls – deserved to be declined in disgust. But no, he accepts, he goes and he loves it – the glittering party acquiring a piquant edge when a protester in the gallery hurls hundreds of anti-Vietnam leaflets onto the throng of white-tied gentlemen waltzing their elegantly gowned partners around the dance floor below – the entire spectacle, from protest to the prankster's arrest, captured on national television. "It was the most wonderful evening I've ever spent," he writes. "I arrived back at the hotel, after dancing the whole length of the Belvedere Park, at ten past seven just when the night porter was going home … It is now my ambition to escort my Mummy to the Wiener Opernball with her fabulous long white dress, or perhaps her turquoise one! I don't think Kit, with all his swish parties in aristocratic London, can match up to this one! It was simply fantastic."

Later in the year, in July, I travelled to Vienna and spent a few days with Gerald before his return to England. Through the British Council he helped me find a job as an English tutor to a teenager whose family lived in a remote village near Graz in southern Austria. Vienna was hot and I was pleased to escape into the countryside. But those few days in the capital turned into a happy reunion – my brother leading me on a whirlwind tour of the sights, effervescing with gossip and information, introducing me to his favourite cafés. He did not take me to Christ Church. I did not meet Father Peter. No hint of his troubles.

*

Squeezed snugly on the Backs by its grander cousins Trinity and Clare, Trinity Hall – one of the smallest and oldest of the Cambridge colleges – hummed, all abuzz. The scrum around the porters' lodge was chaotic but good humoured, voices raised in nervous excitement; mothers, fathers, their sons dragging cases, trunks, boxes and all the paraphernalia of freshers arriving for the new term. It was early October, a chilly afternoon, and waiting his turn, one nineteen year old stood taking in the scene in front of him. He had travelled up from Kent alone and felt a little lost in the melee – his parents deciding to stay behind. One family group caught his eye: father – tall, straight-backed, moustached, his overcoat emphasizing a military bearing; mother – dark, striking, elegant, a fox stole about her shoulders; and son – in tweed jacket and tie, reflecting the handsome Mediterranean looks of his mother. Their animated chatter made the diffident young man feel a little envious; that he could not share the excitement with his own family.

Eventually, the porters directed the new undergraduates to their rooms – Peter Judd to Staircase A; Gerald with Etty and Peter to Staircase S. As they crossed Front Court, the intimate – even cosy – stateliness of its honeyed Georgian architecture filled them with pride and a reassuring sense of anticipation. Later Gerald would recite the words of Henry James: "If I were called upon to mention the prettiest corner of the world, I should draw a thoughtful sigh and point the way to the gardens of Trinity Hall."

But that sense of reassurance very quickly melted away. After a week, Gerald scrawled a hurried postcard home: "The atmosphere is pressurized and highly competitive," he writes. "One's afraid to get left behind … Work is far too much to cope with at present, and the blasé attitude of some scholars hardly helps. So many talented and clever people everywhere – unbelievable!" The alarm button in Taunton bounced straight up to me in London. From the kitchen table in Westbourne Terrace, I wrote a soothing note to Etty and Peter: "Don't worry about Gerald," I said, promising to visit him at the weekend. "He's just been taken slightly aback that there may be other people in this world as good or even better than him intellectually! At school, he was the best. Now he's in among the best of the rest of the schools in Great Britain – so naturally he's feeling the push. Once he gets used to the pressure he'll think nothing of it."

It was an easy prediction to make. Catching his breath, the rhythms of life at Cambridge soon became a pleasure and an inspiration in equal measure. One evening, a few weeks into that first term, he and Peter Judd were dining in Hall when they found themselves seated next to each other. After they had eaten, Gerald invited his new acquaintance back to his room for coffee. "That's wonderful!" he said pointing at his gramophone and an LP of Benjamin Britten's *Missa Brevis*. "Put it on while I get the coffee." Peter gently lifted the stylus onto the turntable. Within seconds Gerald had burst back into the room in a state of agitation. "You idiot!" he bawled. "You've put it on the wrong speed." An unpromising start. But from this faltering introduction – fondly remembered thirty-nine years on by the present Dean of Chelmsford – there sprang an enduring friendship, one which was undemanding but mutually pastoral where each man, in his own way, looked out for the well-being of the other.

At the end of their first year, the new-found chums, like a pair of romantic poets setting out on the grand tour, packed themselves off to Florence and Renaissance Tuscany for a holiday. Peter suspected Gerald's sexual tendencies from the beginning but, for now, there was no hint, no mention of the moral battle raging inside him. That was to come later. At Trinity Hall, Gerald mixed with a racy crowd – a social elite from which his shy friend felt excluded. He recalls one evening in the college bar when Gerald made a rakish entrance calling loudly for someone to lend him a condom – he'd met a girl, he needed equipping. One member of his circle dug into his pockets and, lifting his arm in the air with a flourish, called: "Gerald! Have two!" In Florence there were no such displays of sexual brio. Florence was cast as a moment of artistic purity and the pursuit of the aesthetic. In the tent they shared that summer, the two were scrupulously private – never dreaming of changing in front of one another. Meanwhile, in neighbouring tents, the occupants were kept awake at night by the Cambridge pair indulging in high-minded debates on art, literature and philosophy. "Our conversations," the Dean confessed, "were fearfully pretentious!"

*

It had been a good year, 1969. I had graduated and bagged a plum job in a leading London advertising agency, and Gerald was happily settled in Cambridge. As he entered his second year that autumn – billeted now in student lodgings in Bateman Street – all seemed to be well. And at Trinity Hall, the College had appointed a new Chaplain, The Reverend Dr. Anthony Phillips, whom Gerald liked. He enjoyed taking Holy Communion in the intimate atmosphere of the small fourteenth century chapel and one Sunday, after a little firm coaxing, he persuaded his reluctant travelling companion to join him. This, an extraordinary turn of fate, became a signal moment in the life of a reserved young man who, one day, was destined to rise to a position of substance within the Anglican Church. Peter Judd found the experience intensely moving and it set him on a journey which began with his spiritual reawakening, led to theological college after Cambridge and his eventual ordination into the priesthood.

But all was not well with Gerald. While his friend now opened his soul to the light of divine revelation, my brother's path seemed set on an opposite journey – a gradual descent into spiritual darkness. He became withdrawn and depressed – swallowed up in a black hole created by an existence which had turned insatiably promiscuous. Inevitably, it served to reinforce his feelings of self-hatred, a state of mind relieved to an extent by his growing involvement with the University's theatre and drama groups, and by his love of good music. The oscillations in his humour swung between extremes. When the pendulum rose to a high, he was Gerald The Big Personality; Gerald the much loved, larger-than-life character. After an evening listening to a major orchestral production of Berlioz' *Symphonie fantastique* at Ely Cathedral, his college friends gathered in the pub. Enthusing about the performance over their drinks, suddenly one of them realized their messmate was missing. "Where's Gerald?" He cried. A question answered instantly by Gerald's purveyor of condoms: "Oh! He's back in his room masturbating over Berlioz!" he cracked.

But among the reminiscences of the Dean, the memory of Gerald's state of despair still weighs on his conscience. One afternoon, as a small kindness,

My maternal grandparents. Thanassaki and Fifi Rosi.

Molly Guiver, Louise's mother.

Peter Guiver, Louise's father.

Machi and Etty Rosi.

Louise Guiver, my future wife.

Peter and Etty on their wedding day. Athens, 2nd June, 1946.

that I shall have a "Foreign
daughter in law. I shall love
her all the more & try to make
up to her, the loss of her
beautiful country, for our
Land is everything, but these
days. with its Austerity,
everything — & shabbiness &
poor rations — The parcel
You tell me of has not yet
arrived, but I have Theo's photo
framed & she is by Tom side

My advice as to what + how much
to tell ones wife is — always tell her
the truth — about everything — Whenever
She asks for — a wife wants to be
at one with her husband, not
be put off with excuses — That
denies trust & causes dissension —
Does she know about Tom Father
He was a fine man, & you have
no reason to be ashamed, for you
all Tom Brains from him, he
was a most unselfish noble &
fine character, but should never
to have married —

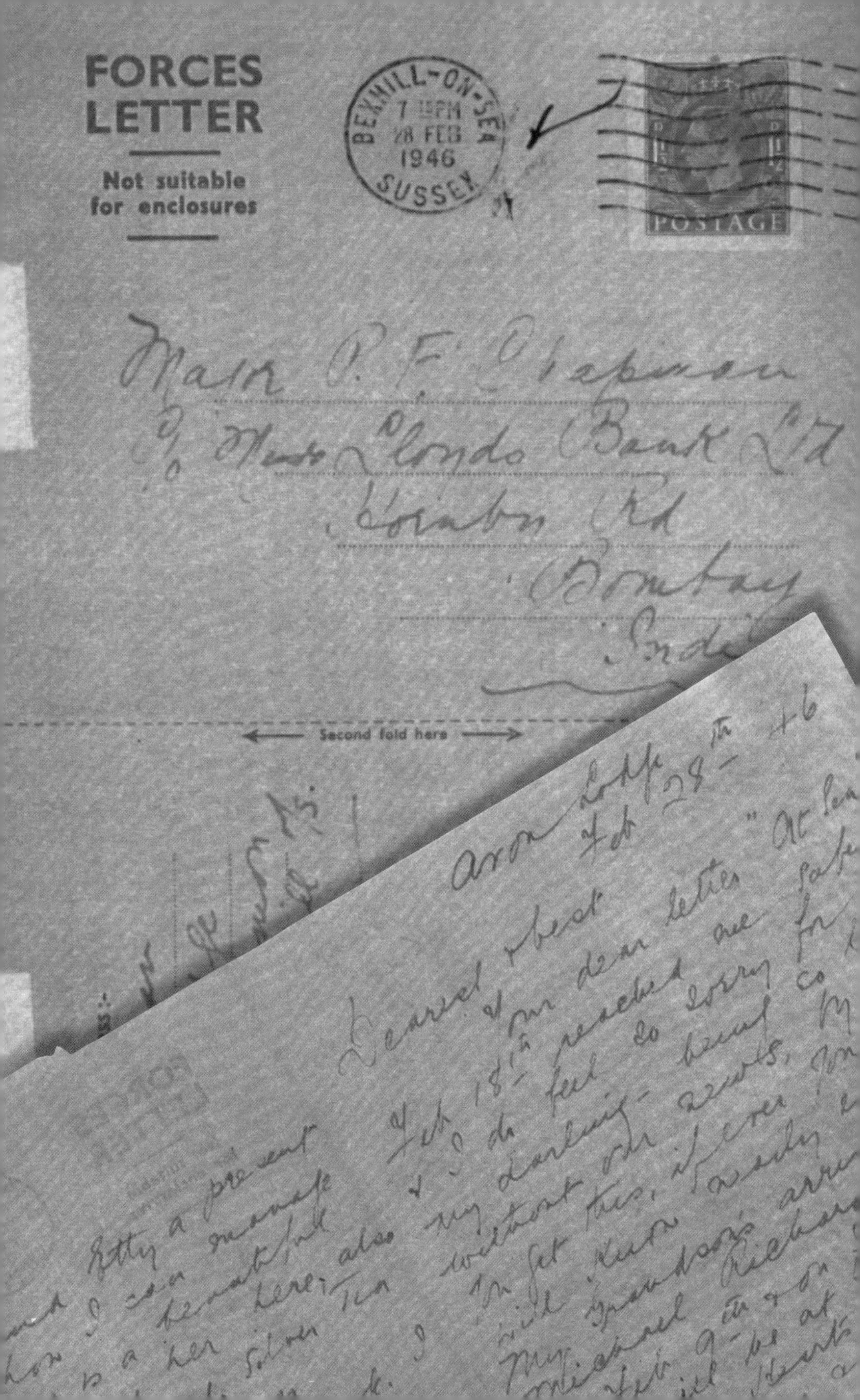

BEXHILL-ON-SEA
7 15 PM
28 FEB
1946
SUSSEX

POSTAGE

Major P. F. Chapman
℅ West Lloyds Bank Ltd
Colaba Rd
Bombay
India

← Second fold here →

Avon Lodge Feb 28th 46

Dearest & best

Feb 18th our dear letter "At Sea"
reached me safe
I do feel so sorry for
my darling — brief co
without our news, you
will turn readers
my grandson's arri
Michael Richard
Feb 9th & on
will be at Berk

Betty a present
I can manage
Berkshill
her silver Tea

Previous spread: "Dearest & best". Nell's revelatory letter to Peter, her favourite son, after his engagement to Etty in February 1946. The letter begins to untangle the mystery surrounding Henry Prüger's death.

Images of Etty, my mother, in some of her many dresses.

32, Queen Olga Street, Salonica. 7ᵗʰ November 1950. Gerald's first birthday. Four snapshots: from looks of bewilderment to expressions of enchantment of joy.

he bought his chum an LP of Benjamin Britten's *Rejoice in the Lamb*. When he called on him in Bateman Street, he found Gerald icy pale, washed out, asleep in his bed. Wishing him better, he scribbled a note and placed the LP by his bedside before leaving the house. "I had the distinct feeling that he might try to take his life," Peter Judd told me. "I should have woken him and talked through his problems. If I wasn't as young and naïve as I was, I would have put a lot more effort into that. Gerald needed help and I didn't do enough. But then I don't think he wanted to tell anybody."

In fact Gerald did tell somebody. But only after a bizarre incident which occurred late one night on his way home. He was walking down Bateman Street when he spotted three girls standing framed in the window of a garishly illuminated room. When they saw him, they dropped their knickers and paraded their neatly trimmed pudenda in a lubricious display of sexual promise. It was an unambiguous invitation to party. Gerald pressed on down the street towards his lodgings. Disturbed by the scene he had witnessed, it now sparked the terrible realization that, in spite of the girls' open blandishments, he had felt not the remotest sense of sexual arousal. He could bear it no more and went to see his college chaplain, Anthony Phillips.

Once again, Gerald was in crisis. In my own mind, I imagine that in turning to Dr. Phillips, Gerald perhaps was expecting the kind of sympathetic rescue he received from Peter Spink in Vienna. But his new confessor's attitude proved more robust, more temporal and pragmatic. He referred him to the Cambridge Counselling Service who put him in touch with an eminent London-based psychoanalyst, the Viennese doctor, Lothair Rubinstein. For my brother, the struggle he confronted was to work out what was going on in his life. He was indulging his appetite for homosexual sex but he did not automatically think of himself as homosexual. Society, convention, his upbringing, his faith had conditioned him into believing his raging passions were unnatural and evil. So his referral to Rubinstein offered him fresh hope of finding a passage out of his moral swamp, to finding his sixth-former's vision of "truth and beauty" which would lead him "to a more balanced and worthwhile life."

But for Etty and Peter, the idea of their son submitting to psychoanalysis was as alien as it was frightening. They were in shock. How could it be? Handsome, happy Geraldo, a psychiatric case? And who exactly was this Freudian Dr. Rubinstein? The notion that his sexuality might lie somewhere at the heart of the matter was not a consideration – certainly not to Etty. Their immediate response was to seek a meeting with Anthony Phillips in his rooms at Trinity Hall.

Like Peter Judd and his wife Judith (Gerald was Peter's best man at their wedding), Anthony and Vicky Phillips have been family friends for almost forty years. Talking to them one spring afternoon, the famous meeting in Anthony's study is one he remembers well. He was joined by Jonathan Steinberg, a history don whom Gerald admired and who was involved in drama and the musical life of the university. Both chaplain and don were clear in their intentions to break the news of Gerald's sexuality as the explanation for his therapy under the care of Dr. Rubinstein. But their attempts to explain – like those of John Rae three years before – went unheard; perhaps because their words were too nuanced for the message to be received or, more certainly, because Etty only heard what she wanted to hear while Peter cast himself adrift, lost in his silence.

The mood and mores of the times would have made communication problematical. This period in our domestic history – between the sixties and the start of the seventies – was a moment of seismic shift in the old social structures. Two and a half years after homosexuality was decriminalized and also with the passing of the Abortion Act in 1967, the age of majority fell from twenty-one to eighteen. Attitudes and behaviour were in a state of awkward transition. Even everyday English usage found itself bereft of a comfortable, demotic language to draw on in this shifting social climate. Words like 'gay' and expressions like 'coming out' did not exist. And the language that did exist tended to be universally pejorative – words like 'poof' and 'queer' and so on. So open discussion of homosexuality remained taboo. It was there, assumed, even accepted – but it was a subject removed from polite conversation. At Cambridge, as Gerald discovered, it was rife. Most undergraduates came from single-sex public schools and now found themselves thrust into the all-male environment of their colleges. Few had much experience of girls – although there was the vague acknowledgement of all that happening in its own good time; with a career and marriage; with growing up.

The accepted convention, then, was to keep quiet, never to discuss. In making the break, Gerald was unusual – his distress finally driving him to seek help, leaving Anthony and Jonathan Steinberg with the decision to confront the issue, gently but directly, with his parents. "Etty dominated the conversation," Anthony told me. "Peter was almost silent – both of them shocked that Gerald had been referred to a psychoanalyst in London. She was desperate for him to find a girlfriend and kept repeating herself: 'Is it a phase?', 'Will it pass?' and she kept asking me 'Why? Why?' In the end, I think, she clung to the idea that homosexuality in young men was a passing phase which, in those days, tended to be the prevailing view."

Etty left Cambridge comforted. Peter less so. But she, at least, had convinced herself again that whatever his problems, Gerald would come through – her belief sustained by the certain knowledge that this was only "a passing phase". For her this was affirmation enough. Soon he would find a nice girl and all would be well - όλα ωραία, όλα καλά.

That Gerald, if inclined, could have stepped out with a host of female admirers cannot be in doubt. Vicky Phillips echoes Daphne Rae's observations about his attractiveness to women. "He was like a Greek god!" she exclaimed when we met. "You were aware of him immediately he came into a room – very charismatic and very like Etty." Her husband and the Dean, on the other hand, were intrigued by the relationship between Etty and Gerald – both clergymen quick to remark upon the intensity of the bond between mother and son. "Etty adored him," observed Anthony. "There was something there which was almost overpowering." Peter Judd went further: "Etty, I think, was in love with Gerald," he told me. "She was over-involved – I think she found him terribly exciting sexually. He was her Greek boy – the Greek world she had lost. You were the Austro-Hungarian boy, your father's boy."

It took me a moment to absorb what Peter was saying. "Are you telling me," I asked him, "that my mother's relationship with Gerald was more than loving?"

"I felt there was a sexual frisson there," he replied. "That was my intuition. In his presence, she once showed me a photograph of him on a beach in Greece. She made a comment about his 'magnificent hairy legs'. It was a comment that seemed quite explicit and has stuck in my mind ever since."

*

Gerald spent twelve months commuting to and from Dr. Rubinstein's Hampstead consulting rooms. It was expensive therapy but Peter and Etty were determined to support their son with whatever it took to see him overcome his crisis. Their unquestioning faith was now invested in the good doctor – his Viennese roots somehow endowing him with an aura of mystical power. I too became as much aware of these visits as my parents; the name "Rubinstein" a constant call in family discussions about Gerald, but a name never invoked in the context of his sexuality. The problems were emotional; Gerald was "finding himself" and Dr. Rubinstein was helping him. Meanwhile Gerald grew close to his interlocutor. He felt a strong bond and, with it, a confidence that he would find a way through his problems and be "cured". But it was not to be. In their final session together, Gerald sat listening in a state of alarm while the eminent psychoanalyst delivered his devastating diagnosis. Gerald, he declared, was irrevocably homosexual. "The question now," he said, "is how do you live the rest of your life in this certain knowledge?"

An emphatic, definitive confirmation of his homosexuality was not what Gerald was expecting. Hopes that he might change were now dashed, along with the prevailing notion of the times that homosexuality in young men was a "passing phase". But in spite of the initial shock, Rubinstein's declaration brought relief. After the years of guilt, depression and denial, this was a turning point and the beginning of Gerald's acceptance of the way he was made. It had been a painful process and if the result was largely beneficent, it also brought a serious casualty in its wake. He could no longer reconcile his being with his faith and he turned his back on the Church. I write these words hesitantly because, deep down, the need of his faith, I believe, remained ingrained in his soul. And for him, the answer to this dilemma – a kind of moral tension stirring in his subconscious – was to turn to the friend he most trusted. Now in their final year at Cambridge and with Gerald eschewing his faith, Peter Judd's path was already set for theological college and the priesthood. The shy, reserved undergraduate dragged reluctantly to Holy Communion two years before, became the close confidant of the theatrical, arty student who was drifting away from his avowed attachment to High Anglican tradition.

It was at this richly ironic moment – when Gerald decided, before anyone, to confide first in Peter and tell him the outcome of his analysis – that their lifelong friendship seemed to be sealed. Gerald's relationships, sexual or not, tended to be fired with an intensity which invariably burnt out – broken or in tears. That was in the nature of my brother's mercurial character. His friendship with Peter was different. It endured – the only one to do so outside the love of his own family – because it was conducted in an atmosphere of calm, trust and quiet sanity. For the would-be priest Gerald certainly injected colour and dash into the sobriety of a minister's life but Peter also found himself confronted with an early opportunity to come to grips with one of the most intractable questions of his chosen vocation: the Church of England's attitude to homosexuality. "My close friendship with Gerald," the Dean told me, "influenced my thinking from the beginning. I was going into the Church; it was important for me to understand it. At the time, the received wisdom suggested it had all to do with upbringing and the stereotype of mum deeply involved with son which caused it – or the remote, non-communicative father. The truth is no-one really knows the answer.

"Homosexuality would not be such a difficult problem if it were perfectly clear that a person's sexuality is a given. If it was given like the colour of your eyes, then the question for the Christian is how do you live a moral life with brown eyes. It's as simple as that. But it hasn't reached that point – although the evidence would seem to be moving that way. But when Gerald and I were at Cambridge, nobody talked about it; people knew even less than they do now. People thought it was nurtured – this is what parents did to their children." Listening to Peter Judd, I was reminded of Gerald's favourite gay joke. On the wall of a public lavatory someone had scrawled the words: "My mother made me a homosexual." Underneath, someone else wrote: "If I give her the wool, will she make me one?"

In Taunton, Etty and Peter remained oblivious of Rubinstein's final diagnosis. As did I in London. It didn't matter. Gerald seemed contented. More at ease with life.

*

Gerald's graduation in the summer of '71 was a cause for jubilation for Etty – a moment to dress up and party. Her boy's Upper Second came attached to a roll-call of theatrical credits: leading Shakespearean parts interlaced with his own productions of modern plays including *The Caretaker* and, at last, *Murder in the Cathedral*. Now he was planning to stage the British Premiere of *Godot Has Come* for the Edinburgh Festival Fringe – a controversial play by the obscure Yugoslav playwright Miodrag Bulatovic, a sequel to Samuel Beckett's *Waiting for Godot*. Meanwhile, his last acting role at Cambridge was as Mercutio in *Romeo and Juliet* – an event Etty and Peter attended with their "erudite" friends the du Canns, Edward being the distinguished High Tory and Member for Taunton. The party settled themselves into the luxurious surroundings of the Garden House Hotel where, after the play, they gathered for dinner with some of Gerald's pals, Peter Judd among them. At the sight of her Geraldo sweeping into the dining room, Etty took him in her arms: "You were wooonderful!" she exclaimed, and the fêting of her star son began.

That evening Etty's vivacity was playing on full volume – and with good cause. Gerald's success at Cambridge had been sweetened for her by the intervention of his chaplain – and both he and Vicky Phillips had become new friends. She had been touched and reassured by Anthony's letter to her: "I'm convinced Rubinstein has done him much good," he wrote, "he's more mature and wiser. Of course, he's not reached his goal – but he's a different person from this time last year." And then, to the family's delight, there had been the happy announcement from her eldest. The διάδοχος – her "son and heir" – had just become engaged to an enchanting girl and Etty was riding on clouds of excitement at the prospect of a grand winter wedding in London. For now, there were the holidays in Greece to look forward to and Gerald was set to join his aunt Machi and her husband Petros at Diodati for a few weeks before returning to Cambridge to begin rehearsals on his Edinburgh play. Louise and I would follow in August, joining Etty and Peter – our first introduction to Diodati, their new summer hideaway.

Amid the excitement, one member of the family was less buoyed by Gerald's graduation. Peter – bewildered by the outcome and value of Rubinstein's therapy – agonized about his younger son's future. In the peace and quiet of Diodati, he thought, Gerald might be more receptive to a father's advice. He wrote a lengthy letter gently touching on the uncertainties of a career in the theatre and the need to lay the foundations for a secure future. My brother received this "v. long and interesting letter" in early July and in a nine-page response ignored the contents, offering instead a deliciously gossipy tour d'horizon of the sexual adventures of the island's expat community. For good measure, he also threw in his own holiday reading: *Sexual Life in Ancient Greece*. "A very boring book," he noted, "which solemnly quotes all the literary instances of bestiality and the like!" By page nine he had the good grace to acknowledge his flippancy – knowing perfectly well that his attitude would offend his father – and changed his tone: "It may seem an insult," he wrote "not to answer the many basically important points raised by your letter: perhaps another time … I think I must just press ahead and see what happens. But I could not forgive myself if I never tried to do the one thing that engages me fully, emotionally and intellectually." He finished on the issue uppermost in his parents' brooding minds: "Also, as far as the long term is concerned, questions of marriage, family, etc; though these are important, I hardly think they are pressing just at this moment."

A month later, while we were holidaying in Diodati, Gerald wrote to all of us from Cambridge. With only three weeks before the first performance of *Godot Has Come*, his rehearsals were running on a punishing schedule of eight hours' work a day. He was exhausted. "But I think it's going to be quite fun in the end," he says anticipating our arrival in Edinburgh. Reading this letter – as with all Gerald's correspondence – is like holding a mirror to his life. For him a letter is hardly worth writing unless it is infused with drama – life, death (and sex) on every page. A teasing, effervescing paragraph about the imminent birth of Anthony and Vicky Phillips' child – "I shall go out today and buy a little fluffy toy for the baby" – is followed by the news of the sudden death of Lothair Rubinstein at a convention in Vienna. He was speaking at a seminar and collapsed. Gerald is shocked. His analyst was only sixty-two. "I must say it's an awful blow," he tells us, "because it means starting again, though the benefit I've had already doesn't mean a completely new start. Personally I am upset because I respected him and liked him – he was always so kind and encouraging. So he'll be very difficult to replace: *if* I feel I need to replace him, which in a way I do: I think I *do* want to continue nonetheless."

Gerald's uncertainty is never resolved. Rubinstein is replaced, but never equalled. And his letter ends on a note which will have brought little comfort to his father: "There's still no news about jobs, from anywhere. I don't know what's going to happen. Anyway – see you in Edinburgh …"

*

We arrived in Charlotte Square, Robert Adam's famous landmark off Princes Street at teatime – the interior of the Roxburghe Hotel failing to match the Georgian splendour of its location. Observing the proprieties of the day, my father had reserved single rooms for Louise and me. We changed and shortly after seven a taxi drove us to the University Union in Teviot Row. Gerald greeted us, fizzing with nervous excitement. He led the way to our seats and rushed off back stage.

The play – banned behind the Iron Curtain – is a bleak satire on political tyranny: the toing and froing of a "blood" train transporting its victims providing a sinister symbol of authoritarian oppression. When Godot shows up, he turns out to be no saviour but a naïve cove who's been fired three times for his idleness – hardly a liberator for whom it was worth waiting. Instead we are presented with an extreme vision of humanity cruelly reduced to conditioned, mechanical objects. Five years before, when the play was premiered in Paris, Le Monde commented: "Le monde de Bulatovic croule sous les vomissements, les excréments, le sordide et le grotesque." And for Gerald's family, this evening in Edinburgh was no life enhancing experience. Peter walked out – hurt and horrified by the spectacle he was witnessing on stage.

Later, in a touching letter of thanks for both her holiday in Greece and the trip to Edinburgh, Louise attempted to console her future father-in-law, suggesting to him that for Gerald, now starting out in his career, it was inevitable that he would be attracted to the challenge of a controversial play. I doubt Peter was convinced, but he did at least have one happy consolation to look forward to – a family wedding in December.

*

On the eve of our marriage, Gerald wrote to his friend Peter Judd.

Claridges, London
2-12-1971

Dear Peter,

I thought this notepaper would "amuse" you! The whole family is here to-night, and we're celebrating my brother's wedding. I'm best man (a misnomer for a start!) and have to deliver myself of some dire speech at the reception, which, of course, is also here! I have decided, (in my speech), to condemn the whole show as subversive, socially, but above all sexually. Needless to say, I shall not get drunk: I never do on such miserable occasions, it's far too painful.

Anyway, I've also decided to get thinner, to discipline my lascivious body. But how can I? We had strawberries for dinner. Strawberries! What a pain, - for the strawberry pickers in mid-winter. Most thoughtless. This whole place is

thoughtless: it's designed to torment the staff in every possible way: there's even a
buzzer for the waiter on the desk here.

"Godot has Come" went down OK in Edinburgh perhaps, but here [at the Cockpit
Theatre, London] it was absolutely panned. The Times, Guardian and Punch all
hated it; Fin. Times quite liked it, and there are several more reviews to come, all
of which I'm dreading. You might have read about it. I was very upset of course,
but perhaps it was best to get it all over and done with: I had to get slated some
time or another I suppose.

<u>*Do*</u> *please get in touch because I'd love to meet you sometime over the Christmas*
period.

Please write.

Yrs.

Gerald

When the Dean showed me this letter, I collapsed with laughter. This was
Gerald at his most wilful and perverse. Gerald being arch and ironic. Gerald
in a display of mock indignation – that he should be complicit at an event
which he saw as a capitalist conspiracy against the workers of the world. A
piece of disgusting bourgeois theatre in which he had to perform for the sake
of the family. We often fell into bouts of political fisticuffs – him in the red
corner, me in the blue – noisy sparring matches which never betrayed any
trace of malice. Finally, our arguments exhausted, I'd challenge him: "Come
the revolution, Gerald," I'd say, "blindfolded, my back against the wall,
will you be the first to pull the trigger?" Of course, he loved the pomp and
ceremony of the wedding, the champagne and the canapés, the buzzer on the
desk to summon the butler, and the sheer indulgence of eating strawberries
in winter. And he loved his family – glad of us especially on this occasion
because we had invited Anthony Phillips to wave the Anglican standard beside
the Catholic establishment at the Church of our Lady of the Assumption
in Soho. Anthony's brief was to deliver the address, just as Gerald's was to
make an amusing speech at the reception – a Cantabrigian dimension to the
proceedings which Etty found very pleasing.

But life post-Cambridge was proving to be a struggle. While he searched for a job, Gerald needed the family's support. Before the wedding, he came to live with me in Camden Town and I persuaded my bosses at Grey Advertising to take him on in the television production office. "I'm working temporarily at my brother's advertising agency," he tells Peter Judd, "and hating it."

Gerald's first professional posting – as assistant director at the Theatre Royal in York – was a long time coming. Meantime, Peter kept him afloat on a runnel of cheques while Etty tried to persuade him to go for the greater prestige of an opportunity at the Royal Court in Sloane Square. The emotional heat being generated over Gerald's future was intense and he felt exasperated. Before leaving London in April 1972, he wrote privately to his father to explain his need to escape the family nest. "I have felt stifled," he said, "and that is why I must be away, and only return when I want to, when I am ready to. That is also why I'd prefer to be in York than in London. It's not sacrificing my career to my private life: it's not entirely true that the Royal Court is better for me, at this stage, than York. Anyway, York is a nice place, and it's cheaper! London is too near both home and Cambridge. For the first time I feel I can be alone without panicking."

The uncertainties of his career, the loss of Rubinstein and the baggage of family angst he was humping all weighed him down – the letter to Peter gradually descending into a well of sadness, frustration and self-pity. This is his last paragraph:

I'm sorry I must have been so prickly and miserable-looking at home. I hardly seem to offer anything to you: perhaps I feel I don't have much to offer to anyone, or what I have to offer is rejected or ignored. As for 'pretending to be someone else', which is what I was supposed to be doing while at home: well, I can only say that everyone has their own set of masks, and they choose one which is most tolerable to themselves. I think if I 'pretended to be like someone' whom you could like or admire, then that would be intolerable for me. Frankly, I feel a bit of a thorn in the family's side, and unable to share my most important and innermost feelings, something which I know perfectly well I haven't been able to do from about the age of seven onwards, except v. occasionally. No wonder then that there is a kind of aridity at the moment, and that I feel rather lonely when unhappy. But this does not preclude any fruitful relationship, and particularly I appreciate the unflagging support and loyalty you give me in my professional work. This is v. valuable to me.

He signs off: "I hope Mummy has a happy [Greek Orthodox] Easter. Crack a red egg for me won't you?!"

Reading this letter from my brother – seven pages this one – causes me heartache; churns my soul; calls on forgotten memories of past family conflicts. I remember that dreadful sense of panic Etty seemed to inject in both of us – in Louise too: the emotional pressure, the feeling of being controlled, trapped in her will unless you behaved how you were expected to behave. Then there was that pet expression of hers: Etty liked us to be "under her wing" – her possession. Just as she might accuse me of madness when I challenged her – refusing to nestle beneath her downy warmth – so Gerald here was being accused of pretending to be someone else. Yes, he was holding a mask to his face – a veil to his sexual ego. But they wouldn't hear what he was saying – the words of John Rae and Anthony Phillips lost years before. And so Gerald felt isolated, lonely and misunderstood by the very people from whom he craved understanding.

This letter was written four months after Louise and I married – a wedding that had fulfilled Etty's ideal vision. I was working in a smart West End advertising agency. I was well paid; a success – another fulfilled ideal. Obsessed by her own self-image, she wanted her younger son, her Greek Adonis, to be in that image. But these aspirations which Etty now urged upon Gerald only created a set of masks which were "intolerable" to him. It was no wonder he felt alienated at home. How we remember those times – Louise and I – all of us together in Taunton at a weekend: the moments of frustration and anger when he would retreat to his bedroom, bang the door shut and listen to his music. Another paragraph in his letter to his father reads: "Music has been a great compensation in the last three unsettling weeks. I listened to the whole of Wagner's *Ring* on four consecutive nights while in Cambridge, and two piano recitals here this week."

This long note – like the others – lay in its box of Suchard, tucked neatly inside the Harrods hatbox. So, I guess, it's safe to assume that Peter passed the letter to Etty. Not that her reading of its contents would have made the difference he perhaps wished for – but, at least, I can see how difficult these situations were for him. I am sure he understood – but he worshipped his wife and could never gainsay her. To do so would have led to a bitter void. To nowhere. And as for Louise and me, at that time we were less affected, consumed as we were with the headiness of our new life in London.

*

A month after Gerald's desperate appeal to his father, Etty and Peter had installed themselves in Diodati for their annual spring break. By now he had found digs at number 15 St. Mary's in Bootham, close to the centre of York and within walking distance of the Theatre Royal. On pale blue airmail notepaper, he told his parents that he had settled in well; was happier now – busy with a raft of interesting work, from big productions to workshops and lunchtime plays. "The flat's OK," he wrote. "I got my stereo set which will take two years to pay off! Rather expensive, but *really* magnificent." Tensions seemed to be easing and by June he was in a mood for peace gestures. An envelope arrived in Taunton containing "some early heather from the edge of the moors!" – "Mummy's surprise," read the brief message. Now, today, sitting at my table on Aristotle's, I am looking at that sprig of Yorkshire heather: still almost perfectly intact, the violet blush to its tiny flowers a little dulled by the passing of thirty-five years.

*

By the autumn, Gerald's state of equilibrium had evaporated as he slipped into another cruel depression. He turned to the one friend in whom he had complete trust. Travelling home to Taunton for his twenty-third birthday, he wrote to Peter Judd on Castle headed notepaper. "I've been exhausted and very, very depressed in the last week and a half," he began. "I came home to recuperate of my own volition (an unprecedented act that is). I've seen my GP who's given me lots of pills, and my analyst in London who was very kind and helpful. But the depression is something that will be there for a long time, and my own anxieties and terrible guilty worries about my sexual life will remain until I can somehow decide how to come to terms with them and control them: certainly they can never be *resolved* now. There are some things which one can never get over, and which maim for life."

A month later, just before Christmas, Gerald's sense of desolation seemed to have abated – or, at least, it had been displaced by his creative energy and experimental work in the theatre. "I am seeking that elixir," he told his friend, "the *pure communication* where barriers are down totally and one is at one's most vulnerable." These "happenings," as he called his experiments, were a preparatory process for a play he was directing called *Self-Accusation* by Peter Handke. The play was about human vulnerability. "But we can only perform it," he explained, "if we communicate its truth to the retina and soul of every member of the audience. To employ them in this search for the best relationship, where there is *no* embarrassment, and the audience participate therefore voluntarily through *our* effort, and make themselves vulnerable to the experience being enacted before them."

Having defined his ideal for the play, his argument crumbles when, at the end of the letter, he dwells on his own loneliness and vulnerability. "As for alone-ness," he says, "sometimes I wonder at the effort to try and make relationships; why bother and be disappointed? But then part of the 'bother' can be made fun if you half-expect to be disappointed, as long as it never becomes a fantasy – *then*, one is never alone; and the fantasy gnaws into your marrow until you discover that you actually *are* alone: and *that* is tragedy." A bleak and cynical perspective on the value of human relationships? Or a cry of anguish from a troubled brother? And as for the play, it was declared a critical success when it opened in January, so much so Gerald took it on tour: to Harrogate, then to Manchester and, finally, for a week's run at the Young Vic Studio in London.

But Gerald was now beginning to grow bored. He found the atmosphere at work too stuffy and tensions were simmering between him and the Theatre Royal's director, Richard Digby Day. He needed a fresh challenge and set his sights on Leicester where the new Haymarket Theatre was opening in October. Before his move – which came late in July 1973 – Gerald was determined to drive through one last initiative in York, an important project calculated to nudge artistic boundaries to new limits, even if it proved too radical and controversial for the conservative appetites of the local establishment. He was planning to stage *Big Wolf* by Harald Mueller, a play for young people about Vietnamese war orphans, and perform it in the open on a disused site in the run-down Leman Road district of the city. This piece (for which he created "The B52 Company" as the vehicle for its production) was a signal moment in his career because it marked his debut as a pioneer of young people's theatre – the field in which he would ultimately make his reputation. Meanwhile, when *Big Wolf* opened in early July, it immediately ran into trouble. "It's a *very* tough neighbourhood," he tells his parents. "On Sunday we very nearly got involved in a gang fight with one of the boys in the play – an ex-skinhead himself, now reformed as it were. Still, all my lads are very keen and good about it all. Tonight I was advised to have a policeman on duty during the performance!"

For Gerald, the play stood as a successful first experiment in youth theatre and after his move to Leicester, he staged it again, at the Phoenix, before taking it on to a Sunday night presentation at Lincoln's Theatre Royal. This time his cast was drawn from a group of teenagers from the "notorious" New Parks estate in Leicester where the boys had never before seen the inside of a professional theatre.

*

Gerald's stint at the Haymarket was brief – a stepping-stone out of the provinces on his way to London where he knew he could better serve his rising urge to become more politically active. Seventies' Britain was a decade of industrial strife and economic turmoil. Like Harold Wilson, his predecessor as Prime Minister, Edward Heath seemed incapable of taming the overweening power of the unions and by the end of 1973, the miners' work-to-rule had brought the country to its knees with a three-day week, power cuts and misery. Wilson's return to power in 1974 made no difference and after James Callaghan succeeded him two years later, the International Monetary Fund was called in to bail out a near-bankrupt British economy. Meanwhile, the Government's continuing battle with the unions finally descended into its ignominious "winter of discontent" over 1978/79 – grim months which saw our city streets raising plastic mountains of rotting refuse. In parallel to all this industrial and economic woe, society itself was in a state of upheaval in the wake of Harold Wilson's measures to liberalize the laws on abortion, homosexuality and divorce. The loosening of the old social mores and the rattling of class barriers were ushering in a new age of meritocratic, populist power structures: this was a decade for iconoclastic activism. Gay liberation and contemporary British theatre were on the march – both in the van of this revolution in modern manners – and Gerald wanted to be part of it.

His farewell to Leicester was no cheerful swansong. In his bag of final productions, Gerald was drawn to a play which reverberated with his experiences and observations of life in Leman Road and the New Parks estate. He wanted to stir the consciences of his audiences by planting a thick fist in their gut. What he gave them was a raw and brutal morality tale played out on a sink estate in south London where an outburst of group violence – in the stoning to death of a baby in a pram – symbolized issues of social oppression, emotional emptiness and cultural impoverishment: well-established and favourite themes in the politics of Gerald's theatre. The play was *Saved* by Edward Bond, a playwright he greatly admired, and a play first performed at London's Royal Court in 1965 in spite of a ban by the Lord Chamberlain, British theatre's official censor. Then the production caused a storm – of outrage and voluble support in equal doses – and led directly to the Theatres Act of 1968 which, effectively, abolished the censor.

Gerald's production at the Haymarket Studio ran for ten days at the end of January '74 and was pronounced "excellent" by the *Leicester Mercury's* theatre critic: "It rips, rends and gouges its way through the system with the professional expertise of a medieval disemboweller," he wrote, "skilfully dousing the audience with the odd jug of reviving laughter every so often – solely to ensure that they suffer the more exquisitely at the next jab to the vitals." The playwright himself provided a short essay in Gerald's programme notes: "I write about violence as naturally as Jane Austen wrote about manners," he argued. "Violence shapes and obsesses our society, and if we do not stop being violent we have no future … Unless theatre makes these things clear, and makes audiences so hurt or happy they must act on what they understand – it is irrelevant."

Thirteen years later – early in 1987 – Gerald revived his production of *Saved* for Birmingham Rep. It would be the last play he directed in England – a prime example of his life-long preoccupation with contemporary theatre as a medium for the expression of modern social experience.

*

Part Seven

London and New York

Gerald Chapman 1949 – 1987

The idea of being given a platform on which to create his own community theatre group appealed enormously to Gerald. And that this opportunity should come to him with an associate directorship at the Soho Poly Theatre Club also gave the project a strong set of running legs. But his company – which he called 'Bread 'n Butter' – was blighted by bureaucracy and much of 1974 was soaked up in tiresome meetings with the councils of seven London boroughs, dozens of community and social service organizations, arts associations, working parties and the like. The outcome was a tour programme – reduced in vision and ambition – which swept a wide south-easterly arc through Brixton in Lambeth to Thamesmead, Sidcup and New Addington in Croydon.

By August he was fed up – his faith and purpose ebbing away. "London's a big, dirty and exhausting place," he tells Etty and Peter on the eighteenth in a doleful airmail letter posted to Diodati. "I think the provinces attract me more, particularly Yorkshire." In the next sentence, we hear that he has written to the Yale School of Drama about scholarships – "as I think it may be a way of getting to the USA" – and then, that he's toying with the idea of going on the Kathmandu trail. Symptoms of his state of mind – unsettled, unhappy, lonely. A week later – a Sunday – he arranges to meet Peter Judd for lunch at the Swiss Centre in Leicester Square.

His old friend was shocked at the pale and seedy figure staring at him across the bubbling pot of fondue. His manner seemed brash and thoughtless and they fell into an argument about the role of the novel. "I don't read them any more," Gerald snapped. "Pointless escapism! In life there can be no substitute for experience and the reality of people."

"Yes," replied Peter quietly, "you can escape into fiction, but you can also use books to illuminate, and make you question your experiences and the life that you lead."

Gerald changed tack; his friend having gently opened the way to a rush of pent-up emotion. "I've been very frustrated over these past few weeks," he confessed. "I went to a gay bar and picked up a Chinaman – called Chi Chi would you believe! Anyway, we leapt into bed together – unbelievable sex – and now I've got VD!"

After lunch they joined the crowds of tourists milling about Leicester Square and strolled down to the National Portrait Gallery where Peter left him to browse. That evening, the young deacon, just ordained, sat down to complete his journal entry for the day. The meeting with Gerald had disturbed him. "Oh dear," he wrote, "I hope he can find some stability." On the opposite page, he pasted down a pen and ink portrait of John Keble. There was something compelling about the expression in the nineteenth century churchman's face and eyes – a look of peace and serenity which had persuaded Peter to buy the postcard. At the foot of the page, he wrote: "Keble. The face – everything Gerald isn't!"

*

It was during these turbulent moments in Gerald's life – the middle seventies – that we saw more of him. Dominic, our first-born, was approaching his first birthday and we had settled snugly into our tiny two-bed basement in Putney – at number 24A, Oxford Road. They were good years for my brother and me because, at last, we had time to reconnect before, once again, our careers propelled us in different directions: Louise and me to Somerset, and Gerald to find a new life in the United States. What pleased me most was the easy friendship, the loving bond which blossomed swiftly between brother and sister-in-law. I think both were quick to recognize each other's untameable independence of spirit: the streak of rebellion that led to the tensions and feuding which dominated our lives at the Castle but which Gerald avoided by his move to New York.

He loved coming to see us in Putney. Here, his sense of family and home found freedom, unshackled from the feelings of panic and pressure which oppressed him in Taunton. With us he relaxed – arriving, perhaps for dinner or a weekend, in torn jeans and a T-shirt, a Greek woollen sack stuffed with papers, plays and notes slung over his shoulder. His hair greasy, his face spotty – the seediness and pallor that had shocked his best friend worn as a mark of Marxist proletarian fashionability. If I was working late on some client presentation, he would help Louise bath Dom and play with him while she prepared supper – her moussaka a special favourite. And they would sing along to her musicals on our decrepit record player, hamming it up at the top of their voices: *Robert and Elizabeth*, *South Pacific*, *West Side Story*, *My Fair Lady*; Dom, wrapped in his arms waltzing, spinning around the room. It was huge fun – Gerald at play, deserting his lofty intellectual turret to show that he too enjoyed the pleasures of middle-brow middle-England. I can hear his boyish laughter now – still ringing in my ears.

Over dinner, Dom long tucked away in his cot, he would talk to us about his work and, with a fresh bottle of wine on the table, delight in describing his latest sexual encounters – testing, teasing Louise's tolerance with the graphic details. She'd scold him and giggle in disgust. But his problem with VD worried her and in a quieter moment she never shied from speaking to him bluntly, urging him to take more care of himself. In the flat, when he stayed over, she insisted on a strict routine, keeping a purple towel for his use only and instructing him to disinfect the bath after he'd used it. Next day she would cook him breakfast while he took his washing to the launderette. Later, we'd all walk Dom around Wandsworth Park and, on our way back, stop off at Mr. Malik's on the corner to buy a packet of crumpets. Gerald loved crumpets and we'd eat them for tea with plenty of butter and strawberry jam.

This was the private Gerald; a loving, playful brother and uncle who, off duty – away from the posturing and the politics – found moments of real happiness in quotidian family life: in a crumpet and a cup of tea. But sunk deep inside his heart, the other Gerald was now being claimed by the rising tide of gay activism. The Gay Liberation Front, the Campaign for Homosexual Equality and titles like *Gay News* were becoming increasingly vocal and successful in raising their public profile. The arts and theatre scene in London also wanted to play its part, and a founding group – which included Gerald – set up Gay Sweatshop, Britain's only national gay theatre company, with a plan to stage its first season of plays – called *Homosexual Acts* – in 1975.

This great surge of gay opinion, swept forward by its campaigning zeal, led to a new openness and the dismantling of the old taboos. After the years of guilt and self-loathing, and the moral struggle with his sexuality, Gerald felt emboldened – that he was being enfranchised by a reluctant society; that at last it was okay to be gay. But for me, and others close to him, we began to notice a sharper edge to the man we knew. Here now was Gerald the militant proselyte whose strident rhetoric I found deeply unattractive – and I told him so. I disliked being force-fed his creed and, to his credit, he did not misunderstand my objections as a sign of homophobia. While he moderated his tone with me, others were less fortunate. Since leaving Cambridge, he had kept in touch with Anthony Phillips and in the spring of '75, while he was immersed in plays and projects for *Homosexual Acts*, he met his old college chaplain for lunch in Soho. Their meeting began as a jolly and bibulous affair: "I suppose we must have consumed at least two bottles of wine," Anthony told me. But as the afternoon wore on, Gerald began to preach. "He started to push it," he continued. "He wanted me to embrace his gay world and I refused. I have never held the view that homosexuality was a sin and I never condemned Gerald. But I was also not prepared to show a lot of sympathy for his cause." Our conversation paused for a second. "That said," he went on, "perhaps I didn't handle it very well." But Gerald, well-oiled and wilful, was not being too clever either: he invited Anthony to join him at a gay club. Their rendezvous ended disastrously and both men parted company feeling affronted, hurt and rejected. They never saw each other again.

Peter Judd – now a curate in Salford – also came to feel the heat of Gerald's activism. "My life has been quite hectic socially and sexually," he writes in March, just before his Gay Sweatshop production of *Ships* by Alan Wakeman at the Almost Free Theatre. "This has been very important for me these last two months. Together with the season of Homosexual Plays, I've also become more and more confident about my sexuality, and I have decided to tell my parents about it at long last. I'm more militant about the 'Gay Scene' and will not tolerate any put-down at all." A few weeks later, in a second letter running to nine pages, he catalogues all the people he has fallen out with: his father and Anthony Phillips heading the list.

> *Basement Flat*
> *168A Shirland Road*
> *London*
> *W9*

May 1st '75

Dear Peter,

Thank you for writing such a nice and caring letter. With all the hysteria of the past 3 weeks it is very refreshing to receive such a cool, calm sort of response. Life's been very difficult. I went home to Taunton, arriving at 10.10 pm on a Friday night and by 11.10 pm that same night I'd walked out of the hotel and stayed elsewhere. Saturday morning found me back in London. My father and I had the biggest shouting match I've ever experienced – ostensibly about my work. Anyway, we're slowly patching that all up again, and the row has in fact positively contributed towards a better understanding and a coming closer to each other. Meanwhile I've had a sort of running battle with Anthony Phillips whose attitude I find totally unacceptable, just as he finds my "militancy" also totally unacceptable. I'm sorry to say that I took a certain pleasure in being deliberately rude to him. It's unlikely I'll really want to discuss anything with him again quite honestly until such time as he ceases to regard me as a "2nd best" sort of person who labours under a crushing "disability" (to use his phrases). I was very disappointed in him indeed. No doubt the feeling's mutual. At one point he even suggested that homosexuality was the gift of the devil: I think he probably meant it as well.

Various people seem to have left me…I cannot go on much longer like this, scraping away, doing the odd production here and there, not being paid and tiring myself out and being slapped in the face all the time. I have suddenly (and hopefully it'll be temporary) lost all enthusiasm for my work – which at the moment is all I can live for.

[Gerald continues his letter with an angry polemic on sexuality and class, concluding that "homosexuality is not so much a sexual, but rather a social taboo." He ends with another tilt at Anthony Phillips and the "Establishment" he represents.]

Can you conceive of Trinity Hall inviting its Association to the Annual Gathering with the words "all old Hall men together with their ladies and male lovers will be most welcome"??!! No wonder the Establishment feel threatened by us; no wonder the only ultimate role homosexuals can adopt is a militant-looking one.

I must finish now as I am so exhausted these days: I am drained and feel very empty.

My love to Judy.

Bye for now
Gerald xx

It must have been in March, around the date Gerald wrote the first of these letters, that he appeared at the offices of BBDO in Hanover Square – the agency I was with at the time. He was agitated – anxious to probe my thoughts on the vexed question of "telling" Peter and Etty.
"Gerald, why do it?" I asked. "Your private life is your own affair. Why hurt and upset them?"
We argued for a while but to no purpose. He wanted affirmation, comforting, a brother's reassurance and, at first, I would not comply – misjudging his

determination and the depth of his feelings. More than ever now, he yearned to be accepted for the human being he was, sick of the charade he'd been playing with his parents for so many years. In the end I gave way and agreed to travel to Taunton with him that weekend. A family muster: Louise – three months pregnant – Dominic and me; Gerald's nervous lieutenants in support of his mission.

We arrived early on Friday evening – Peter and Etty in high spirits, excited to have all three generations of family under one roof. A table was booked in the restaurant. Wines ordered. Staff briefed – a minder for Dom. But Gerald wanted to do the deed quickly and be done. As we were changing for dinner, he knocked and entered their bedroom. I shall never know how he went about his business but whatever he said, it must have been as brutal as a summary execution. Three doors down, in our bedroom, we heard a great wail, then howls and cries of "Why?" It was like witnessing a Greek tragedy live – a Euripidean chorus in full lament.

Their door opened. It was my father, flushed crimson and grim. He hurried past us and disappeared out of the penthouse – I guess to the privacy of his office downstairs. Gerald followed, retreating to his own room; the door slammed shut. Moments later, Beethoven's Ninth Symphony thundered down the corridor. I could not stand idle for another second and, leaving Louise, I went to console my mother. When I came into her bedroom she was sitting at the dressing table fixing her eyes. She seemed strangely contented and at ease with herself. Then, in the instant she noticed my presence, her head cocked in an expression of exquisite sadness. Etty, the chameleon, now appealed to me in her time of suffering. I kissed her and held her hand. Meanwhile, in our bedroom, Louise was attempting to settle Dom, and as she did so, wondered about the family into which she had married.

After half-an-hour my father returned. "They're ready for us," he said. "We ought to go down. I don't want to keep the staff waiting." I could see how upset he was. The strong, honourable Indian Army officer I had known all my life had the look of a wounded retriever. He was heartbroken and that aura of hurt never really left him. But my mother had transformed herself –

a remarkable trick I saw her perform on many occasions. Out of the pit of despair earlier in the evening, she glided into the restaurant – her family in train – elegantly groomed and gowned, radiating proprietorial confidence and good humour, playing the charming chatelaine to both staff and diners. Όλα ωραία, όλα καλά. *God's in his heaven, All's right with the world!* The public face unblemished.

But, as Gerald's second letter to Peter Judd suggests, this was only the first bout in the three long weeks of tribulation which engulfed his coming-out. After a short pause, he was obliged to return to Taunton. The summons came from Etty. "Daddy is so upset," she whispered on the telephone. "You must come and see him, and make your peace. Alone this time. Don't tell Kit – κρυφά, κρυφά!" [secretly, secretly].

While my mother had evidently taken the news in her stride – her unspoken, maybe unconscious, realization that she was and would always be the only woman in his life – Peter had lapsed into a terrible depression. His son was a good-looking, gifted young man who now looked as if he might be destroying his life and prospects of happiness. He had no stability. He was jobless and broke, his career in disarray. For some months he had been freelancing – scratching a living wherever he could find work. He'd even done a bit of teaching at LAMDA. The news about his sexuality seemed to be the final blow, perhaps because of its ring of finality. Peter knew but he didn't want to believe: his emotions buried like the memories of his father: the truth suggested by others now rawly exposed by his son.

I have no idea what happened when he arrived home late that Friday evening – but it is easy to imagine: Gerald tired, on the defensive and, in his state of mind, spoiling for a fight; Peter weighed by anxiety, nervous of confrontation but determined to face the issues. It would only have required a tiny innocent remark to detonate the "shouting match" which ended in Gerald's abrupt exit.

*

My brother's obsession with the militant politics of the gay movement warped his sense of perspective, as much towards his career as his attitude towards the family. He would be incensed with me for making the point – but my father was right. Gerald was lost in his own wilderness; a barren land during which his work was all fire and propaganda amounting to little of any substance or heart. Then, in the summer of '76, the call came and his life's mission took root. This was the year that heralded Gerald's transition into a role that would evolve into something greater than the radical theatre director he had become. For me, his greatest gift to society came in the person of inspirational teacher-communicator to the constituency in which he felt most committed: young, often troubled, oppressed and marginalized minority groups. And the job that launched him came from the Royal Court – as director of its Young People's Theatre Scheme.

Excited about the prospects, he is eager to tell his friend in a letter that is radical, socially engaging, dynamic! Very Gerald!

YPTS   *Royal Court Young People's Theatre Scheme*
                The Royal Court Theatre
                Sloane Square London SW1   *19.7.76*

Dear Peter,

Thanks for your letter. I started this job about 5 weeks ago : it all happened very suddenly, and of course I'm very pleased that I can hold down a permanent job in London, especially one which allows me a lot of freedom to plan a full, far-reaching policy.

Basically the job entails:-
1) Youth theatre work with local groups of people (usually 15 yrs. +) who have a specific identity – ie. all live in one area, all Asian, all gay, all part of some group etc. I use this identity as a springboard to do a play. Each group will

work with a writer who, by Royal Court standards, is important or worthwhile. The first group is with gay teenagers who are part of a counselling organisation called "Parents Enquiry". Each youth play will tour its area and other areas.

2) *Professional work that opens at the Theatre Upstairs and then tours to the same sort of places as the youth plays go to, as well as round the country.*

3) *The "Activists" club – a young supporters club for 16-22 yr olds based at the R. Court and meeting regularly, organising its own activities, helping out with the youth theatre work.*

4) *Commissioning new writing.*

5) *Extra events – eg. Young Writers Competition (in conjunction with the Young Observer), Young People's Festival (for the Queen's Jubilee) a season of plays entitled "The Young Offender" focusing on different aspects of that theme.*

As you can see the policy is very social-oriented. I've got to get more money for the policy though. I've only got £6,000 for this financial year, out of which my salary is paid for a start. So I'm applying to all sorts of foundations and trusts and things.

Congratulations on the Clare job [Peter had just been appointed Chaplain at Clare College Cambridge]: *it won't be too rarefied will it? – or is that just a myth? All my love, Judith too! – Gerald.*

*

Gerald spent the next four years at the Royal Court and under his direction the Young People's Theatre Scheme took flight. London's schoolteachers were quick to embrace his alternative curriculum as a vehicle for helping pupils find their own voice – and this through an agenda which included programmes on sexism, racism and socialism. His biggest problem was money – or, more precisely, the means of inflating his meagre budget at the Royal Court to do what he wanted to do. But in appealing to "all sorts of foundations and trusts and things", he had to tread lightly. In his drive to raise the visibility of YPTS, he deliberately courted controversy but he had to stir his radical potion in a way that did not poison his sources of finance. There was no guile in his method. He simply applied a rich mix of natural passion and charm, and although he claimed there was never enough, his fund raising efforts attracted a number of willing sponsors, including an annual sum of £1,000 from Lord Sainsbury.

Two initiatives in particular paid tangible evidence to Gerald's artistic success. The group he called the Activists provided a pool of some 150 young actors, writers and enthusiasts who supported his itinerant workshops and his productions in the Garage or the Theatre Upstairs, spaces attached to the Court. And the winners of an annual writing competition for teenagers basked in the prestige of seeing their plays professionally produced and performed on the main stage by their young peers in his Young Writers' Festival. One of Gerald's protégés was a seventeen year old Hackney lad of West Indian descent. Michael McMillan, a member of the Activists, wanted to write a play about 'sus' arrests in London based on his own and his friends' experiences of police harassment. In an arts feature for the Guardian (published in November 1979), Kenneth Rea was struck by the extraordinary volatility of rehearsals when the play went into production. "They are, after all, the real thing," he observed of the cast in McMillan's play. "Rehearsals are seldom calm, occasionally broken by disputes. At a rehearsal I attended, the police came to close the place for the night because there had been a fight between some other boys downstairs. When the play is eventually completed, it should prove both a compelling piece of theatre, and a vindication of the policy of genuinely helping young people to express themselves."

Gerald, of course, was no stranger to these tensions and flashpoints: for him this was théâtre -vérité, theatre as an instrument of politics. "Kids in a fractured community," he once wrote, "should not be offered plays as therapy or diversion but as 'weapons of happiness'. It is in creating as many imaginative contacts as possible between the principal source of these innovations (the Court) and kids that the YPTS is engaging with a yet wider movement to change society."

*

By the end of the decade, Gerald was beginning to grow restless again – an increasing pressure on budgets fuelling constant arguments with his artistic director, Max Stafford-Clark who saw himself as a theatrical Charlemagne. "Running the Royal Court was a bit like reigning over the Holy Roman Empire," he told me. "Within the theatre's hierarchy, Gerald was like an ambitious duke determined to enlarge his dukedom. He was very assertive, always fighting for more money – but never devious about it." Professionally, Stafford-Clark admired his work and one of Gerald's last productions for YPTS was directed on the main stage by his boss. It was *The Arbor* by Andrea Dunbar, a young teenager who, in Max Stafford-Clark's words, came from a "semi-criminalized, semi-vandalized estate just outside Bradford." The play, which like many of these works was autobiographical, tells the story of a schoolgirl pregnancy and her forlorn struggle to save the baby. It was a brilliant success and at the 1980 Young Writers' Festival *Time Out* described the eighteen-year-old playwright's work as a "sensational debut".

But for my brother, life was about to take a dramatic turn. News of his work had travelled and, though he didn't know it, he was a marked man. The composer and lyricist, Stephen Sondheim, had read about Gerald's annual festival at the Royal Court and, in his role as president of the Dramatists' Guild, the professional association of American playwrights, he attempted to persuade a sceptical council to consider a similar scheme in New York. The idea lapsed until 1979 when Sondheim found himself in London at the time of the festival. Twenty-two years later, he would recall his early impressions. "It was an experience so moving and exhilarating," he wrote, "that I returned to the council with renewed vigor."

By June 1980, Gerald was in a state of high excitement. "My life here is about to alter quite dramatically," he tells Peter Judd. "In April I put in my notice and I'm leaving at the end of July. I hope I'll be able to get a job in the USA setting up and running a Young Writers' Festival there – and it all depends, believe it or not, on Stephen Sondheim, the famous lyricist/

composer, whom I'm seeing next week when he arrives in London (staying at the Savoy, my dear!) for the opening of his new big musical *Sweeney Todd*."

A month later he cabled Etty and Peter in Diodati. "AMERICA CONFIRMED," it read.

*

New York City was as unfathomable as it was fabulous – Gerald at once overwhelmed and seduced by its throbbing pulse and the sheer surfeit of life on the streets – bewildered, sometimes, by an overdose of stimuli. He loved sauntering through Chinatown and Little Italy; watching fire-eaters, magicians and the impromptu jazz in Washington Square; dancing in the bars of Greenwich Village: "Boy, are they wild!" he wrote in a postcard home. Not surprising then that his first apartment was nearby, in St. Mark's Place. Returning from work, he'd emerge from the subway – its amazing graffiti an irresistible foil for the dirt and the noise – and walk through Astor Place, glancing left to spot the Empire State Building some twenty-five blocks to the north. Into St. Mark's Place – East 8th Street by any other name – and he entered a quarter which had morphed out of sixties' hippiedom into late-seventies punk. Heading in the direction of his apartment at number 110, he'd pass several leftist and alternative bookshops, record stores and cinemas playing old movies. Then there were the macrobiotic grocers, an Italian baker, two Chinese laundries, a celebrated Jewish Deli and an equally celebrated Ukrainian restaurant which was situated below the headquarters of the Ukrainian Liberation Organization. Past the twenty-four hour newsagent's and a sauna, he'd pause for a few moments to admire the balletic virtuosity of young Puerto Ricans weaving their astonishing patterns in a roller skate disco. Moving on he'd pass the Polish Cultural Centre, its school and St. Stanislaus, its church. And beyond he'd come to the West Indian Reggae music shop, "The University of the Streets" which, according to my brother, was a front for a black American-Muslim nationalist organization. "I see them dressed in their wonderful long robes and colourful little hats," he tells Etty and

Peter, "smoking their dope and hoovering the carpet!" This then was Gerald's neighbourhood – a cultural salmagundi – and it suited him very well.

He had settled happily into his apartment too: "A bit scruffy, but delightful," he reassures his mother and father. "It's very cheap by NY standards – $200 a month, inc. gas and elex." And the food in the city, a favourite topic in any discussion about Gerald's well-being abroad, found particular favour. "I can go up two blocks to 2nd Ave and 7th St to the famous 24 hr. Kiev Deli," he tells them, "and see the whole world before me tucking into their Pastrami, Kasha, Blintzes and all the other delicacies. Actually I really like Pastrami on Rye with mustard and pickles." But, he goes on, there are two English staples which he misses dreadfully: "Of course no one here knows how to make tea," he complains. "You get boiled water and a tea bag! Nor can you get marmalade for less than $3.50."

Three weeks later, in mid-December 1980, Gerald embellished his first impressions in a letter to Louise and me – a note spilling over with his early experiences of life in the city, and in language less cautious than he would dare lay before the eyes of his parents. "Everyone is usually v. kind here – especially the staff at work," he begins, "and when I go out and meet people, either in a disco or some other den of vice (there are two gay saunas near me: I've never seen so many naked men and cocks hanging around in my life before – don't tell M & D that!) then everyone's extremely friendly – and not just to get off with you either." But the friendliness he encountered seemed also to be tempered by his fears of urban mayhem. That December witnessed the savage slaughter of John Lennon outside his home in New York – a murder which shook Gerald's sense of security. His letter to us continues: "The terrible violence of this place is really beginning to unnerve me. Not just the Lennon murder, but every week (I am not exaggerating) there is some appalling event, and I wonder what sort of a place this is to promote this kind of thing?"

Part of the answer to his nervousness he provides himself – both in this correspondence and in the reports he delivers to his new bosses. In fulfilling the brief for Sondheim's Dramatists' Guild – to stage America's first Young Playwrights' Festival – Gerald had to build alliances with New

York's educational establishment, community groups, schools and theatres. It was hectic, exhausting work and it exposed him to a social melting pot – from the dazzle and polish of Big Apple society on the surface, to a rotting and diseased core within. What he saw and experienced often touched his political nerve ends. "Most white and a lot of black middle class kids go to private schools," he writes, "thereby rendering the public schools (the state system) 75% black, Hispanic (i.e. Puerto Rican) or oriental. The result is that the poorest sections of society are ghettoised in the state schools. I can see how easy it would be to live a life of decadence here because society is so fragmented and divided against itself. People isolate themselves, hide in their own ghettoes, be it Harlem, heroin or Broadway successes and the Manhattan intelligentsia/Jewish mafia, and you short circuit the necessary connections which make sense of this society and merely indulge in the narrow references of your chosen milieu."

Gerald's angry politics were not confined to his family. Those who administered the Guild were drawn from an artistic elite which numbered some of America's most famous luminaries – including Jules Feiffer, the Pulitzer prize-winning cartoonist; Mary Rodgers, the accomplished writer and daughter of composer Richard Rodgers; and Ruth Goetz, the playwright and co-author of *The Heiress*. The Guild's executive inhabited "posh offices in the middle of Broadway theatre-land" – at 234 West 44th Street. Indignant or not about the disparate world he found himself bridging, it was an environment in which Gerald felt perfectly at home. "We are on the top floor of the Sardi restaurant building," he writes, "where traditionally first night parties wait up for the reviews to come out. 44th Street is off Times Square, and so each day I see the blinking neon lights, run the gauntlet of all the hustlers and prostitutes, the gamblers and dope dealers, the theatre executives and the tourists. Just to complete the extraordinary kinetic feeling of the area, the Alvin Ailey Ballet co. have their headquarters just opposite the office and you can see them through the big windows rehearsing, pirouetting, jumping, dancing or just lounging around or doing barre exercises in their leotards and tights and leg warmers (it's quite a sexy sight actually! Typical of the whole place). All that is in contrast to the bitter cold and warmly wrapped-up faces leaning into the icy blasts which whip up 44th Street sometimes."

It was in this sophisticated theatrical milieu that Gerald delivered his own icy blast at the annual meeting of the Guild in February 1981. By now he had already run workshops in twenty-two public schools in New York and when he stood up to address the council and members in his first report, he began with the words: "This is not an invitation to a children's tea party. Not everything in the garden is rosy." He illustrated his talk with examples, including a play – a tragic story of a girl who wanted to be a dancer – written by a group of teenagers from the Bronx. "The plays children write," he told his audience, "bear witness to tremendous intimidation and tremendous cultural deprivation. There is great anger, great violence and despair in what young people write." He goes on: "It is the minority groups who provide the most sensitive sounding board to society's rhetorical calls to freedom, creativity and equality. At the age of thirteen, the kind of phrase used by children most often consists of 'It's not fair.' So, you see, they are very aware of the gap between truth and mendacity which adults, later on, smudge. The value of all that we are trying to do with this project is that, at precisely the same time kids are most aware of the double standard society has imposed upon them – when these double standards challenge and conflict with teenagers' own profound and most human feelings of justice and humanity – it is at this time young writers can offer a challenge back."

*

By now the plays – each one competing for a staged production in the Festival – were beginning to trickle onto Gerald's desk. He was pleased. "Some of them are very good," he observed in a letter home. They ranged from an elementary school in the South Bronx where a group of eleven year old girls submitted plays about sex, drugs and prostitution to schools in gentler neighbourhoods where the same age group – its innocence still in flower – offered plays about cats and guinea pigs. The regimes in these schools varied, sometimes to a startling degree. At one – by no means a unique example – the atmosphere within its walls shivered with fear and menace, the older students routinely mugging their juniors. "The discipline is Gestapo-like," Gerald told us, "and the Principal is well to the right of Attila the Hun. Teachers patrol the roof, as well as the corridors and playground, with radio walkie-talkies."

But my brother's gift for reaching out to his fellow human beings transcended these challenges. The schools, the teachers, their students wanted to work with him just as they had done in London. In the office, the Guild had appointed an administrator to assist him in promoting the Festival – now planned for the late autumn. Peggy Hansen became his principal lieutenant and she soon found that working with him was to be a thrilling act of close collaboration with no dividing lines between the Festival's organization and its artistic direction. When I spoke to her after a lapse of twenty years, her affection for my brother, her recollections of their shared experiences, seemed at moments to be caught in the hush of her voice: a few tears shed at the remote end of our telephone line. "Gerald drew me into the work," she said. "He had extraordinary energy and enthusiasm – an optimism that was contagious and it made him inspirational in the classroom. He did not feel bound by conventions or rules and, because of this, I think his appeal to young people was him simply being himself – not anyone else's idea of who he was supposed to be. He was a tremendously caring and supportive person. But he also handled setbacks and disappointments well – they didn't change his world view!"

Sheri M. Goldhirsch, the Artistic Director of Young Playwrights Inc., the organization that runs the project today, was a graduate fresh out of college when she joined the Guild as an administrative assistant in the early years of the Festival. Her memories of Gerald echo those of Peggy Hansen – and again, from across the Atlantic, those of Daphne Rae and Vicky Phillips. "He had this way of walking into a room and absolutely owning it!" she exclaimed. "Gerald always said what he thought and got away with it by charming the pants off everyone with his English accent. But he also had a temper and was never shy about telling people what he thought of them. In the end, he became the face of playwriting in the United States for writers under the age of eighteen." In the heady world of American theatre, my brother was on his way to becoming something of a national treasure.

It was then that disaster struck. Gerald contracted a severe strain of hepatitis and was rushed home to England. The timetable for the Festival – already tight – was now impossible and had to be redrafted with a new date set for April the following year. Meanwhile, his illness kept him away for almost three months; but when he returned to New York in the summer, it was to discover that the trickle had turned to flood with over seven hundred plays received from thirty-one states, twice the number that had ever been submitted to him at the Royal Court.

There was another, more unexpected surprise to come in the aftermath of his hepatitis. Gerald's absence – his time at home – inspired a reawakening of his belief in his parents; the emergence of a kind of peace process after the years of tension and conflict. On the evening of 29th July – the day Prince Charles married Lady Diana Spencer in St. Paul's Cathedral – he sat down to write to his old Cambridge chum. The letter began somewhat playfully with an account of a champagne breakfast he had attended with some of his smarter friends in an apartment on the Upper East Side. "I was amongst a whole bunch of American royalists at 5.00 am today," he tells Peter Judd, half-sneeringly, half-proudly. "One of them was waving a Union Jack in front of the TV and said, 'the Revolution was a mistake; we should have remained in the Empire. For this I'd willingly pay my taxes!' Another said 'A diamond tiara, and no money: that's class!' And as Lady Di's stepmother came in: 'Who's that?' 'She's the Bitch!' And then: 'My God, Princess Anne looks like a hooker!' Well – that's New York for you! Later today all the IRA diehards were protesting outside the British Consulate."

With the gossip of the moment dispensed and after briefing Peter on his life and work, the letter ends with a long paragraph about his illness. "… My mum loved it because she could really pamper me and keep me in bed (I could not move, even stand up, for two or three weeks). Altogether I spent eleven weeks with my parents, and that is the longest time of close proximity to them that I must have spent since I was a little boy. Without it being planned, therefore, these eleven weeks have come to represent a huge development in the life of the family, and in relation to me and them in particular. I could also observe them at close quarters (and become more understanding, admiring and tolerant of them): and that was important. So, with my time in New York, and my big illness, both happening in my 'early-mid-life', as it were, these last eight months have represented quite a big development for me."

Gerald's reincarnated faith in his mother and father – reconciling, in some way, the love he held for his family with the life he had found in New York – speaks of a deeper loneliness within, and of a bitter-sweet homesickness. He misses "England's green and pleasant bowers". He misses his Earl Grey and thick-cut marmalade: the food parcels from home a welcomed gift and a tender reminder of all that he remembered that was good, now so far away. On his return to the city in that hot and humid summer of '81, he gets out to the Long Island beaches, there only to "gaze wistfully across the Ocean!" And his Chinese pianist friend, Joo Ann – mentioned here and there in his correspondence – returns to Singapore leaving him "lonely and bereft." In his letter to Peter Judd he says: "New York is certainly very exciting if not a very nurturing society." Gerald liked to nurture and be nurtured. And his frequent changes of address – St. Mark's Place long abandoned – did little to foster any sense of nurture or home. "This weekend I'm moving – AGAIN!" he tells Etty and Peter in August. "This time I'm near Central Park West, and my bedroom overlooks the Park a bit – on 70th Street."

For those eleven weeks in spring, pale and sick and weakened, he found his nourishment: snug within the Castle's walls at first, then out in the leafy Somerset combes – rediscovering the county's ancient beech woods or the woodsmoke and warm familiarity of a thatched Exmoor inn. A long convalescence which finally ended with a spell on Diodati's terraces beneath the Aegean sun. A time to be a little boy again, under his mother's wing.

*

Loneliness, like an intermittent shadow, now stalked the pages of his letters. Illness and the reconciliation it conferred on his relationship with Etty and Peter made the family's Christmas that year a happy reunion – ending in the New Year with long and tearful farewells. From New York he sent us enlargements of the photographs he had taken over the holiday including "the Oedipal one of Mummy and me in bed." These weeks, his time at home, had also begun to forge a loving bond between uncle and nephews –Dom now eight and Nick turned six. And his affection and regard for Louise had grown, a development my mother was quick to spot. More and more she assumed the wearisome habit of insisting she accompany her younger son every time he wanted to visit us or whenever we wanted an evening alone with him. By now we had occupied our tiny cottage high up in the Blackdown Hills for almost six years. My own working relations with my parents in the hotel were showing the strain and I longed for a few private moments with my brother. Rare though these moments appeared to be, Louise's friendship with her brother-in-law was sealed and in my occasional absences abroad promoting the Castle, Gerald liked to keep in touch with her.

In January '82, I embarked on the second leg of a major sales campaign to promote the Castle in the United States – a three-week tour under the balmy skies of California, sweeping through that gilded seam of America's leisured West Coast from San Francisco southward to Santa Barbara, Beverly Hills, Newport Beach and San Diego. In England - up on our hillside – a barren and monochrome landscape was gripped by cold winds and drifting snow. As my taxi drew away, inching nervously down our icy drive, I looked back, my eyes lighting upon an image that still remains lodged and guilt-torn in my memory. There by our back door stood Louise and Dom and Nick huddled close against the bitter chill, waving forlornly at the disappearing car. Our romantic homestead, equipped with a Rayburn in the kitchen, had no central heating in the bedrooms. At night our breathing condensed and froze on the inside of the windowpanes leaving crazy opaque patterns for us to scrape off in the morning. Later, after my return from California, Louise told me they had abandoned their beds, dragged mattresses downstairs and made a dormitory in front of the log fire in the living room.

Gerald understood and he cared, knowing also he had someone with whom to share his own loneliness.

January 23rd 1982

c/o Dramatists' Guild,
234 West 44th Street
NY NY 10036

Dearest Louise,

You must be feeling a bit lonely with Kit away; I hope it's not too bad. To-day it's very cold and wet, so I'm staying in, listening to Joan Armatrading and Bette Midler. I had Chariots of Fire at top blast as well while doing the vacuuming!

I've been missing England a lot – terribly, in fact! It sort of started last Sunday which was about minus 10°, and I stayed in again and I missed you all, and all the values, the gentleness, graciousness – even the pomposity of England. I've seen quite a lot of my friends. Last Monday I watched episode 1 of "Brideshead Revisited" which is just about to take the USA by storm I suspect. And I've had dinner with various friends: and that's been nice. But there really is no substitute for friendships that are 5 or 10 years old. I miss my Chinese friend, Joo Ann a lot – he's the one in Singapore. It's a bit difficult to have a relationship 4000 miles away! I have yet to meet someone really special here. Oh well.

Back in the Dramatists' Guild office, I've had to put up with the absurd pettiness and legalities and bureaucratic procedures which somehow didn't irritate me so much last year, but which now irritate me a great deal. I'm looking forward to negotiating a new contract, for another year, which will allow me greater freedom. [Gerald was also applying for a Green Card.]

Meanwhile, we're slowly preparing for the Festival – which opens late April. The Puerto Rican girl's play, "The Bronx Zoo" (which I'm doing) has just appeared in a 4th draft, and it's very good: a really street-ethnic sort of play – full of life, laughs and tears etc! I'm also doing a staged reading of a remarkable piece called "Epiphany", a play set in an English Public School, and it centres on a love affair between two boys and how it's bust up by the arrival of a new boy and his sister (who's just visiting). The sister and one of the boys fall madly in love, and the new boy falls for the other boy. It's very authentic (I should know!) which is remarkable considering the author is a girl living in Ohio who got the idea of the play from reading books about it all!

So, I've been busy preparing for all this. On Monday we have a party for all the ten winning playwrights (aged 8 to 18) with their parents etc. On Tuesday a press conference, when Sondheim and myself will face the cameras!

It was so marvellous seeing you and the kids. And I'm sorry that we never said goodbye properly. Write to me again when you can. And give the boys a hug from me. Love – Gerald.

Peggy Hansen recognized Gerald's irritation with the Guild's "bureaucratic procedures". "Employees had to clock in," she told me. "But Gerald didn't bother. He saw the Festival as a separate entity. He had a way of ignoring the office politics and made his own rules!" And so it was that on the twenty-seventh of April, and for the three weeks that followed, Gerald staged his first Young Playwrights' Festival. It took place at the Circle Repertory Company, a theatre in a second floor loft on upper Broadway and attracted universal applause – the New York Drama Critics' Circle awarding the project a Special Citation later in the year.

*

Pressure of work, his life in New York and his illness the previous year seemed to exact their toll as Gerald became more susceptible to viruses and chills, ear aches, acne and even mouth ulcers. Etty and Peter worried about his state of health and fussed constantly with a steady stream of airmail packages containing everything from food and medicines to T-shirts and Bermuda shorts for his holiday in the Caribbean – a break, he said, that returned him to New York "rested and recharged". They had also befriended Ruth Goetz, a senior member of the Guild's council and a regular visitor to London. To her evident dismay, the celebrated playwright suddenly found herself adopted by Etty as a transatlantic bag handler for the benefit of her son. "Ruth's coming to London on September 20th," he tells them at the start of the month. "She very much wants to see you both, but don't give her anything to bring back this time. She was a bit startled last year when you gave her my dinner jacket and the marmalade! I never heard the end of it …"

By this stage in the year, of course, he was busy harvesting a new crop of scripts in preparation for the second festival, a process he was finding increasingly tiresome. "I'm just a bit fed up with reading too many awful plays by young people," he groans, "though this is not any different from reading awful plays by adults. And at least youngsters can be taught: and I mostly enjoy the teaching." But the strain of it all, even his frustrations with the Guild – "an office of lawyers and accountants" – seem to be symptoms of his own ambivalent feelings towards New York, a city so full of contradictions that, at times, it unsettles him. On one occasion he visits some Cuban friends who live in New Jersey just across the Hudson River. "They have the most spectacular view from their living room," he writes, "with the whole of the Manhattan skyline stretching out in front of them, glistening in the evening sun, reflected in the river. Back in Manhattan this warm glow quickly dissipates as you struggle through the crowds and dirt and violence. But then last week I went to see *Midsummer Night's Dream* under the stars in Central Park: and it really was magical."

Gerald's mixed emotions about New York leave him equivocal about his future there. While part of his heart pines for a return to Blighty, the other half remains determined to pursue the expensive business of applying for a Green Card. "In spite of this investment," he tells us, "I still don't really feel at home here and, in some ways, find myself psychologically resisting the urge to do so. It's strange. My life sometimes only seems worth it when I can observe the city from afar (like in New Jersey or the Caribbean), rather than from inside it. That's why I want to live in England, and visit here once a year or so. But that is not likely to happen for at least two years (until my Green Card comes through), and meanwhile I've got to make sense of being here now."

*

THE NEW YORK TIMES, MONDAY, APRIL 18, 1983. "The second annual Young Playwrights Festival is an event that makes one feel hopeful about both the American Theatre and American young people." These opening words from Frank Rich, The Times's powerful theatre critic began a long review which would cement Gerald's reputation and mark his future success. Mr. Rich's enthusiasm seems boundless: "… some of the most gifted adults in the New York Theatre, under the leadership of Gerald Chapman," he continues, "have banded together to mount these plays at a high level few established writers have known this season." And in a final flourish he ends his notice by observing that "today's theatrical establishment has truly given its sweat and blood to the Young Playwrights Festival. It's a selfless gift whose future dividends are incalculable."

Gerald was ecstatic. He wrote immediately to Etty and Peter, carefully folding a copy of Frank Rich's article into the envelope. "Of course it's made everything here crazy with excitement," he gushes. "TV interviews, an article in Time magazine and so on! It was never like this at the Royal Court!" There was much to celebrate and by a lucky coincidence that April happened to take Louise and me to the United States as part of a troupe of hoteliers flying the flag in a major cultural mission headlined *Britain Salutes New York.* We installed ourselves in the hushed and refined luxury of the Ritz-Carlton on Central Park South, and when he came to see us, Gerald took immense pleasure indulging his appetite for the hotel's lavish hospitality. In our suite overlooking the park, the coffee table and sideboard glistened with delectable bonbons and expensive beverages: petit fours and handmade chocolates, exotic fruit plates and champagne. Gerald saw to it that they were properly appreciated.

Meanwhile, Louise and I were hurled into a breathless cycle of lunches, dinners, cocktail parties and presentations – edgily polite gatherings held in locations designed to impress those cynical audiences who have seen it all before. We paraded our British charm and our accents at the New York Stock Exchange, on a yacht cruising up the East River and at a grand mansion in the Hamptons, favourite enclave of the super-rich on the eastern reaches of Long Island. Within a couple of days Louise began to find the whole circus of fake grins, padded shoulders and perfect hair a dreadful bore. So she left me to network New York and appointed Gerald her tour guide. She needed a reality-check and her brother-in-law provided it, brimming as he was with the fun and humour she found entirely absent in the earnestness of our worthy hosts. He took her to Carnegie Hall and in the interval offered her a drink. She never discovered the whereabouts of a bar, instead he led her to a water fountain – complimentary refreshment at the push of a button and a more memorable experience than any cocktail lounge she had visited. Afterwards, supper was a pastrami on rye at the Carnegie Deli on Seventh Avenue and she loved that too.

Next day, the two set off for Times Square. "We'll go on the subway," he announced.

"That's one thing I don't want to do, Gerald," she said. "I'm frightened. We've been told to use cabs."

"If you haven't done the subway, you haven't done New York," he insisted. "Just don't look people in the eye. Hold onto my arm and look purposeful." She folded her musquash coat – the fur turned in – and, placing it over her handbag, seized Gerald's arm as they descended into the bowels of Manhattan to face the dirt and the graffiti. They toured theatreland and he took her to the Rockefeller Center before walking the nine blocks back to the Ritz-Carlton. I was furious with my brother for his irresponsibility. But he laughed it off and popped another chocolate praline into his mouth.

*

Like sunrise over these islands, the New York Times piece illuminated Gerald's gifts and the swell of publicity that followed attracted the attention of a wider world. The Festival went on to be endowed with the prestige of a Drama Critics' Circle Award; the educational arm of Heinemann commissioned him to write a book – *Teaching Young Playwrights*; he conducted workshops as far afield as Michigan, Texas and South Dakota; he was invited to teach at Boston University; and there were invitations to direct plays by theatre companies both in the United States and in Great Britain. His reputation even found a cause in Australia where, in 1985, he was a Guest Director and Tutor at the International Young Playwrights Festival in Sydney, a muster of seventy-two young writers from across the globe: "one of the most exciting things I've ever attended," he claimed in a postcard home.

But the most significant element to enter Gerald's life at this time was the arrival of Ivan whom the family gradually came to hear about during the course of 1984. "Ivan and I are both well," he remarked in July, "enjoying each other's company as we get to know one another more and more." At last, it seemed, Gerald had found his elusive soulmate – that "someone really special" he yearned for in the letter he had written to Louise more than two years before.

That Christmas in Somerset, Ivan came to stay. For us it was the first family Christmas in the company of Gerald's lover; and for Etty and Peter a difficult moment where a cultural void and the accepted proprieties of the times were tested to their limits. But a kind of restrained diplomacy eased the tension on all sides – even if an unfamiliar perspective on the public image of Mr. and Mrs. Chapman and family caused a few provincial eyebrows to rise. For Ivan it was no easier. Twelve years Gerald's junior, he presented himself in Taunton as a twenty-three year old African American with dreadlocks; a moment which would have drained the blood from my father's face if he and Etty had not first met him in New York that summer.

The young Ivan Chatman had been raised by his divorced mum in the borough of Queens – their modest one-bedroomed house in Corona touched by the shadow of the Shea Stadium, home to the New York Mets. She cleaned for a living and supplemented the family income by baby-sitting for the neighbours. But mother, a God-fearing Baptist lady, was ambitious for her son. Determined to see him well educated, she sent him to school in nearby Woodside, a predominantly white area of the borough. Ivan prospered and completed his education at the Fashion Institute of Technology in Manhattan before taking up a career in interior design.

One afternoon in May '84, he visited the bookshop at the Cathedral Church of Saint John the Divine on Amsterdam Avenue and 111th Street. He would often be found there browsing its shelves. He liked the shop's unusual collection of books and, besides, the peace and tranquillity of the cathedral gave him a soul-soothing break from the frenzied streets of the city. By chance that day, Gerald was there too, investigating opportunities for conducting young writers' workshops on the premises. A month later, on his birthday, Gerald gave Ivan Eric Gill's *A Holy Tradition of Working*, an anthology of writings by the controversial sculptor which he bought from the cathedral shop. It was the first gift Ivan received from him – and a book he still treasures and rereads. "It has helped shape my outlook on life," he told me in a long telephone conversation one Sunday evening from his apartment in New York.

This call – a poignant moment for us both – was our first communication in twenty years. We had lost touch and I had spent weeks attempting to track him down only to discover that he still lived at 109 West 74th Street – the same address he and Gerald had shared all that time ago. At the start of our conversation, his opening words were to enquire after Louise and Dom and Nick – and throughout the sixty or more minutes we spoke together what touched me was the obvious affection he held for Louise, much like Gerald's. He remembered the support she gave him, the feeling of a special bond, a "kinship" he called it because with Louise as my wife and Etty as her mother-in-law, he saw himself cast in a similar role as Gerald's partner. "With Etty," he said, "Louise had to live up to such tremendous standards!"

And so as Ivan's life changed course – now to be shared with Gerald's – his first taste of our family came when Peter and Etty arrived in New York on a flying visit shortly after the great romantic encounter at Saint John the Divine. That moment of first meeting etched its impression on the young design student. Gerald had been careful to brief Ivan about his parents, particularly on the more singular characteristics of his mother. He told him about the tribulations of their past relationships – mindful also to balance these old tensions and difficulties with the reconciliation which emerged through his long illness and convalescence in England and Greece. But as eager as he was to prepare him, and as much as Gerald would surely have briefed his parents on Ivan's background, nothing could alert them to Etty's periodic tendency to ambush a conversation with an ill-considered one-liner.

The trigger was Ivan's surname – Chatman. Similar, and for Etty uncomfortably similar, to her own – Chapman. The four had spent an evening at Carnegie Hall and, like Louise's visit the year before, after the show Gerald was keen to introduce his parents to the pleasures of the famous Carnegie Deli. As they strolled the one block down Seventh Avenue chatting amiably, Etty turned to Ivan.

"Chatman?" she asked suddenly apropos of nothing. "How did you get that name?"

"It was my father's name!" came the startled retort.

Gerald winced inwardly at this bizarre exchange, his antennae instantly decoding his mother's naïve prejudice. He waited before delivering his response and when it came it came as a blunt fait accompli. He wanted Etty and Peter to be in no doubt about the importance of his love for Ivan and at supper he announced that the two of them had decided to live together. Etty's reaction was predictable, immediate and emphatic. She did not believe it was a good idea. The heat in the rhetoric was now rising to incendiary levels and an old-fashioned family row was only averted by Peter's quiet calm and firm intervention. For Ivan, this was a moment of extreme awkwardness. Gerald had given him no advance warning of his intention to make an announcement to his parents. "I wish he'd told me," Ivan said. "I had no idea he was going to come out with that." But then, I suspect, neither did Gerald – until his mother's behaviour compelled him to retaliate.

This brief but uncomfortable skirmish brought its benefits. It clarified the order of our lives and set down a new status quo which eased Ivan's arrival at the Castle that Christmas – harmony and goodwill prevailing in concert with the traditions of the season. The only detail to cause a passing flutter of temperament came over the question of the sleeping arrangements. Gerald wanted Ivan to feel part of the family gathering and share his bedroom in the Penthouse – a request which overstepped the line. On this one he had to give way. "Gerald, this is Taunton!" Etty snapped. "This is not New York! What will the staff think?" Peter gently endorsed the mood for decorum and the local gossip industry was held at bay. Meanwhile, Ivan was found a hotel bedroom at the far end of a long corridor on the third floor. "I felt comfortable and secure," he told me. "I'd never been given such a beautiful room to stay in."

Our celebrations passed off well and we all had a happy time. Ivan, at first overawed by the family and the hotel, soon relaxed – and Louise and I found him genuine and kind and immensely likeable company. We had just moved house and on Christmas Day they all came out to us. After lunch we played charades and the shyness we had seen in him at our first meeting the evening before descended into peels of unaffected laughter when Gerald started directing Dom and Nick in an improvised mini-pantomime. Ivan's adoration of Gerald was touching and at the end of the afternoon, exhausted and oblivious to the rest of us, the pair of them sank into a deep sofa holding hands. A mutual, uncomplicated love. Each at ease with the other.

In recalling that Christmas with Ivan on the telephone, I asked him how he remembered my parents. Even with the passage of so many years, his scrupulous politesse and gentleness did not desert him. "They were very gracious and respectful to me," he said. And, after pausing for a second, he added: "Through your father, I came to understand Gerald. He had such dignity."

On their return to New York in early January, Gerald wrote home with his thanks, an almost palpable sense of relief evident between the lines dashed off on a Castle notepad. "We both had a glorious time," he began, "and sorely missed England when, on arriving by bus in Manhattan, we had to put up with aggressive taxi drivers and the street paranoia of this place." The note ends: "The time we spent with you was wonderful. The carrots and shortbread biscuits were lovely – as are all the goodies which now fill our kitchen cupboards." He signs off: "All my love – from us both, Gerald xxx." But, in spite of its hum of contentment, the letter struck one brief chord of mild alarm. He still hadn't finished writing his book – Heinemann's deadline for the manuscript already exceeded by eighteen months. Delivering it before the end of 1985 became a firm New Year's resolution.

But it was not to be. In the late spring Gerald was diagnosed HIV-positive, the deficiency in his white blood cells so great that the onset of Aids was inevitable. At the time, the condition was still a new phenomenon. It struck fear among homosexuals who, in turn, became stigmatized by a censorious public as the disease looked like spiralling into an epidemic across Europe and America. Sitting quietly together in their apartment, Gerald took Ivan's hand and held it gently before he spoke to break the news. As the meaning of his words gradually seeped into his young companion's consciousness, tears of despair welled up into their eyes and they embraced. And as the weeks went by – each trying to come to terms with an uncertain future – the two men slipped into a terrible depression. Gerald convinced himself that Ivan was about to desert him, and when eventually he confessed his cold panic, his lover felt wounded. It was a cathartic moment in their relationship. The younger man had already made a private vow to take care of Gerald whatever the circumstances and he now reassured him that he would remain by his side for ever.

*

In the autumn Gerald returned to England. It was time to face the family – a duty he had delayed for several months on account of his work commitments, the pressure to complete his book and the trip to Sydney for the International Young Playwrights Festival. But before travelling to Taunton, there was another call he wanted to make. On the evening of the twentieth of October, a Sunday evening, Peter Judd and his wife Judith had just settled their children for the night. Young Tom was now almost four, Alice two years behind him. Since their son's birth the family had been living at Hitcham Vicarage in Burnham just west of Slough, the seat of Peter's present ministry. With the children tucked up, mother and father were about to sit down to eat when the telephone rang. It was Gerald.

"This is a surprise!" Peter exclaimed. "Where are you?"

"I'm in London," he replied. "Just landed from New York. On my way home."

"And how are you?" interrupted his friend, already sensing an anxiety in Gerald's voice.

"I need to see you, Peter," he answered. "I'm in deep, deep trouble. Can we meet tomorrow?"

"What's up Gerald?" he asked, alarmed by the ghostly tone of the call.

"I'll tell you when I see you," he said.

The conversation was brief. But the priest knew Gerald in crisis and his response was immediate. They agreed to meet at Cliveden early the following afternoon before his onward journey to Somerset.

Leaving their cars by the kiosk and shop in the National Trust car park, they strolled through the woodland to Canning's Oak overlooking the Thames. The gravel paths were carpeted with fallen leaves – green, yellow, ochre, raw and burnt sienna. And the view through the trees was spellbinding – the river serene and stately, untroubled by time and the affairs of the world, wrapped in veils of autumn foliage.

They were alone – the woodland all theirs as they sat on a bench beneath the oak and gazed down towards the water. They talked for two hours – a long conversation which included a frank discussion about preparing to die. "I've got a year to live," Gerald told Peter. "My immune system is down to seventeen T-cells per thousand – the average minimum is five hundred T-cells per thousand." In his journal Peter noted: "He gets hot flushes as he thinks about it. The prospects are terrifying." And as the afternoon wore on Gerald began to repeat three words like a Vedic hymn: "Nobody told us!" He said.

"Nobody told us!" But the truth at the time was that nobody could tell him because nobody knew. Until then the dangers of unprotected sex and HIV were still obscure.

As the light on the river began to fade, the priest quietly touched a dormant nerve. "What about church?" he asked. Gerald did not reply, silently appealing to his friend to develop his theme. Some years before, he explained, when Judith had been in New York, she visited the Cathedral of Saint John the Divine. She had returned home to tell him that it was a very remarkable place. Did he know it? Peter asked. Of course Gerald did. But not as a place of worship. That had been an aspect of his life he had abandoned at Cambridge. "That is why I'm asking," Peter replied. "Try it. See if you like it." Gerald agreed, promising that he would go on his return to New York.

It was time to leave their bench under the oak tree. But before returning to the car park, Peter – whose instincts and long experience of his Cambridge chum had primed his senses – produced a small booklet and gave it to him. It was a selection of the revelations of Julian of Norwich, the fourteenth century mystic: an unusual and wonderful choice of gift which could only have been offered in the company of a profound and affectionate understanding between giver and receiver. Peter had lived through Gerald's great struggle at university. He had grappled with his self-loathing and his guilt – all the shame and the confusion which had shadowed those difficult years. Now there was a new crisis. And he turned to Julian of Norwich to comfort his old friend. The mystic had lived as a recluse at the time of the Black Death, the terrible epidemic which had swept through England killing almost half its population. She believed in the supreme power of divine love, her theology contrasting dramatically with the accepted teaching of the age which saw the Plague as divine punishment for our sins. In Julian's belief, the suffering of the people was the medium that would draw them closer to God's love – an unconditional love which was all-redeeming. From this belief came her most famous saying: "All shall be well, and all shall be well, and all manner of things shall be well."

*

Gerald drove away from Cliveden comforted – pleased to have seen his friend. But by the time he turned his hire car onto the westbound carriageway of the M4, he was overcome by fear and loneliness. He missed Ivan. And he now had to confront his family.

I remember that October night so well. He arrived at the Castle early in the evening and over supper in the Penthouse spoke to his mother and father. When he had finished he insisted on driving out to us, leaving his parents speechless and distressed. It was now past nine o'clock. We had eaten. Over coffee around our kitchen table, Gerald, Louise and I sat and talked. He told us about Sydney, his return via New Zealand, then Thailand from where he bought me a present. I opened the long slim package to find a sober silk tie in midnight blue shot with thin pearl grey stripes. I have it here now, beside me, feeling its soft smoothness between my thumb and fingers. At the kitchen table that evening, he spoke to us. One hour, two hours – explaining everything in the minutest detail.

I began to feel sick. Taking the tie, I left Louise with Gerald and went to our bedroom to lie down. Opening my wardrobe door, I hung the tie beside three dozen others draped over the metal rack. And, staring at it, I spoke aloud to an empty room. "Gerald! Gerald!" I swore. "I shall wear this at your funeral. But not before that day – whenever it may come."

*

A strange taboo now descended on the family. We talked about Gerald, worried about Gerald, even sought confidential advice from a trusted friend in the medical profession. But the A-word was never uttered. Never. Gerald's disease remained a deep and dark family secret. No one should know. And after a burst of Euripidean wailing, my mother began to recite her favourite Greek mantra όλα ωραία, όλα καλά. She convinced herself that all would be well, eerily echoing the creed of Julian of Norwich. She lit candles in her bedroom and prayed before her holy icons. On her frequent visits to London, the first call after disembarking at Paddington was a short taxi fare to the Greek Orthodox church in Moscow Road. More candles and prayers, incense and icons. She bounced back – reclaiming her famous joie de vivre. Geraldo would live.

But from that black day in October an almost visible change gradually took hold of my father and his spirit retreated, a lifeblood withdrawn. His occasional moments of melancholy, his tendency to lapse into periods of sad reflection became more evident and, at times, made him seem a little remote from the hurly-burly of everyday existence. As a fourteen year old he had lost his beloved father. Now in his seventy-first year he was facing the death of his adored son. He began living a bereavement like a running sore: his innermost feelings a no-go area for anyone but himself. Through it all his Ettylein – "Koutsi Mou" – was his lifeboat; not because she understood or shared his pain or tuned into his distress, but because her gaiety and childlike optimism kept him afloat.

Christmas came and went much as it had done the year before – the family's united determination to celebrate, perhaps, eclipsing the question uppermost in our minds. Would this be Gerald's last? He and Ivan seemed to infuse us with courage and hope more than any emotional support we provided in return. And he had also taken Peter Judd's advice about church. In an upbeat letter, he wrote to his friend in December to wish him and Judith a happy Christmas and, in a flourish of excitement, he described the drug programmes he was being put on – some "unofficial and experimental." "I'm feeling very well," he says. "Ivan and I have started jogging! So far I like it and it makes me feel really great." With the letter he enclosed the service sheets from Saint John the Divine, thanking Peter for encouraging him to go. After a long absence, Gerald had begun to rediscover his faith and he now found himself glorying in the splendour of the liturgy. "It's fairly overwhelming at first," he confesses. "But it's certainly very friendly: not at all stuffy. Female priests of course …"

As the weeks and months slipped by he became more involved with the Cathedral, attending Sunday Eucharist and participating in the Church's calendar of feast days. Ivan – who preferred to sleep late at weekends – recalls the day Gerald joined the pageant for the Feast of St. Francis of Assisi

– swinging open the great Bronze Doors of the West Front to herald in a procession of animals – domestic pets, livestock and beasts from the zoo – all to receive a blessing from the Bishop of New York. "He loved it there," Ivan told me. "This is where he found his inner peace."

As the disease began to invade his body, the long letters home which had become his trademark grew shorter, and he took to writing postcards as a means of reassuring Etty and Peter of his active life and good health. A card from Aspen Colorado in January '86 spills over with enthusiasm: "Had a great week skiing here," he notes. "I was so pleased I could still do it after eighteen years!" In July, a card from the north of Wyoming strikes a more wistful chord: "It's wonderfully beautiful and peaceful," he writes. "The light is so crystalline, and it's dry and not too hot. Very relaxing. Just what I needed." Another in August describes Yellowstone National Park as "utterly spectacular," and ends with the firm reassurance: "I'm feeling fine!" But a letter to Peter Judd four days later is more qualified: "I've developed a couple of spots on my elbows which are cancerous (Kaposi's sarcoma), but my doctor seriously believes they'll not spread. So I'm not too anxious."

As we approached the final months, Gerald's ravaged body refused to overwhelm his extraordinary spirit and will to live. His suffering, stoic in its way, wore a convincing disguise – a sunny deceit to relieve those he loved from the hurt and worry they might be enduring. In September he returned to England once again, not just to see us and the Judd family, but to pursue an invitation he had received to direct Edward Bond's Saved for Birmingham Rep in the New Year. "Don't worry," he tells Etty and Peter on his return to New York. "I'll look after myself. And please look after yourselves too!"

We all travelled to Birmingham to see the play – Gerald's last. We sat amid the bright bare whiteness of the Studio under bright bleak lighting which denied us any hiding place. This was Gerald at his most raw, determined to force his audience to share the moral and emotional rawness of the piece. It was a great critical success, a local critic observing that "the overall picture of an alienated, brutalised society is arguably more recognisable as the present day now than it was twenty years ago."

Shortly after, at the beginning of March 1987, Gerald was admitted to the Beth Israel Medical Center on First Avenue and 16th Street. On the third, a Tuesday, he wrote to his father on the hospital's headed notepaper to wish him "Happy Birthday for the eighth!" He apologized for not sending a proper greetings card. Four short lines ending: "I'll see you soon and I'm much better! All my love and thank you for *everything.*" The message was signed "Geraldo" – followed by five crosses.

I am trying to imagine how I might feel on my birthday if I received a letter from my son, the notepaper stamped with the hospital's neat blue logo. Imprisoned in his cot. His body wired up. The thought consumes me and my vision begins to blur. Raising my eyes, the sea is cloaked in a grey-blue haze of tears. Lost memories of my brother drifting into view.

Eleven days later he wrote to Hitcham Vicarage in Burnham.

109 W.74
NY NY 10023   *Mar 14 1987*

Dear Peter,

Sorry about this scrappy note – no more nice paper left!

Thanks for yr. wonderful letter – you've had some good trips to Florence and the Lake District.

I came out of hospital on Mar 10, only to have to return there this Mon (16th)! They've now isolated the cause of the adrenal failure and have to begin treatment. I'll be in for 5-6 days – then I go home and do the medicine myself with the help of a home-care nurse (it's intravenous, you see). Eventually I'll learn to do it myself and I'll have to continue for 6 months!! But the symptoms that arose this week (the day I left hospital, ironically) which indicate this particular virus (fever, diarrhoea, tummy ache, no appetite) ought to disappear within 2 weeks. Then I can begin to eat properly again and regain weight (I've lost over 20 lbs).

My spirits are high. God is with me always. Ivan's terrific. I have a wonderful network of friends who cook and clean for me. And my parents are at last coming here, very soon.

All my love and thanks. Gerald.

Slowly, too slowly, my father, my mother, Louise, me – even our two boys, Nick now eleven and Dom thirteen – began to confront a reality which, until this moment, lay screened behind its rosy camouflage. Easier that way – helps you cope and get on. Self-delusion, denial, faith, hope – all these are powerful tricks which hold mortality at a comfortable distance – out of sight, out of mind. He was thirty-seven, rising to his prime, indestructible. No more. And so we rallied round, gathered and reinforced our delusions – cheerleaders on a Stygian touchline brandishing brave words down telephone lines; a stream of letters and messages and prayers for Geraldo. Among the shoals of letters swept about my feet is one from Nick. "I hope you come home soon," he begins, "because I miss you very much. I hope you have a nice Easter and get lots of Easter eggs. If you didn't want your Easter eggs do not throw them away. Give them to me and I hope they are chocolate. Love from Nicholas."

*

109 West 74 St.
NY NY 10023   *April 14 1987*

My Dear Daddy,

Your wonderful letter arrived last week, and I've pondered on it a lot. I know I thanked you for it when we spoke at the week-end, but I wanted to respond in writing, however inadequately, as well.

Life is so full of unexpected events, and obviously my illness is one of those. Equally life has certain "rules", like we are all going to die, etc., etc. When the two, the "unexpected" and the "rules" seem to get confused and mixed up we panic and lose our bearings, and wonder if there are any guidelines at all.

I know, both from observation and from what you've told me, that you have faith in some of these guidelines – a faith I share, though we may disagree about the "small print"! And all I can say is that for all of us – Mummy included, of course – a faith in the essential <u>goodness</u> of life, in its extraordinary <u>subtlety</u> and <u>complexity</u> which shift constantly about an essential <u>simplicity</u>, a faith in the communion we share with lovers and friends, (their support, resilience and good humour); above all a faith in God's love and the redemptive experience that, like daily miracles, strengthen and transform us, irrespective of the pain, or how old we are, or how entrenched we may feel, - all of these <u>faiths</u> sustain us, and, blessedly, <u>change</u> us. We no longer have to feel like helpless victims, passive in the face of shifting forces we cannot understand. <u>We</u> can take the initiative and determine, to a great extent, our own destiny. And thus we <u>change</u>, sometimes slowly and imperceptibly, sometimes enormously fast. I've experienced such a fast change these past two months – it's exhausting and exhilarating. And I know that you both have changed, and will continue to do so. I'm sure this realization strengthens your resolve. Your sense of hope in regard to me, your wonderful spirit, after the initial trauma and terror of the first few days here, was an inspiration and source of joy to me too. So, <u>there</u>, in the 10 days we spent together in N.York, was a tremendous change. And this will continue.

I know you feel frustrated at not being able to provide more "active and practical help" to me and in previous letters you spoke of feeling "helpless". Well, I just want to say that you <u>are</u> an active and practical source of help, financially, psychologically and spiritually. And these all contribute to the medical progress, as we know. I rejoice in this for I know that the future is not bleak; I can rely on you, and I can rely on a shared understanding of my life here, and a shared faith in the guidelines I spoke of.

I'm so glad you've planned to go to Diodati. That always invigorates you and you'll return feeling even more changed! And I'm sure that I'll continue to do well and make progress.

I'll sign off now. Once again, thank you for your letter. Thank you for your love. Gerald x

*

109 W.74 St.
NY NY 10023   *May 6 1987*

Dear Peter,
I thought it was about time I wrote and told you how I was doing. Everything is well, so far, thank God. I'm getting stronger every week, put on weight (½ of what I lost already), occasionally put in a few hours in the office, re-started the famous book I've written (my publisher took me out for yet <u>another</u> lunch last week!). They've been v. kind and patient (they know about my illness).

I'm on a very strict medical regime. Every morning I spend 2 hours preparing (mixing with a saline solution) a drug and infusing it intravenously (thro' a catheter implant). So I drip, drip, drip for a good hour, during which I can meditate or write letters or catch up on my reading. It's a good, <u>quiet</u> time. Then I take a whole variety of pills (on some days 5 different kinds!) throughout the day, and night (I have an alarm go off at 2.30 a.m.). But I usually sleep ok – it's gotten much better recently. My feet still hurt a bit – (the neurological pain has lessened but not disappeared) – but I've just discovered that a hot footbath really helps, so I do that now every morning (while I drip!) and before going to bed. It's quite a pampered existence really!

Ivan and I are v. happy. He's enjoying his job a lot. Recently we attended a Healing Workshop together and he made some new friends. This was very good because until recently he'd been isolated, with no-one to confide in. We're planning a holiday in California in July-Aug: we've been invited to stay with friends who are very rich and have a ranch house near Santa Barbara. I've never been anywhere near Los Angeles, so I'm looking forward to it a lot.

Do write when you can. Lots of love, <u>Gerald</u>

P.S. My parents are fine – they're off on a holiday in Greece very soon.

*

109 West 74 St.
NY NY 10023   *May 25 '87*

Dear Peter,

Enclosed is the Cathedral of St. John the Divine's newsletter, which I thought you'd like to see. Yesterday, guess who was preaching?! – Hugh Montefiore!! The week before we had the (Anglican) Bishop of Jerusalem, who's a Palestinian.

I'm still doing pretty well. I'm in the midst of some radiation treatment for a K.S. [Kaposi's Sarcoma] lesion in my mouth, which is already going away. The treatment does tire me and I'll be glad when it's over. My holistic-medicine friends are very against radiation, but I keep a positive attitude towards it. I'm also trying some herbal remedies and acupuncture, and am taking bee pollen and other supplements to cleanse and strengthen me. I've changed my diet a bit too. So, all in all, I think things are going well.

Ivan's fine – he's been depressed lately. His mother has, I think, guessed I've been ill and is now questioning him on this. She's been quite hostile about it all, apparently, and this obviously puts Ivan into a difficult position. He feels badly about being "sick" (he's got the virus, but he's not <u>actually</u> sick) at such a young age. Couple this with my own lack of libido and he naturally feels frustrated. Difficult times. In July/Aug. we're going on a holiday to southern California for 2 or 3 *weeks, and that will really help us, I'm sure. I've never been there before.*

Today is Memorial Day, the official start of summer. The weather's been good and Central Park's beautiful. Ivan and I went on a crazy shopping spree on Saturday: we got a microwave and also a juice extractor. We've tried them out and are pleased with the results. Of course they create even less room for ourselves in our tiny apartment – soon we'll be overwhelmed with modern appliances!

Well, I'll finish now- I send you all my love and hope you all survive election fever, and its end result – God help us all! Love, <u>Gerald</u> x

*

109 West 74 St.
NY NY 10023   *May 31 '87*

Dear Mummy & Daddy,

Here is a memento of a very special occasion today – the dedication of a large-scale copy of this icon in the Cathedral of St. John the Divine. The original icon is in Poland where it is venerated as miraculous, and is known as the Queen of Poland. [Black Madonna of Czestochowa. World famous icon presented by Leon Sliwinski. Dedicated 31 May 1987 The Cathedral Church of St. John the Divine New York, New York.]

You'll get this on your return from Diodati – I hope the journey wasn't too exhausting, and that you find everything ok back at the Castle.

Speak to you soon.

All my love – <u>Gerald</u> xx

*

In late July, Gerald and Ivan travelled to California for their holiday – as guests on the ranch of Maxwell and Juliet Caulfield, their friends near Santa Barbara. They airmailed two postcards to Etty and Peter who had returned to Diodati for their long summer break.

July 28 [The postcard, branded "California", carries an image of a hummingbird.]
Hummingbirds hover above us, amongst the profusion of flowers, and it feels like Nature's blessing us. Perfect weather. Soon we visit Los Angeles and Disneyland. Juliet and Maxwell are so generous and loving. As a result I feel better than I have for weeks. All my love, Geraldo xx.

Aug. 5 [Mickey Mouse in front of Sleeping Beauty Castle]

On Saturday we visited Disneyland – "The happiest place on Earth" – and indeed it was *happy. We felt like 10 yr. olds all day! Los Angeles itself is another matter – a most sprawling and stressful place. So it was good to get back to Juliet and Maxwell's home. All our love, Gerald & Ivan.*

The happiness they shared in California proved as fleeting and as frail as any Disney fantasy. Back in New York, Gerald relapsed – this time with pneumonia – and he was rushed back into hospital. Another crisis he survived. "It was bad for a week," he told Peter Judd, "but I'm now on the up and up. So don't worry. Each time I come back with an even stronger sense of confidence. Lots of prayer, meditation and visualization: it all works."

These months of treatment were like fighting spontaneous fires and, throughout his trial, my brother's concern for Ivan, his family and friends seemed to override his suffering. Only once did his resolve forsake him and it came like a sudden biblical cry from the Cross. He had been recalled for a massive blood transfusion. Late one evening, in his vicarage in Burnham, his friend and confessor received an unexpected call. "I'm in hospital in New York," heaved the anguished voice. "I'm in terrible pain. This place is a hell-hole!" The priest, caught unawares, was shaken. Behind the voice on the telephone, the noise he heard was the sound of bedlam, a ward filled with the screams of its patients. Peter did not know what to do or what to say. "The screams were scary," he told me. "HIV-Aids was new, terrifying. I felt bad that I could do nothing to help. If I had had some warning of his call, I would have been better prepared."

But again Gerald's fortitude prevailed. Even when his physician, the good and kindly Dr. Donald L. Kaminsky, advised him to "put his affairs in order," surrender was not an option to trouble the rest of us. Peggy Hansen, his close colleague at the Dramatists' Guild, was among the many friends who visited him in hospital. "No-one believes I'm going to make it," he told her. "But I know I will. I feel so good and confident." His words, fired with an intense conviction, encouraged her to suggest they hatch a plan to do something interesting together when his health was restored. "Thank you," he replied, "but I don't want to make a promise I may not be able to keep." It was a sad moment she remembers fondly for being typical of the character of the man with whom she had worked.

*

On the morning of Tuesday the twenty-second of September, Gerald's condition deteriorated. By the afternoon he had fallen into a coma, Ivan at his bedside in a private room at the Beth Israel Medical Center. A small portable cassette recorder played tapes they had bought from the Cathedral shop – Kitaro, the Japanese New Age musician and George Winston's folk piano compositions. "Gerald had held me and hugged me the day before," he told me. "He was saying 'goodbye'. Now I just sat there talking to him, reassuring him, telling him I'd take care of everything. But I could feel him slipping away. He looked so thin and emaciated."

In Taunton that evening, at the Castle, I was playing mine host to a group of grey-suited conference delegates in the bar. At about eight o'clock – when they had moved to their table for dinner – I took the lift to the Penthouse.

The door was locked. I rang the bell and Etty appeared, her face drawn and wet with tears. "It's Kaminsky," she hissed. "Gerald's in a coma." In the bedroom, my father was on the telephone – cool; controlled. We were to fly out immediately. I called Louise from the sitting room and then poured two generous whiskies for my father and myself, and a vermouth for my mother. They decided to go to London in the morning – to the Greek Orthodox church in Moscow Road – leaving me to organize the flights and an hotel in New York. I then telephoned Dr. Kaminsky myself – in private. It took an age to track him down. But when we spoke he was patient and kind. "I'm not sure how long Gerald will last," he said. "Perhaps twenty-four hours, maybe longer." He wasn't sure what had happened. In the meantime, they were blasting him with a cocktail of antibiotics.

There was one final issue pressing on all our minds, and one I needed to clear with the doctor. This was the crude matter of dealing with the public relations. How do you launder a stigma? I explained that the social and emotional atmosphere engulfing Aids in Europe was very different from the United States. We needed to agree a position. Kaminsky understood and we rehearsed a number of plausible options: a variety of cancers; leukaemia; even a brain tumour. We settled on leukaemia.

And so on Wednesday morning I briefed my managers and department heads, unscrambled my diary, booked the flights, reserved our rooms at the Pierre. It was late – after nine – when I returned home to find Louise in the bedroom, suitcases and hand luggage already half-filled. The conversation was about death and what to pack for a funeral. I was being frivolous. She scolded my irreverence reminding me that my brother was still alive. "There must always be hope," she said. "Without hope there is no life." "Yes," I replied. "But there is no hope." We recalled Gerald's visit to Ashfield two years before – his gift from Thailand: the silk tie hanging in the wardrobe, pristine, untouched, waiting like a noose to be knotted around my neck. I folded it carefully in tissue paper and laid it in my suitcase.

Ready for bed, the telephone rang – the time now just a few minutes before eleven o'clock. I took it. My mother's voice was broken, barely audible.

Kaminsky had called. It was over. My father could not speak to me. I said nothing, just listened until the line faded and she hung up. At last the news struck me. The fantasy, the illusion evaporated instantly. Gerald was dead. Dead. Dead. Fact.

In New York, Ivan was exhausted. He had kept vigil by Gerald's bed for almost thirty hours. His only nourishment a sandwich ferried in by their mentor and friend Charles Pridemore, the Cathedral's Director of Crisis Ministry. Gerald liked to address him as "Vicar" – a title the Reverend Canon found amusing for its English eccentricity. He had already given him his Last Communion, now he stood in silence and prayed: the dying patient surrounded by medical machinery, a scene relieved only by my brother's quartz crystals arranged on his bed tray.

When the time came, the medics removed the tubes, the catheter, the drips attached to the body, and Ivan removed the oxygen mask from Gerald's face. He was now alone in the room. Lying beside his lover, he held him and kissed him and wept. Later, on his way back to their apartment in a cab, the streets of the city seemed to have turned into a miasma of hopelessness; surreal, uncomprehending. He began talking to himself. "This world has just lost someone so special, so fantastic," he repeated, and repeated again.

*

The alarm woke us at 6.20. Mugs of tea primed our minds for the day ahead. Louise then packed a bag for Nick who was joining Dom's boarding house at school for the time we were away. In the bathroom, I brushed my teeth and sobbed in unison. At home and at school both boys listened to the news solemnly, without comment. Dominic had had his hair shorn into a flat-top, an early act of rebellion. He carried it off well and looked suitably defiant. Gerald would have approved.

Our drive to Heathrow was trouble-free; my mother talking, crying and occasionally laughing all the way up the M4. My father silent, so silent. In the Super Club cabin on BA flight 177 to JFK we wined and lunched ourselves into a state of numbed tranquillity.

It was early evening when we checked into the Pierre. Shortly after, Ivan arrived. More tears. He was in a very bad way. The concierge recommended a place nearby on Madison for dinner. A restaurant which turned out to be a dreadful mistake – the quality of the menu failing to calm the state of our emotions.

On Friday morning, gripping a copy of Gerald's obituary in the New York Times, Louise and I tapped on Peter and Etty's bedroom door. My mother ushered us in, her mood strangely joyful, telling us to sit down as she rejoined Peter in bed, the remains of breakfast on a room-service trolley in the corner. During the night, my father had experienced a mystical revelation and he was eager to tell us about it. In spite of his emotional fatigue and the strains of the journey, he had found it impossible to sleep. Lying in bed, he opened and closed his eyes checking the time displayed by the luminous glow of the digits on his bedside clock. Here below, in his own words, is a written account of the vision he described.

Just after 3.00 am I took Etty into my arms in yet another effort to induce sleep in us both. Gradually my left hand felt a change in the nature of Etty's arm. It grew bigger, harder, male, that of a muscular man. I was lying next to Gerald.

"Gello," I said, and burst into tears.

"Dadsy!" He replied. "Don't grieve, there is <u>no need</u> for it. I'm happy – very happy. I've left behind me my dirty and diseased body which was like a saddle – no, a <u>pack</u> saddle – and a yoke, which have now been lifted off me. At last I am FREE – and SO happy!"

"Have you seen my parents yet?" I asked. "And Pappou and Yaya?"

"No," he replied, "I will soon – but there's plenty of time for that. There is SO MUCH to see – and DO, and LEARN! It will take me all Eternity to cover it! But I ask you all NOT to grieve, there is no need for it. I know that you, Kit and Louise will be alright but do take care of Mumsy, Ivan and Peggy Hansen – they will need help."

Then he vanished and Etty was there once more.

When my father had finished, I stood up and walked across the room to the bathroom; closed the door and wept silently. It was more than I could bear. This revelation, vision, call it what you will, and the wonderful obit in the New York Times struck deep and sent a rush of blood through my arteries.

Forty-one years earlier, in India, a few days before he set sail from Bombay to be reunited with Etty in Athens, Peter had written to her about another vision. That one described her creation by a host of saints and angels who were commanded by God to fashion her into a beautiful incarnation of an ancient Greek goddess. Now Etty had become the medium for Gerald's reincarnation. Deities both! But the mystery bewildered my father and he felt compelled to subject his experience to a little self-examination which, again, he recorded in his hand-written notes.

Was this a dream or perhaps a hallucination emanating from the subconscious, brought on by great tiredness and emotional strain?

I do not know. But the facts are:-

1. *I am certain I was awake and I am not a fanciful person.*

2. *The pillow was wet with my tears. (Could they have been shed in a dream?)*

3. *I have never had a dream which included such a clear and sharp physical contact with a body.*

4. *Some dreams I have recalled fairly clearly on waking, but never one with the crystal clarity of this.*

5. *Gerald repeatedly used the word "grieve". I never use it, my words would be "mourn," or "sorrow," or "be sad about". So why should my subconscious use "grieve"?*

6. *Etty and Ivan I knew, of course, to be particularly shocked and afflicted. But I had only met Peggy Hansen once in my life before this, during our visit to Gerald six months earlier in March. She could hardly have been "on my mind". When we met her three days later at the Memorial Service, she was stricken with sorrow and sorely needed comforting. So I told her about this experience and Gerald's concern for her.*

*

But that Friday left little time for mourning and introspection. There were practical matters to attend to – our first duty to collect Ivan from his apartment. And while he acted as our guide for the day, Louise assumed her role as his chief source of consolation. At the Cathedral we met Charles Pridemore, the "Vicar", and his director of music to plan Gerald's memorial. Etty and Louise agreed to take charge of the flowers. Later, in the afternoon, we met the funeral director at the Beth Israel Medical Center to sign documents relating to Gerald's death certificate and his cremation – a clinical process which, in New York, is conducted by crematorium staff without ceremony, neither relatives nor mourners present. The deceased's ashes are delivered to the church in advance of the service. It is a simple business transaction. Payment in advance. All credit cards accepted.

By Sunday we were set and I now needed time to think about Gerald and what I would say in my "Testimony of Remembrance". I made no notes, just collected my thoughts, ordered them and stored them in my head. To help me exercise my brain, I took a long walk in Central Park. It was a fine, mild autumn day and I found myself enjoying the sheer madness of the place. Two friendly dealers offered me dope. "Hi ya!" they called. "You wan'it, we got it!" I watched some baseball and a volley ball game. Roller skaters ducked and weaved around me doing their thing with small cassette machines and headphones as part of the standard gear. Some of them as high as the birds in the skies over the city.

We rose early on Monday – the morning of Gerald's funeral – our bedroom at the Pierre transformed into a pavilion of flowers. Etty and Louise had had a busy weekend. At 7.30 porters arrived to carry the arrangements to a waiting taxi and mother and daughter-in-law set off for the Cathedral surrounded by their floral cargo. I took my time – showering and shaving carefully, thinking about the words I would speak, searching for lost strength, determined to protect the family's dignity. Louise and Etty soon returned from their mission. We dressed. Slowly, deliberately, I looped Gerald's tie around my neck and shortly after ten o'clock the four of us climbed into a cab and headed for St. John the Divine.

We walked down the length of the nave awestruck by the immensity of a church which reaches out to the world as "a house of prayer for all people". To the right of the choir we found the St. James' Chapel, an imposing Gothic space dedicated to the patron saint of Spain with a succession of magnificent stained glass windows, one depicting famous writers, mystics and artists: Cervantes, St. Teresa of Avila and El Greco among them. The chapel seated a congregation of two hundred and fifty, and it was already filling. My father now drew himself up to his full six feet and four inches – stiffly erect like an officer on parade, insisting that his family observe a code of dignified control. "Hold your heads high," he commanded. "Remember we're British!"

Peggy Hansen was the first to approach us, her tears in flood. All around us emotions were running high. Even the clergy, Gerald's friends, were weeping. I couldn't stand it. Walking out of the chapel, I strode briskly behind the high altar towards the Columbarium to regain some semblance of composure. In my hands I held the order of service. Its front cover ablaze with the dark leonine features of my brother – a radiant portrait my eyes strained to avoid.

Gerald's farewell was a pageant of great beauty and wonder. The organ's prelude – Bach and Albinoni – accompanied a long procession of priests and acolytes, the choir and the Cross. Incense and candles and icons and flowers all about us, this was a rich kaleidoscope of Orthodox, Roman and High-Anglican ritual. At its centre, on a small table in front of the altar, stood an urn draped in an olive green damask shroud. *Throughout the service,* noted my father in his hand-written memoir, *my eyes were on that draped urn. There in front of me were Gerald's ashes. The essence of Gerald, the physical core that not even the cremation fires could destroy. And in my mind's eye I could also see his vital persona, a flame dancing over his ashes, the burnt-clean remnants of his frame, the conveyance of his soul, the carriage of his noble, generous, wonderful and indomitable spirit.*

The choir sang Henry Purcell's *Rejoice in the Lord Alway*, an anthem Gerald and I had sung at school. It had been a great favourite and we often parodied its exuberance around the kitchen table. At the funeral, our comical duet kept tune in my imagination. The Gospel reading followed, then the testimonies

– mine first. When I rose to speak, I turned and saw a silent ocean of faces: a patchwork of colours, creeds and ages, people whose lives my brother had touched and often inspired. It was a heart-warming sight which endowed me with the fluency I had prayed for – my voice reverberating around the chapel, valedictory words, rising and falling, strangely detached from my body. I do not remember exactly what I said but I know that I recalled our childhood together in England and I know that I spoke of his great generosity of spirit, a sentiment repeated by Peggy and an inconsolable Ivan in their tributes to Gerald.

We took Communion. After the Blessing the clergy lit candles, passing them down the ranks of mourners who joined in procession behind the damask draped urn. The cortège moved slowly out of the St. James' Chapel to the Baptistry Columbarium – a quiet, beautiful Gothic octagon leading to an enclosure inlaid with a hundred and twenty marble-faced vaults, each engraved with a name. Canon Pridemore placed the urn in a single open cavity, Gerald's miniature tomb, and spoke the words of the Committal … "Earth to earth, ashes to ashes…"

Then it was over, wrote my father. *We stood a moment in silence. I realized that this was it – the final parting between my dearest and most beloved Gerald and me. I had an overwhelming pain as something almost physical was ripped from me and went to join the ashes in the urn. That part of me is still there and always will remain with Gerald. All I could do was to blow a kiss towards what remained of Gerald and I imagined that from the urn came a whispered "Adieu – Goodbye".*

*

That night we flew home.

Two days later, I climbed the stairs to my study at the top of the house. Louise had been tidying. On my desk I found a small vase filled with flowers from the memorial service. I had no idea she had brought them home with her. Beside the flowers was a small silver-framed photograph of Gerald and me. It remains there today.

*

At eight o'clock on Sunday morning, the twenty-seventh – the day before the funeral – Peter Judd held his own "private" requiem for his friend in Hitcham Church. This was to be his "Special Intention" for the service, an intention which remained unknown to his congregation although he had named Gerald in his prayers for the dead. At the offertory, he placed the collection on the altar – the bread and the wine and next to them Gerald's name. The words he used were these: "Receive, O Lord, we beseech thee, these gifts. Accept in them the sacrifice of ourselves, and of they mercy so perfect us, we pray, that we may be in life and death an offering to thee for ever; through Jesus Christ our Lord. Amen."

Burnham's parish priest went on to become Vicar of Iffley and is now Dean of Chelmsford. He visited Peter and Etty every year on or near the anniversary of Gerald's death. When my parents died, he officiated at their funerals. Today he and I have become friends and keep in touch, meeting in London for a good lunch.

*

Although he was diagnosed HIV-positive in the spring of 1985, Ivan Chatman is well and continues to live in New York City where he pursues his career in interior design. Like Gerald, he reclaimed his faith and, in time, he was baptised at St. John the Divine by the Bishop. He has also registered his wish for his ashes to be interred with Gerald's. On the directory at the entrance to the Columbarium, his name is inscribed on a brass plate below his lost companion's.

Today, Ivan has a new partner. His name is Michiael O'Brien, a paralegal, whom Ivan met five years after Gerald's death.

In our last telephone conversation, Ivan told me that he was still in therapy and still talks about Gerald. "I am happy," he said. "But it's taken a long time to get there. I only knew Gerald for a short time. My love for him was immense."

*

Challenging public prejudice and attitudes towards homosexuality engaged Gerald to the end. Ten months before he died, Peter Judd sent him an academic pamphlet written in 1983 by Elizabeth R. Moberly entitled *Homosexuality: a New Christian Ethic* (published by James Clarke & Co. Ltd., Cambridge). The book attempts to pull together a psychological and theological narrative to "suggest what healing can mean for the homosexual and how it may be achieved" – it's aim: "to promote increased understanding and a wider and more compassionate involvement."

In a long essay to his friend, Gerald dismisses the pamphlet as well-intentioned nonsense. "Being gay is no different from being left-handed," he writes, and then concludes: "Ultimately, the only healing a homosexual needs is the self-acceptance, self-love, self-respect that will alleviate the guilt, repression, self-hatred and fear that social attitudes have tried to instil. For myself, I feel scarred by the fantastic self-hatred I went through between the ages of 15 and 25. And it was only alleviated by finding reciprocal love, and by that love being expressed erotically. The sexual expression was a great act of liberation for me: it was/is an authentic expression of my nature which, I believe, is God-given and blessed. The author would have me believe that it's an expression of sex with my father, or a definite rejection of a loving relationship with my mother. This is utter nonsense!"

*

Gerald's book, *Teaching Young Playwrights* was published by Heinemann in 1990 – his original manuscript skilfully edited and developed by Lisa A. Barnett. In 1991, the book won the American Alliance for Theatre and Education Distinguished Book of the Year Award. In 1993 the book was published in Britain. A review in the Times Educational Supplement on 4th June noted: "This is an authoritative and inspirational work written by a gifted teacher for other teachers to take up and apply ... Chapman shows great respect for the world and worth of the young people to whom he devoted so much of his life and expertise."

Teaching Young Playwrights was reprinted in 2007.

*

Gerald's Young Playwrights' Festival – founded by him in 1981 – prospers today. The organization has taken flight from beneath the wing of the Dramatists' Guild and stands on its own as Young Playwrights Inc. (YPI). Over this time it has been supported by donations from many hundreds of charitable foundations, sponsors and private benefactors running to tens of millions of US dollars. In spite of dozens of imitators across the United States, YPI remains the only professional theatre company dedicated to producing the work of playwrights aged eighteen or under.

Since 1981:

31,000 students from all fifty states have submitted their plays for the competition and received a detailed written evaluation of their work.

52,000 people have attended professional productions of plays by writers aged eighteen or younger in the annual Young Playwrights Festival.

65,000 young people nationwide have studied playwriting in *Write A Play!* workshops.

3,500 teachers have participated in the *Write A Play!* Teacher Training Institute.

10,000 young people have had their first experience of live theatre when the Young Playwrights School Tour came to their school or local community centre.

*

Part Eight

Tribulations of a Family Business

The real hotel
where you can
see Sybil Fawlty

Daily Mail, Saturday March 10, 1979

Diodati - my archipelago. I sit, staring out to sea, and the resinous scent of pine invades my nostrils; sleep-cloaked eyes barely open, my mind drifts back to those dying days of 1987. Almost a dozen years had elapsed since I turned my back on an advertising career; since Louise and I, with our two young boys, had deserted London to begin a new life in Somerset. The prodigal son was returning home to join a business which had, at last, passed into the family's ownership. That was in the spring of '76 – a season of triumph for my sixty-one year old father who had been waiting for this moment since taking up his post as the Castle Hotel's manager a quarter of a century before. Now he was seventy-two: aged, tired, weak, ailing – at the start of his long decline.

Gerald's death was a tragedy which should have bound us more tightly inside the comforting folds of a family's mutual love. But it seemed to have the opposite effect: the stardust which had inhabited our souls now blown away, the radiating beam connecting us switched off. We were filled by silence and darkness – the vital essence of Gerald lost like a tethered line cut, casting each one of us adrift in our own sea-swell of private memories, regrets, thoughts and reminiscences. It seemed to create a collective state of mind more susceptible to tension and conflict, or anyway to fan the embers that smouldered in the grate. My rows with Etty, often over the most trivial matters, became more frequent and acrimonious. Peter, increasingly in his diminished condition, found himself powerless to contain either of us. And Louise's feelings of alienation grew more acute.

Each in our own way we nursed our grief, isolating our sorrow in clam shells. Inevitably the Castle – home to my parents, source of the family's livelihood – became a party to our gathering estrangement, wrapping itself in its own pall of neglect as the rifts between the two generations deepened.

Blindly, we were setting a course for self-destruction. I was sapped of energy; the vision I had conjured for the Castle, the will that had driven me through the Eighties began to dissolve. Whereas my chief role should have been the construction of a future for the family business, sinking foundations to make it secure and strong, the divisions within encouraged me to seek new horizons to excite my senses and challenge my mind. Not the least of these was a commission from the Octopus Publishing Group to write a book about British chefs, their cooking and the gastronomic revival that was taking flight in Great Britain.

*

In 1984 the Castle found itself among a leading group of provincial hotel restaurants awarded a Michelin Star. In that year only eight other hotels outside London could lay claim to this microscopic but prestigious little symbol attached to their name in the guidebook. Today Michelin Stars are a more common currency – a simple consequence of the dramatic rise in the quality of eating out. But in the 1980s, things were very different. The gastronomic view looked out on a barren, withered and inhospitable land. A few of us, a pioneering force of keen palates and sharp noses, the new generation of chefs and restaurateurs, were bent on revolution and I found myself in the thick of the movement – the long dormant renaissance of the British kitchen. As an adopted Westcountryman, I had already begun to proclaim the virtues of local growers and producers (eccentric behaviour at the time) and listed their names on the front page of the Castle's menu. It struck me as an obvious thing to do. After all, the region offered a rich and fecund larder for game, fish and fowl; lamb and beef; fruits, vegetables and herbs; and a fabulous variety of cow, ewe and goat's cheeses. The cartes of provincial dining rooms had become a well-worked joke (the Castle included) and I was determined to change all that.

But I was an innocent – the job of change proved to be a more difficult task than I had anticipated. My experiences as a gourmandizing adman who ran up heroic expense-slips dining in London's swankiest eateries did not equip me with the credentials I needed to sort out my own restaurant. Never mind. From that day in April 1976 when I took up my post in Taunton, I set about reviving a moribund kitchen con brio. The incumbent chef was a fat and idle fellow with a goatee who tested my patience. I fired him and he promptly marched me to an employment tribunal. He lost his case. The next couldn't stand the heat in a kitchen aiming for the stars and quit. The third, an Anton Mosimann protégé from the Dorchester, showed great promise but the man drank. On New Year's Eve he head-butted his sous-chef and I fired him too. The bloodied number two had talent so I promoted him and it was Chris Oakes who became my first successful appointment, leading our kitchen to its Michelin glory in 1984.

This began my long association with a variety of gifted chefs – a breed of human being who could claim, with some justification, to be a species distinct from the rest of us. My relationship with each of them over the past three decades has been at once affectionate and fruitful, chequered and volatile, inspiring and painful. Oakes, the most stable and consistent, was succeeded by Gary Rhodes, the most charismatic of talents and Phil Vickery, the finest of craftsmen. Today Richard Guest is the Castle's master of the stoves, ranking with the most inventive cooks of his generation. All are great chefs in their own right. And all have driven me mad with admiration and exasperation in fairly equal measures.

But then it was bound to be that way. I was an unusual proprietor in that I interfered in their domain and if there is one thing a proud chef resents it is an over-opinionated proprietor. The kitchen is their natural habitat and they prefer to govern it with a fortress-like zeal, at times resisting cooperation with other departments in the hotel or even denying the customers themselves. So I took care with my appointments, emphasizing my expectations with prospective candidates who were required to sign up to my "English Project": a policy of celebrating the region's fresh produce, respecting the seasons and rehabilitating the English table. The Castle, an eight hundred year old landmark, was rooted in the history of the West Country. I wanted our menu to express its regional context and its national heritage in a way that would make it both relevant and attractive to the modern palate. The strategy worked and Messrs. Oakes, Rhodes, Vickery and Guest shed any early scepticism they may have harboured to make the "English Project" their own – each one interpreting the theme in his own individual way.

*

Forging a close working relationship with my chefs, the restaurant became my passion. The times were propitious too – coinciding with Mrs. Thatcher's revolution in "popular capitalism" – the rise of the yuppie running parallel with the rise of its close cousin the foodie. The moniker was coined in 1982 by *Harpers & Queen* and became enshrined in the vernacular two years later when Ann Barr and Paul Levy produced their *Official Foodie Handbook*. These were heady days and regardless of the frustrations and politicking of the family in Taunton, I realized that the Castle had become a platform for my own career advancement. Long before the publication of *Great British Chefs*, the idea of writing a book had begun to stir in my mind – a desire inspired by my admiration for Anthony Blake and Quentin Crewe's classic work *Great Chefs of France* published in 1978. The planted seed was soon nourished by a stroke of good fortune. My efforts to lift the ambitions of a dining room locked in the centre of a sleepy provincial market town intrigued the editor of the trade's principal mouthpiece – *Caterer & Hotelkeeper*. His name was Joe Hyam, a cultured man to whom I owe an enormous debt of gratitude for inviting me to write a regular column in his magazine. It was his encouragement that gave me the confidence to seek out a publisher for my book later in the decade.

If the Castle provided my platform, the magazine column gave me profile and a stage set against which I could strut my stuff on any issue I pleased. Inevitably, my pieces attracted controversy even if, occasionally, Mr. Hyam had to rein me in. Otherwise my targets ranged from tourist boards to catering colleges; smoking policy to service charges; guidebooks, red tape, local authority stupidity and much else. But browsing through the old files, my favourite pitch tended to revolve around matters gastronomical – one essay devoted entirely to the anatomy of a salade niçoise. A recurring theme, I noticed, was chicken. I had a thing about that miserable and much abused battery fowl and in April '85 I launched a campaign for real chicken. Plus ça change. These days the cudgels have been taken up by TV chefs like Hugh Fearnley-Whittingstall, Jamie Oliver and Rick Stein.

The chicken for me has an elemental significance on a Proustian scale. Of all my childhood memories none is more profound than the smell and taste of one particular bird along with the circumstances of its consumption. It is a memory which has been absorbed by my olfactory nerves. It is indelibly etched on my psyche because this chicken came to symbolize all things good and wholesome in my life. And it is to Nanny Jenkins, our round and jolly ginger-haired Scottish carer, to whom I owe this gastronomic rite of passage. I suppose I could not have been more than six years old …

As my parents were taking a holiday, Gerald and I were sent to stay on the Jenkins's farm near Barnstaple in north Devon. The couple lived in a tiny, primitive cottage at the foot of a steep hill. There was no electricity and the plumbing was basic, the lavatory a shed at the back. The unfamiliarity of this isolated stone hovel inspired a mixture of fear and excitement in us – for a week or two we were living an adventure of the Famous Five. Jenkins had no motor car – instead the Welshman's mode of transport was an old trailer drawn by a huge, slow, submissive shire horse for whose lot in life I felt acute sorrow. The poor beast would struggle to haul its load up the steep track from the cottage, the farmer's only method of encouragement being to whip the wretched creature repeatedly to get us to the summit.

But the cruellest shock to the sensibilities of this tender child came when I witnessed the capture and slaughter of a proud and magnificent cockerel. One morning I was drawn by the deafening sounds of domestic birds flapping, squawking and racing around the yard. Jenkins was there leaping and diving like a circus clown. He had selected his victim and his fattened quarry knew it. Finally, the farmer grabbed the fowl in his leather-tough hands, shook it violently and slit its throat. Wings still flailing maniacally in his grip, Jenkins made off quickly, disappearing round the back of the house. For several moments, I stood open-mouthed and awestruck. I could not understand for what purpose this innocent bird had been chosen for such a vicious and gratuitous death.

Jenkins, I decided, was a madman and a murderer. We were all in grave danger and I ran off to find Gerald to warn him. As I rounded the corner of a barn, I stopped frozen in my tracks. There before my eyes, strung up by its legs, was the chicken, a large pool of fresh blood staining the hard, pale earth beneath its severed neck, a feathered corpse hanging motionless in the warm mid-morning sunlight. As my mind grasped the horror, I turned on my heel and ran for my life.

A few days later we ate that bird and to this day it remains the most succulently flavoured, delicious chicken I have ever tasted. The shock of its slaughter became my conversion, my gastronomic epiphany. As the smells of the roasting fowl curled around every nook and cranny of the cottage, the rising tide of its sweet, pungent fragrance – redolent of the farmyard it was reared in – filled me with a new delight. Sitting at Nanny Jenkins's modest kitchen table, I had suddenly discovered the ambrosial pleasures of good food simply prepared from the best raw ingredients. In my enlightenment, Farmer Jenkins now became my hero. And so it was written that, many years later, I would acknowledge the value and importance of our producers by listing their names on the first page of the Castle's menu.

*

Every family has its pet catchphrases – teasing lines that often caricature the person. From the day we married, Louise collected a sackful of hard balls which, now and then, she enjoys lobbing in my direction – a favourite being "Kit, all you think about is lunch!" Or, more provocatively, "Kit, all you're any good at is lunch!" Certainly, the early and mid Seventies – my advertising years – helped to fuel an impression which refused to lie down in the Eighties. How could it? I had become an hotelier and restaurateur and I was on a mission. While lunch and dinner have always been important to me – precious moments in the rhythm of my day – they were hardly indulgences taken at the expense of my determination to develop the business and burnish its reputation. The late-Seventies and Eighties were a period of high activity. There was much to be done. And I was driven, like a man in a terrible hurry.

Today, three decades on, a new-found peace in our existence and the gift of grandchildren have eased the pace and reordered our values. Then it was all go-go-go, a fast lane that was never fast enough. Just recalling those years leaves me breathless: material enough for a personal memoir but that is not the point of this story. An abridged catalogue of my efforts will suffice to illustrate the adrenalin pumping through my veins at the time. As an ex-adman, marketing was my métier and the Castle was ripe for treatment, my father the first to recognize the need to raise our game. I set about my task conscious that location was our severest handicap. Except for visiting business suits and the occasional cricket correspondent in summer, why else would anyone travel to Taunton? But we had a handsome old castle, we had "character", we had personality that comes of independence, and we had style. Encircled by Exmoor, the Quantocks, the Blackdowns and the Somerset Levels, we also sat at the hub of some of England's most beautiful countryside. And hidden within these landscapes there lay an abundance of history and folklore, stately homes and gardens. If the Castle was not a destination in itself, what we offered in it and what there was to see around it gave us half a chance of attracting tourists who might otherwise have continued headlong down the M5 en route to Devon and Cornwall.

Within a few months I had launched a raft of initiatives, special packages and weekend breaks using price or a special occasion as bait. Soon our dank and empty winters were filled with a new vibrancy as a calendar of events for lovers of good music, theatre and fine wine skipped into action. Many of the world's great chamber music ensembles came and still come to perform for us today. Thirty years ago I adopted the Lindsays as our "quartet-in-residence". And when they retired, the Vienna Piano Trio took up their "residency" at the

Castle. Famous actors arrived to entertain us, among them Judi Dench and Michael Williams, Isla Blair and Julian Glover. And when Timothy West and Prunella Scales visited in March '79, the *Daily Mail* picked up the story with a cartoon under the caption: "The real hotel where you can see Sybil Fawlty" – Basil poking his head around the battlements in disgust as Sybil, permed like an erupting storm cloud, strode across our forecourt to the hotel's front door.

And then there were our gastronomic events, inspired in no small measure by the example of my Uncle Michael at the Imperial in Torquay. He set a standard which I sought to surpass by presenting menus to match some of the greatest vintages of the century. At one we pitched a pair of 1945 First Growths against each other. Sitting in a packed dining room, we sniffed and sipped our two glasses: the one filled with Château Mouton Rothschild, the other with Château Latour. Both were pure nectar but arguments about their relative merits raged around the tables. When the vote was called, opinion divided with the Mouton winning a small advantage. At this point, Pamela Vandyke Price – doyenne and indisputable grande dame of the wine writing world – poured scorn on the result and declared that the Latour was unquestionably the more "cerebral" wine!

In those days, black tie was the recognized evening uniform and, of course, as a family we hosted these weekends from our guests' arrival to their farewell. For Etty this was party time – glittering occasions which assumed the splendour of command performances, an opportunity to parade her fabulous wardrobe and dazzle our visitors with her elegance and vivacity. My mother knew how to play the chatelaine as perfectly and as peerlessly as a great diva. Sweeping into the chandeliered Monmouth Room for a concert, greeting people at the opening cocktail reception, or taking her place at table in the restaurant, she commanded the approbation of the house receiving the applause with unalloyed joy. And as if there were some deeper urge to crown the attention paid to her, there would always be a chosen coterie of friends and VIPs who would be invited to join the family for interval drinks or at the "top" table for dinner: a regimented platoon of white-gloved waiting staff lining their path to the banquet. It was pure theatre and a conspicuous display which attracted guarded stares from the unchosen, leaving me just a little uncomfortable.

Peter always appeared more than content with Etty's arrangements. Besides, watching her shine in public made him happy – his transparent pride akin to that of a father for a favourite daughter. Perhaps I was being over-sensitive about the perceptions of our other guests or, perhaps, it was Louise's growing feelings of exclusion on these and other occasions which began to trouble me. With my energies revved up and focused on the business, I was slow to grasp the tangled sub-plot simmering between my mother and my wife. I had started to travel abroad, principally to the United States where I pursued a hectic series of missions aimed at tapping the market for wealthy Americans. A night or two in a twelfth century castle was just the thing they loved. One campaign I devised blatantly exploited America's stereotypical image of the Englishman. Collaborating with two friends, the proprietor of a Kentish manor and the owner of a luxury driver-guide service, we persuaded Jermyn Street to fit us out and British Airways to fly us. Dressed in striped shirts, donning bowler hats and wielding furled umbrellas, we branded ourselves "The Three British Gentlemen" and blitzed the continent, journeying coast to coast and from the Sunbelt States to the Midwest. Over two punishing winter tours we held press lunches, made television appearances, visited local radio stations and attended travel trade shows.

The campaign was an extraordinary success and helped fill our bedrooms in the early Eighties, a period when the UK economy had sunk into deep recession. Its novelty also attracted TV and press attention at home, and in January 1981 Joe Hyam ran a cover feature about us in *Caterer & Hotelkeeper* under the title "One way to sell British hotel rooms to Americans". Later in the year, at an industry awards ceremony, the mission won the British Tourist Authority's top prize for an overseas marketing initiative. The effect of all this accumulating publicity was to spotlight the Castle, boost the hotel's national and international image, and generate more column inches in the press.

By now my father had appointed me managing director of the family firm and while he was looking for an easier life, I had begun adding to my responsibilities by taking on a string of extracurricular duties. I sat on the executive of the West Country Tourist Board and chaired its fifteen-hundred-strong commercial members' group. I became a ministerial appointee to the Exmoor National Park Authority. And I took up a seat on the management committee of Prestige Hotels, a marketing consortium of privately-owned properties, ultimately becoming its chairman. There was more to add to this crowded agenda – too much, I confess, to allow me to pay enough attention to Dom and Nick, growing sons who had embarked on their school careers; and too much to make me properly understand the tensions which had begun to unsettle Louise. At first I dismissed her complaints as generational – the natural tussle that might arise between a mother and daughter-in-law. "Etty means well," I reassured. "Yes, she can be infuriating, I know. She loves you really." But I was being disingenuous, denying a problem I knew existed but which, just then, did not suit the agenda. In the end this would become a problem I could not ignore. If my father was anxious to wind down, Etty certainly was not. As managing director, I was ready to take up the reins and, I felt, it was time to begin involving Louise. But for my mother, life as the chatelaine was too important to allow her fiefdom to be usurped by a rival. The daughter-in-law posed a threat.

Etty's ego was programmed to weave a Byzantine web worthy of her Greek ancestry. The games she played always shone with a veneer of innocence and righteousness which disguised her instinctive cunning, a wily femininity that was extraordinarily accomplished. Certainly she was manipulative and sometimes she could be thoughtless, but her genes possessed no obvious evidence of a malicious nature. Her actions were rarely premeditated or calculated with any sense of practical logic. Etty's make-up, her whole being, was soaked in emotion and driven by the projection of her own self-image. Exotic and colourful, she fascinated people. She played up her Greekness and her Greek accent and charmed her acquaintances by making a virtue of her English solecisms. She was like a technicoloured balloon floating high in the social ether. Prick it and it went bang! Few dared and those who did tended to be members of her family.

Louise, twenty-three years Etty's junior, youthful, beautiful and wise, read the politics from the start and stood well back. For her, home and children came first – and, besides, the terrible skirmishes with Etty at Diodati in the summers before our move to Taunton had left their scars. But we were no longer a family leading separate lives who, once a year, came together for a fortnight's holiday on a balmy Aegean island. Now we had become a family joined in business, working and living in close proximity. Home – our pretty white-washed cottage high up on the Blackdowns – detached us from the Castle by eight miles. But no matter how successfully Louise kept her distance, conflict was inevitable – even if, at the time, we chose to erase that inevitability from our imaginations. With Gerald as with me, Louise shared a fierce independence of mind: resistant of any pressure to conform, impatient to break loose from the post-war rigidity of middle-class mores, refusing to be corralled or controlled by a senior generation who thought they knew best. Her upbringing had been loving but strict, and even the nuns at St. Mary's – her convent school near Ascot – failed to quell her free and occasionally anarchic spirit.

The rebel may have matured and learned the wisdom of discretion but she never lost her fire. In those early years, rarely if ever, was I a witness to my mother's confrontations with Louise. Etty's natural guile made sure of that. In my presence – especially when other people were around us – her devotion to Louise overflowed with love and admiration. She praised her beautiful grandchildren and the way they were being raised; and she praised the wonderful home Louise had created for her family. Out of earshot, and if guests enquired, she explained away her daughter-in-law's absence from this party or that reception by painting an image of Louise as a homemaker with a passion for needlework and baking sponge cakes. In four decades of marriage, I do not recall seeing or sampling a single Louise-baked sponge cake, biscuit or anything else. And her talent with needle and thread did not extend much beyond sewing Cash's nametapes onto the boys' school uniforms. When, on other occasions, these same guests met Louise, they were surprised to find a sophisticated woman with rather more sparkle and fun than the folksy stay-at-home mum they had been led to believe she was.

It was a harmless deceit which amused us both. More irritating was Etty's persistent habit of breaking into Louise's conversations at these social gatherings, especially if the exchanges with her guests looked too animated for the chatelaine's own comfort. My mother's strategy in these situations was simple and effective. She would snatch some poor soul whom she judged the dullest person in the room and, without knowing their name to make an introduction, she would haul the stranger over to Louise, spiriting the other startled visitor away. Any passing compliments made by the hijacked guest about her charming daughter-in-law were hurriedly brushed aside with a nervous laugh. If there were compliments to be dispensed, they were reserved for Etty herself to control.

This possessiveness, her jealous paranoia, became more transparent with Peter and Gerald. Both adored Louise – a fact that might have been just too vexing for my mother's peace of mind. She was never happy to leave Peter alone with Louise. And when Gerald came to see us on his visits from New York, she reacted indignantly to any suggestion of him driving out to Penny's Cottage to spend an evening with us. "Why don't you want me?" she would cry, instantly raising the emotional temperature. "Why do you want to keep me away? He is my son! We are a family all together." And all we craved was a little space. Of course, Gerald was never allowed to stay over.

At moments Etty's obsessive protectionism even extended to me. Occasionally, Louise would bring Dom and Nick into the hotel for tea after school. I sometimes wondered if my mother were not possessed of some sixth sense which alerted her to the children's arrival – but then it was not unusual for Etty, always ready to spy on the comings and goings in the entrance hall, to be flitting from vase to vase making a play of adjusting her flower arrangements. So when Louise and the boys walked in, they were intercepted. The noise and excitement of seeing her grandchildren echoed up the stairwell and any passing guest or member of staff would be introduced with a proud flourish. Eventually, Louise would explain the purpose of their visit. "We've come to see Kit," she'd say.

"Oh don't bother him," my mother would reply. "He's busy. He doesn't want to be disturbed."

"But he's expecting us, Etty," Louise insisted. "We're having tea together."

"No! No! Come and see Pappou," persisted my mother, not listening to a word her daughter-in-law was saying. "He's in the Penthouse. I'll have tea sent up straightaway. The boys must be very hungry."

This artless attempt to deny access to her husband began to breach Louise's line of tolerance. "No, Etty!" She replied tartly. "The boys have come to see Kit. He's working tonight. They won't see him otherwise."

The balloon was pricked! "Why are you behaving like this?" my mother snapped. And with staff and guests shrinking into the shadows of the front hall, Louise suffered the well-rehearsed wails of vituperation she'd heard a hundred times before. "Why are you so prickly? Do you have your periodo? You are so cold and English! Not like me, Continental. Everyone loves Etty – I'm so easy and warm-hearted …"

The apparent innocence of my mother's motives – a desire to spoil her two grandsons, to bring them to Peter – belied her unthinking need to control, her inability to acknowledge Louise's feelings by dismissing her wishes with a silly deceit: "Kit's busy. He doesn't want to be disturbed."

The scene I have described here was repeated time and again and, in the end, Louise stopped bringing the children in for tea. Whether the confrontation was like this one or any other, these incidents, when they occurred, tended to be trivial – indeed, so inconsequential they were quickly forgotten. But at the moment of combustion, the explosion would be ear-splitting. Worse still, if I were rash enough to step into the fire in support of Louise, the row would be volcanic with Etty instantly accusing her of being a "troublemaker". So Louise, like everyone else, was expected to defer – to subscribe to Etty's rule book. But Louise being Louise refused – an attitude which reminds me of my grandmother Nell and her refusal to kiss the hand of her mother-in-law, Amelia Prüger, when Henry brought his family home to Bratislava at the end of the Great War. If Louise failed to display the approbation so willingly lavished on Etty by Peter, her friends and her acquaintances, she would feel

the icy chill of her mother-in-law's disapproval: "You're so cold! So English!
…"

The comments hurt and contributed to a creeping alienation between the
two sides of our family. Like a succession of minor cuts and grazes, sores that
become inflamed and won't heal, these skirmishes – aggravated by Etty's little
lies and deceits – gradually corroded our relationship. Like Nell at the Savoy-
Carlton, Louise retreated – limiting her appearances at the Castle only to the
more important official functions.

*

If there was an unhappy inevitability about the difficulties which now tainted
our relations, a twist of fortune was responsible for exciting these ill-feelings
to a degree which might have been avoided in different circumstances. At the
start of 1976, as Louise and I were preparing our move out of London, the
Fates were spinning a different endgame to the one we had been anticipating.
My father's negotiations to buy the Castle Hotel were well-advanced and the
date set for the deal's completion had been fixed for the twenty-seventh of
February – a deadline agreed with R.G. Spiller's two daughters to whom the
estate had passed after the death of his widow, Mary, in 1972. The deadline
was critical. If my father failed to complete by the agreed date, the sisters
would be free to advertise the sale of the hotel on the open market.

Raising the money to purchase the shares had been a hard two-year slog
and by the middle of 1975, my father was still short by some £20,000. To his
great relief, Louise's father stepped in with an offer. Since the wedding four
years before, our families had grown to know each other and the two Peters,
Guiver and Chapman, got on well. Louise's father – a man who enjoyed
staying in Europe's grandest hotels – admired the Castle and respected my
father's abilities as an hotelier. He understood the importance of the purchase
and he understood its significance in the new path his daughter and son-in-
law were planning. His own firm of chartered surveyors, A & G Guiver in
North London, had been in the ownership of his family since 1810. Now, for

the first time in his life, he decided to break his cardinal rule of never mixing business and family. On the eighteenth of September he wrote to my father confirming his promise to invest £20,000. Peter was overjoyed. At last the balance of funds he needed to complete the deal were in place. Moreover, the date was felicitous for another reason. At six o'clock that evening, at Queen Charlotte's Hospital in Hammersmith, Louise gave birth to our second son, Nicholas. The two Peters had become grandfathers once again.

In the family and on the business front, all seemed to be well. Financial information, the company's accounts were made available, further meetings were held. Then, five months later, on the tenth of February, little more than a fortnight before the deadline, Peter Guiver suddenly withdrew his offer, his letter citing ill-health as the cause. My father was shattered. In his family history he wrote: "Buying the Castle meant everything to me. Failure to do so would leave me not only with very little capital (whatever the new purchasers paid for my existing shares) but with no future and no home for Etty and me. In any case I had come to love the place. I knew every nook of it, every electric circuit and fuse, each valve controlling the water and heating – I knew it intimately. I had been at the Castle twenty-five years, it had been my life's work and was part of me. To love it and then be separated from it was unimaginable, unbearable."

The convulsions inside our two families were seismic. Peter Guiver's decision tore us in half, Louise taking her father's side as I took mine. The row that ensued between us was so terrible we spent twenty-four hours apart: both in shock, we needed time to cool off. With Nick's birth five months before and a clear way forward planned, we found ourselves thrown into a cold vacuum of uncertainty. Our Putney basement in Oxford Road had become too small for a young family of four and we'd sold it – living meanwhile in a Knightsbridge town house lent to us by a friend as a stopgap before relocating to the West Country. Now we felt lost, wondering where to search for a new home: London or Somerset? Were we staying or moving? My job may have been secure, the money good, but I had grown sick of the vacuity of the advertising game. Flogging soap and cans of hairspray struck me as a black art

– a heartless, cynical occupation which offered little more than the promise of a swollen bank balance in exchange for an impoverished soul. Suddenly, my career and my future had become fogbound – Louise and I cast into a state of confusion and bewilderment.

It was Mark, Louise's elder brother, who broke the news to me. I was summoned out of a client meeting in the agency to take the call – a conversation which was brief, apologetic, to the point. Certainly, his father had not been in the best of health, but this was not the reason he had reneged on his promise. The numbers just didn't add up. "My father's advisers have told him it would be imprudent to proceed," Mark explained. "The money for the investment would come out of a family trust which is used to support Granny Guiver. Her security and well-being are paramount. I'm sure you'll agree."

I was stunned into silence and thanked him for his call. Why, I wondered, had it taken his father so long to arrive at this conclusion? Five months! We had opened the Castle's books for him and responded to his questions. Returning to the conference room, I ignored my client's agenda and left my colleagues to run the meeting. My mind was elsewhere, racing wildly in a state of panic.

Granny Guiver, Peter's ninety year old mother, lived in Lowndes Square, a quiet and leafy residential strip off Sloane Street. I remember her as an impish, diminutive figure who amused the younger members of the family – Louise, Mark, me – with her racy sense of humour. She shared an ample apartment with Mrs. Smith, a Scottish lady of Presbyterian rectitude who looked after her as a carer-companion and was the butt of her many jokes. As the principal trustee and a shrewd businessman, Peter Guiver needed little advice from his accountants and solicitors to see that a £20,000 uptake of shares in the Castle Hotel was unlikely to yield a dividend that might even approach the sums he required to support his mother's comfortable lifestyle. The business was showing a lacklustre profit record which, year-on-year, floated hesitantly between three and five percent of turnover. What he needed was income, not long-term capital growth.

But still I kept asking myself the same question. Why had it taken him so long to drop his bombshell? My father-in-law was a particular man, interested in detail, cautious in his judgements. I imagined him as I had seen him many times – hunched over the ancient bureau in his study at number 4 Ennismore Gardens Mews, his cigarette, a Player's Medium Navy Cut, smouldering in the ashtray. He never trusted devices like the electronic calculator and refused to use one. At ease with numbers and preferring his own arithmetic, all his calculations were computed on scraps of paper.

Perhaps, at first, he was reluctant to say 'no', the heart willing him to say 'yes'. Perhaps his advisers took time arriving at their opinions. And having given them, seeing his own judgement confirmed, perhaps he finally realized it would be foolish to proceed. These are all questions Louise, Mark and I have debated ad nauseam. But no matter how slow he was in coming to his decision, other issues had begun to tease his mind. If he went ahead with the investment, the trust would own a minority interest in a business now controlled by the Chapman family. He saw Peter Chapman as a charming, able and professional hotelier – but was unconvinced by his record as a businessman. I was, as yet, untested. And Etty he saw as a worry – a force whose influence might lead to trouble. Five years before, he had had his own minor run-ins with her over the wedding arrangements and on the eve of the big day he and Molly had brooded over their daughter's future. He knew what lay ahead. "She'll have a difficult ride with a mother-in-law like that," he had told his wife. "But if anyone can handle it, my Sparrow will."

In time I came to acknowledge, even admire, my father-in-law's prescience. His handling of the whole affair caused a deal of pain for both families but, in the end, he made the right decision in the best long-term interests of his family. In Taunton, Peter Guiver was declared persona non grata and was never seen entering the Castle Hotel again. Louise's scorecard was handicapped even before our move westward.

*

Sitting at his office desk, my father held his head in his hands as he stared at the letterhead lying on the blotter: 4 Ennismore Gardens Mews, London SW7.

His face was pink with despair. Using the slim paperknife which lay beside his leather-bound inkstand, he had opened the envelope himself first thing that morning. It was now eleven o'clock. Opposite him sat Michael Blackwell, his principal adviser through the long, tortuous negotiations of the past two years. A blunt, wiry Yorkshireman, Blackwell was the chartered accountant's answer to Geoffrey Boycott. Born and raised in the village of Kimberworth north-east of Sheffield, he was a product of Rotherham's famous grammar school – a young man who had travelled far and fast to become a partner in the Taunton firm of A.C. Mole & Sons before he'd turned thirty. Now, at the age of thirty-nine, he had become a substantial presence in the local business community. Looking back across the desk at his client, he did not underestimate the task that confronted them. With only seventeen days left before the end-February deadline, he was determined to rescue the deal from collapse. The loans he had secured from Barclays for the family to buy their parcels of shares were in place, but he accepted there was little point in going back to the bank for more. With the sudden withdrawal of the Guiver trust fund, the challenge now facing the family was to find an alternative source of capital – an investor who already knew the Castle Hotel and respected Peter Chapman, someone who was prepared to step in immediately with the cash.

In his desperation, Peter's first shot was to approach his brother in Torquay – an act he regretted within the forty-eight hours it took Michael to come back with a proposal. His plan was unworkable and served only to rekindle memories of my father's miserable years working for him and his partner Frank Isaacson after the war. "Unfortunately, the terms were unacceptable," noted Peter in a tone of supreme restraint.

Michael Blackwell, meanwhile, pursued a different course. He realized that his best chance of landing this elusive investor lay in a search for a local man with roots in the town and an affinity for the Castle. His target was the head of Stansell's, a well-established Taunton builder and a company first founded in the earlier part of the nineteenth century as decorators and specialists in ecclesiastical restoration. Bill Stansell was the family firm's fifth generation and a man touched by a well-developed sense of civic pride. He saw Taunton as a prosperous market town and he believed in conserving its assets within the locality – a desire he fulfilled by investing in small family businesses to stop them being devoured by some faceless national predator. When the young and resolute accountant presented the share offer to the sixty-six year old grandee, Stansell immediately warmed to the idea of buying a stake in the business. He loved the Castle and his family were regular customers. The notion of this famous wisteria-clad landmark falling into the hands of Grand Metropolitan Hotels or Trusthouse Forte was unthinkable and, besides, the hotel had once been owned by R.G. Spiller, his friendly rival in the building trade. Like Old RG, Bill Stansell also had two daughters – Elizabeth and Julia, both married with children. Mindful of the future interests of his family, he consulted them first before committing to an £18,000 investment in their favour. This left a shortfall of £2,000 which Michael Blackwell and my father's legal adviser, Richard Kennedy, took up with share purchases to the value of £1,000 each. With two days to spare, Peter was now ready to complete the deal. The new company he formed would give his family an eighty-five percent holding in the Castle's share capital.

*

Friday, the twenty-seventh of February 1976: a date in this saga that still trembles in its own surreal sky. All of us – my father, my mother, Louise and me, Gerald, Dominic and Nicholas – gathered together but oddly detached; each preoccupied in our own mini-worlds; each conscious but unaware of the other's involvement. My father with me at the bank; surrounded by functionaries and professionals, attending to the numb bureaucracy of completion. My mother minding her grandsons; fussing and spoiling them; showing them off. Louise with Gerald; driving around the Somerset countryside in search of a new family home.

"Just a formality really," my father reassured us at breakfast. "It shouldn't take too long. Let's all meet in the Penthouse at twelve. I've organized some champagne to be sent up. I can't believe we've made it at last!"

Just before half past eleven, we walked into Barclays Bank on North Street – a short step across the road from the hotel. I sensed my father's nervousness and tried to calm him. Michael Blackwell – rosy cheeked and chirpy after an early morning game of squash – had already arrived and the three of us were ushered into a sparsely furnished, windowless room at the back of the building. When the branch manager walked in, the expression on his face was as grey as the herringbone weave of his suit. "I'm afraid we've hit a problem," he began. "The solicitors acting for the other side are insisting on various requirements which we cannot accept. So I am not in a position to issue the bank's draft in payment of the purchase price."

My father let out a long, heavy sigh, his eyelids drooping mournfully like an old St. Bernard's. What happened next faded into a blur of explanation, claim and counter claim, sharp words from Blackwell and a frenzy of telephone calls to and from solicitors and the local director of Barclays' regional head office in Exeter. We sat in that airless room for over two hours. And all I remember is my father in a state of distress I had never seen before. With his elbows on his lap, hands tightly clasped and breathing deeply, he rocked backwards and forwards in a beige swivel chair. Silent, his dream seemingly evaporating into the bland emptiness of the carpet.

It was a quarter to two when we returned to the hotel. In the Penthouse the family were waiting. The ice had melted in its silver bucket and the champagne was warm. But it hardly mattered – the bank, in thrall to its arcane processes, had finally sanctioned the payment. My father raised his glass to the new firm and over lunch he began to relax, listening to Louise and Gerald's account of their house hunting expedition. Louise had fallen in love with a cottage near the village of Buckland St. Mary in the Blackdown Hills. The property came with two acres of land and was owned by a courtly and earnest American lady who kept horses. She had shown them round. "Gerald was so embarrassing," Louise said. "So nosy – picking things up, putting them down; and reading all the invitations on her mantelpiece!" Everyone laughed.

Next day Louise drove me out to Penny's Cottage and I met the courtly American lady. In the words of the estate agent, she was being "very particular"

Ivan with Gerald. A visit to the Lincoln Memorial in Washington DC.

"Oyez! Oyez! Oyez!" As tudor pageboys, Gerald and I proclaim a refurbished Castle officially open in 1956. Peter and Etty look on anxiously.

Delphi, Greece. My younger brother with his mother. Etty as Audrey Hepburn in *Breakfast at Tiffany's*.

With Nicholas, Uncle Gerald and Dominic on an Aegean beach.

Gerald and Louise on another Aegean beach.

With Gerald. Louise framed this photograph and put it on my desk at home after Gerald's funeral.

Actors Bill Homewood, Prunella Scales and Timothy West with Gerald for a theatrical weekend at the Castle in 1979.

The opening of the new Gents' loo in 1984. With Patrick Litchfield and his famous nudes. The urinals were decorated with sweet peas by Louise.

With Gary Rhodes, the Castle's
Head Chef in the late 1980s.

The Three British Gentlemen. Frederick Pearson (centre), Matthew Bates (right) and I pose in front of Buckingham Palace before our first mission to the United States to persuade Americans to visit Britain.

With Nicholas, Louise and Dominic at Buckingham Palace again. This time to receive the MBE from HM the Queen.

Louise succeeds my mother as the Castle's chatelaine in 1990 – officially, if not entirely in reality.

Autumn 1990. The new board line-up. Michael Blackwell (second left) succeeds my father as Chairman; Ian Fleming, General Manager (left) and Louise are formally elected directors of the company after a mighty struggle.

June 1988. A cover story in the industry's leading trade magazine. The photograph betrays the two factions - staff lining up according to where their loyalties lie. Louise and me to the left. Peter and Etty to the right.

about the suitability of any prospective purchaser to make sure they were worthy of her house. For us the decision to buy was easy and after submitting to a polite interview over tea and cake we won her permission to proceed.

In London on Monday morning I resigned my post in the agency and gave a month's notice. By mid-April we had moved.

*

As a young man, just turned twenty-nine, I did not dwell on the significance of our move. This was not a time for reflection. Rather, this was a moment in the family's history to look forward, to set an ambitious course towards a new horizon. Now I look back on 1976 as a watershed year for each one of us, collectively and individually: a year that defined our future and the beginning of a period which would redefine the dynamic of our relationships with each other. For my father the anxieties of his long battle to win the Castle coincided with Gerald's coming-out. The rows with both parents had been fearful – exacerbated by the militancy of his gay activism which had offended and hurt Peter deeply. At the same time Gerald's career had lost purpose. Professionally he was wallowing in a stagnant pond, going nowhere. In 1976, all this changed. Soon after the ownership of the Castle passed to the family, Gerald arrived at the Royal Court, a move which would establish him as the leading pioneer and exponent of youth theatre in both Britain and the United States. It was also the year which would lead to reconciliation with his mother and father.

The thaw in Gerald's relations with them took a while and only found full expression five years later after Stephen Sondheim had spirited him away to set up a young playwrights' festival in New York. If the Court was the seed from which this peace process germinated; Gerald's confinement at home during his bout of hepatitis saw the shoots of reconciliation come into flower. Writing to his friend Peter Judd at the time, he had described it as a "big development" in his life. He had become "more understanding, admiring and tolerant of them".

Several weeks of his convalescence were spent on holiday with Peter and Etty at Diodati and it was from here that he wrote to Louise and me in late April '81: a classic Geraldian narrative running to fifteen pages – irreverent, entertaining and funny for the first nine; sex never far from his mind. "Not much crumpet on board," he writes describing their flight to Athens, "except one Greek boy with fetching curly hair and that typically fierce-looking sexiness which I find overwhelming…" The final six pages of his letter are devoted to his observations and advice on the gathering strain in my relations with Etty and Peter. Rereading it today in the very place he wrote the letter twenty-six years ago, it is a sibylline commentary as much as one which illustrates the shift in two brothers' relationship with their parents. Whereas his was on the mend, mine was deteriorating.

A hint of Gerald, the changed man, comes early in the letter where he tells us that, arriving in Thessaloniki to visit Machi and Petros, Etty's sister and brother-in-law, he is despatched to a local barber. Gerald's hair had always been a running issue with Etty and a flashpoint between the two of them. On the occasion of their reunion with the Greek branch of the family, she would have insisted that her beautiful son present himself perfectly dressed and properly trimmed. For the first time since childhood, Gerald gives way. "I consented," he notes, "to a haircut by a 'πολί μοδερνο' [very modern] hairdresser gloriously known as 'Adonis of Salonica'. To my surprise it's come out rather well".

Then, on page ten, he turns to our long conversations at home before their departure for Greece. My recent elevation to the post of managing director in the family firm had proved to be a hollow promotion. Nothing had changed. And with Gerald in Taunton recovering from his illness, I had used the opportunity to air my frustrations. Peter and Etty owned their castle, lived in their castle and, for all my father's desire to ease up, my mother was bent on remaining in control of every quotidian detail in the running of the place. I sought Gerald's advice, confident that I would have his sympathy. I was wrong. He had witnessed the signs of family fracture for himself and in robust language, heavy with foreboding, he warns of the consequences, placing the burden of repair on me.

"You think I'm a shit-hole," he begins. *"Well it's easier for me to go along with M & D partly because I staked my independence out very clearly when I came out as gay in 1975, and partly because I see them less often. For you it's a constant daily battle of nerves and family politics. So I sympathise with you and understand why you felt I'd betrayed or reneged on my previously-stated position. But remember, you were always better at arguing with M & D than I was: so the result is that when I'm with them I don't argue any more: I've given up! You've a lot to fight for, not least your family. My only anxiety is that in the relatively new situation of your being 'the boss' in the hotel, the battle may become a war of attrition and that you'll adopt, on both sides, intransigent and inflexible positions, each exploiting the other's failings. What I've seen of you all seems to confirm this move, - there is more tension, and more suspicion and less trust than there was a year ago. My darling Kit – I will say this now and forever shut up, unless you'd like me to talk about it further, - but I honestly believe that I have seen you, M & D, – all 3 of you – become more intolerant and more arrogant about the hotel than at any time before. I believe things could get so bad that there will be a change – it'll be inevitable – and one side or another will back down. And, of course, it will be M & D who'll back down. But at what cost?? Instead of exploiting each other's failings (almost delighting in each other's fuck-ups as a point of professional pride), you should instead exploit each other's strengths, so that you learn from each other, and the business consequently flourishes. I'm not advocating 'family unity' for the sake of it, but unity for the sake of business efficiency. Do not take their criticism personally, and equally don't personalise your criticism of them. It's bloody difficult – and I couldn't do it myself, as I've indicated above. But I think you can do it. And if it doesn't happen the business will harden itself and come between you all like some iron machine and destroy the fragile human links which, we all agree, give the business its distinctiveness. So, humbly, I advise that the burden is actually on you (because you're in the stronger position) to effect a change in these inter-relationships. Give way, a bit, to them: listen: and treat them more as equals rather than as lieutenants. Far from weakening your status I feel this may strengthen it. After all, you are the boss, so people have, ultimately, no choice but to listen and obey, or to leave (or in the case of M & D to shut up); but, as boss,*

you __have__ got the privilege of choice – whether to listen or not to listen. I seriously counsel you to do a teeny-weeny bit more of the former."

Over time, as the events I record unfold, Gerald's words would prove to be a mix of keen observation, prescience and sheer naïvety. Or perhaps I just failed in the task he set me. I may have been "the boss" in name, but if I was in the stronger position to repair the relationship by giving way a little and by listening because I had the "privilege of choice", it never happened as long as Peter and Etty were bunkered in their penthouse. There was no choice. To succeed, giving way and listening must be a bilateral process. I listened but was never listened to – my father powerless as an intermediary between my mother and me. In the end, old age and his infirmity forced the issue and they moved to Avon Lodge, their villa on Blagdon Hill. It was a bitter and sad retreat. Gerald's prophecy that the Castle might become a destructive instrument –"like some iron machine" – would be fulfilled. And at what cost!

*

I brood over these things on Aristotle's; pricked by self-reproach and moments of regret, haunted by the memory of my father's melancholy. Guilt!

In mid-morning, the shade of the pines protects me from a fierce sun. The sea mist at daybreak, a pearly-white frill around the Skopelos littoral, has lifted and a chorus of cicadas stirs our lazy hillside. A single gull glides across an olive oil sea. Meanwhile, Louise has driven to the village to find Patra whose commission in the kitchen today is to prepare mezethes – marinated red peppers, tzatziki – and her famous moussaka for Greek cousins arriving later: Thanos, Machi's son and his wife Santa. Patra knew Gerald all those years ago – her sublime repertoire nourishing his recovery in the spring of '81. She remembers him sitting at the table in Diodati's living room, shutters thrown wide to the terrace. This is where he read his plays, made his notes, wrote his letters. At peace, he would spend hours engrossed in his thoughts and his papers – a habit which irritated Etty who wanted her boy lying under the sun beside her on the beach: much better for his health that way. So she recruited Patra as a reluctant accomplice, instructing her to clean and sweep around his feet – a wily ploy which soon brought him running to mother.

Moments like these found Etty at her happiest – to have her favourite child under her wing: alone, to herself, and available to appear in company linked on one arm while Peter took the other. A winning threesome! Gerald and his mother often mistaken for brother and sister to her huge delight. Of course, it could never be like this for me because I had Louise, a transparent love she could not deny. We had married young, had children young. And quietly stirring at the back of her mind, Etty had registered my attachment to the Guiver family, an association stained by betrayal. Gerald was her perfect Greek boy, unencumbered, pure. I was the fair-haired son with whom she would compete, seeing my marriage to Louise and my position at the Castle as threats to her status as matriarch and chatelaine. I always felt weighed down by the underlying presence of her need to be venerated as a superior being: the residual feelings, perhaps, of a child's devotion to his mother. Though she went through the motions, Etty never seemed quite able to celebrate my achievements and successes (or was I, child-like, too anxious to seek her approval?). No, somehow she would make me feel that in triumph she and Peter should have been the ones lifting the trophy aloft.

Behaving like an ageing star whose limelight is being snatched away, she was gored by this unattractive seam of jealousy and I could never understand it. This was not how a mother was supposed to behave, not how a son was supposed to feel about his mother. How, then, would I fulfil Gerald's dictum? What chance did I have to repair the widening cracks in this relationship? In the years before my father died, we persevered like minor warlords protecting our particular territorial interests, my role as managing director effectively abandoned and replaced by a portfolio of outside interests like my column, the tourist board and Prestige, the consortium of independent hotels. The battlefield at the Castle fell into two camps depending on where the staff's allegiances lay. Publicity and marketing, the kitchen and restaurant fell under my command. Rooms and housekeeping, reception and administration, maintenance and refurbishments were Peter and Etty's province – my mother endowed with the title Director of Aesthetics.

In the summer of 1988, *Caterer & Hotelkeeper* published a cover story about us under the banner "TAUNTON'S STRONGHOLD". But it was the image on the cover of the magazine that told the story. The staff were ranged in two ranks – an inverted V-shape meeting at a point by the hotel's porch. The line to the left was headed by Louise and me. Beside us stood Chef Gary Rhodes with his brigade, and Richard Mills-Roberts, the restaurant manager with his team. On the right, the line was headed by Etty and Peter followed by David Prior, our long-suffering general manager, his assistant and a bevy of receptionists and housekeepers. The line-up was not stage-managed. The staff assumed their positions for the photocall as naturally as the air they breathed.

It was in the latter half of this decade that my career seemed to land on a high – a strange counterpoint amid the turmoil of Gerald's slow and horrible death in New York. But in Taunton, a fair wind had caught our sails. At the stoves, Gary Rhodes had succeeded Chris Oakes and we held our Michelin Star; the Good Hotel Guide made us a gift of a *César* for "best town hotel in Britain"; and at the industry's own ritzy "Oscar" ceremony of '87, my work in promoting British tourism was rewarded with a Catey (one of a number of bronze statuettes presented at *Caterer & Hotelkeeper's* annual awards-fest in London). At the same time, the Octopus Publishing Group commissioned me to write *Great British Chefs* with a contract promising an advance of £10,000 – an opportunity which would open the way to my own television series. And finally, in the Queen's Birthday Honours in June 1989, I was awarded an MBE for services to tourism.

Here for all the world to witness was a success story. The Castle had provided my platform and I had danced on it. Now I was taking my bow. But beneath the grand façade, in the wings behind the glitter and the greasepaint, the platform was a decidedly shaky structure. Taunton's "stronghold" was anything but strong, its foundations floating on shifting sands. The tensions and arguments that tore at our emotions were coming close to collapsing the stage upon which we were meant to be building our livelihoods. The Castle made no money. In the late-Seventies, with a third of our bed stock still without private bathrooms and our public areas looking tired and dated, we had borrowed heavily to fund a major programme of redevelopment. As Director of Aesthetics, Etty had a ball and her extravagance led to these works costing more than the investment could sustain. Room refurbishments were designed by Harrods, furnishings were sourced by Harrods, and from time to time a convoy of green Harrods' pantechnicons would cruise down the M4 and M5 motorways to deliver their expensive wares to our front door.

For me in my role, these matters were no-go areas, considered outside my brief. And here we were struggling to keep the business alive. Denied any real involvement, I was becoming increasingly frustrated and my father appeared entirely complicit in Etty's choice of schemes regardless of the cost, and regardless of a weak financial position which, I know, gave him sleepless nights. He was chairman of the family business but incapable of stamping his foot and saying no!

*

Reflecting on the events of the Eighties, I see now how Gerald's long agony and tragic end blinded us to reason; anaesthetized our senses to help us cope, our hearts and minds dressed in black. The complete family was no longer, and it left an open wound where suppurating tensions simply multiplied. The Castle became a divided city state where an ailing king and his ambitious queen were mourning the loss of their favourite child. They had grown wary of their other son, the ambitious first-born and heir apparent, and his wife whose family had betrayed them.

This is a Greek drama. The prologue is done. It is time to tell the tale.

*

Part Nine

An Iron Machine

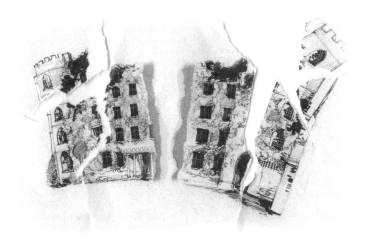

Michael Blackwell sat back in his chair drawing deeply on his pipe. He stared intently at the spotlit wall behind me where a set of twelve sepia-tinted prints depicted the sad story of two doomed lovers. Photographed by Sarah Moon, it had been a calendar inspired by the era of F. Scott Fitzgerald's *The Great Gatsby*. BBDO, my old agency, had produced it for my clients, S.C. Johnson, to coincide with the release of the movie starring Robert Redford: a lingering souvenir of my advertising past. We had just eaten a plate of sandwiches prepared by the kitchen and as he listened to what I was saying, wisps of smoke hung motionless over my office desk, a round white pedestal table by a first-floor window overlooking Castle Bow.

On the day we were meeting – a Tuesday in April 1988 – Etty and Peter were away in London and I needed some space; I needed to talk. Over the previous dozen years, since the formation of the new company, the Yorkshireman had become more important to the hotel than simply the professional who acted as its finance director. He was now the family's confidant and a go-between with an impossible diplomatic role to play. Before settling down to business, he wanted to hear the background to a story he had read on the front page of Friday's *Somerset County Gazette*, Taunton's weekly newspaper.

"Chambermaid accuses hotel over sacking," read the headline under the smiling face of seventeen year old Heidi Draper. Etty had fired her – a summary dismissal made in a fit of pique because the girl had refused to work her day off. At the time neither the head housekeeper nor David Prior, the general manager, was consulted. "When I was working on Easter Sunday," Heidi told the *Gazette's* reporter, "Mrs. Etty Chapman asked me if I could work the following day. I told her I couldn't because I had arranged to go out with my brother whom I don't see very often because he lives in Surrey."

When the story broke, Etty exploded into an hysterical fever. She had lost face! All the town appeared to have read the piece. Now our shining Castle had been royally smeared as an unsympathetic, ill-tempered employer and the only defence David Prior could muster when the reporter telephoned was a limp "no comment". But by the time I sat down for my meeting with Michael Blackwell, the storm had passed. Young Heidi had been paid off and, the *Gazette* told us, she had found a similar job with another Taunton hotel. She remains one of the few ex-employees of the Castle who dared to say "boo" to Mrs. Chapman!

Michael raised an eyebrow and another cloud of pipe smoke curled towards the ceiling. "Let's move on," he said. "We have bigger problems on our hands. The half-year results are dreadful."

"Yes," I replied, "I know. And my problem is that I'm not sure how much more I can take of this business."

"What do you mean?" he growled.

"For the first time since Louise and I moved down from London, Michael, I'm seriously of a mood to resign, jack it all in and sell up. That's how low relations with my parents have sunk."

I was angry and hurt. For several weeks I had ignored my mother, frozen her out, and a private heart-to-heart with my father had only led to another fracas with Etty and a wretched forty-eight hours of fallout for him. In the journal I kept during these turbulent years, I noted: "M, her behaviour and her hyped-up state of mind is driving me round the bend. Louise is being wonderful – calming me down – but she's pretty fed up as well."

The trouble began when Richard Mills-Roberts, my restaurant manager, came to see me. I had recruited him as an assistant, and for eight years he had worked successfully with me supporting the development of the restaurant alongside chefs Oakes and Rhodes. He was a good man. Now, suddenly, my mother had made a direct attempt to subvert him. She had started to brief against me and other members of the management team, including David Prior who had decided to move on after eighteen years of loyal service to my father. Richard, still in his twenties, sat down in front of me in a state of bewilderment. He had hesitated to knock at my door but the manner of Etty's clandestine approach shocked him into action. She had cornered him in his office, imposing her own fanciful omertà to secure his silence. "If Christopher comes in," she declared, "we'll tell him we are discussing the new blue baizes for the trestle tables."

The young man, pinned to his chair, sat speechless as my mother unburdened herself on him. Sitting nervously in my office a few days later, he gave me a near-verbatim account of her pitch: the gist of her words recorded in my diaries. "My husband," she told Richard, "has worked here for over thirty years and thinks the place is falling to bits at the moment. Prior doesn't care any more because he's leaving. Simon Casson's work [a junior manager] has deteriorated because of his affair with Sîan [a receptionist]. And Christopher has lost interest in the hotel – he's never here."

A week later I was still bristling with fury and yet I held my peace because of Richard's understandable fears of a backlash from Etty. But my anger and my unhappiness were complicated by something else. An overwhelming malaise had taken hold and had gripped me for the past six or seven months – since Gerald: his long illness and slow death still fresh in our minds. My journal transcribes five lines from Book Three of Wordsworth's Prelude which, for me, seemed to express my state of mind.

Rotted as by a charm, my life became
A floating island, an amphibious thing,
Unsound, of spungy texture, yet withal,
Not wanting a fair face of water-weeds
And pleasant flowers.

Continuing, I write: "I ask myself if I will ever snap out of this dreadful feeling of ennui. All my drive and enthusiasm for life seem to have evaporated. Is it just Gerald? An expression of grief? Is it something else? I don't know. I just feel incredibly lazy about my existence and the future. All I seem to want is an easy and peaceful life – indulging myself in small pleasures, little treats.

"And yet I have nothing to complain about and everything to live for. Few can be as fortunate. I have a wonderful wife, healthy and beautiful children, and a good and happy family – both on my side and Louise's. My father has given me the Castle – it has its problems (and my mother!) but it is a fine asset and something to be genuinely proud about. We have a lovely home, we have a privileged lifestyle and we have the means and support to enjoy life. We are blessed. The Angels are on our side. I should not complain. For Gerald's sake, in his memory and for the joy and life he gave to young people, I must pull myself out of this pit and look forward."

I wrote these words ten days before Richard Mills-Roberts made his revelations. Now I felt betrayed and, in the end, I was overtaken by my brewing anger and hurt pride – a terrible mistake. Mindless of the recriminations, I was determined to see my father and try – yet again – to put a stop to Etty's infernal meddling. For days I hesitated, Louise cautioning, doubtful that much would be achieved. I was worried about him, the reality of his condition staring at me every day – too old and too tired to grapple with fraught issues like these. But I wanted to talk to him, to share my feelings with a father I loved and admired. My history of confrontations with Etty, his wife and the evergreen woman he worshipped, was driving a wedge between us and I had begun to feel the chill more and more: a creeping alienation which I found disturbing and unsettling. I needed to reconnect with him – at least to win his understanding.

His office lay just beyond mine – at the end of a narrow passage on the right. Each morning I would hear him shuffling along the corridor and down a short flight of stairs – his breathing audible, laboured, rhythmic. He was now seventy-three and unsteady on his pins. He had no need to arrive at his desk at precisely nine o'clock: always immaculately suited, shoes polished, tie knotted just so. But this had been his routine for thirty-eight years and Etty insisted he keep to it. There was something tragicomic about this weary ritual which, in all its absurdity, upset me. My mother's power over him was now absolute. If she had instructed him to rest in bed for a while or call for his post to be sent up to the penthouse, he would have accepted her will. But she refused to permit any variation in his routine. Appearances had to be maintained; the edifice of the regime and its outward sign of authority had to be perpetuated. Denying his declining health, Etty believed the face of the family and its honour came first.

*

I waited twenty minutes, giving him time to settle down to his post. He liked to open his own letters with his long slim paperknife leaving the empty envelopes in a neat pile for his secretary to tear off the stamps which were collected and sent to a charity. We agreed to meet later in the morning. Etty would be out, lunching with a friend.

At midday, office door closed, we talked – my father listening carefully to my appeal, his pale watery eyes gazing at me like old crystal pools. I began by confessing my feelings of malaise – how I seemed to have lost my energy and enthusiasm for the job. "I just feel trapped," I explained. "I don't feel I'm getting anywhere and it's not helped by Mummy. I'm afraid she can be very indiscreet with members of staff sometimes."

"Kit," he interrupted, "you really should not believe all the things the staff tell you. You have been away a lot. Now there's your book. If you were more involved with the hotel, you wouldn't have these problems."

"Well, I'm sorry Daddy," I replied, "I can't really agree and this problem's for real. I have no reason to disbelieve it." As I described my meeting with Mills-Roberts, I sensed a flicker of understanding as if my story might just be plausible. He had been desperately worried about the company's finances and in some late-night outburst with Etty he had probably been too free with his words. Agitated by his distress, she had flown to the nearest available pair of ears.

"Comments like these from Mummy," I continued, "aren't helpful. They are divisive and it's demoralizing when staff are buttonholed like that. Richard was quite shocked."

"Well, I'll talk to her," he said sighing. "But you know what she's like. She really doesn't mean it in the way you describe."

"Maybe not," I said. "But sometimes she behaves a little naïvely. Almost like a little girl."

"But that is part of her charm!"

"Well, I feel quite strongly it's inappropriate for her to talk in these terms to a junior manager."

"Kit, I've said I'll talk to her and I will." Then, in an uncharacteristic afterthought, he added: "You will never understand how difficult it can be for me sometimes."

"I imagine it must be," I said gently. "But I wish she would try to understand that her interference in the running of the hotel can sometimes be damaging."

"The only way round your mother," he replied, "is through kindness and love, you know that. You've been very cold towards her lately and she feels it. I wish you would come upstairs and just give her a big hug. You'll get nowhere by bashing her!" We laughed.

"I love her very much as a mother," I said, "but the way she behaves sometimes can alienate her family. I find it very difficult to cope with. You keep saying that you want me to get on and run this place. How can I? She makes it impossible for me!"

We continued talking for a while – about the state of the business, the burden of our borrowings, about the need to cut an excessive payroll and about David Prior's departure. Again my father urged me to consider taking on the day-to-day management myself, anyway for six months before the appointment of a new general manager. It might help to re-engage my energies, he suggested, and it would have the advantage of saving a salary. If he could have devised a guaranteed route to open conflict with Etty, this might be it! Besides, I had signed a contract with Octopus and my publisher was expecting me to deliver a manuscript by the New Year. I had ten months to research and write the book – a project which would see me travelling for days and weeks across Britain.

By now it was almost one o'clock and we decided to take a table for lunch in a quiet corner of the restaurant. There were other things on my mind and this seemed a good opportunity to air them. As we took our seats, my father's chair creaked under his weight – a loose hind leg – and a waiter rushed forward to replace it with another from the table next-door. Recently we had spent a vast sum of money, £80,000, redecorating the room, a scheme which included replacing the old furniture with seventy Harrods-supplied Louis XV-style bergère chairs. While their great elegance had pleased Etty, their impractical design – more suited to a lady's boudoir than a working restaurant – was driving us crazy. Their straight, spindly legs failed to cope with the strain of constant use and kept breaking. They were an expensive mistake which cost us another small fortune as job lots of chairs were taken out of commission and sent for serial repair. My father groaned. "These bloody chairs!" he muttered as the waiter made off to find us the menus. "We're just fighting a losing battle."

We settled down and when our food arrived I began by reminding him of a conversation he, Michael Blackwell and I had had some weeks before about the disposal of a small parcel of company shares David Prior had bought. At the meeting we agreed that the best solution must be to keep the shares in the family and allow Louise to buy them. By now Dom was approaching his fifteenth birthday, Nick his thirteenth. After her years in the wilderness, I was determined to see Louise involved in the hotel. She would be a great asset and I wanted her formally appointed a director – a move openly supported by Michael: my turn now to suggest how my lost enthusiasm for the business might be re-energized. My father remembered the conversation but he seemed reluctant to make a commitment. He needed time to think – the spectre of Etty looming in his imagination. It was getting late and I could see that he was tiring. I worried that I may have overplayed my hand. He needed his afternoon rest.

*

The row with my mother was a grotesque music hall turn overheard by everyone in the corridor – secretaries, accounts and administration cowering in their corners. She didn't even bother to close my office door. And when I had done, the histrionics were so wild passers-by in Castle Bow must have been witnesses to the commotion.

Early that morning I had arrived to find an envelope lying on my desk. Opening it I found a five-page letter from my father, hand-written on the back of old arrivals and departures lists. It was a kind and fatherly note reiterating his thoughts on our meeting and what I should do to shed my present torpor. He meant well but once again he had failed to see the problem and his words were lost on me. No mention either of Louise, or the disposal of Prior's shareholding. Later, when he came downstairs, he seemed depressed, mawkish even, and when I enquired he told me he had had two sleepless nights. Etty in turmoil. "Frankly, Kit," he said, "life's just not worth living!" Moments later, he shuffled back up the corridor and did not reappear.

It must have been ten-thirty or eleven when she burst in and erupted over my desk. "How can you treat your father like this?" she ranted. "You upset him so much. He hasn't slept for two nights."

"Why do you blame me?" I replied. "We had a very good talk together. This affair is all your making."

"You believe everyone except your own mother," she snapped, glaring at me with rage. "Mills-Roberts is lying. That's the truth. You are a fool to believe the staff. He just wants to stir trouble."

"Well, I do believe him," I said, my throat tightening with emotion. "He has no reason to make trouble and he is not the first person to come and see me. You have this terrible habit of pinning staff in corners and saying things which are totally out of order. I'm fed up with it and it's got to stop."

"How dare you talk to me like that," she screamed. "I'll speak to who I want! Who do you think you are? Are you mad?"

"I'm your son. If I'm mad, you gave me my madness." Overwhelmed by my sense of outrage, I was losing control.

"You want to get rid of us. Go on say it! Confess it to me! You want to be 'king of the Castle'!"

"Mummy, you are a bloody liability to this company and I've had enough of it!"

"Eeeee! You think you can rule us? Your father gave you this place on a plate!"

"The way we're going, the bank – *not me* – will be getting this place on a plate!"

"Why don't you shoot me then?" she screeched. "Go on shoot me!"

"Now you're being hysterical! For God's sake grow up! You're behaving like a very silly spoilt little child!"

"Christopher, how dare you speak to your mother like that!"

"Don't you see what you're doing, Mummy? Don't you see that you're alienating your own family?"

"Eeeee! Alienating? Me? You really are mad!"

I was finished. "Mummy, please get out of my office," I shouted. "Just go! I'm busy!"

She stormed out, slamming the door.

*

Tapping his pipe, Blackwell sat impassively listening to my account of the feud which was now tearing the family apart. He stared again at the set of sepia prints on my wall. "Oh dear," he said at last. "And what about Richard? I suppose he got it in the neck from your mother?"

"Yes," I replied. "He was given a good mauling and then she hauled him up before my father to apologise! Quite what for I don't know!"

"How did he feel about that?" Michael asked.

"I'd warned him in advance that I would be speaking to my father," I said. "Richard's a toughie. He was braced for the reaction – said he could handle it."

"And did he?"

"I think he must have done. A few days later she decided to kiss and make up with a peace offering. He told me she'd given him a bottle of wine! A typical Etty manoeuvre!"

Michael had read my mood but he wanted to move the discussion on and bring it to earth. "Look Kit," he said, "these spats do not make for a promising future. As things stand, I can't see the business making any profit again this year. Our cash flow is dire and although the bank is being very supportive, it can't go on forever. I'm going to have to ask for another extension to our overdraft facility. It's getting serious."

"So much for my plans to redevelop the garage block!" I said referring to proposals I had drawn up to demolish and rebuild a motley patchwork of redundant outbuildings.

"Not a hope," he said. "Not with our level of bank debt! The only way you'll get your cookery theatre and leisure centre is by bringing in a partner with a very substantial investment."

"We've discussed this in the past," I said. "I'm not terribly keen to dilute the family's shareholding."

"Then are you really serious about selling?" he asked looking at me directly. "You mentioned it a moment ago and it sounds as if your career is taking on a life of its own."

"Well, yes" I muttered. "I'm so fed up that's how I'm feeling at the moment – and the book's an exciting new outlet for me. But then I love this old place. I grew up here and with all the effort we've put in, I'd like to see it work. So would Louise."

I paused to call for some coffee. Outside on the street a child was bawling its head off as his mother struggled to settle him into his buggy. Workers returning to their offices after the lunch break hurried past, disappearing under the Bow, the medieval arched gateway to the Castle. Michael glanced at his watch. "I need to be going shortly," he said as a waiter came in with the tray of coffee.

"There's just one more thing I need to talk about," I said when the door closed again. "We've got a board meeting in a couple of weeks and at some point I'd like to settle the question of Prior's shareholding and clear the way for Louise to join the board. Perhaps another private chat between you, me and my father?"

"Kit," he replied, "you know I'm with you on this one but it's going to be difficult."

"You mean they just don't want her," I groaned. "It's so depressing!"

"Your father's less of a problem," he said glancing at his watch again. "But the current state of relations between you all doesn't help. You'll have to leave it with me for the time being. Now I really must be going."

*

The board meeting we held that May was a grim affair in spite of a picture sketched by the official minutes which is so anodyne as to suggest we were living in a fantasy world. The half-year results were showing a "loss of £52,000" and it was agreed that "every effort should continue to be made to contain costs particularly in view of the need to meet the loan repayments [to the bank] due in the year". Item 4 on the agenda examined our weak cash flow position which reflected "heavier spending on overheads resulting in higher than expected borrowings". And against this bleak background the board held a grand debate on the purchase of a new entrance hall carpet. My father had obtained quotations from three Taunton-based companies and one from Harrods, each firm receiving an identical specification. Of course the Knightsbridge store's price tag ran ahead of the others by a good £700 and although some of us raised our voices in opposition, the contract was awarded to Harrods "on the grounds of past service and status with suppliers". With her husband's support, once again Etty had won the day!

As chairman, the strain on my father at these meetings was visible. There was something almost heroic about the statesmanlike posture he assumed – his noble attempt to appear in command even though the fragility of his pose was obvious. Proceedings were conducted with a friendly formality – a genteel politesse occasionally spiced by a trill of airy frivolity from Etty. Neither David Prior, nor Elizabeth Williams – Bill Stansell's daughter who represented the minority shareholders – were inclined to upset or challenge the wisdom of the chair. And while Michael Blackwell doggedly presented the financial realities of our predicament, he was reluctant to press his case. As for me, I just felt isolated and disenfranchised, my mind often slipping out of the boardroom and into my other life: the book, my publisher, the chefs still to be interviewed.

After two wearying hours, the agenda lurched towards its end with Any Other Business and I raised the question of Prior's shareholding. His departure from the hotel was now imminent, a price had been agreed for the purchase of his stock and it was time to get the issue out into the open. Perhaps I should not have been surprised by my father's reaction because my question instantly touched a sensitive nerve.

"I've decided to buy the shares myself," he said, his face flushing pink with irritation. "I'm going to put them in trust for Dominic and Nicholas!"
"But Michael, you and I had discussed ..."
"Kit," he interrupted, "I've made my decision and I'm adamant!"
The chairman moved swiftly to close the meeting. And when the minutes were circulated some weeks later, they contained no reference to the disposal of David Prior's shares.

Again I saw my father's attitude as a calculated move to exclude Louise from the affairs of the company. Again I saw him as Etty's willing fender, her protector and co-conspirator. After his death, Gerald's shareholding had been put in trust for Dom and Nick, a good decision which had pleased me greatly. In March, when David presented us with his resignation, we had agreed that his small parcel of shares should be offered to Louise – a topic I had touched on with my father at our lunch together. His hesitancy then had been turned by Etty into a blunt refusal.

Two days after the board meeting, I went to my father and raised the issue once more. I asked him for another private conversation with Michael who was coming into the hotel that afternoon to report on his latest discussions with the bank. At a quarter to five, when Michael walked into my office, I used the spare minutes before our rendezvous to rehearse my case.
"Frankly, Kit," he said, "I'm very surprised at the action your father is taking. He did not consult me and, if anything, Prior's shares should be offered to the board for shareholders to take up on a pro rata basis. But like you, I believe it's time Louise got involved with this business and that's why I think she should pick up these shares."
"Well let's have another go," I replied. "We'd better get going. He's waiting

for us upstairs."

Within a few minutes I was to learn that I had made two tactical misjudgements in setting up this meeting. The first was to call for another discussion about David's shares when my father, Michael and I were meeting anyway to talk finance. The second was to agree to meet in the penthouse – an arrangement which suited Peter. He and Etty would have just returned from their afternoon walk and he liked a cup of tea at this time. So at five o'clock when Michael and I stepped into their sitting room, we found both David Prior and Etty already installed either side of him: she on her small scalloped sofa, he on a low cushioned ottoman and, between them, my father in his tall winged armchair. I had been outmanoeuvred – my mission spiked. Like a game of charades the meeting proceeded – my mother oblivious to Michael's commentary on his session with the bank and the need for an extension of our overdraft facility to prop up the rickety state of our cash flow. I sat in silence, listening, quietly fuming – a moment I remember as much for the evening sun which streamed into that sky-perched room half-blinding my eyes.

When Michael had finished and the moment came for us to leave, Etty turned towards me in an expansive play for all to witness. "Christopher," she said in her meekest, sweetest and most conciliatory voice, "I have just received some beautiful carpet samples from Harrods. Shall we sit down and choose one together?"

*

Through the summer and early autumn of 1988 the business limped on to deliver another crushing loss at the end of our financial year. Meanwhile friends in the trade, my fellow hoteliers in the Prestige consortium, were making hay – recording high occupancies and healthy profits. For much of this time I was absent visiting my "Great British Chefs", listening to their stories, deconstructing their kitchens. I travelled from Scotland and the English Lakes to South Devon, London and East Anglia to compile my first volume of profiles on eighteen top cooks (a second book would follow in the mid-Nineties). My aim was to do for Britain what Quentin Crewe had done in his brilliant appreciation of the three-star chefs of France a decade before; except that this is where the comparison ends. In 1988 Britain's only three-star grandees were two Frenchmen, Albert Roux at Le Gavroche in London and his brother Michel at the Waterside Inn on the Thames at Bray. My chefs were a more eclectic breed, each chosen to illustrate the nation's gastronomic revival, from great pioneers like Francis Coulson at Sharrow Bay and John Tovey at Miller Howe to a selection of young revolutionaries – Alastair Little, Simon Hopkinson, Rowley Leigh, Shaun Hill and others – my own Gary Rhodes among them.

So the writing of the book became my private retreat, a kind of creative sanctuary breathing freedom into my veins. But in the relief that absence brought from the constant feuding and from the battle to see Louise embraced in the business, I denied my proper responsibilities, ignoring the looming crisis which would engulf us in the months to come. And although the book distracted me from my duties in Taunton, it did little to palliate the emotional burden I seemed to carry – a dull sense of oppression I find difficult to explain. I became obsessed by the sheer drama of my relationship with Etty and Peter.

We avoided Greece that summer, preferring to take Dom and Nick on our own family holiday in the South of France where Molly, my mother-in-law now widowed, kept a flower-strewn balcony on a jaw of red rock overlooking the Bay of Cannes. Rereading my diary entries for August, Louise and I seem to have spent hours of our time talking about the Castle, our future and the senior generation. "I have this awful feeling," I wrote, obviously troubled by my mother's state of mind, "that she is becoming progressively more manic, more obsessive, more overbearing. Is she going a little mad I ask myself? I dread her return to the Castle [Peter and Etty spent their Augusts at Diodati]. What kind of emotional upheaval will I find on my return from France? George Elworthy [David Prior's successor] was telling me today that Valerie Harper [the head housekeeper] is already worrying about it. So is he. So am I."

But the worries came and went. We were on holiday and it was one of our happiest. In Miramar or nearby Théoule, the boys – teenagers now – swam and skied, and with them, we endured the pain and pleasure of visits to the rackety amusement parks at La Napoule and Antibes. And when Molly minded them for us, Louise and I drove into the hills to rediscover our favourite village restaurants – at Mougins, Valbonne, Pégomas, Auribeau and St. Paul. These were special moments and we talked endlessly about our dreams and the problems of coping with ageing parents. Towards the end, as the day of our return to England drew closer, my preoccupations resurfaced. "What's to be?" I asked myself, writing on Molly's terrace on the twenty-fifth. "I just don't know. Peace has been struck for the present by way of an unspoken and uneasy truce, admirably assisted by separation. How long will it last? I fear trouble this autumn – more turmoil which does us no good and, in particular, is deeply wounding to D. He is now in his twilight years … a sad man and so surely my duty is to bring him some joy, to try to relieve him of the misery of watching his beloved wife and first-born son waging war on one another. The Castle, the business has laid siege to our love."

A few days later, shortly after nine o'clock in the morning, I wrote my final journal entry of the holiday … "Here I sit," I began, "enclosed by oleanders and geraniums, the sun shining and a gentle breeze dancing around the tasselled fringes of the blue parasols. I don't feel properly awake. I can't really recall anything we have done this week other than a wonderful tour of the Gorges du Loup on Monday when the day began dull and then turned bright. I'm in a haze of mixed emotions – contented after my coffee and croissant, feeling guilty for not feeling full of beans and suffering bolts of panic each time I contemplate the consequences of our return home in two days' time. I'm just not ready to face it all."

*

The agenda for day one of my return included a closed-door session with Blackwell and my father to discuss our cheerless trading situation, meetings with a demoralized management team who were instructed to make staff cuts, and a heart-to-heart with Mrs. Harper who came to me with another complaint about Etty's interference in the housekeeping department. Soon after I was away again – this time to North Yorkshire and Staddlebridge to interview the McCoy brothers at the Tontine Inn, a solitary curiosity on a busy trunk road with a riotous interior which tossed Victoriana, art deco and chinoiserie into a forest of hanging foliage: a restaurant *Punch* likened to "a Chinese opium den" and one which Egon Ronay ranked among his top ten in Great Britain.

I was sorry to leave the McCoys – the whimsy of the place appealed to me, its kitsch backcloth inspiring a kind of burlesque theatrical production for their refined and luxuriant gastronomy. As I headed south on the A19 towards the A1, the September sunshine seemed to ambush my mind, opening its dark store of memories, suddenly overwhelming me with thoughts of Gerald. I suppose it must have been the road signs for York which prompted this rush of emotion. "York," and again, "York", and another, "York": the repetition needlessly reminding me of the start of his career; hinting then at New "York" and its end. Silly mind games scrambling the imagination. How he would have loved the Tontine Inn. In exactly seven days, on the twenty-third, we would be marking the first anniversary of his death, a date I could not account for in the confusion of my soul.

I should have been in jollier spirits. I was heading for London and the wedding of Louise's great school chum the following afternoon. Anne Snead-Cox was descended from ancient Catholic stock which had weathered the Reformation, the boundaries of her family's substantial estate in Herefordshire still largely intact after half a millennium. She was marrying an Ulster Protestant – a dashing fellow, Mike Allen, who divided his time as an ICI executive and as a company commander with 4 Para, the Territorial battalion of the Parachute Regiment. They had met on a group skiing holiday and, drawing short straws on the first evening, had been obliged to share the last double bed in the chalet. Four days of polite restraint, they claim, was as much as they could endure before their passions erupted!

The embossed invitation said noon at the Church of the Immaculate Conception in Farm Street. Fortified by a good pork sausage and a glass of Buck's Fizz, Louise and I set off with Dom and Nick shortly after eleven. As our cab rounded Berkeley Square, it seemed that the whole of Mayfair had turned out in morning dress and extravagant millinery to celebrate the day. The church filled and as the bride made her entrance the surge of the organ and the voices of the choir raised us to our feet. The atmosphere inside this sacred place struck me like a storm and again lost memories of Gerald came flooding into my head. I gripped Louise's hand and when the choir rose to sing Handel's *Zadoc the Priest*, I struggled to control my tears. This was an anthem Gerald and I had sung at school and like Purcell's *Rejoice in the Lord Alway* at his funeral, *Zadoc* was another favourite we loved to parody on our walks or after supper at home.

Even today, these wild flushes of emotion still lie in wait and surprise me. There is a feeling I have for my brother, a sheepish, guilty feeling, which I find unnerving. Then as now I find I miss him more in death than in the years he was alive; and I feel ashamed to have to admit it to myself. In life I took him for granted and only since his death have I come to recognize the depth of my affection for him. His handsome portrait – the one that smiled up at me from the order of service at Saint John the Divine – is everywhere: on the book shelves in the living room at Diodati; on the staircase leading to our bedroom in Somerset; and beside the desk in my study at home. There, on a low pine table, it belongs as one of a trinity of mementos – the others being his silver christening mug engraved "Gerald 12.2.50" and the small silver-framed photograph of the two of us which Louise gave me on our return from New York. But it is the large single portrait which transfixes me. Displayed like an icon in each of its locations, I stare at it every day: greet it, talk to it, occasionally harangue it for not answering back. And all I get in return are those kind, crinkled, intelligent eyes smiling back at me from beneath a rich mane of black curls.

After we had left Taunton School, we were both consumed by the hurly-burly of our separate lives, and because of this, most of my memories of

Gerald are contained within the years of our childhood and youth. They tumble into my head in their tens and hundreds: playing "tanks" in bed, eiderdowns covering our heads, the shaft of a cricket bat sticking out over a pile of pillows firing at a make-believe enemy; chasing an oval ball in a field on the Blackdowns with our daddy; clowning in the shallow end of the town's municipal pool after the swimming coach had released us from our interminable lengths; bossy me sending baby brother off in search of string, sticks, scissors, crates and other materials for our camps in the hotel's garden; crumpets for tea, the butter and jam oozing through his chubby fingers; hot chocolate in Gindelwald after ski school; his teasing; his clever impersonations; his laughter.

The singing – our jokey duets – came later but like the shared experiences of our childhood, that memory is anchored in the spirit of those early years. It was as if we had invented a private world of our own, giving a kind of exclusivity of access to each other, an unconscious feeling which was quietly whispering "we are blood brothers – a unique state – precious – immutable." Childhood memories stick and they accumulate like pebbles gathered on a beach. For me they became the invisible touchstones of an unspoken, unbreakable sibling bond. And only in death was the bond broken, leaving me disentitled, less than the person I was before.

When Louise and I were married, the quality and nature of this sibling relationship might have been threatened. But astonishingly it wasn't. Somehow it was strengthened even though, in our twenties and thirties, we saw less of one another, each in our different fields madly ploughing our individual furrows. Gerald loved Louise as a sister and she him as a brother. He would look forward to visiting us in Putney, then in Somerset, where he felt at home – a homeliness free of the ceremony, fuss and ritual imposed by life at the Castle. Louise did not expect him to wash his hair or change his shirt. Both shared the same sense of fun and independence, of rebellion even – a reluctance to submit to convention, and that made me happy. They were instinctive qualities bedded deep in their nature, cementing their special kinship.

And what of our attitude to homosexuals and homosexuality? Neither

Louise nor I were conscious that this should be important in our relationship with Gerald. If we had any residual prejudices – and we did – he made them irrelevant. And in observing him confront his demons through the 1970s, he helped us to understand the many and complex shades of human sexual behaviour. He never challenged us, never lectured us. In Louise's presence as much as my own, there were no inhibitions; he knew he was free to express his feelings – his passions and foibles aired in serious discussion or amid gales of laughter. Yet always – whenever he visited – he was scrupulous in his respect of our home and the presence of two young children.

*

The twenty-third of September 1988 fell on a Friday. At midday we gathered in the entrance hall – Peter, Etty, Louise, me – and we walked the short half-mile to St. George's, Taunton's principal Catholic church, a cavernous space I've never much liked, its walls hung with heavy woodcarvings depicting the Stations of the Cross. By right we should have attended St. Mary Magdalene, an Anglican parish church built of Ham Hill stone in the fifteenth century and Somerset's most magnificent, its soaring multi-pinnacled and ornamented tower crowning the end of Hammet Street. As children this is where we were taken every Sunday morning, its square interior divided by a nave and double aisles, its gilded angels and medieval masks filling me with awe. But on this occasion St. Mary's was dismissed because the church did not subscribe to the Orthodox habit of lighting candles. At St. George's we were free to light as many as we chose. And so we did – ten in all, a grandiose act inspired by the certain belief that the brighter the illumination the closer we would be drawn to Gerald's spirit. My father and mother sat together in a pew behind us: he silently praying, she sobbing. I remained unmoved, sitting next to Louise, lost in my thoughts while she knelt and prayed for what seemed a long time. On our way out, we found the porch scattered with dead flowers and limp, dingy wreaths, debris from a recent funeral. A church attendant asked us if they were ours. We stared at him in bewilderment, shook our heads and returned to the hotel.

That evening, at home, Louise and I talked again about my lost brother. A year had passed, twelve long months; an age all in the blink of an eye. Where had that year gone? The living Gerald still lived, inhabiting our hearts and minds; vital, full of energy, with us and around us. Then, in a sudden change of tack as if to change the subject, Louise said something which startled me – a comment I found shocking only because her observation had never really occurred to me before. "Since his death", she said, "you're a changed man, Kit. You seem to have lost so much of your joie. He wouldn't have wanted that." I conceded that she was probably right. How awful, I thought, a symptom of my general malaise. And I promised to try to shake myself out of my dark dream and lighten up.

*

Perhaps the anniversary was a watershed. The onset of winter surprised me with two new opportunities which, miraculously, had the effect of cheering me up. The first was a chance meeting with a television producer who was intrigued by my book and wondered how it might be adapted into a series of programmes showcasing Britain's gastronomic renaissance. The second emerged out of a casual conversation with a well-connected Californian couple who were taken by my ideas for a tour of the United States with a group of chefs drawn from the book. Meanwhile, the writing of *Great British Chefs* was making good progress and my publisher seemed pleased, confident now that the decision she had made to commission an unknown author might pay off. I had reached a point where I was beginning to think about the book's introduction – a long essay with an historical perspective which sought to define the origins and influences of our culinary revival. To help me with this task, I was determined to win an audience with Elizabeth David, our greatest living food writer and a much-garlanded grande dame of English letters whose prose I worshipped for its purity, its evocative beauty and its simple descriptive power. More to the point, she was ideally placed to provide the historical context I needed for my introduction. Indeed, she was an important part of that context. With recipes gathered from around the Mediterranean, she had rekindled the impoverished palates of a rationed and war-weary generation of chefs and amateur restaurateurs who suddenly discovered fresh inspiration from the pages of her early books.

At first she refused to see me, her letter in reply to mine saying she did not do interviews. I persisted and in early December I visited Mrs. David at 24 Halsey Street, her Chelsea terrace home. As the taxi drew up outside the house – butterflies dancing wildly in my stomach – I spotted two shadows moving across the basement window. She had asked me to arrive at five o'clock and go downstairs – not to come to the front door. It was already dark and by the time I had paid the cabby and turned to descend the steep steps, a blind had been drawn. I pressed the bell to the basement door and a woman ushered me into a narrow passageway. And there at the end of the corridor, by the entrance to her kitchen, she stood: a diminutive figure, unsteady on her feet, more elderly than I had anticipated. She greeted me politely and we sat down at her kitchen table. By now the other woman had disappeared. Perched uncomfortably in her chaotic basement, engulfed by toppling piles of books, bottles, glasses, papers and magazines, a camp bed in the corner barely distinguishable beneath the hillocks of print matter, I found myself alone with Elizabeth David.

I might have expected a cup of tea but it was not offered. On the table between us stood two glasses and a bottle of Sancerre, half-drunk, which she asked me to taste before pouring. A test. The wine was fine and after objecting to a taped interview on my cassette recorder, we began to talk. I asked her questions about the development of the British restaurant scene, about chefs and their cooking since the end of the war, but she was of little practical help. Now seventy-five years old, she was out of touch, more absorbed by her own scholarly interests. We finished the wine and she despatched me to the fridge to find a second bottle. I poured her a fresh glass. "This one's got more life," she declared and with that our conversation drifted away from its agenda and the reason I had come to see her. She wasn't interested. But there was a warmth, a playfulness in her voice and about her eyes, and I soon gathered that what she really wanted was a good old-fashioned gossip about our contemporaries in the food world. At which point I abandoned the interview and settled down to enjoy the wine and her company.

Each time I topped up our glasses, her views became more wicked. She was making mischief, enjoying the moment, and before long I learned that there were precious few people in our trade she held in any admiration. Among those whom she did were the Roux brothers, Jane Grigson and Simon Hopkinson whose restaurant Bibendum was a personal favourite. These aside, Mrs. David treated me to a long catalogue of her bêtes noires. She described one cookery writer as "very pretty" but found her recipes "too fancy". Another's were "terribly boring". A well known foodie author was branded "ugly" and "a name dropper who knows nothing about food". Various editors of the *Good Food Guide* were also her targets; one was pronounced "poisonous", a successor deemed "pompous" and a third, who "knew nothing" when he first started to edit the Guide, "had improved a lot". A number of London's most celebrated chefs also attracted her waspish contempt. Where she "hated" the cooking of one, she despised another Michelin-starred chef for being "too full of himself".

By seven o'clock she was noticeably tipsy. Again she invited me to draw another bottle of Sancerre from the fridge but I declined. Besides we had been joined by her lodger, an American academic, who was escorting her to a do in Covent Garden and I had a train to catch. Before saying our goodbyes, she presented me with a signed copy of her new 1988 edition of *Mediterranean Food*, her first book originally published by John Lehmann in 1950. Then slowly, unsteadily, she led the way upstairs to the ground floor, each tread – each corner of each tread – piled with more books, hundreds of them, many with annotated slips of paper tucked between their pages. At the front door we said farewell and I promised to send her a copy of my book when it was published.

In the taxi bound for Paddington, my head fizzed with the experience of the previous two hours. My mission had been a complete failure yet my encounter with Mrs. David remains one of the most memorable in my life.

On the train journey home, my time passed happily in the company of her *Book of Mediterranean Food*. For the umpteenth time I read again that famous passage from the introduction to the 1950 edition: "anyone who has lived for long in Greece will be familiar with the sound of air gruesomely whistling through sheep's lungs frying in oil."

After Castle Cary I closed the book and spent the final minutes of the journey in thought. Why? I asked myself. What was so remarkable about my meeting with Mrs. David? Here was a high-minded woman, a Fellow of the Royal Society of Literature, who had agreed to talk about her subject and mine but who, on acquaintance, chose to while away two hours being spectacularly rude about the good and the great of our trade. Gradually, a feeling I had resisted crept into my thoughts. Her warmth, her playfulness suggested that she was enjoying my company. She liked me. A great beauty in her time, here now was a seventy-five year old lady behaving like a garrulous teenager, flirting with a strange man thirty-four years her junior. Should I have been shocked or flattered? I didn't know. At Taunton I left the train a little light-headed, undeservedly contented with my day.

Next morning I sent her flowers, a gesture which set in motion a brief, even affectionate, correspondence. I was fortunate to be favoured. The book was being printed in Hong Kong and would be published in October. My greatest wish was that she might agree to attend the launch party. And come the day she did – but only after first reading the book to endow it with her private seal of approval. Sadly for me that evening, less approving voices came from Etty and Peter who objected to the preface. My transgression was to impugn the family's honour by daring to reveal that: "I grew up over the shop and my mother had no need to cook ... because our dining room table was admirably served by a dumb waiter."

*

Christmas 1988, the second after Gerald, was much the same as the first except that this year the festivities were even more muted. Another undeclared truce did its best to veil the constant state of tension between mother and son, the fragility of the business swept under the carpet for the duration of the holiday. As usual, all the customary rituals and family traditions were faithfully observed beginning with the singing, in German, of *Stille Nacht, Heilige Nacht* (*Silent Night*) around Etty's candle-lit tree in the penthouse. And as we sang along to an LP, arms linked in a manner prescribed when my parents were children in Bratislava and Salonica, our only thoughts were for him, his presence hanging like an invisible pall around the room; Louise and I wishing he'd just leap out from behind a curtain and raise a laugh.

On the afternoon of that Christmas Eve, before changing to go into the hotel, I sat alone in my study writing my journal, listening to the Festival of Nine Lessons and Carols from King's College Cambridge on Radio 4. By the third verse of *Once in Royal David's City*, I was in tears – the small silver-framed photograph of the two of us held tightly in my hands. Again I imagined myself with him, singing those verses as choristers at school. At the end of the service, there was an unscheduled news bulletin with a short broadcast from the Queen – an additional message to her annual Christmas broadcast to the Commonwealth which had been pre-recorded some time before. She wanted to lead the nation in a moment of reflection on three terrible tragedies which had befallen the world in recent weeks: the Armenian earthquake, the Clapham rail crash, and finally Lockerbie. Just three days before, PanAm flight 103, en route from London to New York, had fallen out of the sky in a fireball, killing all its passengers and crew, and eleven inhabitants of the Scottish border town. "Sabotage is suspected," I noted in my journal, "but the investigators have found no proof yet. What misery at this time of celebration."

Shortly after, as the family linked arms to sing *Silent Night*, our thoughts were no longer with the victims and bereaved of Lockerbie. Times of celebration tend also to be times of remembrance, a moment to reflect on lost loved ones. And so I was relieved to see Christmas pass into the New Year, always a moment when a fickle world wakes up to new hope and the belief that all will be well as our leaders tempt fate with their rash pronouncements.

This New Year was no exception, a valedictory President Reagan declaring that in 1989 the world was a safer place! As for us, the family and the Castle, 1989 would be a year of cruel decision.

*

> '... oh! yet
> Stands the Church clock at ten to three?
> And is there honey still for tea?'
> Rupert Brooke

In memory of my brother Gerald for whom afternoon tea was most important.

The dedication was my final duty and, to my publisher's relief, I delivered the manuscript to the March deadline. Eerily, two days later, an unsolicited envelope arrived from New York. In it I found a cheque for $10,000, the proceeds of a life insurance policy taken out by Gerald naming me as beneficiary. His gift was a surprise – at once comforting and poignant – and I took it as a positive omen for the exciting prospects which seemed to be unravelling in the wake of the book.

By early April I had heard from my well-connected Californian friends who faxed to confirm that the wine producing fraternity of the Napa Valley was "wildly enthusiastic" about my scheme to lead a team of British chefs on a tour of the United States where they would present a series of dinners in a number of major cities across the country. This was an ambitious promotion which would only succeed on the back of sponsorship support from hotels, airlines and other like-minded associates including the Californian wine trade. The aim was to persuade doubting Americans that at last they had another reason to visit Britain. In addition to satisfying their fascination for our castles, stately manors and gardens, they could now eat well. With Richard Shepherd from Langan's Brasserie on board and primed to lead a brigade of star names drawn from the book, my plan was to mount the campaign in January 1990. News that we had won the support of the Napa vineyards was an encouraging start.

Meanwhile, my chance encounter with the producer I had met in Taunton before Christmas had developed into more detailed talks about a possible TV series. Edward Adcock was a suave ex-Thames Television cameraman with an immaculately manicured beard and an affection for black cashmere polo necks. He had set up his own production company and was hungry for a first commission. The notion of a gastronomic travelogue celebrating the richness and diversity of Britain's natural larder appealed to him. I would write and front it – presenting a different theme for each week of the series – and we would invite a guest chef for each programme to demonstrate a variety of dishes on the chosen theme. Soon after meeting him, my enthusiasm for the project soared when he introduced me to Chris Kay, the director he wanted for the films. In stark contrast to Edward's cool, Chris was sartorially shambolic – a mercurial but loveable, hairy Scotsman whose working wardrobe amounted to a collection of garishly patterned and coloured short-sleeved shirts. It didn't matter. His credits as a film-maker were what impressed me and in particular the fact that he had directed the final two series of *Take Six Cooks*, the hugely popular foodie features of the 1980s.

The three of us got on famously and my next task was to draft a synopsis for six half-hour programmes against which the other two could plan budgets and schedules. By mid-April we were ready to take our proposal to a potential broadcaster and we headed first for the offices of HTV West in Bristol where we met the company's director of programmes, Derek Clarke. We were in luck. My first shot at this game hit its target and we left with a promise that *Simply the Best – A Celebration of British Food* would be put to the commissioning editors at Channel 4 and some of the larger ITV companies. Four weeks later, on Louise's birthday, Edward called me. Subject to a screen test, I was in business and by the end of June we had started to shoot the opening sequences of "Edible Flowers" on location in Dartmouth and South Devon.

Rereading my journal for this period, the entry for Sunday, 25th June borders on the euphoric. "Everything seems to be going my way," I wrote. "It all seems to be coming good. I have been on a bit of a high and I daren't believe my good fortune." As the filming got under way, Octopus began pumping up their publicity plans for the book. I had made presentations to the sales force and their marketing people were boasting that W.H. Smith had been persuaded to list *Great British Chefs* in their Christmas catalogue. The logistics for my chefs' tour of the United States were falling into place too. British Airways had agreed to fly us across the Atlantic and they were in talks with United about the internal flights. Four Seasons Hotels in New York, Chicago and San Francisco had promised complimentary bedrooms and a favourable response was expected from the other cities soon. Finally, eight days before, on June 17th, the Birthday Honours List was published announcing my MBE – simple confirmation after the baroque formality of the letter I had received from 10 Downing Street in May informing me that the Prime Minister was minded "to submit your name to the Queen with a recommendation that Her Majesty may be graciously pleased to approve that you be appointed a Member of the Order of the British Empire".

The rush to my head was thrilling. But the terrible truth was that my euphoria glowed like a hot air balloon in the night sky – much of it born of bitterness, resentment and rejection. As the Castle's fortunes continued to slide – our losses for the year touching £60,000 – I had gone AWOL, an absentee managing director neglecting the family business in favour of an unknown parcel of projects which now consumed huge volumes of my time. My father's sleepless nights became more frequent – worrying that he had failed his old friend Bill Stansell because the minority shareholders hadn't seen a dividend in thirteen years. Occasionally I sat in his office and he pleaded with me to return and reassert my authority. I told him I couldn't and I told him why. Still Louise was denied admittance to the inner circle and my squabbles with Etty saw no pause – her wilful attempts to subvert my decisions sometimes appearing like guerrilla tactics, ambush and surprise being a particular speciality. Better then to stay away – write my film scripts, meet my American sponsors, anything to avoid another verbal brawl with my mother whose maddening behaviour was shredding staff morale. I now mourned the departure of David Prior, my parents' pliant puppet, who endured eighteen years of Etty's giddy manipulation. He was succeeded by a small parade of general managers whose life expectancy was reduced to as many months. And now, mindless of the dangers, I had sunk into a black hole of my own making. The more I stayed away, the more I compromised my own authority and credibility – Peter was right there. But then all of us shared in this ludicrous state of affairs. We were all writing our own suicide mission – heading for the abyss, behaving like arrogant lemmings blind to the fall.

Perversely, my absences served to fuel rather than calm the disharmony between Etty and me. I worried about the disaffection she was fomenting in the hotel, especially with the department heads and Ian Fleming, an intelligent young man and the incumbent general manager. But all my attempts to stay her hand ended in denials and tantrums. She, on her side, became intensely curious about my activities. Jealous of my extracurricular success, dazzled by what she saw as a glamorous new existence, she was obsessed with keeping track of my movements and would do so slyly to avoid asking me any direct questions. Her strategy was to tiptoe into my office and leaf through my desk diary at times when she knew I was away. Then Gill, my secretary, would be obliged to face a gentle interrogation on my whereabouts – questions which she parried with an air of polite discretion. Before leaving the office, Etty would whisper her customary command, "Don't say I said anything," sealing the words with her trademark gesture: a raised forefinger drawn sharply down over her tightly pursed lips.

On occasions this furtive show of envy spilled over in ways which affected the staff. If she chose, she would actively disrupt the best laid plans. And in so doing Etty knew she would be upsetting me – her game an artless form of subversion by proxy. One lunchtime that spring the object of her animus was directed at a major fund-raising event organized by the Taunton Constituency Conservative Association at which local business chiefs were paying a handsome premium to sit at a well laid table with Lord Young, Mrs. Thatcher's favourite cabinet minister and the Secretary of State for Trade and Industry. I had been asked to organize it and I was included among the invited guests – a detail which irritated Etty, indignant that she and Peter had been overlooked. The planning for this party had to be meticulous and minutely timed – his lordship was on a tight schedule. With Chef Gary Rhodes, I was briefed to devise a suitably grand four-course menu with fine wines to match. This was to be a gastronomic production set at a splendidly decorated table crowned by a large floral display commissioned by the client in Tory blue and white.

At noon on a sunny Friday in May, half an hour before the off, I gathered Ian Fleming and his team in the restaurant for a final briefing before joining the organizers in the Castle's rose garden to greet Lord Young and our guests with magnums of champagne. Meanwhile, Etty took up her post in the entrance hall to observe the comings and goings and, by the by, to rearrange the floral display for the party. Mr. Fleming's polite protests that my mother's actions were not what the client had ordered were abruptly dismissed. She was Director of Aesthetics and any challenge to her judgement in this department was, of course, unwise. Fleming retreated.

In the garden jollity abounded, the spirits of Somerset's top people buoyed by the Bollinger, the beautifully crafted canapés and the affable, urbane presence of Lord Young. On cue, at five to one, we passed from lawn to table. And the moment I stepped into the restaurant I spotted the adjustments to the floral display. I glared at Fleming. He shrugged his shoulders. I raised my eyes to the ceiling. And no one else noticed. Lunch proceeded happily to the complete satisfaction of the local Tory establishment. But with all the merriment and political banter in the restaurant, I was unaware of my mother's activities in the entrance hall where she was still keeping watch. While the lunch had been a success, Ian Fleming was having a terrible day. When a small party of hungry businessmen walked into the hotel asking for a table, he had to explain there was none. As the group left Etty pounced on the beleaguered general manager and, in full view of receptionists and waiting staff, delivered a public dressing-down on his decision to turn away good business.

"Mrs. Chapman," he pleaded, "I'm afraid we have no table. And they were not prepared to wait – they wanted to sit down straight away."

"My husband will be furious with you," she continued ignoring his point and immediately adopting her tactic of invoking Peter. "You know what he says. We can't afford to turn business away."

Ian was on a loser again. In Mrs. Chapman's eyes, he had compounded his earlier felony of contradicting her over the flower arrangements. This time he took refuge in the kitchen and watched Gary Rhodes's soufflés rise out of the pastry ovens.

If refusing the businessmen their table was an offence punishable by public humiliation, worse was the failure of the staff to deliver meals promptly to the penthouse regardless of the circumstances. For me this became another running sore and there were moments when I wondered for whose benefit we were running the hotel. Inevitably, it was also a source of frequent annoyance to my team whose first obligation, one supposed, was to look after our guests. But then such was the contrariness of the chatelaine. On the Saturday evening after the Lord Young party, I came into the hotel to perform mine host's duty – a job I enjoyed and one, I am sure, influenced by my early years of observing Uncle Michael's style and dash as he glided from table to table in his dining room at the Imperial. On this particular Saturday, short-staffed and with a full house, kitchen and restaurant were under immense pressure. While I circulated on a mission of gladness and joy to soothe our impatient diners, Chef Rhodes was struggling to get his Michelin starred specialities away from the hotplate.

At ten past nine, at the height of the service, Etty telephoned a very hard-pressed restaurant manager. "Where is Mr. Chapman's supper?" she demanded. "He ordered it an hour ago – a fillet steak!"

"Mrs. Chapman," replied the manager, "I do apologize but Chef has not had time to cook it yet."

"Well, he wants it now! Immediately! Tell Chef!"

That evening my parents were unaware of my presence downstairs and when I phoned back, the exchange with my mother was blunt and factual. After she had hung up on me, I reassured both chef and restaurant manager and returned to my tour of the tables. Next day, my diary entry erupted with frustration: "Why Mrs. Chapman can't cook a bloody steak in her immaculate penthouse kitchen is beyond me," I stormed. "So, once again, we are in a state of cold war. As ever, it will all blow over. And, as usual, I suppose I shall have to back off in the name of family peace and harmony."

At times, in our moments of truce, I tried to explain the importance of separating "home" and "hotel" – but she could see no difference. "The Castle is my home," she would say. "And I'll do what I want in my home." Etty was like an eternal child, somehow unable to bridge the gulf between her charmed life in pre-war Salonica and the life of an hotel in 1980s Britain. For her they were the same. She saw no distinction between the staff at the Castle and the retinue of faithful domestic servants in Queen Olga Street who indulged every whim of her father's favourite child – his "koutzi mou".

This gulf between then and now, my mother's reluctance to recognize the difference, was as much a reflection of her upbringing as it was a resistance to the way the world had changed in its attitudes to class and a once deferential society. In this she was no different from others of her generation. The incident over Peter's fillet steak was a tiny example, but nothing illustrates my parents' attachment to the Old Order, its rituals and snobberies, like Etty's devotion to her regular dinner parties. These Saturday soirées in the penthouse were glittering affairs – invitations willingly accepted in the certain knowledge that the food would be superior to the home Aga, the wines of a higher order and the party conducted in a style Somerset's reduced county mafia could no longer afford themselves, the cooks, butlers and parlourmaids long absent from their exquisite crumbling piles.

The staff seconded to penthouse duty were hand-picked which, to the restaurant manager's dismay, denied him his best people downstairs and so imposed an additional and costly burden on the evening service. For the waiters selected to attend Mrs. Chapman's party, this was a singular honour, elevating them to her favoured elite. The procedure for the dinner ran to a well-rehearsed schedule. Guests were greeted at the Castle's front door by the duty manager and escorted up to the penthouse drawing room where the party – ten, perhaps twelve – gathered for drinks. Gentlemen in black tie, ladies – bejewelled, rouged and powdered – in long frocks. White-gloved waiters offered drinks on silver trays. At an unseen command, dinner was announced and the sliding doors separating drawing room from dining room parted ceremoniously to reveal a glowing wonderland of silver and crystal set on a candlelit Georgian table. The party would gasp with delight and Etty would beam, radiant in her gown. Wine poured, the first course – having travelled safely up four floors by dumb waiter – came to table: the waiters briefed to eschew their usual silver service and adopt the "butler" style of service where guests help themselves from proffered salvers. And so the dinner made its courtly progress until coffee when Etty would rise and lead her flock of females to her bedroom where they would gossip and reapply their powder and rouge while the men were left to talk politics in a fog of cigar smoke as the brandy and port decanters circulated the table – clockwise always, *never* the other way!

These grand dinners were perfectly good fun – but, like the conduct of our upbringing, they were performed like a religious rite and, for me, they came to symbolize the formality of my relationship with my parents in all its distances, conventions and separateness: parent/child; young/old; master/servant. Everything Gerald, Louise and I – and our generation – yearned to break away from. We challenged the Old Order but it still created an atmosphere which persisted into adulthood. As a child I was controlled. As a man in his early forties, approaching middle age, the atmosphere was the same: a suffocating sense of restriction issuing from a parent's need to control, reluctant to see the middle aged child take wing. And when he did, the parent's guarded reaction was shock; surprise; resentment; suspicion; jealousy. The frustration and disappointment I felt inspired a train of confused emotions, the most evident being a growing rejection of my Greekness, an antagonism towards anything Greek.

On our visits to the country, I began to find myself too easily irritated by the smallest things. I hated Greece's petty officialdom, its bureaucracy and its inefficiencies. I hated the food. The only Greek I admired was my Aunt Machi, Etty's sister. She was a wonderful cook; she taught me to read the language; and she taught me the country's history and culture. She understood me and I loved her. But by now we had abandoned any thoughts of holidaying at Diodati and, instead, Louise and I headed off to other islands. And then, when Etty insisted on following us, I turned my back on the motherland, preferring to summer in Tuscany or the South of France – my disaffection with Greece bordering on the xenophobic.

Today, this moment, sitting on Aristotle's, sniffing the heady scent of Diodati's pines, marvelling at the sapphire blue of the Aegean Sea and the serenity of its islands, this sixty year old wonders where he was two decades ago.

*

With the approach of autumn 1989, the family and the business entered a period of uncertainty. Peter's health was declining and doctors, consultants and a variety of medical tests did little to stem his permanent state of fatigue. I could feel his spirit fading too. Etty worried and turned to me for hugs, kisses and consolation. On the second anniversary of Gerald's death, she told me that if her Peter died, she would throw herself off the parapet of the Castle. Her little melodrama made me angry and I told her not to be so silly. In the hotel, our finances looked increasingly precarious. In essence the money had run out and even my mother's aesthetic appetites had to be curbed, the convoys of Harrods pantechnicons no longer finding their way west along the M4. As a final insult to the proud reputation we had built, the editors of the AA Hotel Guide decided to demote us from four stars to three. Slowly, the cold realities of our predicament were rising to the surface of our collective consciousness.

My father, Michael Blackwell and even Louise were gently pointing fingers at me. I had neglected the business for too long and it had lost its way, lacking in clear leadership and what they saw as the essential ingredient of personality – a Chapman in charge. All of us were feeling vulnerable, fearful of the future; acknowledging the problem, knowing what needed to be done but, curiously, powerless to fix it. I was too deeply embedded in my own agenda to jettison any of my projects. The filming of *Simply the Best* was approaching completion with a second series in prospect. *Great British Chefs* was about to be launched. And Richard Shepherd and I had a confirmed itinerary for our pre-Christmas recce of five US cities in advance of our chefs' tour in the

New Year. Almost ten years had elapsed since my father had appointed me managing director of the family firm. It now seemed a little late in the day to drop everything and take up the job expected of me. Within this brewing storm I had fallen upon serendipity and I was determined to follow its path. I may have been walking towards an empty horizon, I didn't know, but now there was no turning back.

On the last Thursday in October – the evening of my book launch – Louise and I walked into Bibendum's Oyster Bar on the Fulham Road to be greeted by the news that Octopus had decided to reprint a further ten thousand copies of *Great British Chefs*. The trade had snapped the book up and I was thrilled. The reviews in the press had been enthusiastic, Elizabeth David was there to congratulate me and I had been flattered by an invitation to join Melvyn Bragg on BBC Radio 4's *Start the Week*. The gathering crisis in Taunton was the last thing on my mind.

Exactly one month later, on the day before Richard Shepherd and I flew out to New York, Louise, Dominic, Nicholas and I walked across the vast inner courtyard of Buckingham Palace. We were there for my investiture. As the family were escorted to their seats in the ballroom, I waited with my fellow MBEs, corralled behind silk ropes in gilt and marble pens to distinguish us from the OBEs, the CBEs and the knights. When, at last, my name was called, I stepped forward, turned to face the Queen, bowed and approached the dais where she hooked the medal on my lapel. "And what do you do?" she asked. Before an audience of a thousand in the Palace's magnificent ballroom, with a military band playing softly in the gallery and awed by the colour and pageantry of the occasion, this brief moment struck me as a uniquely intimate and personal exchange between my sovereign and me. Her question was put in the manner of a much loved great aunt to her favourite great nephew and for a few seconds I forgot that I was one of some hundreds she was investing that morning. I began to gabble with excitement about my trip to the United States until suddenly she took my hand, shook it and gently pushed me backwards. Only then did it dawn on me that with so many of her subjects to process, this grand spectacle had to be conducted with the unremitting efficiency of a production line.

*

By mid-afternoon the following day, Richard Shepherd and I had checked into our rooms at the Plaza in Manhattan. After a quick change we walked across to the Pierre for our first briefing session with the hotel's management, PRs and chefs – a highly professional team, all of them enthusiastic about our mission in January. It was a pattern we found in our dealings with all five of the Four Seasons Hotels we sat down with – for after New York, our itinerary led us to Washington DC, Chicago, Houston and, finally, San Francisco where we would link up with our Napa Valley associates.

Next morning I awoke early and shortly before eight I set off for Amsterdam Avenue and St. John the Divine. Outside it was bitterly cold. I needed some flowers and on the way to the cathedral I asked the cab driver to stop by a florist. We found a small boutique on the Upper West Side and I bought a dozen red roses which the shop assistant arranged in a plastic vase with some gypsophila. By now the significance of what I was about to do began to affect me. I was thankful to be alone. Buying the flowers, realizing their purpose, unsettled me and I struggled to keep myself in control.

The church – huge, imposing, solid and silent – was empty. Hugging the vase, I made my way slowly to the Columbarium. There I laid the flowers beneath the square marble slab facing the vault which enclosed his ashes and those of a stranger. The engraved names read *Chapman* and *Stewart*. Nothing else. Space comes at a premium in New York – but at the entrance to the Columbarium a wall of brass plates etches the details of the deceased. It was peaceful, beautiful and I was alone. I stayed there for forty-five minutes, perhaps an hour, and I wept as I have never wept in my entire life. At the funeral there were too many people. Before leaving, I wrote a message on the small blank card the shop assistant had put with the roses. Funny thing to write a note but I just wanted to: "Hi Geraldo. I love you. I miss you. We all do and always will. Your old bro Kit."

Back on Amsterdam the wind was biting. It was freezing. Wrapping my scarf around my neck, I headed south looking for a cab. The walk did me good. At the Plaza I went straight to my room and ordered coffee. With a long list of telephone calls to make, it was time to get on with the job. After lunch in the hotel's famous Oyster Bar, Richard and I gathered our bags and took a taxi out to La Guardia for our flight to Washington DC.

*

Christmas that year trembled with nervous tension. A whiff of hysteria hung over the family like acid rain. No sooner had I returned from America and I could taste the sulphurous atmosphere. With a sheaf of notes lying on his desk, my father recited a dirgeful catalogue of errors and follies perpetrated by our management team. He looked tired and old – his complexion grey and opaque as a winter mist. Again he appealed for my return to the hotel full-time, to take a grip of the place. After a while Michael Blackwell joined us to discuss the business. The results in October and November had been disastrous and he was applying to the bank for another increase in our overdraft facility – a further £100,000. We had two tough options, he told us, either sell or take the hotel downmarket. We were tripping over the edge.

Three days later we met again, this time in the penthouse with Etty present. The shock of our predicament had seeped into their bones – emotions racing, my mother and father barely able to disguise their panic. Peter had rehearsed his pitch – more Etty's pitch than his own – and he repeated it again and again. He wanted Michael and me to be very clear about their feelings, to understand that the Castle was *their home*. Any notion of leaving was inconceivable. The Castle was their life and the only solution to our problem was for me to return to the business and reimpose a more hands-on "Chapman style" of management. I kept silent. We had been here before. What I found unnerving, even tragic, about this comfortless meeting was my father's apparent inability to imagine any life for himself and Etty outside the Castle Hotel. The prospect seemed to fill them with terror. And so, after ninety minutes of grim debate we arrived at a hesitant conclusion – that we would give the business another year and that I would do my best to pull it round.

Later, in private, I spoke to my father and reaffirmed my promise but I also explained that Etty's interferences in the day-to-day running of the hotel made success almost impossible. Once again I asked him to consider bringing Louise onto the board and giving her a role. She would be a great asset, I said, and a wonderful support for me. Peter understood, his tacit agreement evident in his eyes. He had grown to love his daughter-in-law and respected her – but he never dared express his approval too boldly. Without much discussion, we both acknowledged that the arrangement I was suggesting would never work – it was a sure recipe for conflict. We were trapped and, meanwhile, the business was slipping away.

As if the Fates were intent on spinning their own web around our destiny, the crisis inside the family coincided with another on the outside. The conjunction of the two seemed uncanny – like a signal to me. On our return flight from San Francisco, Richard Shepherd and I had celebrated the end to a successful trip. Finally, all the details for January's tour had fallen into place. We were ready – until, that is, a telephone call from California in mid-December brought home the unexpected news that the mission had been aborted. Months of painstaking effort and planning now collapsed like a house of cards. For reasons lost in a grubby game of accusation and counter-accusation, our two principal sponsors, the wineries and the hotels had had a spectacular falling-out, and after a bout of urgent transatlantic calls, I realized that our grand tour of British chefs to America was broken beyond repair. Besides, I was now too busy fighting fires at home to embroil myself in a row on the other side of the world.

At the Castle, events were unravelling faster than I had anticipated. On Tuesday morning, December 19th, the family gathered formally as a board for a third meeting. After the decision of the previous week, its purpose was to discuss in detail how we should proceed, the cuts that needed to be made, and the marketing action to be taken. But to Michael Blackwell's surprise, and to my own, we never came close to addressing the advertised agenda. My father had spent the weekend thinking deeply about the future and he was now resigned to throwing in the towel, to selling the hotel. The decision was his alone. He saw no practical way forward without my full-blooded support and involvement in the business. To make it work, he knew what I wanted and deep down he wanted it for me. Of course he made no references to his private discussions with Etty and, after failing to persuade her, he saw no hope of Louise being accepted onto the board. Etty had protested again, seeing my wishes as an attempt to sideline her. "You want us out!" she would say. "You want to be king of the Castle!" My mother could neither see nor accept that the time had come to pass the baton on to a new generation. Neither could she see that to do so might be a cause for celebration. She was having none of it. Home and hotel, penthouse and Castle – as long as she was in residence, her position would remain impregnable.

Now, with no future to excite their imaginations, my parents were, understandably, in a distressed state. As I watched them at the boardroom table, my own emotions came in waves of relief, guilt and pity. At last the boil was being lanced. But in their eyes, I had been the cause of the family's unhappiness and it pained me now to see them lament the life they held so dear; the life which they were being forced to surrender. I watched and I saw my father's frailty; my mother's naivety and child-like bewilderment. The talk revolved around what would happen and Michael did his best to reassure them that they would be secure. To emphasize the point, he wrote the word SECURITY large and bold on a sheet of paper. They were terrified of packing up and leaving the penthouse – the Castle, their home. Peter wanted to know how much we might get for the place; how much tax he might have to pay; what he would be left with; even whether a prospective purchaser might allow them to continue living in the penthouse. They both cried. But although I felt for their distress, somehow I sensed that, underneath it, my father was quite sanguine about the decision he had taken. His worry and his sadness were for Etty who was being much less philosophical about his decision to quit.

For now, there was little more to be said or done. Christmas was upon us and we agreed to reconvene in the New Year to appoint an agent for the sale and to discuss the best way of handling the public relations, particularly with the staff. Meanwhile, our decision would remain a closely guarded secret.

The season of goodwill brought little comfort and joy to the family. For a moment Louise and I thought it might pass off happily, aided, we hoped, by the soothing influence and gentleness of Molly, my dear mother-in-law. But in the event her calming presence failed us. As usual we gathered in the penthouse on Christmas Eve. With Etty and Peter sotto voce and subdued – the brittle silence of their mood reverberating around us – I took care not to ignite any emotional fires while Molly, Dom, Nick and Louise kept the chatter light and easy. Christmas Day, again by tradition, was celebrated at Ashfield – our house in the foothills of the Quantocks and our home for the past five years. It was here that the equilibrium of the previous evening crashed into a torrent of hysterics. My journal records that Etty was spoiling for a showdown on the theme that this was their last Christmas at the Castle and it was all my fault. "She got her way," I wrote, "and made the most of it".

She had started to fuss around me in the kitchen, attempting to be helpful, ignoring my pleas to sit down and talk to the boys. As I began to carve the bird, she leapt to my side, manically rearranging the plates on the hotplate, exchanging the ones at the top of the pile with those at the bottom. I snapped at her again and she sat down in a deep sulk. When we were all seated – wine poured, the roast turkey looking deliciously succulent before us – Molly attempted to lift the gloom that had infected the table. "Christopher," she said cheerily, "Etty's a little upset. Why don't you apologize to her?" The touchpaper was lit. Etty immediately dissolved into tears, rushed out of the kitchen and hid in our bedroom. There she stayed, slumped theatrically on our bed to await the delegations of peacemakers. First my father. Then me. Eventually, after our devotional caresses, hugs and kisses, she returned to the table. My journal entry concludes: "But she continued to make the most of her pique which reached its climax when she turned to me, saying in Greek I was to blame for the fact that they were having to leave the Castle. I held my peace, laughing off her nasty little jibe." Peter retreated into his shell for the rest of the afternoon. Only later, when we settled down to watch *Crocodile Dundee*, did the atmosphere lighten.

*

In the second week of the new decade, we appointed Humberts Leisure as agents for the sale of the Castle Hotel. My father called a staff meeting. And I issued a press release to the trade, local and regional media, and to the news services. HTV carried the story on their early evening bulletin. Word spread with wild speculation on the likely sale price. Figures of £7 and £9 million were rife. Our agents advised us to seek offers "in excess of £5 million".

*

Part Ten

Palace Revolution

Dom and Nick on the little red chair. Late 1970s

Diodati – Summer 2008

There is in the house a child's chair, wood-crafted and painted pillar-box red with a rush-woven seat. For many years it stood forgotten in a corner of Diodati's living room – an incidental ledge, useful for stacking board games, books, CDs. This summer the chair has emerged from its corner, in demand again after three decades of obscurity. Back in the Seventies, Dom and Nick would compete to sit on it. Lying on the table in front of me, an old photograph of the two brothers taken, I would guess in 1978, stares up at me. They are sitting on the main terrace, both perched on the edges of the chair, nudging each other for space: Nick, three, in a blue and white striped sailor's vest; Dom, five, clutching Sooty's friend Sweep, his favourite glove puppet – both sporting dark glasses on their sun-bleached heads. An adorable moment captured for the family album.

Last year, Louise and I became grandparents. And today, as I write these words, Oliver who has just woken from his morning sleep, is sitting on the same chair eating a banana. A week ago, Daniel was doing much the same with a chocolate biscuit. The continuing cycle of family life fills us with a sense of contentment. In January 2007, Helena, Dom's wife, gave birth to Daniel and in May, Nick's wife Annabel was delivered of Oliver. The two young cousins are the fourth generation of Chapmans to fall under Diodati's magic spell. Now the little red chair has passed into family folklore – a symbol of Peter and Etty's legacy to their descendants, a reminder of their gift and our good fortune. If they could see their great-grandsons chuckling merrily on the terraces they created here, I know they would be as thrilled and proud as we are.

Watching Daniel and Ollie at play, I gradually come to realize that I have now arrived at a unique stage in my own life, as has Louise in hers. No one is privileged with a better view of the colours, shades and textures of the family canvas than us. Our new-found maturity allows us to gaze forward – hearts overflowing with hopes and expectations – at our sons and grandchildren while we also look back like bookkeepers at a family which has been the subject of this memoir. Grandfathers and grandmothers command the advantage of perspective. Spanning the generations, we suddenly become the links between the past and the future, auditing the triumphs and failures, strengths and flaws of those who have gone before, using that knowledge to guide and advise our young. But I am not writing this book as a cautionary tale for my grandchildren. It exists simply as a record for them to learn a little about who they are and from where they came. A family dominated by a strong male line but one whose women have played a remarkable role in our destinies: from the formidable Amelia Prüger, Henry's mother; to the stoic wisdom and kindliness of Nell, my grandmother; to Etty, Daniel and Ollie's great-grandmother, an extraordinary influence in our lives and for all her mercurial madness, a loving parent. Now I must return to my story.

*

The long months of 1990 unfolded like a bad dream. It was a year which would prove to be the most turbulent in the family's history. The economy slipped into recession and, as property values shrank, our hopes of a sale "in excess of £5 million" became a fantasy. By the end of July we were stranded – haemorrhaging cash from an open wound, our losses for the year running at £125,000. Staff morale had hit rock-bottom. Gary Rhodes had resigned. We were in a mess!

In the early weeks of the marketing process, a number of buyers submitted their offers – big names among them – but they soon faded away. At the beginning of May we were left with one serious player, a Norwegian family. They were keen to pursue the deal and we agreed a price of £4.4 million with a promise to complete the transaction by August. Three weeks later, we received an abrupt note from their solicitors with a revision to their bid. They were now offering £3.5 million. The lawyers exchanged curt faxes but our charming Norwegian family had been listening to the advice of their professionals. The collapse of the market and our miserable trading figures told the tale and they would not budge.

When the news came through, Etty and Peter were in Greece taking their spring break at Diodati. The strain of the negotiations had begun to exact a heavy toll on my father and he was in a mood to accept. But I refused to sell on these terms. The sudden £900,000 cut in the offer was a slap in the face and I felt insulted. An alarm bell inside my head shook me awake and I started to ask myself whether I wanted a sale anyway. Books? Television? Vague ideas of opening a restaurant of my own? Were these the makings of a bright new career after I had invested so much effort in the Castle – raising it from a humdrum provincial hotel to a destination with a national and international profile? I was determined not to give the business away for a risible sum just because my parents now wanted to be rid of the place. Gerald and I had grown up here and it had served me royally as a platform for all my work. Was I really prepared to throw out that effort, that success over so many years in return for a piffling price tag and an uncertain future? The feuding inside the family had distracted me from the very real belief I had in the Castle and I felt she deserved better. With Etty and Peter away, I began a series of conversations with Michael Blackwell about the future of the hotel and how I saw it. My diaries from this period read as though he and I were plotting a palace revolution and, in a way, I suppose we were. "Somehow," I wrote, "they must be persuaded to step down. Otherwise the future will be grim."

But thoughts of withdrawing the hotel from the market and our clandestine plans for regime change stalled when, shortly after their return from Greece, Peter took an unexpected call from a man who introduced himself as Bill Honey of Clipper Hotels. Mr. Honey was making a casual enquiry to ask if the Castle was still for sale and, five days later, he checked in for an overnight visit as our guest. There was nothing casual about Mr. Honey's interest. His late appearance on the scene had been nicely calculated and my parents, for their part, could not wait to make his acquaintance. Preparations for his arrival were intense: best room, best linen, best bathrobes, flowers, fruit, all the usual VIP accessories were put in place. Mr. Honey's welcome reception was also carefully orchestrated. I would greet him, escort him to the penthouse for drinks with my parents and then take him down to the restaurant for dinner. Minutes before meeting him, I was summoned upstairs by my father. There had been a change of plan.

"I've decided that Etty should join you for dinner," he announced. "I'll make my excuses and say I have a meeting to go to."

"Why?" I asked.

"Because that is what your father wants," Etty snapped. "Don't argue with him!"

"I don't want you to talk too much business," he interrupted. "That can wait until tomorrow morning. Mummy will humour him, flirt with him!"

"What!" I exclaimed. "I think that's the silliest bloody idea! The man is here on business. The last thing he needs is my mother flirting with him!"

This mad plan had been hatched by Etty and I had no intention of being part of a game which was now descending into drawing room farce. Such was my father's state of mind, his desperation to find a buyer for the hotel, that she had come up with the crazy notion that her siren charms would seduce Mr. Honey into making an attractive offer. To my relief, they backed down and my evening with Bill Honey passed off well enough. He was a soft-spoken accountant whose avuncular, cuddly tone of voice disguised a sharp business cunning. He gave away very little, preferring to observe and to listen. Next morning we met – Michael Blackwell, my father, me – and Mr. Honey. He was polite and solicitous, listening to the needs and expectations of the family. He floated the idea of a part-shares, part-cash deal and promised to draft some options for us to consider. All very reasonable; almost comforting. But at the end of July we were still waiting to receive his written proposals. Like the others, Mr. Honey and Clipper Hotels had faded away.

*

The stresses of the sale on my father had now become a great worry to me. His doctors appeared to be on permanent call for one complaint or another. The antibiotics they prescribed for his virus infections depressed him and he was constantly breathless. I feared for his life. Etty's attitude to his condition was breathtakingly naïve but entirely in character. Of course she worried terribly – Peter was her "rock" after all – but she lived in a blissful state of denial about his declining health. I looked on at my father's increasing helplessness, his near-total dependence on her. She saw him still as the strong, vital man she had married, the man who had rescued the Castle from its post-war gloom, a great patriarch whose presence was inviolate. She saw no reason for him to change his old routine.

Our vain adventure in the marketplace and now my desire to keep the hotel and his to sell at almost any price seemed to upset the balance of my relationship with him. The bond of love and trust between us was, I think, impaired, if only to a degree. I yearned for the freedom to assume full control and he, encouraged by Etty, resented my ambition. Forty years before, he had breathed new life into the Castle. It was his creation, his child. Now, like a death wish, he wanted it to die with him. His feelings towards me were also affected by my fights with Etty. She was and always would be his "Grecian Goddess", the woman he worshipped, and he never understood why I did not admire her virtues as he did. These things hurt him deeply – the memory of Gerald magnifying his private pain. He was reaching the end of his life and all he prayed for was peace of mind and harmony within his family. Being rid of the Castle, he concluded, would give him this precious prize.

But we were not rid of the Castle and, meanwhile, the business was tipping over the cliff. It was time to think the unthinkable. Like a pair of conspirators, Michael Blackwell and I met again and decided to reactivate our plan. Peter and Etty would be asked to step down and hand the reins to me; Michael would take over as chairman of the company; Louise would join the board as an executive director with an active role in the management of the hotel; and Ian Fleming, our hard-pressed general manager, would also be promoted to the board. Michael agreed to write a formal proposal outlining our intentions which he would present to my father on their return from Greece at the end of August. To help him draft the paper, I provided some hand-written thoughts of my own:

PRIVATE (Please destroy after reading.)   _21st August, 1990_

Michael – _Herewith some notes following our many discussions._
Our immediate objectives must be:-
1. _To relieve my father of ALL responsibilities relating to the management of the hotel. To allow him to retire properly. To create the circumstances to allow him to enjoy life. To take all steps to ensure his peace of mind and good health. To give him the confidence that the hotel will be properly managed._
2. _To persuade my mother to step down completely in the best interests, primarily, of my father – but also in the interests of the long term future of the business. Now is the time to hand over willingly and enthusiastically to the second generation. If she or my father insist on her continued involvement in the hotel in any form, it will be counterproductive, it will cause family conflict – and, indeed, it will alienate her family._
3. _To suggest and encourage constructive outside interests for my parents. "What do we do with ourselves?" will be a major problem._
4. _To attempt to persuade them of the desirability of welcoming Louise into the business – ideally, as a full board member NOW because:-_
   a) _It will help to formalise the new regime – the "new-look" management team – in the eyes and minds of a depressed staff who desperately need remotivating._
   b) _She will be welcomed by the staff and they will understand her role better if she is clearly identified as an executive director._
   c) _It will help convince staff and public that we mean to take the Castle forward positively in the long term._
   d) _It will motivate me. (And, believe me, just at the moment, I need a hell of_

a lot of motivating!)

5. *To make a formal and public announcement to staff and media <u>as soon as</u>*
   <u>possible</u>. We must clear the air quickly and effectively. And the announcement
   must be positive, bullish and newsworthy. To this end, my parents must be
   persuaded of the wisdom of the new board structure with you as chairman and
   with Ian's and Louise's promotion as directors. I accept the principle of my
   parents' involvement as <u>non-executive</u> directors. But equally, they should be
   prepared to welcome Louise onto the board. If they do not, Louise will stand
   back. For my father's sake, family harmony is of the <u>utmost</u> importance and
   I do not want to do anything to upset him. However, if my mother's attitude
   on this issue is negative, I shall – quite frankly – be pretty upset. Nevertheless,
   I would accept the situation – (with difficulty!).

Kit

The Blackwell manifesto entitled "Plan for the future 1990" went through several drafts before he and I were satisfied. Sweet language and comforting words were minimal. This was a serious document which, for my parents, would read like a decree from a revolutionary council – my mother cast as the Marie Antoinette of the piece. If our action amounted to a bloodless coup, I had no doubt that the corridors and hallways of the Castle would flow in rivers of wailing and spilt emotion. To give the plan substance, it had to be underpinned. We needed to rally more allies to the cause and I turned to Peter's doctors for support. At first I thought they might object but they were quick to become willing co-conspirators, happy to confirm that our decisions could only be in the best interests of his health.

*

Twenty-four hours after returning from their summer holiday at Diodati, my father met Michael in the privacy of his office at A.C. Mole & Sons in Taunton. The news of our plan came as a terrible shock. After forty years at the Castle, Peter told the accountant, he and Etty were to be made exiles in their penthouse – in effect they were being placed under house arrest. As for me, he had little confidence in my ability to run the hotel. The cool Yorkshireman held firm, resisting this great outpouring of rage and emotion, and by the end of a long session my father could do little more than accept the inevitability of the plan. But this was only the beginning. In the weeks that followed, the bloodletting would rise to a level even I had not anticipated.

For the next few days the battle lines fell silent. Louise invited Peter and Etty to lunch at Ashfield on the first Sunday after their return from Greece – a moment for them to see Nick and Dom, their grandsons. I feared the worst but in the event the family spent a happy afternoon together. It was glaringly transparent to me that my father had avoided showing the Blackwell plan to my mother, nor had he even discussed it with her. Within himself he was reconciled to standing down – a process he had wanted to begin ten years before when he appointed me managing director. But now he was no longer thinking of himself. Frightened of Etty's reaction, his outburst in Michael's office had come as an instinctive response – more on her behalf than his own. He knew she would oppose any attempt to make her surrender her position to Louise. The task that confronted him – to sell the new regime to his beloved wife – was impossible. It would become a heavy emotional burden on him and so for the time being he was keeping quiet.

The first salvos were exchanged two days later: for now just three of us – Michael, Peter and me. My father had sunk into a mournful state of melancholy and disillusion. We sat like priests in a confessional listening to him express his deep sense of personal failure with the business. Michael gently reminded him of his considerable achievements at the Castle, and in the industry and local community. But the mood changed when we turned to the vexed question of Etty's future. My father was determined to fight her corner and, directing his fire at me, he began searching for a compromise.

"Kit," he stammered, "I am hurt and disappointed at your refusal to contemplate working with your mother."

"But you know it won't work, Daddy" I said. "We've been trying for fourteen years and look where it's got us."

"Well we should try again. Why don't we agree to a three-month trial period and see how it goes?"

"A trial can be as long or as short as you like," I insisted, "you know perfectly well it'll end in tears, and that won't do you, your happiness or your health any good!"

"Well I've spoken to her and she is willing to give it a go." By now it was obvious that Etty still had not seen Michael Blackwell's document. My father was buying time, looking for a way out, desperate to avoid a fracas.

"Daddy, we've had this conversation dozens of times in the past. She is impossible to work with and she is a liability to this business. For your sake and her family's, she should have the sense and good grace to stand down with you."

This first meeting was a sideshow, a minor skirmish. Real battle was joined forty-eight hours later – on Thursday August thirtieth. The setting, like so many of our dreadful confrontations, was the penthouse. My mother, her eyes fired like spitting embers, sat opposite me while Michael quietly mined the interior of his pipe. My father, flushed pink in the cheeks, settled himself in his tall wing chair. By now he had given Etty a fuller account of our intentions, although she was still unaware of the existence of a written plan. In her hands she held a pen and pad – the notes she had been writing clearly visible. What followed was a heavy bombardment; a sustained tirade of accusations; the detailing of past wrongdoings: my aggression, my rudeness, my troublemaking with a host of ex-employees, Richard Mills-Roberts topping the bill.

I kept silent. Michael looked aghast. My father held a hand to his forehead in dismay. Not once did she refer to the plight of the business or what might be done, nor did she show concern for the needs of her seventy-five year old husband, his health or his well-being. At the end, Peter handed her a copy of the Blackwell proposal. "I think you should read this," he whispered. An uncomfortable hush fell in the room. When she had finished reading the document she said: "You make this a fait accompli!" and, in a limp gesture of defiance, she cast the paper to one side. Then, suddenly aware of Michael's presence in the room, she changed her tone – anxious that the family's adviser should be in no doubt of her love for her son. "I understand, Christopher," she said looking adoringly at me. "And you know I would never dream of standing in your way." It was a classic deceit, perfectly played. For a second, I shut my eyes and ears in wonder. Turning now to Michael she said: "But of course Peter and I could not possibly continue living in the penthouse. We will have to find a house."

"Of course Etty," he said anticipating where this was leading, "but you understand that as far the business is concerned, we are in no position to fund a house purchase for you."

"Why not?" she replied. "After forty years, it is the least we deserve. My Peter must be looked after. It is your duty!"

"Etty, the company is in deep trouble – mortgaged to the hilt. It cannot sustain any more borrowings. The bank would not buy it, nor would the minority shareholders."

"But the money must be found," she insisted. "Even poor people are given mortgages!"

"Mummy," I interrupted realizing the futility of pursuing this line, "Surely there are good practical reasons for staying here? It is your home and we would look after you. There is also more to life than the Castle Hotel. There are so many things you could do and enjoy – even write the book you have always said you would love to do."

"Christopher," she snapped haughtily, "stop making a marketing presentation! I'll do what I want."

We were getting nowhere. Again my father suggested finding some role for Etty to play. He objected to my intransigence, reducing the whole argument down to what he saw as a simple question of who did the flowers in the hotel. But if I had learned anything during my years at the Castle, it was the sure knowledge that the chatelaine who arranged the flowers was a ubiquitous figure who wielded huge influence! After two and a half hours we stopped. Nothing had been resolved. My parents asked for time to think.

The weekend passed – guns silent. On Monday morning my father called me into his office. As I closed the door I glanced across his desk and saw a grey, tired wreck. Etty had cast her net of emotional coercion and drawn him in. The pressure had been intense and he was choking with despair. "She has threatened to go and live in Greece," he said. "Can I appeal to you one last time to allow your mother to continue her involvement in the hotel?" His strength had deserted him; he was powerless to stand against her will. I found myself wedged between a well-conceived plan to rescue the business and my father's peace of mind. It was a simple choice and I gave in immediately – unable to see him suffer any more. Back at my desk I telephoned Blackwell straightaway and called another meeting for later that morning. "For my father's sake, we have no choice," I told him. "It will lead to trouble – but we'll just have to manage it."

Again we met in the penthouse. Again she made her demands for a house. On this occasion, I was less free with my sympathy and understanding. Finally, I put forward my compromise. "You are just going to have to accept that the company will not buy you a house," I said. "Stay here and continue to do the flowers as before. That's what you want, I think. And that's fine with me."

A glint of triumph flashed across her eyes. "But what about Louise?" she asked meekly. "Will she mind?"

"Louise won't mind in the least, I can assure you."

"And why do you want Louise 'welcomed' onto the board?"

"Well, don't you think that would be a nice thing to do?" I suggested. "She's not been involved in the business until now."

"But Louise and her family have always been welcome at the Castle!"

Michael tried to explain. My mother's hypocrisy was now irritating me and, without thinking, I committed the cardinal error of opening an old wound. "Mummy, you know perfectly well that Louise's appointment to the board has been refused in the past!"

My father winced and Etty threw up her arms in protest. "Eeee! What are you saying!" she shrilled angrily. "I have never blocked Louise's appointment to the board!"

"Kit, this was my decision," interrupted Peter leaping instantly to her defence. "It was me. I alone vetoed Louise's appointment."

The meeting disintegrated and once again I was pilloried as the villain in the play.

*

One week later, on Monday 10th September, the board of the Castle Hotel (Taunton) Ltd. gathered for its monthly meeting. All five directors were present: Mr. Peter Chapman (Chairman), Mrs. Etty Chapman, Mr. Christopher Chapman, Mrs. Elizabeth Williams [representing the Stansell family's minority interest] and Mr. Michael Blackwell (Secretary). The minutes of that meeting record the following resolutions:

- *Sale of Hotel. All offers had now been withdrawn and, in the circumstances, it was agreed that the hotel should be taken off the market. Proposed by Mrs. Elizabeth Williams.*
- *"Plan for the Future 1990". The paper was discussed at length and adopted in its entirety, in particular, Mr. Peter Chapman will retire as Chairman on 15th October, the 40th anniversary of his commencing work at the hotel. Mr. Michael Blackwell will be appointed in his place.*
- *Mrs. Etty Chapman proposed Mrs. Louise Chapman be invited to serve on the Board of Directors.*
- *Mr. Christopher Chapman proposed Mr. Ian Fleming be appointed to the Board of Directors.*

*

Those autumn weeks of 1990 groaned with bitterness and tension. Our board meeting had been a masked ritual of hollow words, a showcase of empty unanimity. On the surface we played our parts, issued grand statements about the future, held staff meetings. I organized a photocall with the chairman-designate and the new directors, despatched my press releases and lunched the editor of the *Somerset County Gazette*. He obliged with a prominent report in his paper on September 21st and the trade press and other media followed suit.

Beneath the surface, the waters ran ice cold. At the end of the month, I sat down to write my journal. "So much has happened," I began, "all with a gloss of predictability I find deeply depressing. A state of cold war has descended on my relations with M and D. It's bad, very bad. M's hysteria, her egotism, her vanity and the inability of her mind to marshal any vision for the future or see the need for a new order in the way we manage the affairs of the Castle are alienating me from the filial affection she craves. She has lost one son. She is near the point of losing another in spirit. But the real casualty is my father. He is suffering horribly from this dreadful conflict between mother and son. He can't cope. He doesn't know how. And she is making his life hell. The other day he confessed – swearing me to silence – that he had had to desert her for five hours. He just needed a break and passed the time driving around the Somerset countryside. 'She thinks you don't love her,' he pleaded. 'Please go and see her and give her a kiss!' Then the old mantra: 'life's not worth living if we don't have family harmony.' But filial affection is not like tap water and I'm damned if I'm going to turn on some phoney display just to encourage my mother in her own self-conceit."

The decision – my famous compromise – to provide a role for Etty under the new board structure ran into trouble from the start and, inevitably, this was the cause which soured rather than soothed relations inside the family. With Louise's arrival on the management team, Peter drew up new job descriptions – a list of duties which were duly apportioned between his wife and their daughter-in-law. When the chairman-designate saw these, he sighed and shook his head in dismay. "This is farcical!" he declared.

"Yes, it is," I said. "But let's accept it for now and get on with the job of relaunching the business."

In essence, Etty retained all her old duties. On the flower-front, Louise (Constance Spry trained with career credits at the Savoy, the Dorchester and other top West End hotels) was relegated to small vases for the restaurant tables – a task previously held by my mother's part-time assistant. This little charade was annoying but I was unconcerned because Louise and I had discussed a variety of ideas of our own. She was keen to do a real job for the Castle and I wanted to see her profile raised in the local community as part of my relaunch plans. But my father's list of "Louise's Duties" did include one essential job. If Etty was designated Director of Aesthetics, Louise was now adopted in the more prosaic role of Director of Maintenance (a responsibility my mother was delighted to shed). As a first step the board asked her to draw up a schedule of repair works in the hotel's public areas and bedrooms – a job she set about in the company of Mrs. Harper, the head housekeeper.

Louise's findings were a revelation. She discovered that much of the hotel had lapsed into a poor decorative state; worse, to her horror she saw that many of the bedrooms had been stripped of their best pieces of furniture: pictures, lamps, coffee tables, mirrors, desks, chairs and much else – the gaps filled, here and there, with old items snatched from different parts of the building. In the expectation of a sale and unknown to me, Etty had spirited these items out of the hotel and stored them in the "Rumpus Room", an airy space in a lost corner of the garage block where Gerald and I had played as children. When I checked, I felt like Ali Baba opening his cave to find it stacked with hidden treasure – and Harrods' treasure at that! Here was a secret storeroom standing ready to furnish the beautiful new home my parents were going to buy after the Castle was sold.

The mindset had not changed. They had not come to terms with their new circumstances: that, after all, the hotel was not to be sold; that we were relaunching, rebuilding, looking to a new future with a new team. These were the saddest days. I was less sympathetic then, my impatience and determination to turn the business obscuring the shock – trauma even – of recent events on my parents. Now their impulsive behaviour was damaging their pride and their dignity. Looking back at that time, I think I was being a little blind and insensitive to their distress.

I called Michael. The furniture was company property; it had to be returned. He telephoned and spoke to my father – and the following morning, Saturday, I was summoned to the penthouse. They were both in their bedroom, my mother at her dressing table applying her make-up, my father pacing up and down in a state of nerves. I sat on a corner of the bed.

"Blackwell called last night," he said. "I gather you've been speaking to him."

"Yes, that's right."

"Look Kit, I want to make it absolutely clear to you that your mother and I want to sell."

"But the board decided three weeks ago to withdraw the hotel from the market. You were part of that decision. It was unanimous."

"I don't care. We're fed up – miserable. We want to get out regardless of your plans and ideas."

"Well I'm sorry, I simply can't accept that."

"Don't interrupt Kit!" interjected Etty. "Listen to what your father is saying!"

Peter continued: "I want you to call Michael on Monday and get him to instruct the agents to find a buyer."

"No, I won't do that," I insisted. "What's more important is getting all this furniture back into the hotel."

"That's nothing. It's only a few items from the hall and a couple of chairs."

"But I've been to the Rumpus Room. I've seen for myself how much stuff has come out of the bedrooms. It's got to go back. All of it."

Etty exploded: "How dare you poke your nose in there! Who do you think you are? That room is private. It is none of your business!"

"What do you mean it's private! That's utterly ridiculous! All that furniture belongs to the hotel and it's got to be returned to the bedrooms."

With the eruption of another terrible row, Peter retreated into his shell. I stood up and walked out, my mother calling after me. But by early the following week the Castle's lost furniture had been retrieved, each item restored to its proper place.

There had been a host of other upsets in the wake of the board meeting and the press announcements. The new order was being given a rough ride by the *ancien régime* – inconsequential issues magnified into grand soap opera. Ian Fleming came to see me. "The staff can't see that there's been any change," he said. "Mrs. Chapman is still Queen Bee!"

*

October fifteenth is a landmark anniversary in the history of this family. In 1950 it was the date Peter Chapman took up his post as resident manager at the Castle Hotel for its proprietor, Mr. R.G. Spiller. Four decades on, it was a date that deserved to be recognized with a celebration to mark his many achievements: for rebuilding a rusting hulk through the hard years of post-war austerity and establishing it as an important local institution; for the service he gave his community; and, as a hugely respected and trusted hotelier, for the service he gave his industry. But my father wanted no celebration, no fuss. In its place, the day was mired by sadness and self-pity. "Like an old soldier, I just want to fade away," he told me. My journal entry for the fifteenth sweeps me up in his maudlin state. "This should be a moment to celebrate," I write. "He has achieved so much. He is a great man. But all he wants is to nurse his hurt. Now I feel a sense of guilt. I seem to have brought him no joy; only pain. That's wrong. But how much am I to blame?"

Strangely, the anniversary also served as a watershed. Relations eased themselves into another undeclared truce, and the uncertainties and pressures of the past six months began to subside. To my father's evident relief, Michael Blackwell took the chair while Louise, Ian Fleming and I set about the running of the hotel regardless of Etty's capricious interventions. We had to move on – and with some urgency. It was a grind, but a labour we took on zealously in the face of a deepening recession and inflation racing at over ten percent. Britain had just joined the ERM – the European exchange rate mechanism – and although the Chancellor, John Major, had cut interest rates by one percent, I could see little relief from our difficulties: the company's total debt was touching £700,000 and rising. All about us, businesses, large and small, were going to the wall. Our very public excursion into the hotel market had cost us dear, damaging trade and our customers' goodwill. Trimming costs was only part of the answer, the bigger task was to reclaim the confidence of our lost customers and reassert our reputation.

By the third week of November our recovery plan was set to go. So was Mrs. Thatcher, who resigned as Prime Minister on Thursday the twenty-second; the same day a jubilant Dominic, now seventeen, passed his driving test and the same week that the *Somerset County Gazette* published a massive spread across two pages of its paper to announce a fabulous menu of appetizing new initiatives from the Castle Hotel. Supported by thirty small advertisements from our suppliers, the feature cost us nothing and raised the curtain on a major campaign to promote a variety of recession-busting deals: from winter breaks and seminar packages for corporates to wine offers and fixed-price lunch and dinner menus. But the real attraction of the piece came with the unveiling of two eye-catching ideas aimed at raising the profile of a fresh, young team, which included the arrival of a gifted new chef. The first was a dining club which offered its members a series of gastronomic evenings, each featuring an entertaining speaker who was willing to accept our hospitality in lieu of a fee. The club was an instant success and over the years our speakers have included wits and mavericks from the world of politics, the media and show business: Auberon Waugh, Bernard Ingham, Julian Critchley, Ned Sherrin, Clement Freud, Maureen Lipman and Derek Nimmo among them. The second idea was Louise's "lifestyle workshops", a programme of morning talks-cum-demonstrations organized and hosted by her and aimed at Somerset's ladies-who-lunch. Themes included health and beauty, interior design, floral display and cookery – each session concluding with a long gossipy lunch. Louise soon earned herself a name as a consummate hostess with the additional bonus that both initiatives provided a platform to launch our new head chef, Phil Vickery, whom I wanted to establish quickly as a rising star in his own right after the departure of Gary Rhodes.

But the central plank of our campaign was the launch of *Castle Times*, a twice-yearly newsletter bursting with images of our celebrity visitors and crammed with activities, deals and events. In the face of economic gloom and the rumble of war breaking over the Gulf, I wanted to breathe a little optimism and fun into the air. The back page listed all our offers in the style of a booking form. I baptised my PA "Dining Club Secretary". And we despatched the glossy A4 publication to nine thousand addresses on our database. The response was overwhelming and Gill struggled to cope with the flood of enquiries and bookings. Colleagues, staff and customers loved it. At last we had begun our long, stony trek to recovery – a halting start which coincided with the Castle's summary demotion in the 1991 edition of the Egon Ronay Guide. Not unexpectedly, Mr. Ronay complained about our "dated rooms" and "patchy service". Yes, this was going to be a hard-run marathon.

Meanwhile, in the penthouse the reaction to *Castle Times* was muted and, at times, indignant. One item in our first edition featured a list of wine offers accompanied by tasting notes which I invited Peter to write. Foolishly, I overlooked my obligation to match his exposure with an equally prominent puff for Etty – a diplomatic omission inflamed by a full page article devoted to Louise's lifestyle workshops, a piece richly graced with a fetching image of a radiant Mrs. Chapman junior. In my naïvety, I had assumed that the purpose of the newsletter was to avoid making homilies to the past. Its purpose, I thought, was to launch a new washes-whiter formula, a bright new "ring of confidence". Oh dear! The message from the penthouse was one of "shock" and I was roundly accused of wilfully excluding my mother. Once again I found myself on a mission to restore peace and "family harmony". The second edition of *Castle Times*, published in the spring of '91, carried a full page exclusive on Peter and Etty's "40 Glorious Years" at the Castle – a florid tribute written by Rosie Inge, the newsletter's editor. My father may have felt like an old soldier but my mother was determined to make sure that neither he nor she would be fading away. To seal the moment of their belated anniversary, I threw a lunch party in their honour. Etty was thrilled at the attention we lavished on her, especially when she saw her name enshrined at the heart of the menu. The main course was billed "Chargrilled Souvlaki Georgette", a flattering tease which shot straight over her head – the "Georgette" of the dish folded into its saucing as a rich, spicy, lemony emulsion which seemed appropriate.

*

I was relieved to see 1990 out. These were strange times. As a nation, the mood was fearful, a population in the grip of uncertainty – all in our own ways worried about our livelihoods, our security, the future. Mrs. Thatcher had left Downing Street in tears – an extraordinary end to an extraordinary era in British politics which divided the country between those who adored her and those who loathed her. An untested John Major had entered Number 10 to become Prime Minister with a grim economic battle to fight on the home front and the prospect of a war to wage in the Middle East. With the stresses of division inside our family, the problems of ageing parents and a business in deep trouble, the events nationally and across the globe contributed to our own sense of unease and anxiety. It affected us in odd, tangible ways – at moments touching us literally.

One Sunday in December I set off on a long walk through the beech woods near Ashfield – Caruso and Bollinger, our two retrievers, at my side. We were alone, the sublime hush broken by a soft breeze playing in the branches of the trees and the rustle of dead leaves disturbed by the curiosity of the dogs. Suddenly, my peace was shattered – the thunderous throb of rotor blades breaking the silence as a Sea King helicopter pitched over the brow of the hill and hovered above my head – on exercise, I assumed, from its base at Yeovilton. It was a menacing presence which brought home the reality of the coming conflict in the Gulf. I gazed up into a clear winter sky over rural England and stared at a military machine dressed in the buff camouflage paint of the desert. There, a hundred feet above me, was a mighty instrument of resistance against the tyranny of Saddam Hussein, one tiny element of the allied force gathering to expel the Iraqi army from Kuwait.

Three weeks later, on the morning of Thursday seventeenth January, I awoke early. The illuminated digits on our bedside clock read 5.59 am. I flicked the switch of the radio and a voice announced that *Farming Today* had been cancelled owing to events in the Gulf. The voice handed over to Brian Redhead in the Today studio and as the pips bleeping the hour faded, a sombre Redhead told us that war had broken out. By now Louise was wide awake. Listening to the news of the first allied air attacks on Iraq, I took her in my arms – two anxious people among millions across the world riveted to the unfolding drama. Soon after, the United States was claiming that it had "decimated" Iraq's air power but within a week the euphoria was tempered as the sheer scale of the task began to dawn on our leaders. The first casualties had been announced and already our television screens were portraying the spectacle of captured British and American pilots being paraded as humiliated pawns of Saddam's propaganda.

At home the conflict produced its own entirely passive and incidental casualties – and I was among them. The massive media coverage now consuming the nation put an abrupt stop to my television series, *Simply the Best*, which had been launched to the press at BAFTA in December with the network screening of the first episode seven days before the outbreak of war. It was an interruption which would last some months before the programmes were brought back in April. But our paymasters at HTV in Bristol seemed pleased with our work, and Edward Adcock, Chris Kay and I soon had a second series of films in commission.

In Taunton the flush of publicity generated by my TV debut inspired less pleasure. One trade magazine article in particular – resurrecting the tribulations of the aborted sale – upset my parents. "Still king of the Castle" shouted the headline and it stung them. To my bewilderment and distress, my father's reaction was almost violent. "How much more of this am I going to suffer," he cried. "It's a bloody insult!"

That evening at home I told Louise. "I don't understand it," I said. "Everything I do these days seems to upset him. The smallest things …"

"Kit, I'm afraid it's his age," she said. "And deep down he's a little jealous of you."

"I can't believe for a moment that my own father would be jealous of me."

"It's all wrapped up with his feelings of failure. His father was a famous hotelier and Michael made a huge success of the Imperial. He feels overshadowed by both of them. In his mind's eye he sees all his brother's character and showmanship in you."

"And Etty just pumps him up. I know she does!"

"Well, it's the reason she constantly tries to promote him … push him forward."

My mother's influence over my father had become absolute. She had taken complete control of his life, his being, his psyche and I could not get near him. He was no longer his own man, no longer my real father. He had turned himself into a cipher – guarded and careful to do nothing that might shake the fragile balance of their relationship. But there were one or two occasions when he and I managed to rediscover the joy of each other's company – snatched, rare moments far away from the caged servitude of his office or the penthouse where a private conversation would be hijacked, toppled and redirected to conform to her agenda. Our best escape was the Garrick Club where I had become a member – an alien environment for Etty but a haven of civilization for my father who loved lunching in its lofty spaces amid the rich theatrical portraiture of Zoffany, De Wilde, George Clint and a host of other artists of late-Georgian England. I make these trips to London sound like a regular occurrence. They weren't. In all there were only two, perhaps three, occasions when he and I shared a favourite table in the Coffee Room – beneath Johan Zoffany's unfinished portrait of David Garrick. But these were precious moments and I remember them well. Infused by the esprit of the club, he came alive again, animated in conversation like a man unshackled. It was wonderful to see him so obviously at ease and having fun. Although his hearing had become a real problem, I would sit next to him and find myself enjoying the company of a forgotten father – rediscovering his quiet wisdom, his gentle humour, his great humanity. My journal at the time noted: "I adore and revere him." Then contrasting him with Etty, the next sentence reads: "M, on the other hand, continues to send me crackers. She inspires the most unnaturally violent emotions in me which is worrying. I think she is (slightly) mad – and it would appear to be getting worse."

Two months later, my suspicions seemed to be edging towards a growing conviction of her weakened state of mind. "It seems quite clear to me," I wrote, "that M is getting more and more batty these days." Etty's indiscretions had always been an embarrassment to me but now her loose tongue was rising to new levels of silliness. She had taken to telling friends, passing acquaintances and even strangers that her son wanted them "out of the Castle" – a shameless accusation she often repeated in my presence. "We still want to sell," she would tell them, and if any hapless businessman showed enough concern for the family's predicament, she would encourage them to speak to Peter with an offer for their shares. She was out of control and her behaviour was undermining the confidence of the staff who were at a loss to know what to believe. But something else was happening to her – something more fundamental and it was turning my frustrations into a mounting concern for her mental well-being.

For all his infirmities, his age and his emotional outbursts, my father was the sweetest, sanest man I knew. Etty, twelve years younger and still only sixty-four, had reached a stage where she seemed incapable of grasping the simplest notions of everyday life. Her mind wandered. She wouldn't listen and so she couldn't connect with us. Everything had to be repeated and explained –then repeated and explained again. And still she wouldn't understand. Or if she thought she had, she would get the wrong end of the stick and our conversation would collapse in confusion. As with Peter, her hearing was failing, but where my father could still communicate, Etty was finding it difficult to absorb information at any rational level. Her ability to focus on anything for very long had never been good – a deficit brilliantly concealed behind her electrically charged personality. At times this volatile energy, tangled with her random, quixotic mind, exhausted us – a reason, I am sure, why Peter created his cliff-top eyrie at the foot of Diodati's pine wood: a place of retreat away from Etty's hype.

So it was no surprise to me that, by the autumn of that year, 1991, Ian Fleming had thrown in the towel. Poor man had had enough. Etty was delighted. To his credit, Ian had put up a polite resistance to her tiresome meddling which had not endeared him to her. And now, once again, I set out in search of a new general manager. The timing was not ideal. We had ended our financial year with another thumping loss and, with no sign of any "green shoots" on the economic landscape, an unyielding recession was driving us towards another round of cost cuts. We were not alone. Misery was all about us and the hotel industry at large was struggling to survive. One candidate for the job – the manager of Raymond Blanc's Manoir aux Quat' Saisons near Oxford – arrived late one evening because he had spent all afternoon making several members of his staff redundant. At lunch the following day, Etty and Peter were eager to hear how the interview had gone. "He arrived very late last night," my mother began. "Not a good start."

"He was delayed," I explained, "because he had spent the afternoon making a number of people redundant."

"Oh!" she said. "He had a meeting in London?"

"No, no," I replied. "He had to make a number of his staff redundant."

"Ah! He's just been made redundant!"

"No, no, no!" I repeated; and again I tried to explain.

Some weeks later – after a series of interviews – I appointed Fleming's successor. Richard Delany was a charming fellow with a pedigree of experience in top country house hotels, both in Great Britain and the United States. Louise liked him too, and if we had a point of hesitation, it was the obvious one. Was he man enough for the job? Would he be able to cope with Etty? But then the same doubts would have arisen whomever we selected.

*

Young Richard Delany coped very well but twenty-one months later, in the early autumn of 1993, he followed the way of Ian Fleming and resigned – a sad decision but one which Louise and I greeted without much surprise. Together we had fought to weather a bitter recession and at last the nation was beginning to see those long-promised "green shoots" after a period which had laid us prostrate and staring into the abyss. Never in our history had we been so close to insolvency. Our accumulated losses over the previous five years ran to a shade under £500,000, our debt had soared to £920,000 and the bank had demanded a valuation of the business before lending us any more cash. To survive the crisis, we had been forced to cut deep into our running costs. The year before, I had watched as a long queue of employees filed into Delany's office to collect their redundancy notices. For the first time ever we closed the hotel for two weeks in January. Even so there were moments when our affliction looked terminal.

Alongside the cull, we imposed strict operating rules to control every penny of our expenditure. Desirable purchases were vetoed – each item had to pass the test of necessity. It was a regime that dragged Richard and me into a greater conflict with Etty and Peter who saw no reason to interrupt their own way of life – to consider, perhaps, curtailing their lavish entertaining or to stop charging their visits to the vineyards of Burgundy and Bordeaux as necessary business travel. Our pleas and complaints were dismissed as petty and trivial. In his role as chairman, Michael Blackwell also courted disapproval when he dared to suggest that they might like to make their own breakfast. After all the penthouse was equipped with a functioning kitchen. And was their domestic help really required to work five mornings a week? Could not Etty herself water the potted plants on their terrace rather than rely on the hotel to perform this task? All these minor requests were met with high indignation. They felt insulted and the chairman found that he too was falling from grace.

Old age and circumstance – a recession that fuelled existing antagonisms – induced a siege mentality. The penthouse became the redoubt of their last stand. Confrontation became more frequent and more bitter, descending into a spiral of mistrust – their overwhelming emotion, especially in my father, lost in deep feelings of rejection: that Louise and I ignored them, no longer respected them, nor showed them the attention they deserved. Minor, innocent omissions on our part exploded into great dramas. As at Christmas, Peter and Etty always joined the family at Ashfield for lunch on Easter Day. It was a given. It was understood. But by now sensitivities had become so delicate that on this Easter Day my father refused to come because we had omitted to observe the courtesy of issuing a formal invitation. Louise's family were with us for the weekend – Molly, her mother, Mark, her brother, and his wife Diana. They tried to intercede – pleaded with Peter and Etty as we had done – but my father would not be moved. Self-pitying and ridiculous in its way but a very real example of his emotional state of mind. From centre stage my parents had been cast into the wings – trapped and cramped there; but not quite, because they still lived on top of their castle, in part a symbol of their power and authority, in part a gilded cage from which they yearned to escape. Although control of the company had shifted, they could not see it, would not recognize it. With the support of a strong chairman, Louise and I were in charge now, even if there were times when it did not always feel that way.

Gerald's prophecy was coming home. The words of his letter, written from Diodati a dozen years before, returned to haunt me. *"I believe things could get so bad,"* he wrote, *"that there will be a change – it'll be inevitable – and one side or another will back down. And, of course, it will be M & D who'll back down. But at what cost??"* And further on he predicts *"… the business will harden itself and come between you all like some iron machine and destroy the fragile human links which, we all agree, give the business its distinctiveness."*

*

It was a board meeting in October '93 that heralded the bloodiest episode in the affairs of this family – an otherwise loving, generous, noble-hearted family that found itself at odds over a business. This was the beginning of the end: the senior generation's defiant last stand against the determination of the Castle's junior custodians to restore a very sick baby to full health and build a future. The economic signals were propitious and the hotel was showing signs of new life – enough to give us the confidence to embark on a modest programme of redecorations. At the board's request, Louise once again presented a report on essential works required in a number of bedrooms and public areas. The touchpaper was lit. Etty's reaction was immediate. The suggestion that Louise might have a hand in these renovations was anathema to her – a direct challenge to her authority as Director of Aesthetics. Besides, she told the meeting, she had already bought new wallpaper for the redecoration of the reception office – a purchase made at Harrods, we discovered! Michael Blackwell and I were furious. A heated argument ensued and the chairman declared that nothing would happen without proper quotations. Louise and I agreed to draw up specifications for the works and put them out to tender. Like so much else in my family, these refurbishments assumed the proportions of a major cause célèbre. In the end my mother threw her papers across the table and stormed out of the room.

For Louise this meeting, the latest in a series of pitched battles with Etty, was the last straw. When I returned home that evening, she presented me with a draft letter of resignation. It was addressed to the chairman.

14th October, 1993

Dear Michael,

It is with great sadness that I have to give my resignation from the board. I feel my contribution is totally undermined and patronized by Etty Chapman. I feel frustrated and inhibited to do the jobs that are needed. I simply cannot work under the same roof any more. I am very sorry to have to say this but I know it is the right thing to do for my own sanity and health.

Sincerely, Louise Chapman

The letter was never delivered. It remains in its draft form, tucked away with my diaries.

Next day my father came to see me in my office. He was in a mood to talk and so was I. For him, much as for the rest of us, the events of the previous day had been an embarrassment. For the first time in our many conversations over the years, all his customary defences were dismantled – he opened up, sympathetic, wearily understanding of our problem.

"Yesterday's meeting was pretty dreadful," I said gently. "Louise is mortified by the way she was treated. She feels very hurt."

"I know," my father replied. "It was awful. What can I say? After the meeting I told your mother she had behaved foolishly and that she should apologize."

"Daddy, please believe me; like you, all I want for this family is peace and harmony. But at the moment my emotions, like yours, are shredded – wrung out – shot to pieces. This is a horrible thing to say but I feel little affection for her. I just find it impossible to relate to her as my mother. I look on her more as a spoilt baby sister who always has to have her way."

"I know, Kit. That's your mother I'm afraid. I don't know what to suggest."

"Should I try talking to her?"

"No. There's no point at the moment. You'll get nowhere because you can't reason with her. You know what she's like. Nothing is ever gained by criticizing her or attacking her. She will only resist. The only route is to appeal to her heart and she'll be putty in your hands."

"I'm sorry Daddy but I've given up pretending. I just don't have it in me to pretend to worship and adore her any more!"

"Well, you'll have to," he said emphatically.

"Okay!" I replied. "I'll try. I promise I'll try."

We talked for a while longer and he reassured me that Louise could press ahead with her plans to redecorate the third-floor bedrooms. "But feed your mother a few crumbs, Kit," he added. "Let her do the reception office. Please! She is sending me bonkers over these refurbishments!" Before leaving my office, he finished with one last revelation. "You know Kit," he said, "whenever you and I have these talks, she always asks what we discussed and whether or not we talked about her!"

I smiled. "Well, paranoia is a Greek word after all!" He smiled in return and stood up to go.

*

This affectionate exchange between father and son, this private moment of glasnost, was short-lived. Never to recur. Etty chose to ignore the board's decision and attempted to hijack the tendering process – a deceitful ploy to orchestrate the redecorations to her own tune rather than to Louise's. My father had little choice but to fall into line behind her. While I boiled inwardly, he descended into one of his periodic depressions, turning bulldog-like and silent, pinning the cause of his distress on me. Although I was meant to be in control of the project, I now had my doubts – my fears coloured by

Etty's profligacy in the Eighties, excesses which paid no regard to budgetary discipline. "Budget!" she would cry. "What is budget?" We had nearly bled to death and now, at last, our fortunes were turning. I was not prepared to stand by and allow her to run away with this one. Just a few days after our fateful board meeting, a small incident in the hotel was enough to rouse my anxieties. A couple staying in a first-floor bedroom spilt a bottle of ink on the bedspread. It was ruined and had to be replaced. In 1986, the hotel purchased the cover from Harrods for £650. When my father called the Knightsbridge store for a bespoke quilted replacement, he was quoted £900! I said no! And Louise found an attractive alternative locally: a throwover cover for only £30. It was a compelling signal that times had changed. "These days," I noted in my diary entry for October 24th, "my relationship with my mother is almost permanently arctic."

Understanding and explaining my feelings at this time is painfully difficult. Retelling the incident that follows awakens past memories which lay a great weight on my heart and make me shudder with shame and regret. My nervous state, gathering in force, was like an angry, turbulent sea. This was the extraordinary effect she had on me. I saw Etty's deceitfulness as yet another small cut, another small act of betrayal, and thoughts of appealing to her heart, as my father had asked, simply vanished beneath the waves. My reaction was to ignore her, to freeze her out of the picture and get on with the job. In the end, my icy posture irritated her and she decided to confront me. The exchange was fatal – her aggression provoking me, stupidly, to rise to her bait.

"What's the matter? What's wrong?" she began, glaring at me from the other side of my desk. "You want a row! You love rows! So let's get it over with!"

"If you don't know what's wrong, you never will," I retorted.

"Oh! You're being so trivial, like a child in kindergarten." Rich coming from her, I thought, before she blurted out her stock line: "Why don't you shoot me? Go on, shoot me!"

I tried to explain myself but it was hopeless, and our confrontation disintegrated in a blaze of fire. I accused her of being a Machiavellian force in the business and she railed against me for talking to Louise and Michael Blackwell behind her back. "You should never run your own mother down!" she screamed. "Never!" "And you're obsessed with what other people think of you," I shouted. "You never give a thought to our relationship. What is more important to you? Your involvement in this hotel or the happiness of your family? If you had the sense and good grace to step down, Daddy would have what he wants most – his peace of mind …"

"How dare you! I look after your father. I know him better than you. This is his business – he created it – and *you* are the one who is hurting him. *You* want to destroy him! *You* are killing him!"

I was purple with rage and, consumed by the moment, I allowed my darkest feelings to rise up and spill out in words which should never have been uttered: "You've lost one son," I said, "now you have destroyed your relationship with me!"

*

Bitter, angry, wounded, I drove home and remained there with Louise for the rest of the day. The pair of us had lived through these bouts of emotional upheaval too often; they drained the blood out of my face, leaving me ashen and exhausted. Louise was wonderful – always good at bringing sense to my muddled mind, always soothing the violence in my wracked soul. That afternoon, with Caruso and Bollinger in tow, I set off for King's Cliff – the two-mile stretch of beech wood near our house. I walked along the leaf-strewn footpaths as the autumn sun forged a brilliant arcade of amber and yellow light through the trees. On the high ridge above the forest, a single roe deer stood and stared for a moment before darting into the undergrowth. I began to think of Gerald. Memories of our years together swept over me like racing clouds: the vitality of his company, his fun, his friendship with Louise … and yes, his confrontations with Etty and Peter. He had understood. Now, again, I needed to talk to him; I needed his advice, to share the fury and unhappiness burning inside me. On this hike through King's Cliff Wood, I desperately wanted my brother to be there, walking by my side. I began to sob – sharp, uncontrollable, choking sobs. Where was he? Could he see me? Touch me? What might he say to me? In my fantasy, I willed him to appear at my elbow. To sweep through the trees and stand in my path. To burst out of the sky in a shaft of sunlight. To erupt out of the ground before me. Gerald, where are you? I need you. God, did I wail!

A group of ramblers came into view forcing me to compose myself. But I could not stop thinking about my dead brother. Again I kept willing him to appear and eventually I had to pause to catch my breath. Sitting on the rotting stump of a tree, I listened to the sing-song trickle of the stream below me. I sat motionless, in awe of my surroundings, and almost at once the weight on my aching heart lifted. Body and mind – riven by a raging storm moments before – had come to rest in a state of perfect calm. It was beautiful. And perhaps, just at that moment, Gerald was there beside me.

*

The summons to the penthouse was not long in coming and, like a wicked schoolboy called for a caning in the headmaster's study, I presented myself. My father sat hunched in his chair – lugubrious, panting with the strain – and Etty crouched by his side, looking martyred. I attempted to have my say first, directing my words at him.

"Look, I can't tell you how much I regret the row with Mummy the other day. I hate hurting you and upsetting you. I want you to know that."

"You behaved abominably," he said bitterly. "You should have the guts and the courtesy to apologize to your mother now."

"This has nothing to do with guts." I replied. "I should never have said what I said but she provoked me and behaved every bit as abominably as I did."

"Have you any idea of the effect you have had on us because of what you said? … the loss of Gerald. Have you any idea how much that hurt us?"

"I know, I know. And I'm so sorry…"

"Kit, you behaved like an IRA terrorist!" he gasped. "You're as bad as Gerry Adams!"

"You see what you are doing!" said Etty sharply. "You're murdering your father!"

I ignored her ridiculous accusation and tried to explain our predicament. In vain. The problem was all mine, they said, and I had to change my attitude towards them. Old clichés were repeated … I made an issue of petty and trivial incidents … The hotel was their creation … They were not going to be made redundant. In a last stand, again I tried to touch on the demands of the business, the need to control costs: "Don't teach your father to suck eggs!" Etty cried.

I fell silent. There was no more to say. My father was in a terrible state and my mother sat basking quietly in the glow of her moral victory. When I returned to my office, I felt numb with shock. This had been the blackest of confrontations and it had ended in schism, each of us emotional casualties bearing irreparable wounds. My father came away with the deepest scars. Cruelly, I had reopened the wound he had nursed since Gerald's death, a deep hurt that would never heal. It was this, I am sure, that changed our relationship. Etty may have lost my love – the natural devotion a son might have for his mother – but in parallel, I was losing the love and trust and confidence of my father – a man I adored and respected. This is the scar I bear, and it still troubles me today.

*

For the weeks that followed a sinister hush descended on the family. Like injured foxes holed up in our lairs, there was little or no contact. When we surfaced to face each other across a boardroom, the temperature rose and fell over the sensitive issue of expenditure. As the economy emerged from recession and with our plans to start spending money on the hotel again, the old guard reacted to having the purse strings snatched from their control. Fighting Etty's corner in the refurbishment programme, my father argued for a Wilton carpet and a £400 oak dado rail in the reception office – a proposal the board rejected. We also noted that after only one month of the new financial year, my parents had spent sixty percent of the "directors' travel and entertainment" budget. These and many other issues rankled, raising tensions which the chairman had to referee. In the face of this bitter cold war, I worked hard to repair my fences with Peter, but all I received in return was a sense of his suppressed hostility towards me. "It is so desperately sad," I wrote in December, "that this gulf exists between us – an animosity he directs so vehemently against me. They are living in another age – incapable of grasping the commercial reality within which we now have to work."

That year they spent Christmas in Salonica – with Machi, Petros and our Greek family – a secret arrangement made two months before they revealed their intentions to us. Louise and I heard forty-eight hours before their departure and we wondered how they might have reacted if we had hatched a secret plan to spend the holiday with Molly, Mark and Diana in London. The heavens would have fallen in and we would have stood indicted of treason!

On the afternoon before their flight out of Heathrow, a receptionist came searching for me. "There is a very important note from Mr. Chapman on your desk," she said. "He wants you to go to your office straightaway." I knew instantly that this was the overture to another little charade. I was being set up and when I reached my office, I burst out laughing. There on my desk, piled like skyscrapers, lay our Christmas gifts – all neatly labelled to Louise, Dom, Nick, Molly and me. There in the centre of the room lay their Trojan horse! Dutifully, I tapped on my father's office door and when I entered I found them both waiting for me. Barely able to contain my amusement, I made my speech of thanks and after an embarrassed shuffle, Etty clasped me around my waist and laid her head on my chest. It was an embrace that begged to be returned and one given not as a mother might hug her son but like that of a guilty child craving the approval of an elder brother whom she knows she has crossed.

"I love you, I love you," she whispered. "Do you love me?"

"Yes," I lied.

"Say it! Say it!" She pleaded.

"I love you," I stuttered in desperation.

"Let's forget," she said. "You will forget, won't you?"

"Mummy," I replied feeling the agitation rise in my throat, "I can't turn my emotions on and off like a light switch."

"Kit," interrupted my father, "please say those three magic words."

"I've said them," I replied misunderstanding him.

"No, no. Say you're sorry."

Turning again towards Etty I spoke the words required of me with as much sincerity as I was able to muster, "I am sorry!" She replied that she was sorry too and muttered something incoherent about the IRA and peace in Northern Ireland. I left the office relieved that it was done. A Christmas truce had been successfully negotiated.

The absence of parents and my escape from the emotional burden which habitually attended our Christmas celebrations should have released me into a state of beneficence and joy. But ours was a shallow truce. Unknown to me, in the days before their departure, the seasonal cup of peace and goodwill had been filling with the poison of Etty's latest mutterings to the staff. Those colleagues closest to me were outraged by her behaviour, not least my faithful secretary Gill who, shocked by the gossip spinning about the corridors of the hotel, decided to confide in me with her own first-hand experience of my mother's loose tongue. On one occasion Louise had been her target. "Don't be deceived by her sweet exterior," she told Gill, "she is as hard as steel underneath!" And of me she said: "When my Peter goes, he will kick me out, out, out!"

Again I felt betrayed. The touching scene of reconciliation in my father's office had been a sham. But by the end of Christmas my despair had turned to guilt. On the twenty-eighth of December, in my study at Ashfield, I sat down to record my thoughts: "They would have expected that act of loving duty – a telephone call on Christmas Day," I wrote. "I made none. So I am damned. In the end, all the anger, hurt and confusion swilling about my breast could not induce me to commit what would have been a cynical act of hypocrisy. But in this family pretence rather than an honest heart is the preferred expedient. Duty is indivisible and pays no heed to feeling. It was my clear duty as their son to telephone them. And these past few days I have reeled like a drunk between duty and feeling."

Of course, I paid a price for my sin. Just after New Year, within minutes of their return from Greece, I was subjected to a brief interrogation. "Where was everybody?" my mother asked as I stepped into her bedroom. "Daddy had to carry in the suitcases himself!" Their arrival at lunchtime had not been greeted with the dutiful obeisance expected of management and staff.

"We're busy!" I replied. "A big party to look after in the dining room."

"Did you try to telephone us at Christmas?" she asked coming to the point which had really exercised her.

"No!" I said.

"Did you leave a message at the hotel?"

"No!"

"Did you try to call us at New Year?"

"No!"

And that put an end to it … We moved on.

*

Part Eleven

Old Truths Never Die

Peter Chapman 1915 – 1997

1994 was a good year; a good year for one thrilling reason. After a prolonged era of annual losses running into five and six figures, in 1994 the Castle's accounts registered a modest profit of £3,937. We had turned the corner. The price I paid for this pyrrhic success was to witness the collapse of my relationship with my parents and if there needs to be an apportioning of blame, I have come to acknowledge that I must bear at least an equal share. But we had slain the dragon. The spectre of insolvency passed and there was now the prospect of securing the business for our future and, perhaps, for future generations of the family. Around us, Louise and I built a strong team and we all worked well together. I had promoted Andrew Grahame, our restaurant manager, to succeed Delany as general manager. It was a risky appointment but Andrew grew into his new role quickly and soon proved something of a commercial dynamo with a natural chutzpah which infected the staff. Phil Vickery also had stepped out of the shadow of Gary Rhodes to shine in his own right at the head of his kitchen brigade. By now we had reclaimed our lost Michelin Star and the 1994 edition of the Good Food Guide had catapulted the Castle into its listing of the top forty restaurants in Great Britain. We were on a roll, all of us super-charged with a new spirit and determination to win.

Meanwhile, my own extracurricular life had seen the screening of a second series of *Simply the Best* on the ITV network and Channel 4, the production of a package of vocational training videos which I wrote and presented for the hotel industry, and the winning of two new commissions. The first came from my publisher for a new volume of *Great British Chefs*, and the second from the BBC who invited me to compile and present a special two-hour feature on gastronomy and the arts for BBC Radio 2's *Arts Programme*. In between the high drama of the Chapmans at the Castle, these projects were a welcome distraction.

But if the principal excitement of the year was the Castle's move into an elusive profit, our relief was tempered by the heavy debt burden which still imposed a dangerous load on our books. Confidence had to be balanced with caution. Budgets were finely chiselled and closely monitored. And inevitably these strictures led to more trouble. Where Mrs. Chapman Jnr. managed her budgets with creative parsimony, fitting out her office for example with carpet remnants from an attic, discarded hotel furniture and wallpaper from a seconds shop, Mrs. Chapman Snr. suddenly decided to redecorate her bedroom in the Penthouse (with wallpaper from Harrods) at a cost of £2,000 for which there had been no budget allocated. "Do you expect your parents to live in a slum?" snapped my father when I queried the expenditure. I backed away and when I postponed the refurbishment of the reception office, Etty accused me of being a "tyrant!" "What do you want to do," she cried, "kill your father with a heart attack?"

With Michael Blackwell's knowledge and support, the issue was raised formally at April's board meeting. My father, whom I had also warned, responded with a long, rambling and emotional speech expressing his indignation. At the end he stood up. "The Castle is MY hotel!" he proclaimed and walked out of the room. The chairman tried to stop him but he would not return. This gave Etty her cue and she launched into a garbled diatribe – a public regurgitation of all my past crimes. Another meeting ended in chaos and for the first time I saw Michael come close to losing his Yorkshire cool.

But the objection to Etty's unbudgeted spending spree soon revealed itself to be a lesser cause of my father's petulant exit from the boardroom. His parting shot – "The Castle is MY hotel!" – had been spoken with a fury and an emphasis which betrayed his fragile state of mind. Our meeting that April morning coincided with the publication of an adulatory review of the Castle in *The Times*, a major feature written by Jonathan Meades, its feared restaurant critic. Meades, in his innocence, had pierced my father's bleeding heart by referring to me as "the Castle's owner" and, worse, by making no reference to

Etty and Peter. "The man who effected [Gary] Rhodes's metamorphosis," he wrote referring to the rising stardom of my last chef, "is the Castle's owner, Kit Chapman. The guy possesses some blissful knack. He replaced Rhodes with another native of Kent, Philip Vickery, who was, sure enough, a gifted young chef. He then proceeded to do a makeover. Vickery now stands alongside his predecessor; he is every bit as good. The amazing thing about Chapman the impresario is that he directs rather than moulds. He has encouraged Vickery in such a way that the chef has arrived at an idiom that is all his own ..." Once again, a fabulous splash of publicity had inspired deep offence.

But I must not be too harsh in my judgements. My feelings at the time were of despair and sadness. To see my father in this weakened state was dreadful. He was no longer the father I knew: strong, clear-sighted, fair-minded, wise; and always ready to encourage and support his two sons in their endeavours. Never jealous, never self-pitying. Now, in his eightieth year, he saw me as a threat; still expecting to be in control, unable to come to terms with the reality that his powers and his influence were ebbing away.

Some weeks later, before Louise and I left for our holiday in Tuscany, I decided to try once more to reach him, this time by letter.

The Castle at Taunton – 4th June 1994

My dearest Daddy,

I have thought long and hard about writing this letter and I am still unsure whether it is the right thing to do. But as communication between us seems so difficult these days, I thought at least I should attempt to say a few words.

I think – I know – that we can agree that relations within the family have sunk to an all time low and I am genuinely anxious to seek whatever solution to heal the wounds and restore happiness between us all.

It is blindingly clear that the root of all the conflict is the business. In recent years, the pressures have increased and the strains have shown in our personal relationships. But, in truth, there has always been an element of conflict. Now this dreadful family feuding is something of an open secret and it is affecting the fabric and morale of the staff in the hotel. It is also tearing us apart. Somehow, we must find a way of putting an end to it all and that means talking openly to one another. Papering over the cracks after a dispute flares up is no solution. If we are not prepared to tackle our problems together, the wounds will continue to fester and continue to be inflamed from time to time.

We are all anxious to set the business back on its feet. I am convinced that there is a future here and I want to do my best to make it happen. Who knows what will become of Dom and Nick? But I do feel strongly that, if we can pull through, the option to take the Castle on to the third generation should, at least, be available to them. Of course they may not want it. I am exerting no pressure and it would be quite wrong to talk to them in these terms. It is far too early. However, the thought remains and if it ever came to pass, this would be your great legacy.

I have now committed eighteen years of my life to this place and I do love it. In thirteen years, I will be sixty! By that time, we shall know where Dom and Nick stand. They will be in their thirties. If one of them wants to take over, I shall stand down. Meanwhile, my only concerns are to see the fortunes of the business restored and to rebuild family harmony.

To achieve this, something has to give – otherwise our problems will worsen. None of the solutions is easy, but as I see it, our only hope is to grasp that nettle. Either Louise and I must stand down. Or you and Mummy retire. Or we all resign and leave the management of the hotel to a board of non-family and non-executive directors. As we all know, selling is not a viable option at present and, for the reasons I have given, I am very keen to soldier on. Not least, I am acutely aware and sensitive to your own feelings – and the need to underpin your own security and peace of mind for the future. To do this with any hope of success, the business must be managed by a united and motivated board. At present we have neither.

With Louise in 2000. The millennium marks the coming of a new generation.

The watercolour of Dürnstein on the Danube. Nell's birthday gift to Peter in March 1952 to remind him of happier times "with Daddy".

Peter's 80th birthday party. Seated – Aunt Tim; Peter and his brother, Michael. Standing – Louise; me; Etty and cousin Nicky.

With my Uncle Petros and Etty's sister, my Aunt Machi in front of the Rotonda in Salonica.

The third Avon Lodge. Peter and Etty's final home on the Blackdown Hills, south of Taunton.

Alice Hodges, Etty's long-suffering housekeeper, on the terrace at Avon Lodge.

Daniel, our first grandchild.

Oliver and Kitty.

Dominic and Helena on their wedding day in New Zealand. March 2008. With Daniel aged one.

With Nick and Ollie on the terrace at Diodati.

Annabel and Nick at Diodati.

Ollie on the little red chair, Diodati.

Patra with Taxiarchis, our gardener, at Diodati.

Mark, Louise's brother, and his wife, Diana.

Granny Louise with Ollie.

Louise and her two boys, Nick and Dom as young teenagers.

Newly engaged with Louise. St Tropez 1971.

Uncle Mark with his two little nephews, Dom and Nick.

The archipelago taken from Artistotle's Terrace at Diodati.

The back terrace, Diodati.

My father. A favourite portrait taken
in the Penthouse at the Castle.

I hope that we shall be able to talk the issues through when we return from Italy. In the end, this difficult and unsettling problem is for us to resolve alone. No one else can help.

All my love, Kit

*

I cannot say whether my father received this letter. If he did, I do not know if he read it, nor how he reacted to it. The letter was never discussed. On our return from Italy, he suffered a stroke and was rushed to the private wing of Musgrove Park Hospital in Taunton. It happened on a Thursday in early July and twenty-four hours elapsed before Etty broke the news to us. I was to blame, she told me, and she attempted to stop us from visiting him. A call to the ward sister helped me to understand his condition. It was grave. He was undergoing tests. His speech was impaired; he had lost almost all feeling in his right arm and he was having some difficulty controlling his waterworks – but this was improving. I thanked the nurse and said we were on our way. Louise followed half-an-hour later.

My mother and I found him sitting in an armchair by a window. I sat beside him and held his hand. Struggling with his words, he turned towards me. "If this heals the family rift," he stuttered, "it will have been worthwhile." He paused and I tried to reassure him. "Please look after Mummy for me," he added. I promised I would.

*

In time the crisis passed but recovery was slow. Etty refused to listen to the doctors who made the mistake of overlooking "her Peter's" immortality His condition, she insisted, had nothing to do with his age. Instead she continued to blame me – accusations that came in sporadic outbursts which I ignored. Towards the end of the year, I promised him lunch at the Garrick Club, a treat he looked forward to with almost child-like enthusiasm; but a week before our journey to London, he called it off – the thought of trains and taxis and the commotion of a big city unsettling him. Inevitably, my father's decline and disengagement from the business affected Etty who began to lose her appetite for the day-to-day routines of the hotel – a shift which finally allowed Louise to come into her own. To my delight, I soon noticed that she had transformed the atmosphere in the place: it became more relaxed; the staff were happier people; she spent time with them, listening to them; and they grew to love her.

But in sinking herself into the hurly-burly of hotel life, Louise also came to learn that the Castle was an elderly and demanding mistress. Through the recession of the early-Nineties the old lady had been neglected and the moment had come to restore her lost allure. Maintaining the fabric of the place – from its carapace to its intestines – was a major task. Breakdowns, breakages and systems' failures were as much a daily staple as the urgent need to replace interiors and organize refurbishment schemes. To cope – and steering clear of big contractors – Louise assembled a disparate group of independent specialists; local painters and decorators, carpenters, plumbers and electricians, tilers, carpet layers and soft furnishers. This merry band of men and women became her private army. She led them and nurtured them, hectored them and stroked them. In return, they became fiercely loyal to her. And if sometimes she rejected their quotations for being a little fanciful, they dutifully adjusted their prices. Her negotiating skills became legendary in the building trade where she was quickly dubbed Louise "Discount" Chapman.

The contrast in management style and budgetary discipline between the two Mrs. Chapmans was the difference between night and day, penury and liquidity. A major drain on the hotel's limited resources suddenly vanished. To this day, Louise's mindful approach, matched by her flare and eye for design, has saved the business huge sums of money and she, meanwhile, has continued to present the Castle as one of the most civilized and welcoming hotels in England. Her watchwords are colour, freshness and light above any desire to make a boutique fashion statement. To walk into one of Louise's newly decorated bedrooms is to raise a smile of pleasure on the face of the unsuspecting guest; her aim to create a sense of home rather than hotel. And so by the mid-Nineties her involvement with the hotel became total – her time minding the domestic hearth less urgent now that our two boys had matured into young men. While Dominic, now twenty-one, was hoisting a rucksack on his back to embark on a two-year odyssey around the world, Nicholas, nineteen, had already begun his studies at Oxford Brookes University.

*

It was not until early 1995, six months after my father's stroke, that Louise and I came to learn the true significance of Etty's withdrawal from the day-to-day affairs of the hotel. The news, like a bomblet falling out of an empty sky, was brought to me one damp morning when Andrew Grahame tapped at the open door of my office.

"Can I ask you something?" he said furtively.

"Of course," I replied. "Come in and sit down."

"Are your parents moving out?"

"No!" I said, stunned by his question. "Not that I am aware."

"Well, there's been quite a lot of gossip around the hotel. And yesterday some fitters called to ask about the installation of cupboards in Mr. and Mrs. Chapman's new house."

I could not believe what I was hearing. A little later my mother walked into my office and this time it was my turn to catch her unawares.

"I hear you've bought a house! You're moving out. Is that right?"

"Who told you?" she cried. "How do you know?"

"I know! The hotel is buzzing with the news!"

"It's a surprise! We wanted to make it a big surprise," she stammered nervously and rushed out of the room.

That afternoon I telephoned Michael Blackwell. He gasped in disbelief. My parents' little secret had been spun into a clumsy grandstanding gesture; this was their final admission of defeat, a final act of defiance in the long and bloody battle for control of the Castle Hotel. It was their dramatic way of signalling the end. And they had done it without a moment's thought for the consequences to the business. Five years before, in the prelude to Louise's arrival on the board and Michael's succession as chairman, Etty had demanded that the company provide them with a house. If they had found the wherewithal to buy a new home now, they certainly would have had the means then – and the family might have been spared the emotional turmoil of an irretrievable breakdown between the generations. But now, five years on, they had made their move and it landed us with a host of problems which we could have worked through if their intentions had been made plain six months earlier. Suddenly, the business faced the prospect of underwriting their pension – a sum Blackwell set modestly at an annual rate of £60,000 to keep them in the style to which they had become accustomed. And the Penthouse? What was to become of the Penthouse? It offered a fabulous new facility for the hotel but it was being stripped bare and we had laid no plans and set no budget to refurnish it nor to reconfigure its three bedrooms to make them suitable for hotel use. With no advance warning, we were now presented with a major new undertaking which would require a fresh injection of cash at a time when we were working to reduce our borrowings.

Once again I felt hurt and betrayed. Once again Etty had manipulated her husband – too ill and too frail to expose the sham of her Byzantine obsession with secrecy. We had spent Christmas and New Year together; even so they had kept silent – a wilful act of deception which left Louise and me nettled and perplexed. When they began the great move out to Avon Lodge, their hillside idyll on the slopes of the Blackdowns, it was conducted in slow, gradual stages. As a halfway house, they took a suite of bedrooms in the hotel until the works at Avon Lodge were complete and the Penthouse was cleared. Meanwhile, we needed to press ahead with our plans to recommission this large duplex space which was promising to become a valuable asset to the business. So I asked my parents for permission to grant Louise access to measure up for curtains and carpets as an essential step in her refurbishment programme. They refused. I was accused of hounding them out of the building and Michael Blackwell finally lost his temper. "All I've had is insults from them," he told me.

*

By March they were gone; the atmosphere cleared like breaking sunshine after a storm and we began to look forward to running the Castle unhindered. No sense of triumph, just an overwhelming feeling of relief and freedom. Then, on the eighth, the family paused to set aside its differences and gathered reunited to celebrate a landmark moment – my father's eightieth birthday. "He has become a grand old man," I noted in my diary. "But his years weigh heavily upon him. He looks like an ancient sage burdened with sorrow, pain, exhaustion, anguish. Now I hope he finds the peace and tranquillity he seeks." To mark the great day, I threw a small lunch party. We were seven: my Uncle Michael and Aunt Tim from Torquay; my cousin Nicky, Peter's favourite god-daughter, and the four of us. My father chose the menu – a celeriac and saffron soup with truffle oil, a roast rack of lamb and, to finish, a passion fruit soufflé. The wines were left to me and I decided that if there were ever an occasion to do something spectacular, this was it. We began with Krug 1982, followed by two vintages of Château Lafite-Rothschild, the '70, then the '61, and with the soufflé, we drank a glass of Château d'Yquem '76. Not one of these wines disappointed. They were all huge, fabulous and voluptuous. I had decanted the pair of clarets two hours before we sat down and for a while the '70 overshadowed the '61, but as the older wine developed in the glass, it began to display its greatness.

The wines set the tone and provided a focus for an unforgettable day. My father, I think, was touched by the arrangements I had made for him and by the middle of the afternoon we were all in high spirits. Uncle Michael, now eighty-three, could hardly walk and had to be lifted in and out of his chair. But while he may have lost the use of his legs, the Imperial's old matinee idol had not lost his eye for a pretty woman. He flirted openly with Louise and insisted on sitting next to her. At the end of lunch, when the time came for Michael and Tim to return to Torquay, he embraced Etty tightly and as he clasped her waist, he toppled over on his back taking her with him. In a scene of pure slapstick, my father leapt to Etty's rescue and when he stooped down to lift her, he could not pick himself up. There on the floor of a private room at the Castle Hotel, sprawled like toddlers at play, lay Etty and the two octogenarian brothers! Mercifully, there were no broken bones. The younger generation rallied to bring the party to its feet and we all returned home in good humour. Fine wine, fine fun!

*

We had to wait for our first glimpse of Avon Lodge; an invitation which was withheld until Easter Sunday – a date falling in mid-April that year. Louise and I remember it as a slightly strained and joyless occasion, an experience resonating more with a guided visit to a show house than Easter with the family at home. As we turned into the driveway and dipped in a steep arc towards the house, our eyes were struck by a lush hanging garden – trimmed, mowed and pruned to perfection; an immaculate model for any leafy suburb. Beyond, the escarpment fell away to reveal an epic landscape which stretched across the Vale of Taunton Deane to the Quantock Hills in the far distance. This was their Diodati in England, I thought. The Aegean Sea exchanged for the wonder of Somerset's pastoral beauty; a second villa – itself Mediterranean in style – etched snugly into a hillside that looked out on a world of peace and loveliness. My father had chosen well.

Louise and I had hoped we might eat there but with no local cook to understudy Patra in Greece, and even though we offered to prepare lunch for them, Etty refused. She had never lifted a saucepan in her life and had no intention of starting now. So the paschal lamb – roasted by tradition for the family at Ashfield – was replaced by a sterile show tour and a glass of fizz before we decamped to the village pub for a truly execrable meal. But that Easter Sunday, it was not the pub that left its impression on me, nor the panoramic views from the house, nor the careful displays of French silver and Georgian furniture; nor even the polish on the candelabra and the salvers, the walnut, the mahogany and the rosewood. No. What moved me to the core was the changed appearance and manner of my father. "D seems so frail these days," I wrote. "He does not talk much. Although I am sure he is very happy and at peace in his new home, he looks so sad and lost – half in this world, half in another. He appears well, in fact very well, and his face has assumed a rather sweet cherubic, saintly glow. What bothers me terribly is that M does not seem to be remotely aware of his frailty. She is as exhaustingly energetic as ever!"

Peter's arrival at Avon Lodge was his final homecoming. It also embraced a state of mind I do not believe Etty ever understood. The name he chose for the new house echoed with memories of a lost age of contentment, of happier times. It assumed a profound significance in his imagination, carrying with it powerful associations of home, love, comfort, harmony. Avon Lodge was an umbilical reconnection, a return to the bosom of the mother he adored. In his family history, he recalls his early childhood on the Thames at Pangbourne – the original Avon Lodge – where he describes his first recollection of his parents: "I was sitting on a potty at the top of a flight of stairs," he tells us. The two watercolours of the house, commissioned by Nell in 1917, now hanging on the walls of the landing outside our bedroom, were Peter's private joy – his memorial to a family at peace in a time of war. On neat lawns sloping to the banks of the river, figures dressed in white linen gaze across the water to his mother and her sister Fan reclining in their punt. It was a romanticized ideal of family life. And then Nell's cottage in Little Common near Bexhill in Sussex – the second Avon Lodge. This was the home he returned to after India and a second war had separated mother and son for ten long years. It was his sweetest homecoming.

From then Avon Lodge became a name and an idea which, like Diodati, filled his heart with a sense of peace and safety, a sanctuary from the tumultuous events which had shaken his life: the buried secrets of his father's suicide which he could not bring himself to share with Etty; the war and post-war years of struggle and breakdown; his coming to terms with Gerald's homosexuality, then Aids and finally death; and last, the family's long and bitter conflict over the Castle. These episodes had hurt him deeply. So his return to Avon Lodge, reincarnated in the Blackdown Hills, was a return to mother whose protection would heal the wounds inflicted by the unhappiness and failures of his final years at the Castle. Perversely, that grief became identified with the tragedy of Bratislava; the death and shame of his famous father, Henry Prüger, and the ultimate collapse of the family business. The trauma of the fourteen-year-old schoolboy, suddenly called home in the summer of 1929, was transferred to the elderly hotelier – himself an hotelier's son – searching for an escape and finding it at last in the home he always knew as Avon Lodge.

*

As the months passed, Louise and I came to learn that Etty's idea of home was very different from Peter's. For her Avon Lodge was no homecoming, and with the onset of winter the novelty of the new house began to recede as the burden of domestic life and the need to cope with Peter's declining health seemed to overwhelm her. These were practicalities she could do without, that were better dealt with by others. And for all its charms and the splendour of its outlook, Avon Lodge did not carry the public prestige of the Castle Hotel where, with its large retinue of butlers and cooks, valets and housemaids, she had once held court as its elegant and glamorous chatelaine. The Castle was her home. That was where she belonged, and she resented her exile in the Blackdown Hills. Not that she was cast adrift to fend for herself. Heaven forbid! A new brigade of servants – albeit part-time – was employed to take care of the house and the garden. Chief among them was Alice Hodges, a good and honest woman whose many ancestors had been lain to rest in the churchyards of these hills and whose ties to the local community and the parish church of St. Peter and St. Paul at Churchstanton remain as enduringly steadfast as the Blackdowns' ancient beechwoods. In time Mrs. Hodges would prove a loyal and indispensable friend – her fortitude and her sense of duty prevailing against the onset of the gathering extremes in Etty's behaviour.

My mother's unwilling displacement from the social limelight of the Castle to her home in bucolic exile induced within her a new bitterness of spirit, a characteristic she aimed – often with raw venom – at those closest and dearest: Louise and me, of course; also my father who occasionally resisted her more outrageous demands before a tantrum forced him to capitulate; and her sister Machi in Salonica with whom she quarrelled regularly on the telephone before slamming the receiver down. But it was poor Alice who took the brunt of her frustrated outbursts and there were days when she would return home to the family's farmhouse near Smeatharpe distraught and in tears. In spite of her difficulties she persevered, comforted by the kindly influence of Peter who saw what was happening. "Mr. Chapman is a perfect gentleman," she once confided. "He often protects me from your mother's sharp tongue."

Etty's obsessive-compulsive disposition, her selfishness and her need to control suddenly became magnified. To preserve her self-image, she invented a life of permanent rush to convey the impression of urgency and business purpose where she, the chatelaine, was still in command. "Alice! I must go, I must go!" she would say. "I have important things to do at the hotel today. They need me there." And out she would dash leaving Alice a list of instructions which in themselves were a self-inflicted tyranny where every detail had to be observed to the tiniest speck of dust. For my mother, the slightest imperfection in the housekeeping or the smallest interruption to the domestic routine were intolerable. In the garden she hurled a small fortune at a team of professional horticulturalists to create and maintain a prize exhibit, a Chelsea showpiece. And in the house Alice found herself permanently on trial with a regime that bordered on the fanatical. Even the bookshelves had to be dismantled on a strict monthly rota; then wiped down before each volume was carefully dusted and replaced in its proper position – a job which took two days. And when, one bitter winter's morning, she called to say that she would not be coming to work because the farmhouse was snowed in and the track to the main road was impassable, Etty refused to listen.

"But Alice you must come. There is all the ironing to do."

"I'm sorry Mrs. Chapman, I really cannot get out of the house. It won't hurt if the ironing waits for a day."

"Alice you *must* come," she insisted. "I need you. You can thumb a lift from the main road!"

"Mrs. Chapman, the roads are really icy and dangerous up here. Very little is moving. I'm sorry but it's impossible for me to come. I'll do the ironing tomorrow, I promise. Just as soon as our lane's been cleared and the gritters have made the roads safe."

But in the end Etty had her way and the ironing was done – a task that claimed priority over the exercise of a little understanding and some rudimentary common sense. In spite of the weather conditions and the hazards on the roads, she despatched a reluctant Peter to collect Alice from the top of her lane.

This was my mother – guardian to a host of idiosyncratic habits which grew in eccentricity with her advancing years as age and disenchantment with her circumstances detached her from the domestic universe of most ordinary human beings. But then my mother was no ordinary human being. When she offered to support Alice's jumble sale at Churchstanton's annual bazaar, her contribution amounted to a gift of four or five empty boxes: a Harrods hat box, a dress box and some empty chocolate boxes from Fortnum & Mason! A gesture made less in parsimony and more in blissful ignorance of the ways of church bazaars. And then there were the weekly refuse collections at the house, a service Etty considered hopelessly inadequate. Instead, she and Peter would drive into Taunton each day and deposit a black bin liner in one of the hotel skips before settling down to some lunch in the restaurant. And when they set off again to take their afternoon walk in the hills – though my father was no longer in any fit state to do so – Etty would gather small sticks and twigs by the roadside, bundle them up and arrange a neat stack on the grass verge before beginning the process all over again. Her way, I supposed, of tidying up the countryside.

*

Etty's exile did not immunize the Castle from her more subversive habits, but what it gave us was the freedom to rebuild a crippled family business and by the middle of the decade we were making respectable profits. Then in 1996 we started paying dividends for the first time in the company's history and by the following year we had reduced our appalling debt burden by almost half. At last the hotel was rolling forward, poised to reinvest in schemes to develop new facilities for the coming millennium: a modern brasserie to replace our scruffy town centre pub and eight more hotel bedrooms to add to the existing stock of thirty-six. But it was also during this period that our driving enthusiasms were blighted by a serious reversal of fortune. Andrew Grahame, my lively-minded general manager, fell ill with cancer – non-Hodgkin's lymphoma – a desperate condition which put him out of action for over a year. After he had endured months of treatment and palliative care, the doctors declared his case terminal. Then, to the astonishment of us all, the patient's ordeal slowly turned into an extraordinary and complete recovery. His unexpected homeward journey was declared miraculous – a resurrection Andrew owed to the quiet faith he had placed in the powers of his uncle Arthur, a spiritual healer from the Grahame family's home in Derby.

When eventually he returned to his desk, Andrew took up his old post like a man reborn – possessed of a new life force and charged with energy levels I was astonished to see. It was a great relief. For twelve difficult months I had been left without the support of my most senior lieutenant. Any distraction from our purpose was unwelcome, especially if it came as interference from a meddlesome mother. Etty sensed the pressures on her son's hectic schedule and revelled in my problems. It was as if she set out wilfully to provoke me, to undermine me, to punish me for usurping her sacred throne. She may have lost her power base in the penthouse but she still had an ability to disrupt the equilibrium of the hotel by ambushing us when we least expected it, sending managers and department heads into a state of turmoil. No longer queen bee, she adopted the tactics of a zealous insurgent just to remind me of the old order. One day, with no warning, she introduced me to a young Greek lad. This was Costa, Patra's teenage child and Etty's godson who, at my mother's invitation, had flown over to England to work at the hotel. Costa was a sweet boy but there was no job vacancy. Besides, he spoke no English and had never travelled beyond his island home, still less to a foreign land famous for its wet and chilly climate. Within three days he was on a return flight to

Greece having suffered a miserable introduction to the big wide world for which Etty held me to blame. One afternoon I overheard her talking in shrill whispers to an assistant manager on the first-floor landing. "You know my son gets peeved," she hissed, pinning the young man to the banisters. "My husband will tell you. He knows him so well … and he gets peeved. You know why? Because he did not know about Costa. So that peeves him." Later I confronted her, but she denied everything, accusing me, instead, of terrorizing Peter.

Some days after this little episode, she marched into my office. "Is anything the matter?" she asked, my father stooped and wobbling unsteadily at her side.

"No," I replied.

"Have I done anything to upset you?"

"No!"

"I'd rather you told me," she insisted. How many times, I asked myself, had I played this ridiculous charade? I ignored her fatuous enquiry and my father changed the subject.

"Kit, can you tell us the arrangements for your book launch?" he asked referring to the imminent publication of *Great British Chefs 2*. "We would love to come."

At moments like these – and they were many – Louise was quick to soothe my rage, reminding me of how it was before, that now we were in control, and that there was no advantage to be gained by wasting my emotional energy on Etty's giddiness. These were minor irritations, diversionary skirmishes rather than serious attacks on the business. Yet she was my mother and she possessed some demonic, some primeval authority over my emotions which swallowed me whole. Flashpoints came and went with exhausting regularity – my father often covering for her foolish games by accepting the blame. Her spontaneous demands for Michelin-starred meals to be ferried out to Avon Lodge (because she hated Alice's home cooking even though Peter loved it), or her insistence on free bedrooms for her friends at musical weekends when we were fully booked, would drive me mad. Rereading my diaries around these times, the tone and language of my words seem horribly extreme in the context of her selfish little peccadillos. In November '95, the monumental row that erupted over her calls for a meals-on-wheels service out of the hotel's kitchens ended in bitter recriminations – the voice of Peter, as usual, raised as her protecting shield. I was to be disinherited, she told me, and again she repeated the old song that the Castle had been given to me "on a plate". Again I reminded her that my inheritance had come as a broken business and a mountain of debt for which her extravagances were uniquely responsible. In my diary entry for the twenty-sixth of that month, I wrote:

"M is desperately trying to suck up to me as if nothing has happened. I brush her off and keep her brusquely at a distance. I am so hurt and so angry I cannot even bring myself to be in her presence. I have nothing more to give, not even forgiveness. Like the mindless, petulant, spoilt child that she is, she thinks her abuses one week can be swept under the carpet and forgotten the next. She keeps popping into my office, all smiles, aching for a friendly audience – but I have none of it. I have had enough.

"She went to see Blackwell the other day and told him to give me 'a rocket'! He said he wouldn't. The meeting was a non-event. Oh, she is so silly. And inside myself, I just rage in a fury – despairing of this ludicrous woman who calls herself my mother; who demands my love and total devotion at any cost."

Two weeks later, in December, Molly died. It was a terrible shock. Her death had not been expected. The tears we shed flowed freely – mine for a mother-in-law I revered and loved as if she were my own. And in a way she was. Her funeral was held at the Brompton Oratory, a Requiem Mass at the High Altar. Mark, Louise's brother, asked me to say a few words of farewell on behalf of the family. As with Gerald's in New York, I wore the silk tie he had given me a decade before and I delivered my valedictory address without notes. My father was too unwell to travel, but Etty was there to hear my tribute. I recalled Molly's natural wisdom and her selfless devotion to her family; a thanksgiving for a woman who was a rare and adored mother-figure to all of us; her son and daughter, their spouses, her grandchildren: Mark and Diana, Louise and me, Edward and Henry, Dominic and Nicholas.

Some weeks later, in February, we flew to the South of France with her ashes. When we arrived, the locals were celebrating their annual Festival of Mimosa and we drove along a coast road ablaze with yellow buds. The cemetery at Théoule-sur-Mer lies on a steep hillside overlooking a secluded valley of the Esterel, its tombs tiered in long terraces hewn out of the rock. It was here that we reunited Molly with Peter, her husband. Frère René, the priest from Le Trayas, recited a few brief prayers. Louise placed her mother's wedding ring and some flowers on the casket. And we said our final goodbyes.

*

That year, 1996, the close proximity of life and death, the significance of one and the inevitability of the other, surfaced in our collective consciousness and lingered over us like moving shadows of light and darkness – first in the South of France and later in Greece. As we gathered in front of the open tomb on that sunlit hillside in February, our imaginations were unsettled by fears of the sight of Peter Guiver's coffin that had lain undisturbed behind its engraved marble slab for a dozen years. When we saw it, our ghostly imaginings subsided – our eyes falling upon an ordinary coffin which may have lost its varnish and grown a few cobwebs but was otherwise perfectly preserved. As we stared into the gaping concrete chamber, our thoughts turned from the gaunt spectre of death to the happiness of two lives spent together – a moment also to reflect on the blessings Molly and Peter brought to their family. The love they nurtured for one another may have been different in character from Etty's and Peter's but both couples shared the rare quality of total and unshakeable mutual devotion, a love which remained steadfast for the half-centuries of their marriages. The follies and frictions which had caused the two families' estrangement when we moved to Somerset in 1976 were of lesser consequence. Louise's good fortune and mine was to inherit our parents' capacity for absolute love; a greater gift than any other a parent might bestow on their offspring.

And so it was in 1996 that Etty and Peter invited us to Greece to celebrate their golden wedding anniversary – a date which fell on the second of June. This was to be a family affair and they asked us to join them at Diodati. Louise and I agreed although we knew we would have to confront an uneasy reunion with a house that had been the cause of so much conflict and ill feeling and a place we now avoided in favour of holidays in Tuscany. We also harboured doubts about the wisdom of the whole enterprise – feelings Alice shared with us. My father was not a well man and it had become obvious that he was no longer in any fit state to travel. Etty, of course, dismissed our concerns. She refused to listen and it was only then that I began to understand there may have been a more fundamental reason for her blind belief in Peter's eternal vigour. In her heart, her Peter possessed all the might and durability of a mature English oak. For a time, I had attributed this stubborn denial of his poor health to her selfishness. I now saw it was the cold fear of his death that consumed her and the only way she could deal with it was to deny his mortality. As for my ailing father, he had little to say. Besides, this was a special moment in his life with his beloved Koutzi Mou and he would not dream of denying her happiness.

With the mission confirmed, our plan was to honour the anniversary celebrations but extend our break by flying to Athens before the end of May. This would give us a few days to visit the great antiquities in Delphi, Olympia and Epidauros before travelling on to the island and Diodati. In the event our tour of classical Greece was aborted. Two days before our departure, Etty called from the Makedonia Palace Hotel in Salonica. In the early hours of the morning, shortly after their arrival, Peter had been rushed by ambulance to the intensive care unit of the city's Ahepa Hospital with pneumonia. He had also suffered a mild heart attack.

After a night in Athens, Louise and I took a mid-morning flight to Salonica which carried us over an Aegean Sea glinting with the lambent light of a crystal sky. The island was on our flight path and within minutes, its familiar contours and lush green vegetation came into view. "Will he ever see it again?" I asked, half to myself. "Will he ever return to Diodati?" Louise squeezed my hand. Seconds later the island faded from sight as the aircraft tracked northward to

Salonica. At the arrivals' gate Etty met us with a trolley, her nerves crackling with electricity. She wouldn't stop talking – repeating herself, asking the same questions – and by the time we checked into the hotel we were already exhausted. The Makedonia Palace is the city's five-star showpiece – all marble and modern and efficient in the American way. When we arrived the lobby was a chattering hubbub of well-pressed suits and expensive coiffures – a large conference, the receptionist told us, of European Union parliamentarians. We dropped our bags and a taxi hurried us to the hospital.

The Ahepa was a shock – a grim institution showing its age. Built on the university campus by the United States after the war, the structure and fabric of this respected teaching hospital had not been touched in fifty years – or so it seemed. The horror of the place drew me out in a cold sweat. This was bedlam; the noise indescribable; the corridors crammed with people; the walls peeling paint; an aura of panic and confusion everywhere. We climbed a staircase in search of the emergency ward and when we got there they told us Peter had been moved to the cardiac wing. Eventually we found him. He looked a desperately sad sight but the moment he spotted us I sensed his relief and his spirits lifted. "No one in this place knows what they're doing!" he bawled. "But I'm buggered if they're going to get the better of me!" They had parked him in a small ward which had once been a private room with its own lavatory and shower. Now the loo had lost its seat and the room accommodated three beds with barely enough space to jam two meagre cabinets between its three patients. My father occupied the far bed by a window, affording him the luxury of a ledge to store his washing kit.

Etty shot off to find a doctor, a nurse, anyone who might comfort her with guarantees of her Peter's swift return to health. In the room, the space around his bed was so cramped, Louise retreated to the corridor outside to give me a few moments alone with him.

"Ever since I was admitted," he said, "I've not had a hot drink. What I'd like more than anything else is a decent cup of tea."

"That's terrible," I replied. "Why haven't you asked the nurses or Mummy to make you some tea."

"They don't listen. And your mother just fusses about my eating. The meals here are foul and she gives me food I just don't want to eat. But I'm not hungry. Anyway I'm constipated. I haven't been for five days."

"Well, from now on Louise and I will make your tea. And I'll speak to the nurses about the other thing."

When Etty returned from her mission, I moved to the end of the bed and she sat by him. Suddenly the contents of her room service tray – breakfast that morning – appeared out of a carrier bag. She produced a Danish pastry and began tearing it apart, pressing morsels to his mouth like a dotty motorist feeding a parking meter. I was horrified.

"Mummy, he doesn't want it!" I said.

"Don't interfere, Kit. He is my husband. He needs to eat!"

I felt a rising swell of emotion and walked out of the room to join Louise in the corridor. I was struck by the suffering, the bravery and the helpless determination of this wonderful man – my father. His life was so precious to me but his death seemed to be calling out in silent whispers in my head. I was angry – with the hospital, with his miserable circumstances, with Etty's thoughtlessness. And it dawned on me that if my father was to have any chance of surviving this crisis, his family were essential auxiliaries in his care. I held Louise. "You must be strong," she said. "He needs you now."

"Yes," I replied. "I know."

Before leaving, I spoke to the nursing staff about his bowel problem. They were very sweet and understanding and promised to give him an enema. Back at the Makedonia Palace, we unpacked and ate a light lunch on the terrace, its sweeping views of the city's waterfront and the Bay of Salonica bathed in the afternoon sunlight. By now Etty was wearing us out with her endless, meaningless, repetitive chatter. Finally, she exhausted herself and retired to her room for a siesta. Shortly after, a carton of fresh milk and a supply of tea bags in hand, Louise and I returned to the hospital.

We found Peter lying in his own soiled sheets. They had given him his enema – no screens, no curtains, no privacy – but having done the job, the nurses had not cleaned him up, nor had they remade his bed with fresh linen. I called them – not by ringing a bell at his bedside because there was none – but by physically shouting down the corridor! A male nurse appeared, apologized and between the three of us, we completed the task that should have been done two hours before. Even then Louise had to prompt the young orderly to treat my father's bedsores with an ointment or cream. At the hospital store we bought a pack of adult Pampers but before slipping one on the nurse had to remove his catheter. It was an excruciating operation. I held my father's hand and told him to squeeze hard. He did, and I could feel the tremors of pain coursing through his racked limbs. The agony etched into his face – eyes tight shut, teeth gritted – still lives with me today. But for Peter there was more at stake to his humiliating ordeal than coping with the pain. He was an old soldier, an Indian Army officer, part of the liberating forces in Northern Greece at the end of the war. There were questions of honour and dignity and pride to be observed here. To cry out with pain would have been a mark of defeat. Instead, when the nurse had finished, he said: "Thank you!" And turning to me, he said: "Now they've cut my cock off!" We laughed. As the tension and pain eased, he wanted to sleep. His cup of tea would have to wait.

Next day, Louise and I were at his bedside by eight – an inhospitable hour for Etty whose morning routine demanded time at the dressing table before she was fit to appear in public. On the cardiac wing, a kind lady in the kitchen gave us access to hot water and we made Peter's first cup of English Breakfast Tea. We lifted his back and held his shoulders to give him the support he needed. Grasping the cup in both hands, he drank the hot liquid slowly, deliberately.

"Thank you," he said holding Louise's hand. "I've never enjoyed a cup of tea more in my life."

"How are things?" I asked gently.

"Okay," he replied. "But this bed's difficult. I can't stick my feet out because of the board across the end. And I need a fresh nappy!"

"We'll fix it," I said and left the ward in search of help. We waited impatiently until the young male orderly arrived, followed by two female assistants who announced that they had found a spare bed with an open end. The three nurses launched into an earnest debate about the best method of moving the beds with the minimum of fuss. Within moments, the discussion had descended into a wild-eyed argument – hands and arms gesticulating like flashing sabres over Peter's limp frame. In my best Greek, I told them to calm down. "Aren't you ashamed of yourselves?" I snapped. "Behaving like this in front of an English gentleman! Can't you see how ill and weak my father is?"

The male orderly gave way to his female colleagues. They promptly banished the other two patients to the corridor, wheeling their beds out to allow Peter's new bed to be rolled in and parked alongside the old. With a fresh Pamper laid out on the clean linen, all five of us lifted Peter in unison, transferring him from one bed to the other. Changed and settled, he raised a foot in the air and wiggled his toes in a victory salute as the nurses wheeled the old bed out and readmitted the ward's other two occupants. For the Ahepa, this complex manoeuvre had been a logistical triumph. For us it felt like being active participants in a Greek television sitcom.

That evening, when we returned to the hospital, my father's condition had deteriorated. He was in a very low state – so bad I resigned myself to facing the end. The haunted look on Etty's face was chilling – suddenly the prospect of his imminent death dawned on her and she began to cry. "I want to be with him all night," she whispered. His breathing was fitful, his body heaving with the struggle. We stood and watched over him in silence, lost in our own private thoughts. Each time he grunted or gasped or yawned, Etty reacted in fright and clung to my hand. In time he seemed to settle and, with the encouragement of the night sister, we returned to the hotel.

With no word from the Ahepa, Louise and I did not know what to expect on our tea run early the next morning. Deep inside myself I feared the worst. But when we arrived on the ward, our precious patient was sitting bolt upright on the edge of his bed, back towards us, staring out of the window. Peter was very much alive and in good spirits. The crisis had passed. "I slept well," he told me. "For the first time I actually feel rested." I sat with him while Louise made his tea and prepared a plate of fresh fruit, halving and de-pipping the grapes to make them easier to eat.

Later that Thursday morning – at about eleven, after we had collected Etty – we learned that the department's senior consultant, the university's professor of cardiology, had granted us an audience. Thus far we had found the professor a shadowy figure, remote to the point of inaccessibility. His vast suite of offices was guarded by a team of shrill secretaries who acted as his doorkeepers. When at last we were admitted, we entered an ornately-panelled and air-conditioned office hung with the grand calligraphy of his certificates and diplomas. The odd thing is that as we sat before the great man seated behind his great desk, my memory of the professor himself is completely void – my eyes and my mind overwhelmed by the magnificence of our surroundings when just a few steps along the corridor my sick father was lying in his cramped and airless little room. But in spite of my misgivings about the hospital, I now had to concede that – for all his display of self-importance – this man had saved my father's life. He showed us the X-rays. The lungs had cleared and he was happy for Peter to return to England after a brief convalescence at the Makedonia Palace. Monday, he said, would be fine. But meanwhile, just for good measure, he should remain in hospital one more night.

After our final evening visit to Peter, we decided to eat out for the first time since our arrival. All week we had shuttled furiously between hotel and cardiac ward – our time otherwise occupied with Etty's family; my aunt Machi and her husband Petros, my cousin Thanos and his wife Santa. At last we could relax – Vivat Peter! – and we took ourselves off for a taste of Salonica's bustling restaurant scene. We began at Totti's, a fashionable open-air café on Aristotelous Square where we stopped for an ouzo and some meze. Etty was in euphoric mood and by the time she had finished her first drink any notion of the crisis Peter had so narrowly survived evaporated.

"Tomorrow," she announced, her voice rising with excitement, "he will be out of that horrible place. We will drink *champagna*! We will have a party!"

"Mummy, I don't think that's a very good idea," I said.

"Why not? Of course we must celebrate. The doctor said he can come home."

"Yes," I groaned, "but he's still very weak and he needs time to rebuild his strength. He will want to rest. The last thing he needs is a party with all the family."

"Christopher, don't speak to me like that! Stop treating me like a five year-old child!"

"I'm only telling you he'll want time to rest quietly without a lot of fuss and people around him."

"I'm not going to listen to you," she said and stood up. "I'm going!"

Emotions were running high and like all Etty's tantrums this one was heading for confusion and farce unless it was halted. I stepped away and Louise took over, gradually talking her down with the expedients she understood best – flattery and sympathy; casting me with the demons and her among the angels. When she had regained some semblance of control, we found dinner in a nearby taverna – Louise working hard to dispel Etty's martyred looks by laughing off the tiff with a gentle tease. But Etty was never one to be teased and when she lost the thread, her favourite defence was always to mis-hear or half-hear or simply cast her raft adrift and land on another planet. "Etty, you know Kit's a bit of a wind-up merchant really," Louise quipped as the food arrived. "Yes," replied my mother, "I like the wine very much."

*

Next day, Friday, we performed our last early morning tea run and again Louise prepared Peter's plate of fresh fruit.

"When's Etty coming?" he asked. "I need my clothes."

"We'll pick her up in a while," I said. "She's packing a bag for you. Is there anything you want me to ask her to bring?"

"I'd like to wear a jacket. My blazer if possible." I agreed to tell her. Then a sudden look of impatience crossed his face and he said, "I need to get out of here, Kit. Let's go for a stroll down the corridor."

We helped him out of bed and I passed him his walking stick. Barefoot and clad only in his pyjama top and a nappy, he set off towards the wing's reception desk – Louise and I at his side. For this comically attired Englishman, our gentle stroll would be no casual walkabout. This was a one-man victory parade; a demonstration of the triumph of life over death. Brandishing his stick like a conqueror's standard, he progressed down the long corridor, smiling and greeting the staff who stared back in bewilderment. "Καλημέρα!" he called. "Καλημέρα! Καλημέρα!" [Good morning! Good morning!]

"Daddy, aren't your feet cold on this floor?" I said, at once sharing his elation and feeling mildly embarrassed.

"Of course they are!" He replied. "But so what? Look at everybody. They think I'm quite mad."

He had battled against the odds and won the day. And he wanted the hospital to know.

Later, when we returned with his clothes, he refused to allow Etty to help him dress. Examining himself carefully in the bathroom mirror, he adjusted the silk handkerchief in the top pocket of his blazer which my mother then readjusted as we left the ward. The staff seemed genuinely sorry to see him leave and offered to take him to our waiting car in a wheelchair – a kind gesture he politely declined. And when he shuffled into the lobby of the Makedonia Palace Hotel, walking stick in hand, his first instinct was not to head for the elevators. First he went to greet the receptionists, the concierge and the porters. They knew him well and their smiles of welcome were the kind of smiles born of a natural high regard for a fellow human being whose manners and thoughtful ways belonged in another age.

My father had overcome his great ordeal – one more trial in the many that life had put his way. For that week, Louise and I had watched over him as observers in an unfolding drama – a week which lives on in our memories. What we witnessed was the essence of the man, his attitudes to life, his beliefs. An example of principles and practice as one truth. A week which resounded with the voices of my upbringing: "Boys of spirit, boys of will ..." The importance of self-control; of hard work and perseverance ... "Never shirk, never give in ..." The dictum of Henry Prüger, the father he loved and the man who ultimately failed to meet the test of his own high principles. Michael never forgave his father for abandoning Nell and the family. Peter did, and he would make good. Courage and dignity lay at the heart of his pantheon of values and as I watched him shuffling across the lobby of the Makedonia Palace, blazered and erect, I recalled his words in New York before Gerald's funeral: "Hold your heads high," he had said. "Remember we're British!" The irony of his parentage and mine never once crossing his mind.

Today the beliefs my father lived by sound hackneyed, almost jingoistic – certainly a currency of values society appears to have lost or discarded. But as we watched him in his bed at the Ahepa, we were moved by his spirit – his flashes of humour – and by his nobility. On a raw, graphic canvas, we saw the strength of the man and the depth of the resources he was able to draw on to survive. He had inherited his mother's stoicism, a quality Etty did not possess. While he would succumb to her whims and her wiles, he knew she still needed him and he was not yet ready to wave farewell. In good times or bad, and even in his frail condition, she relied on his moral strength and direction in the way a loving daughter might look up to her father. "My Peter is my rock," she would say. And of course he would return her devotion like a doting father for his favourite child. Seven months earlier Etty herself had fallen ill with pneumonia and had spent a week in the hushed care of Taunton's Nuffield, a Ritz among hospitals compared to the Ahepa. "For the first time," Alice had told me, "I saw Mr. Chapman crying. He took me in his arms, he was so worried." His little Etty, his Koutzi Mou meant the world to him.

*

To my discredit, before leaving England I had packed Gerald's silk tie in readiness for a Greek funeral. Now my faithlessness was rewarded with the celebration of Etty and Peter's golden wedding anniversary which fell two days after Peter left hospital, on Sunday. The family muster planned for Diodati had been long forgotten and instead we gathered for a convivial lunch at the house of Thanos and Santa in a quiet suburb south-east of Salonica. There were ten of us around the dining room table with one absentee. As I had predicted, Peter stayed away and, to my relief, Etty respected his wishes. She gave him an early lunch in the hotel before tucking him up in bed to sleep for the afternoon.

That morning Machi had taken Louise and me on a short expedition to three of the city's historic sights: first to the massive basilica church of Agia Sophia; then to Panagia Ahiropíitos, a restored fifth century church named after its miraculous icon "not made by human hand"; and finally to the Rotonda, a vast fourth century mausoleum later converted into a Christian church by Theodosius the Great, the Roman emperor and ruler of the Eastern Empire. Over lunch Machi was eager to continue her tutorial – echoes of my childhood when she had taught Gerald and me to read Greek and appreciate the nation's history from its classical and Byzantine eras to the Ottoman's four-hundred year occupation. But we did not get very far. Etty had always felt a little threatened by her sister's erudition – irritated by her high-mindedness – and with this, her special day, she was not going to allow Machi to command the stage. We let it pass and celebrated the health of the anniversary couple.

*

Our journey home on Monday was trouble-free. Like an old trooper, my father coped well and accepted his free rides in an airport wheelchair without a murmur. The flight out of Thessaloniki touched down at seven in the evening and rather than complete the final leg to Somerset, we spent the night at Heathrow's Ramada. Peter went straight to bed, exhausted, and Louise and I ate supper in the hotel's brasserie. At ten, midnight Greek time, we spotted Etty and Peter having a drink in the bar – my mother, evidently, still in party mood. I buried my face in despair and we headed for bed.

Back at Avon Lodge, the doctor called in on Tuesday evening. He examined Peter and advised him to cancel his planned return to Greece in July. Etty protested. Diodati, the island, the sea, the sun were the best tonic for her Peter. She knew best. They would be going. Next morning she appeared at the Castle, hijacked Peter's old secretary and drove her back to Avon Lodge to take dictation; thank-you letters to the Ahepa, the Makedonia Palace and others, notes I could easily have handled on his behalf. She then returned to the hotel with Peter for lunch – he pale from his exertions – leaving Avon Lodge to a hurt and tearful Alice who had already prepared his lunch before discovering that Etty had binned the bouquet of flowers she had bought to wish them a happy wedding anniversary. We were back to the old routine.

*

In September, four weeks after their long break at Diodati, we faced a second crisis. Peter had another stroke. He lost the ability to swallow and his life-line became an intravenous drip. "This is a major setback," the consultant told Etty. "I think you will need to prepare yourself." She wailed, Louise consoled and I watched by his bedside. Miraculously, he made a second recovery – and it occurred to me that it was he, not she, who was doing the preparing. A year on, in the summer of '97, against all medical and filial advice, he followed Etty to Diodati one last time, and in December they returned to Thessaloniki for Christmas – Etty blind to the dangers. But then he seemed keen to go – a kind of unspoken desire to say a final farewell to the family who had found him the girl he loved; a goodbye to the town he associated most with his happiness. On Christmas Eve I took a call from their bedroom at the Makedonia Palace Hotel. He was not feeling well and wanted to return home early. He knew he was dying. By the afternoon of the twenty-eighth, a Sunday, they were safely back at Avon Lodge but within a few hours of settling in, Peter was rushed to Musgrove Park Hospital. We found him in the admissions ward, in a small private room off the reception area – Etty in tears beside him. He was lying motionless supported by a dozen pillows; drip; oxygen mask; his skin pale grey-green; his watery eyes blinking slowly in recognition. I kissed his forehead and held his hand. "Pneumonia," said the nurse.

Next morning I went to see him. I needed time alone before Etty arrived. Louise, Dom, Nick followed later. We would all be there. But for now, for a few precious moments, I sat alone in that small room: a private communion with my father, an urgent desire to let him know that I loved him. More, I felt a terrible need for absolution, or at least a signal of his understanding and forgiveness for the feuding which had driven a wedge in our relationship. We didn't talk. I just sat at his side holding his hand. He gripped mine gently. It was communication enough – a sign anyway of his love. "I'm thirsty," he whispered at last. Holding his head in my right hand and with a plastic beaker in the other, I gave him a little water. A final gesture; an offering of peace. That afternoon he slipped quietly away.

*

The funeral was held on Thursday the eighth of January at St. Mary Magdalene, Taunton's parish church where, as children, we were taught to worship. Peter Judd, Gerald's Cambridge contemporary, now Provost of Chelmsford, read the Sentences and led the service. My tribute, hand-written in a large leather-bound exercise book, spoke more of the nature of the man who was my father than of his career and service to his industry and his community. I paid tribute to Etty, their marriage and their enduring love – a flame which never trembled in fifty-one years. And I ended with these words: "… He saw humility as a necessary virtue in life – as a conduit to truth. He held a deep understanding of a universe beyond the idols and icons of a consumerist age. Peter Chapman achieved much; but he was never famous. He did not achieve the greatness acquired by public recognition. What my father had was greatness of spirit. Greatness of heart. Nobility and humanity."

The committal took place at the Church of St. Peter and St. Paul in Churchstanton, by a quiet plot in a far corner of the churchyard. We had returned him to the pastoral tranquility of the Blackdown Hills, his favourite corner of Somerset.

*

Part Twelve

Epilogue

Sunrise over the archipelago

Ashfield House – Winter 2008/09

I began this story two and a half years ago, my hope in its telling has been that it might lead me to some new understanding of my family; that the journey might reveal a forgotten truth which made sense to me and, through it, bring me to a reconciliation I never achieved when my parents were alive – although, I think, by the end, I found it with my father. Etty is the greater difficulty and she troubles me still. Five years after her death, the emotional oblivion that descended on me then has not lifted. She continues to haunt me and the harder I try to ease the shackles binding us as mother and son, the tighter I feel their grip. My father's death, at the moment it came, was calm and peaceful. All the family were gathered together. There was a gentleness about his passing, a serenity. The death of Etty was very different.

The moment, St. Valentine's Day 2004, was interrupted by a sudden and violent encounter just before dawn – a surreal experience I cannot explain. She died unexpectedly and alone in her bed at Netherclay House, a care home near Taunton, while Louise and I were taking a short break in the South of France. We were staying in St. Paul de Vence, at the Hotel Saint-Paul, and shortly after five o'clock in the morning I was jerked awake by a terrible aching pain like a hot stone bearing down on my heart. The pain was accompanied by a deep sense of panic centred on Etty. This was all about Etty. But in spite of the pain, this intensely physical ache, my heart felt empty – as if it had been wrenched from my breast. Suddenly, my heart had become a void space. Minutes later, I fell asleep again – the pain clearing as abruptly as it had roused me. By eight-thirty Netherclay had telephoned to break the news, a call followed by another from Etty's GP who needed to sign her death certificate. "In these circumstances," he explained, "you may want to call for a post-mortem." I told him that would not be necessary and we agreed the certificate would give Alzheimer's disease as her cause of death.

The doctor was doing his job. The death certificate did not lie. But there was another truth. The real cause of Etty's death was her desire to die. The will to live had deserted her years before. After Peter, the world she knew vanished forever; and as the months and years passed, as the well of sympathy she drew on from her friends trickled dry, she grew more lonely, wretched and withdrawn. At her funeral in Churchstanton, few of her old friends attended. And unlike the funerals of my brother, my father and Molly, my mother-in-law, I felt ill-equipped to speak – words in tribute from me would have sounded too hollow. Instead, I invited Louise's brother Mark to speak on behalf of the family. Five days later I received a letter from Peter Judd, now Dean of Chelmsford, who had returned once again to take the service and lead the committal. "I thought Mark spoke with warmth and gentle realism," he wrote. And then "… it also seems right that Etty didn't want to struggle on any more."

For a while I dwelt on these words – for it seemed to me that as much as Etty wanted to end her struggle, it would not have been in her nature to leave the stage without striking the last blow. And when it came, she ambushed my sleep through the medium of a paranormal force – there to deliver one final act of defiance, a cry of rage and despair worthy of an Olympian feud. When he was alive, my father often accused us of being uncomfortably similar in temperament. In the *Iliad*, Zeus says to Ares, his son "… thou enjoyest nothing but strife, war and battles. Thou hast the obstinate and unmanageable disposition of thy mother Hera, whom I can scarcely control with my words."

Whereas my "vision" remains a puzzle to me, its drama characterizes the conundrum that defined my relationship with Etty. A part of her wanted to remind me of her matriarchal power and in doing so it ignited the violent emotions which smouldered inside us; for me a mother who oppressed my heart, for her a son who was heartless. What I experienced was unpleasant and disturbing, its message confusing and contradictory. On one level she was threatening me with a war she would wage from beyond the grave. She loved me but I had not learned to love her. I was cursed with the evil eye and this was my punishment. On another level I was hearing her desperate cries, echoed by my own – a shifting kaleidoscope of negative and positive feelings, of beneficent and malign intentions which confirmed, for good or ill, the intensity of the bond between mother and son. For me it was a need for her unconditional affection, yet I came to feel its compromise in a million little ways; all sharpened by her jealousy of Louise whom she saw as a challenge to her role as supreme mother-matriarch. Gerald's rise as favourite son only became evident after Louise and I moved to Somerset by which time Etty's instincts had absorbed the satisfying notion that she would always be the only woman in my brother's life. Gerald, from his teenage years and with the growing awareness of his sexuality, became the rebel activist and iconoclast. I was more conservative, the more politically conventional, and the closer adherent to the middle-class values of my father. Before Louise and before Gerald's coming-out, Etty's great mantra was to hail me proudly as διάδοχος – her son and heir, her crown prince.

But as my expectations of a mother fell short in Etty, so were her needs left unfulfilled in me. With Gerald gone, then her Peter, I was all she had – and I didn't match the standard some Mediterranean mothers expect of their sons – an absolute and unquestioning devotion and deference to her position. For the first twelve months or so after my father's death, and to her credit, she invented a life for herself built around a group of local friends whom she lunched each day at the Castle. Occasionally she went to London to shop and have her hair done, stopping each time to light a candle at the Greek Orthodox church in Moscow Road before returning home. Her trips abroad were limited to one annual visit to Greece but in July 2000 she cut short her stay at Diodati after a terrible quarrel with Machi. Without her Peter, the peace of the house and the joy of the island had lost their magic and she never returned.

I was slow to spot the early stages of her dementia – the muddled thoughts and words, the tantrums and mood swings seemed little more than the frustrating, capricious, spoilt habits of the mother I had always known. But the deterioration of her mind soon became apparent and the medical diagnosis was made. Her driving – never good – became more erratic and dangerous, forcing me to sell her scratched and dented VW Golf. Of course my decision sparked a fierce row and, unhelpfully, I suggested she might like to exchange the car for a bicycle. "I have never ridden a bicycle," she protested. "Even when I was a child, I did not have a bicycle. Papa's chauffeur took us to school!" The rows over one issue or another were endless. Her occasional firings and re-hirings of Alice became more frequent. Cash withdrawals from her bank ran into many hundreds of pounds a week – money she could not account for; money I saw disappearing into the pockets of drug-dependent beggars under Castle Bow and greedy taxi drivers who saw no reason to help her distinguish between the denominations of large banknotes and small. Fifty pounds or five – to Etty they were all the same. In the end our kindly family solicitor arranged an enduring power of attorney which was formally registered with the Court of Protection and I assumed control of my mother's affairs.

Coping with Etty's dementia was demanding. With Alice's help and Louise's and a supporting cast of carers who came and went like phantoms, I dealt with it dutifully – but there was no sense of loving in the exercise of my duty. It was an obligation which I fulfilled in her best interests but an obligation weighed down by my entrenched feelings of alienation. At a time when Etty needed a son's love more than anything else, all I could offer was my duty and an empty heart. For my mother, much as she received all the practical care and attention she might wish for, it could never have been enough. The missing ingredient – her craving to be admired and adored – was never satisfied. The spotlight she had bathed in – her life force from the day she was born – had faded away. Those she revered and depended on, those who had indulged her and had raised a pedestal on which to adore her, had died. Her son was a poor substitute, unable to step into the hallowed shoes of her father, Thanassaki, much less into those of her husband – her Peter.

With the advance of the disease, our problems grew more acute. The ideal solution, we believed, was to arrange permanent, round-the-clock care and companionship at home and, through an agency, we found a saintly man called George whom Etty appeared to like. On the day George was due to move into Avon Lodge I bought a small car to give him the freedom to take her out and about. At last our plans were coming good and Alice, Louise and I began to breathe more easily. Too soon! Next morning a breathless George telephoned to say that Etty had evicted him from the house with all his belongings and she had bolted the door against him. Later the same day, I met George, apologized, paid him his fees and returned the blue Polo to the local VW dealer. Once again we were forced back to the uncertainties of a system which relied on an endless relay of jobbing carers. And when the police called in the middle of the night to say that they had found my mother half-naked flagging down passing cars on the main road, we realized that our options were exhausted.

Her time as a resident of Netherclay House ran to little more than two months. We installed her in a large, light and airy room which we furnished with favourite and familiar pieces from Avon Lodge. It was comfortable, the staff kind and caring. But for Etty this was the coup de grâce. She stopped eating in any meaningful sense; she refused to engage in the life of the home; she withdrew further into herself, preferring to keep to her bedroom. I remember visiting once only to find her lying curled forlornly on her bed in semi-darkness, curtains drawn against the daylight. I tried sitting with her in the dining room to encourage her to eat. The other residents at the table – a lively and amusing bunch – were friendly towards her, interested in her, but she pretended not to hear. When it suited, she could still deploy her famous hauteur. Neither had she lost her old antagonism towards me – I was to blame for everything. On one occasion, as I led her to the dining room for supper, she started shouting at me: "I don't trust you!" She screamed. "I don't trust you!" Everyone jumped, startled by her outburst. An incoherent cry from the heart that was trying to say: "You don't love me! I know you don't love me!" In the end she died of chronic loneliness – isolated in an alien world, her death hastened by near-starvation and a desire simply to rejoin those who loved her: her papa and mama, and her Peter.

*

I am struggling to arrive at a conclusion here – as if the result might lift the veil on one of life's great mysteries and make everything clear. But nothing in life is fully resolved. There are no perfect conclusions. The best we can do is bring a little order to the stage play to help us understand, accept, forgive where forgiveness is due, and move on. Parents and families are fascinating and complex organisms, but they also form the rootstock of our existence. Their duty is to feed and nurture their young – a function which is failing miserably in parts of our society today. If, with all my good fortune and privilege, my complaint is an aching heart caused by a profound sense that something important went missing in my life, what hope is there for the many thousands of abused innocents living in violent households around Britain?

Etty would never and could never recognize the emotional pain and hurt she inflicted on Louise and me. A shimmering, shining butterfly living in a world of her own make-believe, she simply was not aware. And therefore, because she knew no better, and because the child in her was never allowed to grow up, we must forgive. And if the child in me held expectations of my mother which left me crushed when they went unfulfilled, the adult son has to accept and understand, and never look for his wounds to be endorsed. Etty was and always will be the princess in her castle, the supremely elegant and vivacious chatelaine, narcissistic and indomitable, and adored and admired by all her court.

In her coffin, lying at peace, she was dressed in role – ready to meet her prince at the ball. A pink chiffon evening dress with puffed sleeves and an empire line; a gold clutch bag and matching evening shoes; a black velvet ribbon around her slender neck. And her gold crucifix in her hand.

❈❈❈

One unsolved mystery remains in the telling of this story. What are the true facts behind the tragic fate of Henry Prüger? What were the circumstances of his suicide? To a degree I have hesitated in my pursuit of an answer, knowing that I am treading on family sensibilities. In the absence of any conclusive evidence, my cousins Nicky and Alex would prefer me to allow the memory of our famous grandfather to rest undisturbed. Even after eighty years, the tumult of his death touches hidden sores which are still keenly felt. But the mystery won't lie down. On a Sunday morning some weeks ago, I was reading the newspapers in the kitchen when a sudden crash and clatter of an object falling had me rushing into our drawing room. At first I saw nothing. And then I spotted a small framed painting which had tumbled to the floor. The strings attached to the frame had perished. It was a watercolour measuring twelve inches by nine retrieved from Avon Lodge after Etty's death and it depicted a fortress perched on a craggy hillside behind a medieval town lying on the banks of a river. In the past I had shown little interest in it. Now the picture was begging for my attention. On the back of the frame, I discovered that this had been a birthday present from Nell to her youngest son, just turned thirty-seven. Her hand-written inscription reads:

To my dear Peter in Memory of Happy Hours spent in Dürnstein Austria. March 8th 1952.

Do you remember how we all, with Daddy, spent the night there, & you climbed up to the Castle where King Richard I was hidden & his man Blondel found him - & you gathered stones to take back with you to Dover College!!! I think you also stayed there when you rowed down the Danube!

The Painter of this picture, H.S_____, is a relation of Daddy's.

The discovery of this forgotten heirloom with its hidden message tells us a little more about Nell and her relationship with the family. Her nostalgic inscription, written on brown wrapping paper and pasted to the back of the picture, shows how anxious she was to keep a happier past alive in Peter's mind. For her, memories of Bratislava, home life and particularly "Daddy" were there to be celebrated, not swept aside and buried. Understandable then, that she should wish to give the painting to Peter rather than her elder son Michael who chose to erase all memories of his upbringing and even to deny his father's name. Twenty-five years after he was christened Henry Prüger, eldest son of Henry his father, he was reincarnated Michael Chapman.

Mother however was reluctant to adopt the new moniker and continued to address her son as Henry.

In August 1996, twenty-eight months before my uncle's death, and many more years before I fell upon HP's suicide note in my father's black deed box, I visited Michael in Torquay to record an interview about his early life. I was curious and, I confess, I rather hero-worshipped him as the star hotelier of his generation and the man whose style and glamour transformed the Imperial into a world-class hotel. Now I wanted to learn more about the family's history and his perspective on my grandfather who had been built into such a legendary figure in my own imagination. At eighty-five, my uncle Michael was pretty frail, and although he was pleased to see me and happy to talk, I soon gathered that Bratislava was a no-go area, a derelict place wiped out of existence, out of mind. My agenda was restricted to his life in Torquay, to his career and his achievements. The subject of Henry Prüger and the Savoy-Carlton Hotel was a void and he insisted that he did not hold any of his late-father's personal papers and documents. "I find this very puzzling," I noted in my journal. "Some deep psychological barrier is holding him in check. Something is stopping him from talking about HP, his father, and I don't know what it is."

Whereas Peter spoke openly and proudly about his "Daddy", Michael refused. The common denominator between the two – and indeed Tony, their middle brother – was their attitude to the suicide. This traumatic episode, its significance, its truth, became a buried secret. A family shame to be denied. And it happened when the brothers were impressionable teenagers, still at school, leaving all three young men scarred so deeply that it would affect the rest of their lives and the lives of their descendants.

With the limited evidence in my possession – confirmed by Nell's letter to Peter after his engagement to Etty in 1946 – I have suggested that HP struggled with his own homosexual tendencies, and that the suicide may have been triggered by a moment of madness at a time when he was under extreme financial pressure. In her letter of twenty-eighth February, Nell's advice to Peter was that he must "always tell her [Etty] the truth – about everything."

Nell then went on to ask her son a blunt question: "Does she know about your Father?" And, she continued: "He was a fine man and you have no reason to be ashamed ... he was a most <u>unselfish</u>, noble and fine character, but should never have married."

The opening sentence of Henry's desperate letter to his mysterious confidante Hilda hints at some cataclysmic incident rather than a protracted crisis like an illness, disability or financial burden. "A terrible folly of mine smashed all what we possessed," he writes. If another woman was involved, I cannot believe Nell would have worked so hard to promote her husband's memory in such warm and glowing phrases – "a fine man ... unselfish ... noble" ... "no reason to be ashamed". If she harboured any resentment, any ill-feelings or regrets; if she felt that Henry had betrayed her; or if she was in any way ashamed of him, I doubt she would have wanted to send her son a family heirloom for his birthday just to remind him of "Happy Hours spent in Dürnstein ... with Daddy". And if HP's "terrible folly" was connected to his difficult financial situation, any scandal would have been exposed. Besides, after his death, Nell took control of the Savoy-Carlton's reconstruction, refinanced the project and, finally, realized her husband's dream until the long depression of the Thirties overcame her, the banks foreclosed and she returned to England with Maky.

Henry's letter ends ... "my heart aches for my poor Girl, my boys & my brothers & sisters; it is too terrible for words". Certainly, the entire family must have been traumatized by this tragedy. HP was head of the family, the eldest brother. His vision and his drive had created an immense landmark in the centre of Bratislava. His brothers and sisters and their families were involved in this great enterprise; each had their part to play in the management of the hotel – its 250 bedrooms, its two cafés and three restaurants, its nightclub and its Winter Garden. So how did they feel? What was their attitude towards Nell and her three teenage sons? Is it possible that in the weeks and months following HP's death, their grief and shock turned to bitterness and anger? Disgust, even, that the head of the family, this dynamic force who created a monster, had let them down, had deserted them – and, possibly, in a manner which brought shame on the Prüger name? In his family history, Peter relives the terror of a day when, alone in the house, he took a telephone call from his uncle Max warning him that "The Flying Dutchmen" – the notorious squads of city bailiffs – were on their way to strip the villa of all its contents. Panic-stricken and isolated, Peter spent the next couple of hours finding hiding places for the family's valuables. The bailiffs never came, nor did uncle Max or any other member of the family to stand by their terrified young nephew.

This now is all conjecture. But I have a distinct feeling that Henry's death and the pressures over the Savoy-Carlton's future imposed a great strain on relations between Nell, the spirited and independently-minded Englishwoman who was never quite accepted by the Prügers, and the rest of HP's family – a strain which led to an estrangement between us and them, a cooling of relations which is still apparent within some branches of this large and far-flung clan. If my suspicions have any foundation, if the Prüger family's attitude towards Nell and her sons turned sour, my conjecture may – in part – go some way in explaining Michael's decision to turn his back on Bratislava and break with the family name. Nell also, in her many letters and notes to Peter, Etty and her family, is silent on the question of the Prügers – a grand silence which suggests that she too ruled them out of her life. Instead, she determines to stand by her husband and defend his character against any possible recrimination by promoting his nobility and unselfishness.

If my contention is true – that HP struggled with his sexual identity – I believe Nell would have known about it for a long time and had come to terms with his gay tendencies for the sake of her children. The letter of February 1946 again – where she advises Peter "as to what and how much to tell ones (sic) wife" – states emphatically that "a wife wants to be at one with her husband, not to be put off with excuses – that denies trust and causes dissension". Though my evidence is inconclusive, in my view it is compelling, but in airing it – even after eighty years – I know that I am stirring deep waters inside my family.

My cousins Nicky and Alex – Uncle Michael and Aunt Tim's eldest and youngest – do not approve, preferring me to perpetuate the long silence rather than see our grandfather's memory diminished for lack of hard proof. I believe it is time to explore the truth – after all we now live in a society where issues like homosexuality no longer carry the social stigma of previous generations. Henry Prüger's greatness stands as a matter of record, and the family's pride in him, both as an hotelier and as a father of three sons, is clearly evident in the firm position Nell adopted. But in my desire to present a balanced view, I do not want to ignore my cousins' objections. In an exchange of emails with Alex, who is himself gay, he suggests that HP's suicide may have been the result of "the total emotional meltdown of an extremely proud man." He continues: "… to have succumbed & killed himself was an act of enormous weakness on his part … however, just maybe, in a moment of self-pity he thought it more honourable than bankruptcy." This is certainly a plausible theory but, to me, it makes no sense in the context of Henry's choice of words and tone of voice in the suicide note. If he had had some kind of emotional or mental crisis, his note to Hilda, I think, would have been very different. He may even have addressed it to his wife. Equally, this proposition hardly rings true in the context of Nell's revealing letter to Peter.

In his emails to me, Alex was also remarkably candid about the longer term effects of these events. "For my part," he writes, "I came to realize that grandfather's suicide had tragically scarred my father & thereby forever limited his relationship with his family … he was never able to share his pain & forever hid this truth. However with time I was able to understand Michael's hurt & accept what he was able give."

*

In my search for enlightenment – my curiosity awakened soon after I began writing – the time had come for me to visit Bratislava, and in October 2007 Louise and I set off to find this city which had been the scene of so much family drama. We travelled with my cousin Nicky who spoke German and had kept in touch with some of our now distant relations, the scions of Henry Prüger's brothers and sisters. On her last visit to Bratislava, two years before, Nicky had joined her son Patrick who was completing some business in the city and she decided to use the opportunity to locate the old family home and estate in the hills a short drive from the centre. She had never been before, and to help her find the property she arranged to meet our second cousins, Julius Prüger and his sister Eva, the grandchildren of Julius, Henry's younger brother. Over a polite and agreeable lunch, the conversation turned to Henry's and Nell's house, and before long Nicky realized that she had made an unwelcome request. Julius was reluctant to show her the property, somehow suspicious of her motives. "I had to insist," she told me. "After all, this was our grandparents' family home. But he was not at ease with the idea – it bothered him!"

It was for this reason that, in October 2007, we decided not to alert any family members to our arrival. Nicky, and now I, had been touched by the feeling that Henry's direct descendants were not entirely welcome in Bratislava. By 1937 Nell had abandoned the Villa – parcels of land already sold off to cope with the Savoy-Carlton's debts and the boys' education – and she had journeyed home. Now we were feeling her sense of estrangement – exiles who had dared to break with the proud house of Prüger and adopt an Englishwoman's maiden name.

*

As we drew up to the border on our drive from Vienna Airport, Bratislava loomed out of a grey sky to our left – the city dominated by the solid mass of its Castle – a huge square block, turrets like cigar stubs rising over its four corners. It was instantly recognizable from dozens of photographs and postcards in the family archive. We had arrived at that corner of the map of Europe where Austria meets Hungary meets Slovakia. Border crossings are strange places – often sinister and menacing. This one was comical. The Cold War long dead, Slovakia and Hungary are now members of the European Union and this border, soon to be dismantled, was a flimsy construction with a canopy reaching across the road like a giant turquoise caterpillar. But the approach and drive through the outer limits of Bratislava were pure Iron

Curtain: tall, grim concrete tenements; light traffic; people in dark clothes going about their business muffled up against the afternoon chill. Images of Richard Burton in *The Spy who came in from the Cold*.

Once we had crossed the Danube and reached the city's heart, the atmosphere changed and the new, emerging Bratislava revealed herself: expensive motor cars, chic designer shops – Armani, D&G, they are all here – as is Tesco whose arrival would appear to have won special favour, the store marked in capitals on the tourist's street plans. The grand promenade (Hviezdoslavovo Námestie) is dominated by two buildings: the city's handsome baroque opera house and the Savoy-Carlton. This was Henry Prüger's dream standing before my eyes, its rooftop still crowned by a giant 'busy bee', the hotel today rebranded the Radisson SAS Carlton. It made an impressive sight and filled me with a strange proprietorial pride I had no right to claim.

We checked in and soon after set off on foot for the cemetery, stopping on our way at a small florist's to buy three long-stemmed roses – one each in the names of Michael, Tony and Peter. We paused for ten minutes to step inside the chapel of the Holy Cross, the church attached to the great cemetery of St. Andreas. There we found a dozen people kneeling in prayer while a body of unseen voices chanted the liturgy from behind the rood screen. Leaving the chapel, we entered the cemetery by a set of black wrought iron gates and found ourselves in a vast, green, tranquil space dotted with grand memorials, shrubs and conifers. Here funerals travel first class and the dead are given space to breathe!

It had been fourteen years since Nicky's last visit to the grave but her memory did not desert her now and she guided us through a labyrinth of pathways to find the Prüger plot. She had given me no inkling of what to expect, and what I saw when we arrived caught me by surprise. I stood, feet fixed to the ground, and stared in wonder. This was no ordinary family plot. This was a neat and well-ordered terrace in black granite – a line of polished headstones dedicated to the family. The first, a heavy cross, commemorated Heinrich Prüger who died in 1898 and the formidable Amelie, his wife, who died twenty-four years later – my great grandparents. Then a sculpted slab dedicated to Robert Stockinger, the husband of Luise, Heinrich and Amelie's youngest daughter. And next to him, the graves of my grandfather Henry Prüger and his brother Julius. Like the others, HP's granite cross was engraved in a deep Gothic script: "Henry Prüger 1867-1929." And beneath the dates we found the inscription "Requiescat in pace!" We noted the etched exclamation mark! "The busy bee is laid to rest," observed Louise. But the most striking thing about all these headstones was to see them – eight decades on and more – maintained in pristine condition, their gold leaf inscriptions shining fresh and new. Someone, a member of the family, was seeing to the work and paying for it. I asked Nicky who this might be. "I don't know," she said. "Cousin Julius perhaps." We tied the three roses together, laid them on grandpapa's grave and stood in silence for a few moments. When we set off to return to the hotel, the day was closing in and it was getting cold. That evening we dined in the Carlton's Opera Brasserie and drank a very potable Slovakian Cabernet Sauvignon.

Next morning, after a late breakfast, we decided to take a drive out to the Villa – Henry's and Nell's house in the Slavin district of the city which, in the 1920s, had been surrounded by acres of parkland and gardens. The house and its estate were Nell's joy. Peter, in his history, tells us that his mother could never have worked in the hotel because it "would have created difficulties" with the other members of the Prüger family. "Therefore," he continues, "she decided to devote herself to her husband, her children and home, and used [the house] to distance herself from those members of the family with whom she found it difficult to be sociable." Then, in the mid-twenties, when the three boys were away at school, HP bought several more acres of land which Nell transformed into a substantial market garden, managing it as a business with the support of six full-time gardeners. "This was Nell's domain," writes Peter, "and she ran it with flair and success," supplying flowers to the Savoy-Carlton and many of the city's florists.

Our driver's name was Milos and he spoke no English, neither was his grasp of Bratislava's geography good enough to locate the house in the Slavin hills. But together, with the help of our maps and a Google Earth printout, we arrived at our destination. It was an unhappy discovery, made sadder by a heavy sky and relentless showers which had been falling on the city since daybreak. Milos parked his Mercedes and Nicky, Louise and I set out in the pouring rain, each clutching a Carlton Hotel umbrella too flimsy to protect us from a chilly breeze. There was little to see. From the road, the Villa looked shabby and run-down, a once handsome family home now partitioned into flats. All that was left for us to do was to walk the perimeter and peer through the property's fences and railings. What remained of Henry Prüger's original estate had been divided into twenty plots now owned by the City of Bratislava. And the little we could see appeared derelict and overgrown – although I think I glimpsed traces of what appeared to be the ruins of old greenhouses and growing frames. Soaked to our bones, we returned to the car and Milos drove us back to town. At the concierge's desk we returned the mangled remains and snapped spines of our umbrellas with the limp offer of an apology. And after drying out and changing, we lunched in an excellent little café next door –the exact spot where, eighty years ago, HP's brother Julius had run the much larger Café Savoy, an imposing brasserie with tables spilling out onto the promenade.

With the limited time we had left, and while Nicky and Louise set off to explore the town, I spent several hours wading through archive material in search of my grandfather – but there was little I had not already seen. And while the Carlton's solicitous management put me in touch with three local historians, all were indisposed or unavailable.

*

I had come to Bratislava to solve the mystery of Henry Prüger's suicide and I came away none the wiser. Thinking about it, I came to the conclusion that my search for the answers to my questions were unlikely to come from an historian. This was a family matter. And the answers lie buried somewhere in the souls of its late senior members. Michael and Peter went to their graves with their secret still safe. They didn't even tell their wives. The only relation who might have shed some light on this puzzle before he died was Robi Stockinger in Linz, the son of Henry's youngest sister Luise. Nicky had been close to Robi but by the time I started asking my questions, he was in his late eighties and Nicky, understandably, felt unable to approach him.

So I returned once more to the press cuttings of July 1929 and, in particular, to the long obituary by Eugen Holly for *Die Grenzbote*, Bratislava's principal daily. Herr Holly had observed Henry Prüger and his great mission over many years and –family aside – he was the only independent voice I had found to cast light on Henry, the man. The headline to his article – "The Tragedy of a Solitary Man" – immediately hinted at a new perspective.

The feature opens with a hymn of praise to the Savoy-Carlton and its creator, describing HP as a "grand seigneur", a man of honour and a man of influence.

> *"… every person of note who passed through Pressburg and wished to stay overnight inevitably became a guest of the 'Savoy-Carlton'. It was quite simply the hotel in Pressburg. The 'Savoy-Carlton' was the chosen resting place of Government ministers on a visit to Slovakia (as it still is today); in the great hall of this building the Slovakian cereal kings and potato barons conferred together; the blonde head of Luise Esterhazy is sometimes to be seen within these walls, as are other great actresses well known to us; here one sees the captains of industry who have passed through Pressburg when journeying to Cannes or to Belgrade; here one finds the concentrated, pulsating life of this expanding city. This was the realm of Henry Prüger, who ended a brilliant life – not brilliantly, but honourably – in a space in the roof of his own hotel…*
>
> *"… he was a 'grand seigneur' of the kind which will soon cease to exist, one of the last who had a truly chivalrous heart and a head which thought upon the grand scale – and who was nevertheless aware of the smallest details of the vast enterprise in his charge. He was well known in Vienna, as he was in Prague; in Paris, London, Melbourne, all over the world. Closed doors were opened in response to his letter of recommendation emblazoned with the symbol of the 'busy bee'."*

Herr Holly goes on to develop his theme, outlining HP's distinguished career, his marriage to "an Englishwoman" (unnamed!) and the education of his sons "in England". But for all Prüger's wealth and influence, he describes him as an "essentially solitary man … [who] had so much energy bottled within him that he thought – or wanted to think – for everybody else". The picture emerging is of a proud, even arrogant, man; obsessed about detail and something of a control freak; a loner and a bit of a dandy "whom one could see walking through [the] streets with yellow gloves on his sinewy hands … with a carnation in his buttonhole … a phenomenon rather than a mere pedestrian …"

Finally, in a concluding paragraph trembling with atmosphere and figurative symbolism, Herr Holly alludes to a personality he sees as deeply flawed: honourable certainly, but enclosed, introverted, unable to seek advice from others – a means, perhaps, of controlling his own demons but ultimately exposing his vulnerability.

"One realises that, in spite of his millions (which he literally acquired by his own labours), in spite of his influence and power, Prüger was really to be pitied. For life is never perfect. Always and everywhere, in the houses in which good people live, there are recesses and cavities which present a danger to honourable men – to those who are unwilling to compromise, who rely only on themselves, and who are therefore always threatened. It was into such a hollow attic space in the highest storey of Pressburg's grand hotel, that this man finally crept and sought his end. A man who had offered his hand to kings and salesmen. And who always remained a loner in the business of grand hotels."

⁂

On the eleventh of September 2001 – a date seared into the history of our new millennium – Dominic, Nicholas and his girlfriend Annabel, Louise and I checked into the Makedonia Palace Hotel in Thessaloniki. Our mission this time was to journey on to the island and spend three days at Diodati; a necessary tour of inspection to decide what was to be done with the house Etty had now abandoned; her heart lost in a muddle of memories – memories of countless evenings spent with her Peter gazing out over the pine trees to a violet sea. I was for selling the property – a mood influenced by my sense of alienation and a long-held desire to sever my ties with Greece the motherland. But the notion of being rid of Diodati raised howls of dissent from the two boys. And so, as Louise and I had become self-imposed exiles for the better part of a decade, the moment had come for us to return. To see and to decide our way for the future.

After a casual lunch on Aristotelous Square, we walked back to the hotel, wandering first down the length of Tsimiski, Salonica's principal thoroughfare and a street famous for its smart shops, corner kiosks and murderous traffic. It could not have been later than three thirty when we stepped inside the marble halls of the Makedonia Palace to collect our room keys from the reception desk. Upstairs Louise sat out on the balcony while I checked our car hire and ferry bookings before stretching out on the bed to read. Moments later, a tap on the door and Dom burst into our room barefoot, clad only in a T-shirt and his underpants.

"Quick!" He shouted. "Switch on CNN. The world's at war! New York's burning!"

The images were apocalyptic. The World Trade Center had just been hit, its North Tower billowing smoke. It was approaching nine in the morning local time and in Lower Manhattan thousands of people were hurrying to their places of work. We sat transfixed and confused in front of the television screen, unaware that we were about to witness a second catastrophe. At three minutes after the hour, we watched in horror as United Airlines Flight 175 smashed into the South Tower.

In my recollections of that afternoon in Salonica, and among the many images imprinted on all our minds, one for me seems to express the full horror of the human toll inside those buildings. Two thousand seven hundred and fifty-two innocent souls perished that day and thousands more have suffered as victims, as friends and relations, as work colleagues and members of the emergency teams. But it is the image of "the falling man", tumbling down the side of the North Tower, that gave me a brief sense of the panic, terror and inferno raging within, out of sight of CNN's cameras. A terror that drove one man, believed to be a forty-three year old restaurant employee, to choose an alternative death.

That evening dinner with Machi, Petros, Thanos and Santa was a muted affair. It was also an evening I recall for another reason. Before we ate I asked for an ouzo and Petros called for some wine. When the waiter arrived with our drinks and set them down, I lit a cigarette. I had always smoked – perhaps ten a day – and until that moment I had had no real inclination to quit. But now, sitting at a pavement table in a pretty side street in the middle of Salonica, I took one drag and immediately stubbed it out. I have not smoked since.

At ten the following morning Hertz delivered our people-carrier and we struck south along the fast coastal highway linking northern Greece with Athens, skirting Mount Olympus, until we reached the port of Volos – a journey of about two hours. Long lines of trucks, wagons, camper vans and cars queued in serried ranks on the dockside; uniformed officials blew their whistles and waved their arms furiously, and one by one we were admitted into the cavernous abdomen of the island ferry. Later that afternoon we emerged blinking, disgorged onto a sunlit harbour, and for a second my heart leapt as I set eyes on the once familiar sight of the town's untidy pile of whitewashed houses, churches and belfries cascading down to a waterfront lined with busy cafés and colourful tavernas. I was pleased to be back.

It had been eight years since our last visit – in the summer of '93 when Dom had been working the season as an extra hand in a boatyard. Then I felt outraged by my parents' refusal to allow us to use Diodati, referring us instead to a local hotel. We drove out to the house anyway and I had sat on the terrace nursing my sulk, writing my journal, while Louise and Nick rediscovered Puddleduck. Locked out, the house shuttered, I crouched on the terrace's low stone wall with my notebook. "It's beautiful," I wrote. "Peaceful. The view breathtaking. The island I remember from the past." Diodati, I went on to observe is "in perfect nick. Absolutely immaculate. Not a blemish anywhere. ... I feel stung – to think they can't share some of this with their son and his family."

Now, eight years on, we were returning – a strange homecoming to a house where Louise and I felt we had never belonged. As we turned off the main road and onto the Kalamaki peninsula, the car fell silent, all of us tense with expectation, uncertain of what we might find. We followed the track past Kanapitsa – once the clubhouse to the British expat community on the island; past all the villas we used to visit in the merry-go-round of cocktail parties Etty and Peter dragged us to in the seventies. And suddenly we were there, dipping down into our drive.

My first impression was discomforting. The approach to Diodati had changed – somehow it seemed narrower, darker. Trees, bushes and scrub had claimed the fringes of the driveway, creating an eerie overhang of vegetation, the brush scraping the sides and the roof of our people-carrier. And when we drew up to the house, my heart sank. The shining, radiant lady I remembered had lost her charm. Before us, as we unloaded the car, Louise and I saw a ragged, weather-torn shadow of the past. Four Aegean winters had seen to her decline and now Diodati looked forgotten and forlorn. Since Peter's death, Etty had neglected to follow his strict regime of annual maintenance and the house had been allowed to fall into disrepair. It was the saddest sight.

On the main terrace – where I had sat to write my journal – we looked out on a pinewood that had grown at a ferocious rate and was now intent on devouring the villa. One tree hung at a perilous angle over the eaves above our bedroom; another I had known as a sapling thirty years ago had turned into a green monster, overwhelming the terrace, dripping its viscous resin on the stone parapet. And the woodland reaching down to the cliff-top had become an impenetrable jungle, its floor carpeted with a thick layer of pine needles so dry the smallest spark would have set the hillside ablaze, swallowing us in its flames.

Inside, the house looked a little worn and dated, otherwise much as I had known it. But the kitchen was a revelation. When we opened the cupboards, we found them stacked high with foodstuffs, most displaying sell-by dates in the early and mid-nineties. The labels, of course, were vintage Etty – everything had been purchased from Harrods or Fortnum & Mason: turtle soup, caviar, pâté de foie gras, artichokes, prawns, potato salads – tins ballooning, oozing their contents, poised to explode. Another cupboard revealed a dozen jars of Tiptree preserves and marmalades. Another long blue packets of dried spaghetti. The list was endless. The scene depressing.

*

It was Nick who began to bring us round. "Dad," he said when we had gathered on the terrace with a bottle of wine, "your problem is that you're too emotional about the past." Through the trees we stared out at the archipelago glowing amber in the evening light. Soon it would be dark.

"Perhaps I am, Nick." I replied. "Perhaps I am."

"You forget that we've been coming here practically every year since we were born. You and Mum dropped out years ago."

"Yes, I know Nick. And with good reason. But I also know how attached you are to the island. You both have very happy memories and Dom's worked several summers here."

"Well then – think of what we've got here," he insisted. "It's beautiful. Our own little oasis of quiet and beauty in a noisy, wicked world. If you sell Diodati, you'll regret it."

"Yes, okay Nick," Louise interrupted. "But we lead busy lives. Who's going to sort this place out?"

"You are of course Mum! No one else can!"

We all laughed and the decision was made. Next day we set to work in the kitchen, swabbed down the cupboards and removed the offending tins to a skip at the top of the drive. We met Patra for coffee and she put us in touch with the people we needed to bring Diodati back to life. And when we returned in June the following year, the lady had reclaimed her gentle radiance: the house gleamed white, its shutters repainted Mediterranean blue; the woodland had been cleaned and cleared of its scrub; new terracing and pathways had been created; and the garden burst with the brilliant colours of bougainvillea, oleander, geraniums and plumbago; jasmine, hydrangea, gardenias and marguerites. We planted an orange tree, a lemon and half a dozen young olives. And our sainted Patra, wishing to observe Greek

455

Orthodox tradition, made us a gift of two large pots of basil which she placed on the rear terrace, either side of the kitchen door.

At last I felt a sense of calm falling on a once-turbulent heart. At last – with the restoration of the house, its redecoration, Louise's touches – I was beginning to accept my own rehabilitation with a country I had denied for too long. The repentant son had returned, made peace, his love for the motherland reawakened. And ever since that evening on the terrace seven and some years ago, we have all spent our summers here – individually or with our grown-up children and their wives; and now with their children. No restrictions. No prohibitions. Diodati is theirs as much as it is ours.

*

The first decade of the new millennium has brought a shift in the rhythm of our lives. Dom's and Nick's careers have taken flight while a sudden heart scare forced mine to ease up. The boys have married – Nick to Annabel, and Dom to Helena whom he met in London soon after our return from Greece in September 2001. And Louise and I have become grandparents: first to Daniel, then to Oliver, and now – just a few weeks ago – to Kitty, Nick and Annabel's baby daughter, a sister for Oliver. The sheer joy of it – the rush of instant love – has taken me by surprise. Before, my thoughts on becoming a grandfather had been coloured by mild feelings of resentment – and only because the tag suggested the arrival of old age with all its pejorative associations of being "past it" or "over the hill" or, as Louise delights in reminding me, of being "yesterday's man"! Now I know differently and see the transition from one stage in life to this new phase as a rite of passage to be celebrated for its wonder and beauty.

As I come to the end of my story, I look upon it only as the end of the story so far. The thoughts that remain – beyond my pride and happiness – are a preoccupation with the destiny of this family's youngest generation: of Daniel, Oliver, Kitty and, perhaps, of grandchildren as yet unborn. With age and the experience of past lives, I worry and wonder about the future and what it might bring them. Can the past teach us anything about the future? It should do, but too often the lessons of the past are rarely learned and soon forgotten. And with our god-like worship of an ephemeral cyber world – available to us at the flick of a finger – there seems so little of substance to hold onto as ballast. Except, that is, for society's oldest foundation stone – the family – even if that institution is itself under threat. In this family it has proved its worth as the core element above all others to have secured the felicity and wellbeing of its members. And that gives real hope for its future.

Now, with the arrival of grandchildren, the normal ebb and flow of family life has changed: daily routines, priorities, the culture and atmosphere inside the home, even shopping lists change. Louise loves buying toys and clothes while I have bought books and dusted off a box-set of Beatrix Potter I found in the attic. But the issue of books is a battle I seem to be losing against the more compelling attractions of CBeebies and Peppa Pig. Even the characters of Tigger and Pooh are more engaging on a television screen than in the A.A. Milne original. Yet the most striking change in the interplay of family life today is not the invasive power of television; it is the generational shift in the nature of the family's relationships, one to another. The age of deference died with the new freedoms of the Sixties and the democratizing might of popular television. It was that post-war culture of deference which defined Gerald's and my dealings with Etty and Peter in our youth. He cut loose, came out and escaped to New York. For me, marrying Louise at the age of twenty-four was my best escape route from the suffocating strictures of parental expectation. I, along with many of my generation, lived through that era Ian McEwan observes so acutely in his novel *On Chesil Beach* … "when to be young was a social encumbrance, a mark of irrelevance, a faintly embarrassing condition for which marriage was the beginning of a cure." These days, thank God, the old tyranny has been replaced by consideration and mutual respect across the generations, and this has promoted a healthier, more open, more loving dynamic within the family.

*

With the birth of Kitty and the turn of another New Year, the big question absorbing our chatter at the kitchen table has been the future of the family business. With advancing age, time seems bent on overtaking us by stealth, and Louise and I can do little more than look forward to accepting our bus passes with good grace! As with Diodati, the boys' perspective on the Castle is emphatic – they have issued a strict injunction not to sell! So the debate has concentrated on who might pick up the reins, on the understanding that neither the business nor the family's peace and goodwill would survive if both their families were actively involved day-to-day. This is one lesson of the past we have learned.

The irony of the moment is that we find ourselves discussing the succession at a time when the world is spinning headless in a financial cyclone and the economy appears to be descending into its worst downturn in a century. It is now almost twenty years since the last recession when, as a family divided, we squabbled over Louise's appointment to the Castle's board and launched our bid to take control. Then the business had fallen to its knees and was tipping rapidly into insolvency. This time our cash flow is positive, our debt levels modest, and Louise and I sit at the head of a lively and motivated team who are driving an hotel with the grit and the metal to withstand the storm. Over these brief years, we have enjoyed the ups and downs of the ride but when the moment comes for the two of us to step off the carousel, we shall do it freely in the knowledge that the future is in the secure hands of a third generation Chapman. Of course predicting that future is an invidious game, but the wind's direction seems to be pointing towards Nick as the more likely candidate to take command while Dom – forever passionate about blazing his own trail – is more inclined to set up shop with his name above the door rather than one borrowed from his family. In the end, the roll of time and circumstance will dictate the outcome.

Diodati – June 2009

We return and another summer stretches before us. Again I take my seat on Aristotle's. Again I stare in wonder across a silent sea at daybreak – the risen sun casting its fiery pink wand across the water as Homer prescribed. The memories of our early years still linger somewhere in the recesses of my consciousness. But the villa's revival, its new look and feel wrought quietly by Louise, have mellowed those memories of the past. The house, the setting, its scented air, calm heart and mind with their beauty; an elemental simplicity which is transforming; renewing our connection with the beginning, restoring our faith in the family. Diodati is possessed of a healing power I could never have imagined – and in her gentleness she speaks of my mother and father and their creation. The voice could be Nell's speaking of her son in her letters to Etty: "… thank you for loving my Peter," she wrote in February 1946 after their engagement, "thank you most sincerely for making him so happy … [he] is very dear to me." Later, in the same letter, Nell writes: "This devastating and terrible war has ruined so much that was beautiful in our lives, it is up to ourselves, to keep searching for beauty and make our own Happiness – and in as simple a way as possible …"

Peter shared his mother's feelings and I shall always remember his long search for this blend of beauty and simplicity which Nell herself had sought in her life. It took him and Etty many years to find their Aegean idyll – Gerald and I, bored teenagers, following in their wake as they strode across hectares of land in Halkidiki, Thassos, Paros, Rhodes and Crete. And when, at last, they found the perfect hillside, they built their little corner of paradise – their "paradieschen". They made their own happiness.

For Etty Diodati became her romantic sanctuary on Greek soil. Paid for out of the Rosi family inheritance, it made her intensely possessive – the cause of all the years of hurt and exile. But bizarrely, the gifts she bequeathed us were gifts she didn't even know she had to give. She created Diodati with her Peter for him and for herself, and today it is ours – a love affair passed on and shared with her grandsons and their children. Peter would not have discovered this hillside plot and we would not be returning each summer without Etty, without her Greekness and the beneficence of Pappou Thanassaki, my grandfather. And so every year we busy ourselves with new projects. As proud custodians of our island home, there is always something that needs doing: a redecoration; a new plumbing system; re-landscaping and terracing; new planting; an extra shed for inflatables, deck chairs and beach toys. There's always a job to be done. Last summer it was Peter's tiny terrace perched like a nest in the woodland at the head of the cliff above Puddleduck. This was my father's sacred retreat, his secret hideaway where he would sit in the early evening to read, to think or just to dream as he gazed at the islands across the bay. After years of neglect, the terrace had withered into ruin, its stone bench and low retaining wall at the cliff edge reduced to dust and rubble by three-dozen Aegean winters.

In September 2008 we rebuilt "Pappou's View", and in the body of the new stone wall we set an engraved plaque: "In memory of Peter and Etty Chapman who found this place." Now I sit here after a morning's swim, stopping to catch my breath at the end of the climb from Puddleduck – a pause before the steep zigzag trek through the pines to the house. My eyes look down on an aquamarine sea washing the shoreline, a light swell forming eddies and vanishing pools of water between the rocks. Out of the sheer cliff face, two stubborn pine trees, knotted and stubbled and grey, refuse to surrender their priapic pose to the winds. The place, the view beyond remain unchanged. It is as Pappou Peter knew it. And now I too have become a pappou – my new-found status in the family and the stone-set memorial acknowledging the coming and the going of generations; the passing of time. And with it, that elusive peace I have sought has at last become real. The raging heart is stilled. Diodati may still remind us of another age. Etty remains a haunting presence and echoes do not die with the person; they whisper on through time and sometimes return to discomfort me. But echoes fade, and with the villa's rebirth I have come to realize that in this story Diodati has lain "At the still point of the turning world … Where past and future are gathered".*

This sublime retreat – Etty and Peter's discovery – was born of an act of love, a unique token of their unity. Now the power of that love-bond has been transferred to us, embracing the three living generations of this family. This is what I see now: in Louise and me; in Dom and Nick, and in their young families. The stresses and strains of the past, the conflict and the tribulation all melt into nothingness compared to the prize we hold today; the legacy of my parents' extraordinary love affair. Too easily I have forgotten that it was Etty alone who made Peter happy. She was the redeeming angel who saved him from his consuming melancholy, who – innocent of the circumstances – salved the trauma of his father's suicide, who soothed the pain of Gerald's death. Nell saw the vitality of her love for Peter – understood the childlike spirit and energy which transformed him. I didn't. For too long, blinded by my own vanity and driving will, I chose to deny the special gifts Etty brought to her marriage – true love's miracle. Thrown together in the family business, mother and son fought like wild cats, destroying "the fragile human links" Gerald urged me to safeguard in his letter from Diodati in April 1981. Louise too has always been quick to remind me that I am my mother's son, that her volatile temperament runs through my veins – an accusation, a truth, that never fails to sting my pride. And so it is that Diodati dispenses her calm wisdom, gently hinting that peace will only be found when I have stepped down from the pulpit, reminding me also of the words I spoke at St. Mary Magdalene on the day of my father's funeral: "He saw humility," I said, " as a necessary virtue in life – as a conduit to truth."

*Lines from the first of T.S. Eliot's *Four Quartets*.

*

Diodati the great healer. A field of conflict replaced by a garden of sweet smells, peacefulness, and now a memorial. It has been a long convalescence and, like all convalescents, a period of restoration allows time for reflection – to remind us of the swiftness of the passage of time and the brevity of our lives. To remind me of all the unvoiced gifts of parenthood: the love and security of home, an education, books, music, foreign holidays, so much. Gerald and I the fortunate recipients in our childhood. Dominic and Nicholas providing the same for their loved ones today. And in our island home, Louise and I still make tiny discoveries which prompt this sense of continuance. Last week a forgotten cupboard, too tall to reach without a stepladder, revealed a store of wooden coat hangers, old sheets and pillowslips – some torn in fragments for rags. The linens we found were elaborately embroidered with the initials ER – Efpraxia Rosi, my maternal grandmother, my yaya. And the coat hangers were stencilled haphazardly "Fifi" or "Fifi Rosi". Again Diodati quietly unveiling her little treasures; reminding me of Etty; my Greekness – leading me back to the lost love of a motherland I had denied for two decades. Diodati, the enchantress, releasing me from my folly and the long years of self-imposed exile. I had abandoned the first language of my childhood and I have had to relearn it, revelling in its wonderful tongue-tying complexities. I have rediscovered the Greek people, admiring their devotion to family and the fierce rituals of their Orthodox faith where even the local priesthood is a father and son enterprise. I have rediscovered their generosity to strangers, their kindness, their desire to please and their φιλότιμο – a Greek word with no English equivalent expressing this nation's belief in honesty, trust and decency – the social and moral bonds which make a civilized society.

I have returned home.

*

Today we visited Agios Haralambos. The green and craggy mountains of our island are peppered with a scattering of small monasteries. Many are tucked into the folds of their hillsides at the end of rough goat-tracks accessible only on foot, by mule or by four-wheel drive. Ag. Haralambos on the north-east coast is a particular favourite, the saint calling us back every summer. It is a mystical place: tiny, exquisite, perfectly preserved; its white-washed walls fresh and clean, the courtyard's flower beds spilling with geraniums, a flight of stairs leading to a short gallery of cells. We always find ourselves alone here – tourists seldom stray this far – and the only sign of life is a shy community of well-fed cats. In the chapel – simple, polished and pristine – a solitary flame invites pilgrims to light a candle. The visible signals of a human hand – the fresh paint, the watered courtyard, the cats, the flame – make us wonder. The absence of a monk or a caretaker adds to the mystery, leading us to imagine that, perhaps, Ag. Haralambos is inhabited by a mystic hermit, secretly watchful, who emerges from his cell in the early hours and only then attends to his duties about the monastery.

Stooping low under the door, we entered the chapel's gloom. Dropping coins into an empty dish, Louise picked three slim wax candles; I picked three. We lit the tapers and set them in a pair of trinities side-by-side. Peter and Etty and Gerald. Daniel and Oliver and Kitty. Past and future gathered, flames dancing in perfect unison. The purity of this place filling our hearts. The stillness in the air percolating to the soul. We sat and held hands; and inhaled the silence.

Index

Text and picture acknowledgements

The author and publisher would like to thank the following for their kind permission to reproduce copyright material:

Part Six p229	Mr Edward Bond for an extract from a short essay in the programme notes for *Saved* produced by Gerald Chapman and performed at the Haymarket Studio, Leicester in January 1974.
Part Six p229	*The Leicester Mercury* for a review of Mr Edward Bond's play *Saved*, performed at the Haymarket Studio, Leicester in January 1974.
Part Seven p243	Guardian News & Media Ltd for an arts feature by Mr Kenneth Rea published in November 1979.
Part Seven p256	*The New York Times* for an article published on 18th April 1983 written by Mr Frank Rich.
Part Eight p287	*The Daily Mail* for a cartoon by Mr Charles Griffin published on 10th March 1979.
Part Eight p314	*Caterer & Hotelkeeper* for the front cover of the magazine's edition of 9th June 1988.
Part Nine pp340-342	The Estate of Mrs Elizabeth David for a quotation from *A Book of Mediterranean Food* and for the author's words spoken in interview.
Part Ten p379	*The Somerset County Gazette* for various quotations and photographs.
Part Eleven pp402-403	Jonathan Meades for quoting from his restaurant reviews in *The Times*.
Part Twelve p457	Mr Ian McEwan for a quote from *On Chesil Beach*, published by Jonathan Cape. Reprinted by kind permission of the Random House Group.
Part Twelve p460	Faber & Faber for quoting lines from *Four Quartets* by T.S. Eliot.
	Venture Wandsworth for a photograph of Oliver and Kitty Chapman.

Finally, the author and publisher would like to thank David Glen of One Brick Court for his careful reading of the text and his wise counsel.

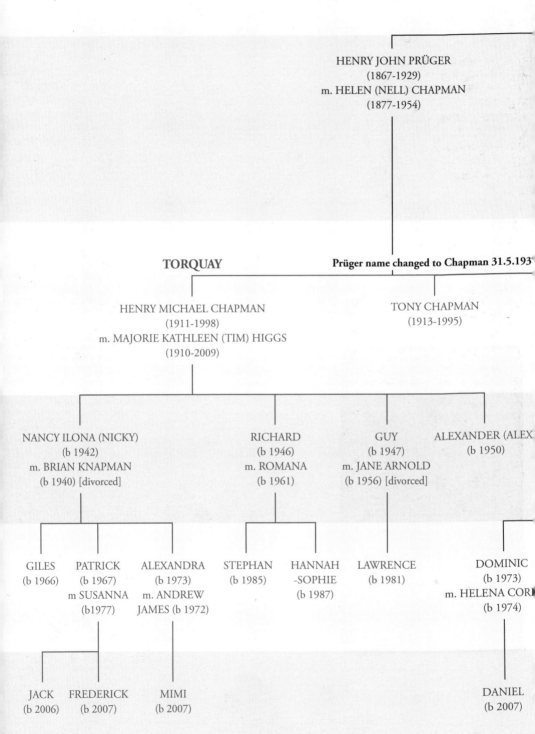

HENRY [HEINRICH] ANTHONY PRÜGER (1834-

HENRY JOHN PRÜGER
(1867-1929)
m. HELEN (NELL) CHAPMAN
(1877-1954)

TORQUAY

Prüger name changed to Chapman 31.5.193'

HENRY MICHAEL CHAPMAN
(1911-1998)
m. MAJORIE KATHLEEN (TIM) HIGGS
(1910-2009)

TONY CHAPMAN
(1913-1995)

NANCY ILONA (NICKY)
(b 1942)
m. BRIAN KNAPMAN
(b 1940) [divorced]

RICHARD
(b 1946)
m. ROMANA
(b 1961)

GUY
(b 1947)
m. JANE ARNOLD
(b 1956) [divorced]

ALEXANDER (ALEX
(b 1950)

GILES
(b 1966)

PATRICK
(b 1967)
m SUSANNA
(b1977)

ALEXANDRA
(b 1973)
m. ANDREW
JAMES (b 1972)

STEPHAN
(b 1985)

HANNAH
-SOPHIE
(b 1987)

LAWRENCE
(b 1981)

DOMINIC
(b 1973)
m. HELENA CORI
(b 1974)

JACK
(b 2006)

FREDERICK
(b 2007)

MIMI
(b 2007)

DANIEL
(b 2007)